Spirits of Protestantism

THE ANTHROPOLOGY OF CHRISTIANITY

Edited by Joel Robbins

1. *Christian Moderns: Freedom and Fetish in the Mission Encounter*, by Webb Keane

2. *A Problem of Presence: Beyond Scripture in an African Church*, by Matthew Engelke

3. *Reason to Believe: Cultural Agency in Latin American Evangelicalism*, by David Smilde

4. *Chanting Down the New Jerusalem: Calypso, Christianity, and Capitalism in the Caribbean*, by Francio Guadeloupe

5. *In God's Image: The Metaculture of Fijian Christianity*, by Matt Tomlinson

6. *Converting Words: Maya in the Age of the Cross*, by William F. Hanks

7. *City of God: Christian Citizenship in Postwar Guatemala*, by Kevin O'Neill

8. *Death in a Church of Life: Moral Passion during Botswana's Time of AIDS*, by Frederick Klaits

9. *Eastern Christians in Anthropological Perspective*, edited by Chris Hann and Hermann Goltz

10. *Studying Global Pentecostalism: Theories and Methods*, by Allan Anderson, Michael Bergunder, Andre Droogers, and Cornelis van der Laan

11. *Holy Hustlers, Schism, and Prophecy: Apostolic Reformation in Botswana*, by Richard Werbner

12. *Moral Ambition: Mobilization and Social Outreach in Evangelical Megachurches*, by Omri Elisha

13. *Spirits of Protestantism: Medicine, Healing, and Liberal Christianity*, by Pamela E. Klassen

Spirits of Protestantism

Medicine, Healing, and Liberal Christianity

Pamela E. Klassen

UNIVERSITY OF CALIFORNIA PRESS
Berkeley · Los Angeles · London

University of California Press, one of the most distinguished university presses in the United States, enriches
lives around the world by advancing scholarship in the
humanities, social sciences, and natural sciences. Its
activities are supported by the UC Press Foundation and
by philanthropic contributions from individuals and
institutions. For more information, visit www.ucpress.edu.

University of California Press
Berkeley and Los Angeles, California

University of California Press, Ltd.
London, England

Library of Congress Cataloging-in-Publication Data

Klassen, Pamela E. (Pamela Edith), 1967–
     Spirits of Protestantism : medicine, healing, and
liberal Christianity / Pamela E. Klassen.
          p.   cm. — (Anthropology of Christianity ; 13)
     Includes bibliographical references and index.
     ISBN 978-0-520-24428-3 (hardcover : alk. paper) —
978-0-520-27099-2 (paperback : alk. paper)
     1. Healing—Religious aspects—Protestant
churches.   2. Protestantism—North America—
History.   3. Protestant churches—North America—
History.   4. Liberalism (Religion)—North America—
History.   I. Title.   II. Title: Medicine, healing, and
liberal Christianity.
  BX4817.K53 2011
  234'.131—dc22

                                        2010053382

Manufactured in the United States of America

20   19   18   17   16   15   14   13   12   11
10   9   8   7   6   5   4   3   2   1

This book is printed on 50# Enterprise Cream, a 30%
post consumer waste, recycled, de- inked fiber and
processed chlorine free. It is acid-free, and meets all
ANSI/NISO (z 39.48) requirements.

For John

Contents

List of Illustrations   ix
Preface   xi
Acknowledgments   xxv

  Introduction: Healing Christians   1
1. Anthropologies of the Spiritual Body   30
2. The Gospel of Health and the Scientific Spirit   58
3. Protestant Experimentalists and the Energy of Love   100
4. Evil Spirits and the Queer Psyche in an Age of Anxiety   137
5. Ritual Proximity and the Healing of History   169
  Conclusion: Critical Condition   209

Notes   219
Archives Consulted   283
Selected Bibliography   285
Index   305

Illustrations

1. Portrait of Dr. Belle Choné Oliver, 1922. / 2

2. Front Cover of Belle Choné Oliver's *Anandi's Question,* 1930. / 2

3. Portrait of The Most Reverend F. H. Du Vernet, Archbishop of Caledonia, ca. 1915. / 5

4. Portrait of Dr. Anna Henry, "pioneer doctor to West China," 1899. / 59

5. Map of United Church Missions, "Missionaries of the United Church of Canada Encircle the World, Preaching, Teaching, and Healing," ca. early 1930s. / 63

6. Dr. George Darby, United Church medical missionary at Rivers Inlet, BC. / 70

7. Belle Choné Oliver (far right) with Christian women physicians at a conference in India. / 107

8. Sherwood Eddy (left) with medium Leonard Stott and Quaker friend Edward C. Wood, ca. mid-1940s. / 127

9. Sanctuary of St. Stephen-in-the-Fields Anglican Church, Toronto, photograph, interior, 1895. / 131

10. Newspaper image of Canon Moore Smith at court. / 140

11. Newspaper image of Reverend Alex Holmes praying for sick child at a Healing Service in Toronto. / 141

12. Photo of Reverend Mervyn Dickinson interviewing men at a Toronto gay bar, November 15, 1965. / 165

13. The grounds of Burrswood Christian Hospital, Tunbridge Wells, England. / 177

14. Labyrinth on the grounds of Vancouver School of Theology, Vancouver, BC, 2007. / 197

15. Derelict St. Michael's Anglican Residential School in Alert Bay, BC, 2007. / 205

Preface

Pathologies of Modernity

The promise of healing is everywhere. Biomedical researchers and charitable foundations race for the cure, self-help books assure their readers that the answer lies within, and a host of alternative therapies channel the energies of the universe to reconcile the traumas of the modern self. The balm of healing is also liberally applied to the wounds of history—be they genocide, apartheid, or racism—when invoked in processes of "truth and reconciliation." It is, in fact, the ubiquity of healing that makes it carry such heavy burdens—mending the body, psyche, and spirit, fending off ever-changing viral and bacterial threats to life, and restoring justice and right relations. A potent tonic of futility and necessity, the promise of healing—whether of mortal bodies or tragic histories—always seems just out of reach.

Nevertheless, hopeful people of all sorts continue to invoke the possibility (or providence) of healing, whether through medical or metaphorical means. The subjects of this book proclaimed healing as the solution to more than one ill: as doctors and nurses they performed the art and science of mending the sick body; as Christian citizens they supported a therapeutic politics in which biomedical care was a public good open to all; and as believers in the spirit they insisted that the science behind biomedicine was itself a gift of divine wisdom. At the heart of early movements for public health care in North America, liberal Protestants became agents of medicalization. They sought to modernize the call of Jesus to his disciples: "Cure the sick, raise the dead, cleanse the lepers, cast out demons. You received without payment; give with-out payment" (Matthew 10:8, NRSV). To be sure, liberal Protestants shied away from taking all of Jesus's words literally. They often con-demned as quacks those Christians who cast out demons or raised the dead. But along with their more "rational" version of Christian moder-nity, liberal Protestants nonetheless practiced a version of spiritual heal-ing by imagining a space in the human body and the body politic for the flow of supernatural spirits and energies that came from without.

Consider, for example, Dr. Belle Choné Oliver (1875–1947), a medical missionary working in India on behalf of the United Church of Canada, who began her career as a young woman dedicated to the double tasks of converting Indians to Christianity and treating their ills with modern medicine. Living in the midst of the Indian colonial struggle, and learning a great deal about the diversity of Indian cultures, she ended her career as a champion of medical education for Indian men and women and as a critic of missions focused on conversion. Her "modern" perspective, how-ever, contained within it an abiding interest in the possibility of "spiritual healing" through a growing diversity of channels. Around the globe in a less prominent corner of the British Empire, the northern British Colum-bia Anglican Diocese of Caledonia, Archbishop Frederick Herbert Du Vernet (1860–1924) practiced his own blend of science and the supernat-ural in which he argued that radio waves could be harnessed as God's healing energies. Drawing from the latest in psychic research and living amidst the traveling spirits of Northwest Coast First Nations, Du Vernet pronounced "spiritual radio" or "radio mind" as an effective therapy attested to by experiment and theology combined.

Attempting to cure the sick in a world wracked by wars and the con-sequences of colonialism, North American liberal Protestants eventu-ally came to see the deep ironies of how their own projects of healing were complicit with the evils they sought to exorcise. While maintaining a commitment to publicly funded biomedical health care, they also be-gan to scrutinize the ways colonial and Christian triumphalism had shaped medical missions, both among First Nations in North America and in the "mission fields" of India, China, and Africa. In the process, they continued the experimental work of Oliver and Du Vernet, opening themselves up to an array of supernatural flows that exceeded dogmati-cally Christian imaginations.

For liberals, the supernatural was not obliterated by the discoveries of naturalistic science, but nor was it spiritual power that knew no earthly or natural bounds. Instead, as Canadian Anglican theologian Eugene

Fairweather contended in "Christianity and the Supernatural," a 1956
lecture he delivered at the Episcopalian General Theological Seminary
in New York City, the supernatural was the path by which God "elevates
human creatures to a true participation in the divine life—an indwelling
of God in man and man in God." Like most liberal Protestants, Fairweather argued for a supernaturalism that could find its way around
both atheistic materialism and Pentecostal miracle-workers: "[I]t repudi-
ates the pretensions of secular humanism without doing violence to the
structure of nature and reason, and sees the true greatness of man in his
natural openness to fulfillment in the 'new being' of grace."[1] Under the
rubric of healing, liberal women and men came up with many ways to
"open" themselves to divine life while also articulating political goals.

Spirits of Protestantism, in short, argues that supernatural liberalism
enabled an imaginative shift whereby liberal Protestants went from considering themselves Christians who combined biomedicine and evangelism to effect "conversions to modernity" to understanding themselves as
complicit in a Christian, scientific, and oftentimes racist imperialism that
was (in the end) pathology dressed as progress.[2] What is more, this Protestant supernatural liberalism—and its attendant hopes for psychic and
spiritual unity throughout the world—can be traced within the ostensibly
secular contours of the anthropology of religion itself.

Many of the claims to healing within "supernatural" liberalism turned
on the question of how the natural human body came to be inhabited by
forces and spirits both good and ill, or what could be called an anthropology of the spiritual body. Underlying the modern discipline of anthropology as the study of humankind are its early Christian theological
roots, in which anthropology was practiced as the study of human nature in its relation to God. This earlier version of anthropology has been
largely forgotten by anthropologists of religion—and by anthropologists
of Christianity—thus constituting amnesia akin to what, in another context, Matthew Engelke called the "epistemological unconscious" of anthropology.[3] Most importantly for my argument, this amnesia contributes to the misrecognition of the continued legacy of Christian theological
categories and modes of argument for anthropological theories of embodiment, ritual, healing, and even medicine.

Anthropologies of the spiritual body underlie the ways people make
sense of the mysteries of transmission, equally baffling from the vantage
point of biomedicine or religious faith: How does a virus pass into or
over one person and not another; how does healing come to this patient
and not that one? How can a mother cradle her feverish child all night

and escape the flu or one cancer patient emerge from his agony to re-mission when another patient succumbs? Healing, like disease, is a question of communicability. Some anthropologies contend that the spirit of God transmits healing power, whereas others understand the medicines, therapies, and persuasive scientific authority of the doctor to bring about healing. Many liberal Protestants, such as Oliver and Du Vernet, combined these two theories of transmission, viewing the tools of medicine and technology as pathways by which the spirit of God was communicated to the vulnerable, imperfect human body.

Firmly committed to the mutuality of biomedicine and Christianity, liberal Protestants thought about "religious healing" in ways that went beyond the miracle, or in other words, the exception to the laws of nature that cannot be explained through rational or technical means. Healing miracles have more often been associated with Roman Catholic or Pentecostal versions of spiritual healing, an association that many twentieth-century Protestants considered to be evidence of the "superstition" of such Christians. But they had their own version of supernaturalism, even if they were convinced that it was not superstition. For liberal Protestants, healing could be communicated quite literally through new technologies that included biomedical techniques of surgery and drugs, but it also included the therapeutic effects of the written word and the spiritual tele-communication of healing radio waves. All of these spiritual technologies were bound together in a supernatural liberalism thought to be made effective by that most mysterious of currents, love, which stretched across the universality of humanity through the difference of cultures, religions, and places.

I have found particularly rich archives for exploring the robust and medicalized supernaturalism of liberal Protestants within the following two groups: the Anglican Church of Canada and the United Church of Canada (the latter church included Methodist, Presbyterian, and Congregationalist influences). These groups offer an ideal site for the rethinking of liberal Protestantism as a movement at once medicalized and enchanted, cosmopolitan and local. On the one hand, Canadian Protestants were inhabitants of a settler colony eagerly establishing the political, economic, and educational institutions that would make it a modern nation. On the other, in the realm of healing in particular, they were deeply shaped by their encounter with First Nations' peoples, as well as by American and British healing movements and a global network of influences stemming from missions to China, India, and to a lesser extent, Africa. These global networks led liberal Protestants across North America and Europe to understand their commitment to human health as beyond nationality precisely because of the psychic and spiritual unity that they considered to bind all human beings together in a holistic and divinely infused cosmos. The coworkers and forebears of such humanitarian medical organizations as the Red Cross and Doctors without Borders, liberal Protestants were just as adept at emergency surgery as at prophylactic prayer. They combined political analysis with religious experimentation to insist that health care was a human right owed by the state to its citizens and sanctioned both by the best models of political economy and the healing works of Jesus.

Accompanied by rhetorics of love and human universality, liberal Protestants moved from medical evangelizers to holistic contemplatives, taking on practices such as yoga and Reiki, a Japanese, energy-based form of healing touch. Their medical missions are no longer rooted in eager evangelism but in a desire for "cross-cultural experience": the three remaining United Church hospitals in northern British Columbia, supported by both church and public funds, focus on "encouraging community independence" while they provide culturally sensitive medical care to largely First Nations' clients.[4] Their definitions of healing have taken on a much broader compass: in the Anglican Church's recent plan for new relations among Indigenous and non-Indigenous Anglicans, "holistic healing" has become a primary goal, along with self-determination for Indigenous Anglicans, historical reparation, justice, and what has been called "A New Agape" that would encourage local and national partnerships.[5] With traditions of socialist critique, scientific spirit, and a sense of Christian *agape*, Canadian liberal Protestants came to question how both biomedicine and Christianity were based on claims to exclusive forms of knowledge and particular modes of the modern as they realized that modernity was a project with which they were intimately, if uncomfortably, engaged.

Keeping their self-awareness in mind, I use "modernity" in a double sense. First, I employ it in the sense that liberal Protestants have used it, to define a particular era in which they lived, one that was characterized by anxiety, violence, the growth of capitalism and liberal democratic welfare states, the rise of science and of anticolonialism, and always, for them, the hopeful possibility of positive change. Second, I adopt critical approaches to modernity as an inescapable, yet plural concept that is at once an historical periodization and a political project.[6] In the end the liberal Protestant and the critical sense of modernity have a good deal of overlap, and paying attention to this overlap is of crucial importance. As Dipesh Chakrabarty puts it, even the most diligent of self-reflexive scholars cannot fully extricate herself from the rhetoric of a "progressive" modernity judged by the standards of democracy and development: "We must, therefore, engage and reengage our ideas of modernity in a spirit of constant vigilance."[7] The pathologies of modernity, then, are not fixed but fluid—what was one generation's healing Christianity looked to a later generation like an imperialist virus, unfaithful to the teachings of Jesus and inadequate to the challenge of transforming toxic structures of power.[8]

My own analysis of shifting Protestant diagnoses of modernity has been shaped by the writings of several twentieth-century philosophers and cultural critics who have made strong arguments that modern structures of living have themselves caused illness and inequity.[9] The skepticism of these works is often directed not at religious modes of healing but at what are considered the sickening effects of biomedicine, or Western-based scientific medicine, operating in conjunction with state or imperial power. Among the most influential of these critiques of biomedicine is Michel Foucault's concept of the disciplinary apparatus of biopower in which he demonstrated the ways that biomedicine is therapy born not only from scientific interventions into the body, but also from political, religious, and economic disciplines of the embodied self that help to define what is considered pathological.[10]

An important influence on Foucault's later work on medicalization was *Medical Nemesis*, the popular critique of biomedicine written by Ivan Illich, an activist, former Catholic priest, and public intellectual. Illich argued that modern medicine had grown so all-powerful as a way of knowing the human body that its modes of diagnosis and technologies of care were literally making people and societies sick. Describing what he called the "religious tenets" of biomedicine, Illich contended that if laypeople did not start to question these tenets, the iatrogenic effects of medicine would take away not only their health, but also their ability to face mortality with dignity.[11] Taking iatrogenesis in another direction, several scholars have pointed to the ways that colonial regimes, including Canada, have used medicine as a tool of conquest, regulating and disciplining the very bodies that were made sick by the diseases brought with and imagined by colonial encounters.[12] The skeptical view of how modern therapies have ended up as pathologies has also taken the form of a critique of "therapeutic culture," for which liberal Protestantism has been offered as a prime example.

Twentieth-century Protestantism, especially in its liberal forms, has long been characterized as having succumbed to therapeutic culture—of having a "theology [that] finally became therapy" in which "self-realization" was more of a goal than overcoming sin.[13] Scholars have argued that a consumerist, therapeutic culture, heavily influenced by the popularization of psychological theories arguing that human beings could transform themselves from within, allowed liberal Protestants to detach themselves from divine authority or absolutes. As the story goes, liberal Protestants replaced sin with subconscious drives, and dispensed with personal responsibility in favor of the guiltless pathologies of psychology. According to sociologist Philip Rieff the "therapeutic ethos" was born when "psychological man" rose from the ashes of Western Christian civilization. For Rieff the perils of therapeutic culture were its rejection of religious institutions that had shaped people as members of a moral community and its fostering of pleasure-seeking individuals: "Religious man was born to be saved; psychological man is born to be pleased. The difference was established long ago, when 'I believe,' the cry of the ascetic, lost precedence to 'one feels,' the caveat of the therapeutic. And if the therapeutic is to win out, then surely the psychotherapist will be his secular spiritual guide."[14] Rieff depicted liberal religious clergy—Protestant, Catholic, and Jewish—as at once submitting to this individualistic therapeutic culture while simultaneously engaging in a hopeless attempt to survive the crises of postwar modernity through political and cultural critique. By becoming anti-institutional "spiritualizers," Rieff argued, liberal clergy fooled themselves into thinking they could break the "outward forms so as to liberate allegedly, the inner meaning of the good, the beautiful, and the true."[15]

Rieff's account of therapeutic culture has been particularly influential in the study of Christianity, psychology, and medicine. Several scholars poised on a fine, if not finessed, line between the writing of history and theology have turned to Rieff in order to depict liberal Protestantism, in particular, as ripe for the incursion of a Jamesian "psychological religion." In Keith Meador's view the seeds of the secular therapeutic—inwardness, latitudinarian spiritualizing, shuffling off doctrinal repression—were already latent in Protestant notions of selfhood, even before psychology set the disease to flourishing.[16] This therapeutic critique joins a persistent refrain in the study of liberal Protestants that paints them as pawns to overweening forces of secularization, in which ideologies of medicine, psychology, and existential philosophy, along with the forces of consumer culture, replaced traditional Christian disciplines of the self with materialistic, liberal individualism.[17]

Although there is some truth to these depictions, the wholesale critique of therapeutic culture is problematic for at least three reasons.

One, the secularization by therapy argument is itself often grounded—if tacitly—in a commitment to a particular vision of what counts as "authentic" Christianity or tradition, by which liberal Protestants fall short. Second, the argument does not engage with the scholarship that has demonstrated how secularity and Christianity are mutually constitutive.[18] Third, the critiques of liberal Protestant secularization are often based on scornful stereotypes of the "belief-based" Protestant, and thus miss the opportunity to consider the energetic and complicated ways that liberal Protestants practiced their own modern supernaturalism in the midst of their love of science.

My interest in liberal Protestants partly comes from what I see to be a lack of imagination when it comes to the analysis of the "liberal subject," especially in its Protestant versions. Anthropologists, political theorists, and other scholars have often worked with a definition of the liberal human subject as an individual invested with autonomy, choice, and freedom of conscience, who is simultaneously willing to grant (or impose) these same freedoms to other individuals under the rubric of tolerance. In some accounts, to be liberal also implies an affinity for Protestantism; liberalism is viewed as a Western political ideology that is "thick with bourgeois Protestant norms."[19] These theoretical accounts of liberalism may work fairly well as a description of the ideal of the liberal subject and rightfully point to the mutual imbrications of Protestantism and power in the empires of North America. They do not, however, account for the messiness of how those who have claimed to be liberal have actually practiced their ideals. Nor do they attend to the diversity of normative claims about self and society at issue within North American Protestantism. As Jeffrey Stout has shown, the sharp critiques of liberalism from theorists and theologians such as Alastair MacIntyre and Stanley Hauerwas have caricatured liberalism as an anti-traditional, rootless cosmopolitanism, requiring little of those who would live under its name. Stout suggests forgoing the term liberalism altogether—without giving up liberal democracy as a tradition—but since "liberalism" is still a live term as a derogatory epithet, a self-description, and a scholarly category, I argue for its continued, if cautious use, realizing that its meaning is not one thing across time or peoples.[20] Considering liberal Protestantism not as a trope but a practice reveals a challenging array of convictions and inconsistencies, solidarities and exclusions that have characterized the lives and communities of men and women who have taken both the advancement and the taming of modernity as their task.

Liberalism, tied as it is to a narrative of secularity as a normative project by which religion is supposedly cleaved apart from political life, makes for an even more complicated subject when combined with religious commitments. Assailed from multiple quarters—including from within—the overly roomy notion of liberalism in its political and religious forms has greatly transformed over the past century moving from a democratic tradition concerned with engaging with a diverse world to a vision derided by conservatives for its unprincipled pliability and critiqued by postcolonial scholars for its unacknowledged Western and Christian assumptions about economy, self, and society. Liberal Protestants, more specifically, have been accused both of heresy and of hegemony; they have been chastised for their lack of true Christian conviction by conservative Protestants, criticized for getting "caught up in the fashionable currents of inclusiveness and ecumenicity" by scholars of American religion, and critiqued by postcolonial scholars for disguising yet more western domination in the language of tolerance and interreligious dialogue.[21] The line between liberalism and liberal Protestantism is fuzzy, but as Michael Warner argues, much of the criticism of both liberalism as a political identity and liberal Protestantism as a religious identity operates with scornfully gendered tropes in place of careful analysis.[22]

Liberal Protestantism is a highly influential form of Christianity rarely attended to by anthropologists, who have little recognized liberal Protestants as anthropological subjects.[23] Theologians in the lineage of Schleiermacher, Rauschenbusch, or Tillich have dominated historical characterizations of Protestant liberalism—critics and defenders alike have considered liberalism an idealistic academic or clergy-led enterprise with a narrow audience. Attention to healing, however, reveals that liberal Protestantism can be found to have many different practitioners when one starts looking: medical missionaries, parish nurses, Christian yoga advocates. A category not especially shaped by official creeds or orthodoxies, liberal Protestantism commenced with a nineteenth- and early twentieth-century openness to scientific modes of critical inquiry, including medical research, adopting, by the end of the century, a growing receptivity to diverse religious traditions, informed, in part, by postcolonial movements of liberation theology in the Americas, Asia, and Africa.

By considering liberal Protestants as "practicing Protestants" with as much ambivalence and complication as other Christians, I open up new avenues for theorizing liberal subjects and liberal modernities.[24] My appeal pushes further Joel Robbins's call for anthropologists to recognize how "the deep structure of anthropological thinking" has made it hard for them to see "convert cultures" as Christian. For my part, I ask anthropologists to see the ways that anthropological thinking is shaped by some of the same cultural and historical forces that have constituted liberal Protestantism's traditions of social critique.[25] The challenge of recognizing liberal Protestants as anthropological subjects, I suggest, is partly the result of the overlapping spatial, intellectual, and political locations and commitments of liberal Protestants and English-speaking academia, including anthropology.

For example the anthropologist Edward Sapir, who for fifteen years worked in Canada among West Coast First Nations at the same time as Du Vernet, argued that the transformations of modernity were particularly tied to "a progressive increase in the radius of communication." Without going all the way to radio mind, Sapir, who came from an Orthodox Jewish family, defined religion by way of reference to Protestant revivalism, Plains Indians' "supernatural medicine," and Nootka notions of the "Supreme Being," coming up with a definition that Du Vernet would likely have endorsed: "Religion is man's never-ceasing attempt to discover a road to spiritual serenity across the perplexities and dangers of daily life."[26] Although not forgoing the Bible, many liberal Protestants had reading lists akin to those of intellectuals like Sapir, including Kant, Marx, Bergson, Freud, and the new literature in "comparative religion." In turn, pioneering anthropologists, such as Franz Boas and Margaret Mead, sometimes came to their conclusions about human nature in direct conversation with practicing Protestants, including Boas's Tsimshian collaborator Odille Morison, an Anglican from Du Vernet's part of British Columbia, and liberal Protestant intellectuals such as Paul Tillich. Protestant supernatural liberalism, like anthropology itself, contributed to a new, modern discourse of "religion" that took shape in the midst of colonial state projects and popularizations of academic prose.[27]

The overlapping critical cultures of anthropology and North American liberal (and liberationist) Christianity have also shaped the work of prominent medical anthropologists. As Mark Lewis Taylor has shown in his analysis of the writings of Paul Farmer and Nancy Scheper Hughes, medical anthropologists who consider their work to require "moral advocacy" turn to "religious-like" language when pushed to the limits of what they can bear as they face the urgency and violence of global cultures of illness, inequity, and suffering. Adopting a liberatory discourse much indebted to the largely Roman Catholic liberation theology found in their fieldwork settings, they blur the line between activist and pro-phetic ethnography."[28] Joel Robbins has addressed this blurry line most directly, in his argument that anthropologists have lost their earlier will-ingness to write about cultural difference in a prescriptive fashion that aims to "get their readers to put difference to use in their own lives."[29] Robbins argues that Christian theology, by contrast, has greater "critical force" precisely because it argues for different ways of living that are meant to directly effect transformations in the lives of its readers.

Robbins makes his argument about anthropology's enfeebled vision by contrast to the bold project of theologian John Milbank—a powerful thinker who has positioned his own critique of the intersection of reli-gion and social theory within the rubric of radical orthodoxy, a group of Christian scholars highly critical of liberal Protestantism.[30] Compared to radical orthodoxy, liberal Protestants and anthropologists share an af-finity largely derived from an historical transformation not discussed by Robbins: whereas there were always anthropologists and missionaries who confronted aspects of colonialism, post-1960s anthropologists and liberal Protestants were both struck in new ways with the awareness that their encounters with difference—in the registers of culture or religion—were profoundly shaped by their own complicity with colonial power. Compared to liberal Protestants, and not to Milbank, anthro-pologists can be seen to have shared a postcolonial trajectory whereby critiques of their authority and power, both from within and without, challenged their willingness or ability to think universally and prescrip-tively. Their optimistic cosmopolitanism chastened, both anthropolo-gists and liberal Protestants have been living with a crisis of faith and a crisis of narrative.

Spirits of Protestantism attends to these overlapping cultures of crisis and critique by examining how liberal Protestants moved from missionary hubris to self-criticism as they sought to alleviate what they considered to be pathologies of modernity via particular techniques and technologies of healing. After an introduction that addresses what I mean by "healing", and situates the groups and methodology at the center of this study, the five chapters of the book take a more or less chronological order. The first chapter, "Strange Places of the Spirit: Anthropologies of the Spiritual Body" has two tasks. First, I argue that constituting liberal Protestantism as the object of anthropological analysis requires showing how liberal Protestants have contributed to setting the terms of the anthropology of religion itself. Reflecting on the awkward kinship between academic an-thropology and theological anthropology, I use both meanings of the term to frame liberal Protestants as "anthropological" subjects. In the process I show how liberal Protestants developed a particular perspective on what it meant to be a "spiritual" body, by drawing on psychological notions of the self and cultivating "spiritual equilibrium," and to a lesser extent, spiritual intervention.

The second chapter, "The Gospel of Health and the Scientific Spirit," details the early twentieth-century liberal Protestant embrace of medical science as a partner to Christian missions and considers the important, and largely neglected, role that liberal Protestants played in the process of medicalization in the first quarter of the century. I argue that this imperialistic alliance was undergirded by an overlapping text-based cosmology in which liberal Protestants understood texts both as talismanic tools of healing and as documents for scientific proof. The third chapter, "Protestant Experimentalists and the Energy of Love," contends with other kinds of mediated supernaturalism, especially the new technology of radio, as liberal Protestants from the 1920s to the 1940s sought tools of healing in forms of energy such as electricity and psychic channels at a time when psychology and psychoanalysis were claiming their share of the human spirit. This experimentalism flourished in such places as Canada, England, the United States, and India at same time that liberal Protestants were beginning to question the ways Christian mission both fostered and was supported by colonialism. Chapter four, "Evil Spirits and Queer Psyches in an Age of Anxiety," follows liberal supernaturalism in North America from the 1950s – 1970s, showing how liberal Protestants tacked between psychological and charismatic understandings of the self to renew their theologies and pastoral practices. Turning to a ubiquitous and vague anthropology of "body, mind, and spirit," liberal Protestants contended with the simultaneous rise of faith healing, charismatic renewal, and psychology as diagnosticians of the moral—or immoral—self. At the same time, they were in the vanguard of a sexual revolution in which the literal "pathologizing" of homosexuality was transformed into a political and religious movement for the celebration of sexual difference.

Finally, the fifth chapter, "Ritual Proximity and the Healing of History" analyzes how contemporary Protestants, in their embrace of yoga, Reiki, and other non-Christian techniques, have rethought and re-embodied questions of what counts as spirit and religious difference in the midst of charges of both appropriation and heresy. In the wake of their acknowledgment that their own historical projects of Christian modernity carried within them pathologies of colonial domination, some liberal Protestants turned to ritual to cultivate a new religious universalism. *Spirits of Protestantism* contributes a new transnational perspective to the growing body of work that has excavated forgotten (maybe even repressed?) traditions of religious liberalism in North America. By reconsidering what counts as the heretical and the hegemonic within the techniques, theologies, and controversies that shaped liberal Protestant discourses of healing over the twentieth century, I provide another genealogy for the work of those political theorists, such as Courtney Jung, who advance a "critical liberalism" grounded in specific political and historical contexts.[31] Tracing anthropologies of the spiritual body inside and outside of medical realms reveals a tradition of supernatural liberalism that has animated both biomedical and spiritual healing practices, and has shaped diverse sensibilities of critique.[32]

Acknowledgments

Writing this book has taken me many unexpected places, both geograph-
ically and intellectually. Along the way, I encountered great generosity of
spirit, for which I am most thankful. I am fortunate to have several stal-
wart friends who are also kindred spirits in the life of the mind and who
have thought through this project with me. Maggie MacDonald has
taken care for both my words and my children and has long inspired me
with her example and friendship. Courtney Bender has graced me with
her keen vision and dry wit, as she pursued her own "energetic" project,
and we worked together on joint ventures—I am grateful for her hospitality on my visits to archives in New York City and for her presence of
mind on all occasions. Amira Mittermaier and Andrea Most have both
shown me just how rich collegial life could be, and their careful and critical readings of the entire manuscript were considerable gifts. More recently, Ruth Marshall has shared with me her unmatched combination of
critical thinking and compassion; her ability to get right to the heart of
any matter, whether that of a philosopher or a teenager, is a remarkable
talent that has been of great help to me on many occasions.

Alan Ackerman read an earlier version of the entire manuscript in our
writers' group (along with Andrea Most and John Marshall), and I am
thankful both for his insightful reading and for the sustenance of that
community of writers. In another writers' group while we shared our
sabbaticals in Tübingen, Germany, Linda Radzik and Bob Shandley read
an early version of chapter two, and I am delighted to acknowledge their

support now that I have finished the entire book. My colleague Kevin O'Neill also read the manuscript and helped me to greater precision at a moment when I needed it most. The Very Rev., the Hon. Lois Wilson, read the entire manuscript and offered excellent suggestions from the perspective of one with intimate knowledge of the United Church. Heather Curtis and two anonymous reviewers for the University of California Press offered detailed and very helpful suggestions for revision—I am especially grateful to Heather for her collegiality and spirit of cooperation. Joel Robbins, the editor of the Anthropology of Christianity Series, has supported this book for many years now, and I have learned a great deal from his remarkable balance of gentle critique.

Other friends and colleagues offered helpful responses to particular chapters or queries, and I am very grateful to the following people for the critical care they took with my work (with the caveat, of course, that I am responsible for all deficiencies): Natalie Zemon Davis, Frances Garrett, Arti Dhand, Alison Falby, Neil ten Kortenaar, Marie Griffith, Christopher White, Jon Roberts, Thomas Hauschild, Susan Sered, Simon Coleman, Ronald Numbers, Charles Stewart, Eric Hirsch, Birgit Meyer, David Morgan, Reid Locklin, Alan Hayes, Tisa Wenger, John Lardas Modern, Phyllis Airhart, Catherine Albanese, and Katie Lofton. Several chapters benefited from audience comments at conferences and invited lectures, including at Eberhard-Karls Universität Tübingen, Northwestern University, the University of Ottawa, the Society for the Anthropology of Religion Conference, the American Society for Church History Annual Meeting, the Canadian Historical Association Annual Meeting, the European Association of Sociology and Anthropology, the American Academy of Religion, the Religion and Media Seminar, and the Social Science Research Council. At the University of Toronto, I benefited from presentations at the Jackman Humanities Institute, the Department of Anthropology, the Centre for the Study of the United States, the Toronto School of Theology Liturgy Seminar, and the Department of Historical Studies. Portions of chapters 2, 3, and 5 were published previously in *Church History*, the *Journal of the American Academy of Religion*, and *History and Anthropology*, and I thank the anonymous readers and editors from these journals for their valuable comments.

Staff members at several archives were extraordinarily helpful during my research process. I am particularly grateful to Martha Smalley of Special Collections at the Yale Divinity School Library, Sharon Larade and Robin Brunelle at the United Church of Canada Archives, Nancy Hurd at the General Synod Archives, Anglican Church of Canada, Sylvia Lassam at the Trinity College Archives, Mary-Anne Nicholls of the Diocese of Toronto Archives, and Ruth Tonkiss Cameron and Seth Kasten at the Burke Library. I also thank the many ministers, priests, parish nurses, yoga instructors, Reiki practitioners, and Anglican and United Church laypeople who welcomed me into their places of worship and sometimes their homes, and shared their stories with me.

When it was at its very early stages, I discussed this book with Karen McCarthy Brown, who first introduced me to the study of religion and healing as my *Doktormutter*. I am very grateful for Karen's support and for the example and insights that her own writings still provide, and lament that illness has kept her from realizing further her creative forays into religion, history, and storytelling.

Many students were an indispensable part of the research for this book. Two of my PhD students, Kerry Fast and Laurel Zwissler, did painstaking work with the church newspapers at the center of the book, and I am very appreciative of how they showed the same standards with their work for me as they did in their own research. Arlene Macdonald also contributed to the development of the book, both as a research assistant and as a scholar who shared my interest in the intersections of Christianity and biomedicine. Amy Fisher traveled to Yale Divinity School with me in search of Sherwood Eddy and to the United Church Archives in search of Belle Oliver and has helped me with the difficult tasks of bringing the manuscript to completion, including the work of compiling the index. Hanna Kienzler, then an MA student at the Eberhard-Karls Universität Tübingen, gave me invaluable help while I was on sabbatical in Germany. University of Toronto MA students Jenny Gilbert and Jenn Bailey also traveled with me to archives in New York City, Waterloo, and Boston, and showed considerable initiative in thinking through the significance of the materials we collected. Both Jenny and Jenn came to the project through the University of Toronto's Research Opportunities Program, an outstanding program that brings together undergraduates and faculty in research teams. Other students who worked with me through ROP and as research assistants include: Emma Sheppard, Lynette Choo, Frances Beswick, Ridhdhi Desai, Amirrtha Srikanthanan, Christine Wu, Eisar al-Sukhni, Meg Mazurek, Krish Parameswaran, Mateen Rokhsefat, Kristin Yee, Sarah Khan, Sandra Kendal, and Sarina Annis.

My research has been generously supported by several foundations and granting agencies. The Connaught Foundation at the University of Toronto supported my work when it was at its earliest stages, and a Standard Research Grant from the Social Sciences and Humanities Research

Council of Canada allowed me to pursue the project more fully. A Humboldt Foundation Research Fellowship supported me at the Institut für Ethnologie at the Eberhard-Karls Universität Tübingen during 2004–2005, and I am especially grateful to my *Gastgeber* (or host), Prof. Dr. Thomas Hauschild, as well as to Prof. Dr. Roland Hardenberg and Prof. Dr. Gabriele Alex, who welcomed me back in 2010–2011. A Fellowship at the Jackman Humanities Institute in 2009–2010 allowed me to finish this book while I started on the next one, and I thank Bob Gibbs, the Director of the JHI, for his confidence in and enthusiasm for my work. I am also very fortunate to be located within two robust and supportive communities at the University of Toronto. The Department for the Study of Religion is among the best places in the world to work as scholar of religion—and an anthropologist of Christianity—and I thank my colleagues, and especially the Chair, John Kloppenborg, for all they do in making it so. Victoria College, my other home within the University, has generously supported my research with travel and research grants, and its Senior Common Room has been a source of all manner of insights for my work.

At the University of California Press, Stan Holwitz, followed by Reed Malcolm, have both been supportive editors, and I am very appreciative of their help in shepherding this book. I am also grateful for the copyediting of Elissa L. Schiff, who not only cleaned up my prose, but also offered me very insightful suggestions for revision. It has also been a pleasure to work with Edward Wade, as well as Kalicia Pivirotto and other University of California Press staff.

Finally, I am deeply grateful to family and friends who have provided me with the support—and optimism—that make my work possible. Fereshteh Hashemi meets every occasion with insight and dignity, and it is a true joy to work (and lunch) with her. Lorraine and Oliver Sutherns have been the best childcare cooperators, and friends, that one could hope for. Susanne and Florian Seiberlich turned our German adventure into an occasion of friendship that continues today. My father, John Klassen, and his wife Vicki Sharp have kept just the right balance of asking after and respectfully not mentioning my work when it was time for more leisurely conversations. My brother Joel has taken care of my children (and me) in ways that I can only hope to return now that he has a family of his own. My mother Susanna Klassen continues to look after me, and my children, with love and unsurpassable hospitality. My children, Magdalene, Isabel, and Georgia (the last two who were born in the midst of this book), are all, in their own remarkable ways, the abiding sources of my energy and hope. I am profoundly grateful to each of them for their abilities to love and be loved. Every word in this book, and many more that he helped to ensure didn't make the cut, has been read multiple times by John Marshall. As my friend, husband, and colleague, he has traveled with me all manner of places, always giving me an irreplaceable equilibrium of critique and love. This book is for him.

Introduction

Healing Christians

When she published her 1930 advice book on how to speak frankly to children about sex, the unmarried Dr. Belle Oliver joined a vanguard of women and men willing to risk censure and censorship in the service of "social hygiene." Writing without the credibility drawn from motherly experience, Oliver nevertheless felt it was her duty to use her medical authority and expertise to bring Indian families both primary medical care and a Christian-inflected reverence for the body. *Anandi's Question* advised mothers and fathers to speak frankly to their four-year-olds about where babies come from, using medically appropriate names for parts of the body. Likening dawning sexuality to the blooming of a flower, Oliver urged parents to teach their children that sex was a strong natural impulse given by God, but one demanding self-control: "Now we must learn to think of sex, not as something that drags people down, but as something holy and good and meant to lift them up. And we must learn to talk of sex reverently in the light of God's presence."[1] At the same time Oliver was coming to question the idea that God's presence might only be felt by those converted to Christianity.

Illustrating *Anandi's Question* with detailed maps of the female reproductive system, Oliver imagined the body with a clinical specificity while she simultaneously infused the flesh with the animating presence of God. Similarly, in her 1942 book *Tales from the Inns of Healing*, Oliver insisted, using the gendered idiom of her day, that "man is not merely a body, but mind and spirit as well." According to Oliver, a healthy body,

FIGURE 1. Portrait of Dr. Belle Choné Oliver, 1922. Courtesy of United Church of Canada Archives, Toronto, Glenna Jamieson Fonds 1988.029P14.

FIGURE 2. Front Cover of Belle Choné Oliver's *Anandi's Question,* 1930.Courtesy of United Church of Canada Archives, Toronto, Glenna Jamieson Fonds, 1988.029C001.18.

mind, and spirit depended on preventive health and the best surgical techniques, but at the same time, prayer would not hurt. Alongside her charts of operations performed and lists of Indian doctors trained, Oliver also related testimonies of healing wrought by prayerful visions of "Swami Jesu." Endorsing "a power of spirit over body in which prayer seems to have made available healing powers of God witnessing to His glory," while also committed to the theological liberalism of her day, Oliver was a practitioner of liberal Protestant supernaturalism.[2]

One of Oliver's colleagues and favorite authors, Harvard philosopher Ernest Hocking, found psychology the best seeding ground for a politically applied supernaturalism: "The disillusioned—not disheartened— liberalism of today turns itself heart and soul to psychological enquiry. . . . 'The Great Society,' whether it is to be ruled, or educated, or saved, or simply lived in, has to be taken as a meeting ground of forces to which we would better apply the name instinctive or passional than simply rational."[3] Psychology cleared a new space for thinking about the human in energetic terms not confined to Christianity, but also not far from the convictions of the liberal Protestant social gospel, which saw the world as a place for Christian social action in the present. When Hocking, a student of William James, led the ecumenical "Rethinking Missions" report in the 1920s, he turned to Oliver for support. Joining a liberal Protestant network of missionaries, medical professionals, educators, and clergy who were increasingly questioning the theological triumphalism, economic ideologies, and political imperialism of Christianity and its colonial missions, Oliver's international activism and medical expertise were also embedded in a supernaturalism in which prayer, visions, and touch were possible routes to healing the body.

Another such supernatural liberal, Archbishop Frederick Du Vernet, presided over a region of forests and mountains that covered over 200,000 square miles of the northern half of British Columbia, and which, according to the spiritual mapping of the Anglican Church, was the Diocese of Caledonia. Here, Du Vernet worked with a population that was mostly First Nations people, along with a growing group of white settlers and a phalanx of clergy and missionaries from rival Christian churches, each with its own spiritual map of the territory. Although remembered as a "strong evangelical leader" by his Anglican chroniclers, Du Vernet shared Belle Oliver's liberal Protestant dispositions in that he supported labor unions, helped to initiate an "ecumenical" Anglican college in Vancouver, and refused to allow "Indian" residential schools in the Diocese at a time when these culture-destroying schools were

expanding throughout the western provinces. Recognized as an eminent churchman, by the end of his life Du Vernet considered himself
an experimental psychologist mapping out new techniques of healing
that brought together the power of electricity with the power of the
Divine.

At the same time that his Protestant colleagues further south in Vancouver and Victoria were engaged in a vicious debate about whether
faith healing was fakery or fact, Du Vernet was writing about his technique of "radio mind" or "spiritual radio," a form of prayer that could
draw down the healing energy of God that coursed through the universe via radio waves. He summed up his work thus: "Perhaps this is
the greatest contribution I have to make to the cause of Science. The
supposed barrier of space between two minds can be effectually annihi-
lated by the power of the imagination working through the fundamental union of all souls in the realm of the subconscious world."[4] Telepathic communication, psychic unity, and divine energies came together
for Du Vernet in a technological supernaturalism that imagined the whole
universe to pulse with the healing vibrations of God.

Neither Oliver nor Du Vernet are remembered for their versions of
supernatural healing, borne of a union of their Christian and scientific
convictions.[5] Historians and anthropologists of Christian healing have
rarely recognized liberal Protestants as dwellers in the spirit or witnesses to the uncanny and have focused instead on those more dramatically convicted by spiritual healing, such as Pentecostals, Christian Scientists, or spiritualists taken with séances and mesmeric healing.[6] Beyond
the sphere of healing, twentieth-century liberal Protestants are often
characterized by their conservative critics, as well as by scholars, as the
most secular of modern Christians, and the very personification of Max
Weber's notion of disenchantment. For Weber, disenchantment was an
historical process that demystified "mysterious incalculable forces," ensuring that "one need no longer have recourse to magical means in order
to master or implore spirits." Going further, Weber considered science
and bureaucracy to be two generative modes of authoritative knowledge
that facilitated *Protestant* disenchantment especially, resulting in "specialists [who were] without spirits" altogether.[7]

As specialists with spirit, Oliver and Du Vernet are but two examples
of a wider network of liberal Protestants whose commitments to science and the social gospel helped bring into being the very institutions
of secular modernity—including hospitals, universities, the Canadian
version of a state-funded health care system, and transnational nongov-

FIGURE 3. Portrait of The Most
Reverend F. H. Du Vernet,
Archbishop of Caledonia, ca.
1915. Courtesy of The General
Synod Archives, Anglican
Church of Canada, Accession
number P7805-2.

ernmental organizations—while they maintained a commitment to the
reality, or at least the possibility, of supernatural intervention in the
world. Their supernaturalism was bred of habits of prayer, convictions
that spiritual energies coursed through the universe and the body, and
for some, a hope that all religions offered paths, via rituals and spiritual·
exercises, to these universal truths.

Liberal Protestants deeply saturated many locations of the secular in
North America—including medicine and anthropology. Canadian "socialized medicine," the specter that has persistently haunted U.S. debates about restructuring health care, is a system that gradually came
into being over the course of the twentieth century partly with the help
of liberal Protestants and Catholics who considered that all people were
equal before God and deserved equal access to medical care. In a world
undergoing medicalization—that is, the rise of biomedicine as the medical approach with the greatest cultural, interpretive, legal, and economic power—liberal Protestants staked their authority on the biomedical turf of hospitals, medical schools, medical missions, and eventually,
psychology clinics. At the same time they also cultivated practices of
spiritual healing dependent on technological metaphors of electricity,

vibrations, and energy, as well as on the spiritual disciplines of other religions. At once bracingly counterintuitive and explicitly political, the liberal Protestant blend of supernaturalism and secular modernity can be found in the middle of many of the twentieth century's fierce contests: anticolonialism, the rise of and challenge to biomedical hegemony, embrace and suspicion of technological innovation, and the depathologizing of homosexuality.

I first came at this project intending to do an ethnographic study focused on new healing movements in the early twenty-first century in a variety of liberal Protestant churches. I wanted to place liberal Protestants within the same "religion and healing" compass that has included other North American groups, such as the Chicago Catholics devoted to St. Jude described by Robert Orsi and the New York Haitian Vodou communities discussed by Karen McCarthy Brown.[8] After attending several prayer and healing services at both an Anglican church and a United church, sitting in on the meetings of a parish nurse health cabinet (in which the nurse seeks advice from congregation members), and stretching my way through sessions of Christian yoga, I came to the realization that the story I had to tell needed to reach further back in time (as did Orsi and Brown, as well). Why were these United Church members now laying hands on each other in the search for healing, when their Presbyterian and Methodist forebears would have spurned such rituals as either "Pentecostal excess" or "Catholic superstition?" Why were Anglicans doing the "downward dog" in full view of the cross, when one hundred years ago such bodily manipulations in a church would have provoked cries of "heretic!" or "heathen!"?

With these questions in mind, my first point of departure was to turn to the church newspapers of the Anglican and United Churches (before 1925 I followed its Methodist wing) starting at the beginning of the twentieth century. What I found was an ongoing debate and discussion about what constituted appropriate practices of healing—and what counted as healing itself. The editorials, letters to the editor, book reviews, articles, and advertisements in the Methodist *Christian Guardian* and the Anglican *Canadian Churchman* (and their later versions) demonstrated the ways healing contributed to fashioning "imagined communities" of North American Protestantism as groups of white, middle-class citizens increasingly transformed by their awareness of and encounter with cultural and religious difference.[9] In addition to their own richness as sources, the newspapers were an indispensable starting point for me to work outwards to texts, debates, and personalities referred to by various authors. This led me to a range of other textual sources, including mission reports, other newspapers, scientific articles, autobiographical and biographical writings, personal papers from the archives of Anglican, Methodist, United Church of Canada, and Christian Science denominations, and the myriad of popular texts on religion and healing written by twentieth-century European and North American clergy and laypeople.[10]

Pairing this historical research with fieldwork gave me a broader perspective in which to understand how, over the course of the twentieth century, liberal Protestants in North America went from being the patrons of medicine in opposition to superstitious heathens and heretical quacks to being seekers of healing via the rituals and epistemologies of these same castigated others. They moved from early convictions about the moral necessity of medical missions and the immoral heresy of new Christian healing-based movements such as Christian Science to later experiments with an eclectic range of spiritual traditions and therapies including Reiki and yoga. How did Protestants of liberal dispositions shift from decrying Christian charlatans and non-Christian superstitions while actively advancing biomedicine to find themselves experimenting with yoga *asanas* and channeling healing energy via the laying on of hands? I answer this question by exploring both the past and the present of liberal Protestant approaches to healing not solely as a form of bodily repair or cure, but as an expansive concept and practice that shifts in meaning and application over the twentieth century. Liberal Protestants used the rubric of healing to understand their role in facilitating the rising authority of biomedicine in a medicalizing culture, to assess and critique varieties of Christian and non-Christian spiritual healing, and to encounter the technologies and techniques of North American therapeutic cultures, such as counseling and psychoanalysis. By the end of the century they also hoped that the notion of healing could be a space of apology and reconciliation in the wake of their part in the colonization of First Nations peoples.

For liberal Protestants in particular, the last one hundred years have been a time of profound hybridity, in Homi Bhabha's sense of cultural and historical mixing that transforms (and subverts) both colonizer and colonized.[11] Their confident missionary triumphalism of the early twentieth century was increasingly chastened by the harsh lessons of two European-based world wars, anticolonial resistance to Western dominance, and a rising discourse of universal human rights. In this (unfinished) transformation from missionary-colonizers to self-critical advocates of social justice, liberal North American Protestants adjudicated how and whether such diverse techniques as yoga, faith healing, medications, telepathy, and psychoanalysis work as Christian practices. Changing understandings of the meaning of religious difference have underwritten these evaluations, as liberal Protestants moved from wanting to exterminate religious differences in the name of a worldwide Christianity to celebrating them with an anthropological valorization of difference, to grappling with their responsibility for "Christian privilege" in a multireligious world.

RESPONSIBILITY, PRIVILEGE, AND THE "LIBERAL" PROTESTANT

Defined in historian Gary Dorrien's terms as those Protestants working toward "a rational and experiential third way between authority-based orthodoxies and secular disbelief," liberal Protestants were also Christians who, not unlike anthropologists, sought the unity of humankind while they acknowledged legitimate differences among people and religions.[12] Not a precise designation, liberalism, in William Hutchison's account of U.S. Protestants, was marked by its willingness to modify doctrine in the light of historical and cultural change, its commitment to the immanence of God in human nature, and its optimistic approach to the possibility of universal human community. At the same time, Protestant liberalism is often depicted as antagonistic to the supernatural as embodied in claims about Jesus's miracles, the Virgin birth, or the possibility of faith healing, viewed in the light of modern science.[13] I argue, however, that liberal Protestants cultivated their own version of supernaturalism, as they cut across Protestant denominations, embracing ecumenism, socialist critique, and sometimes even the scientifically mystical allure of parapsychology. As Belle Oliver, Frederick Du Vernet, and others will demonstrate, their blend of reason and experience was often tempered with a strong current of "immanent" supernaturalism that allowed diverse spiritual irruptions to bubble up within scientific dispositions.

Rooted in reason and experience and hopeful about progress brought by medical discoveries, Protestant liberalism insisted that being a Christian was not just about caring about your own salvation—being a Christian made one responsible to all of humanity. Supported in part by biblical texts, the roots of liberal responsibility also lay in the sense of Christian duty held by missionaries. For example, consider a speech by

Mabel Cartwright at a meeting of the Anglican Women's Auxiliary in Toronto during the spring of 1907, in which she addressed her audience on the necessity to "arise and build" the "City of God."[14] As reported in the Anglican newspaper, the *Canadian Churchman*, she asked rhetorically: "Why are we to build?' Because we have entered into the privilege of those who have—because it is God's purpose—because there is a reflex. Unless we build we are keeping our brothers out of their rights." For a Christian to keep her religion to herself—or to her fellow Christians— was a denial of the equality of humanity and of the responsibility of the white, privileged Christian, since "the soul of the heathen is as precious as the soul of the white man."[15] Extending this responsibility to medical care, the English Anglican missionary Hanna Riddell wrote in the same Anglican newspaper, to appeal for funds for her Japanese leper hospital:

> To appreciate the Leper Hospital properly, one should go first to Honmyo-ji, a Buddhist temple for the worship of Kato Kiyomasa, who is supposed to be specially the deity who succors lepers. It is a scene of misery that, once seen, can never be forgotten. To go from this scene of dirt and misery to the clean, quiet rooms and sunny gardens of the Hospital, and watch the looks of thankful resignation, nay, cheerfulness, on the poor lepers' faces, can only be compared to the change described by Dante in his transit upwards from the infernal regions to the quiet resting-place before entering Paradise.[16]

Riddell's depiction of the stark difference between Buddhist and Christian modes of attending to lepers in their illness was not merely for effect—Riddell was deeply convinced that her Christian faith had called her to travel halfway across the world with the Church Missionary Society. Once there, she spent the rest of her life drawing Japanese and international attention to the plight of lepers—long a focus of Christian missionaries—through building and running the Hospital of the Resurrection of Hope and its Anglican Chapel.[17] With hindsight, the empire-fed, racialized Christian triumphalism that motivated such churchwomen as Mabel Cartwright and Hanna Riddell is obvious. But in the wake of their long-lasting medical clinics, hospitals, and associations not everyone remembers these missionaries as cultural imperialists.[18] The effects of Christian missions have been neither one-way nor predictable.

As pioneers in such realms as hospital and hospice care, medical training for doctors and nurses, public health and preventative medicine, and the export of biomedicine to non-Western countries through medical missions, liberal Protestants have played an important role in the emergence of a biomedical system that is still undecided about whether health care is a capitalist project or a human right, or both.[19] Alongside campaigning for greater access to biomedical health care, liberal Protestants have also experimented with a broad range of explicitly spiritual healing practices that have caused the reflex of privilege to rebound in new directions since Mabel Cartwright reflected on the city of God in 1907. Sharing convictions about the equality of human souls similar to that which emboldened their early twentieth-century forebears on the mission field and in ladies' auxiliaries, many liberal Christians no longer stigmatize Buddhist, Hindu, or First Nations traditions of healing but instead embrace them as wisdom traditions with much to teach biomedically dominated Western Christianity. For example by the turn of the new millennium, Father Patrick, priest of an Anglican Church in downtown Toronto, had opened up his church to yoga, Buddhist-inspired meditation, and Reiki healers. Especially committed to the practice of "Christian Yoga," Father Patrick contended that Christians have much to learn from Eastern religions and much to rediscover of their own traditions of meditative prayer. Blending traditions in his yoga classes, liturgical healing services, and meditation/prayer evenings, Father Patrick considered the "energies of God" to be accessible through many channels. Whereas Father Patrick's post-millenium syncretism easily fits within definitions of liberal Protestants, Mabel Cartwright's missionary triumphalism is less readily defined as such. Nevertheless, she is among its ancestors.

The liberalism that is of interest to me is neither a classic, market-driven economic liberalism nor its more recent version of "neoliberalism." Instead, I understand liberal Protestants to intersect with another culture of liberalism, which has taken the continued questioning of authority (itself a very Protestant mode) as a necessary democratic process. Nikolas Rose reveals a facet of this process in his discussion of "advanced liberalism," which he argues is characterized by "a recurrent diagnosis of failure coupled with a recurrent demand to govern better." For Rose, the "perpetual questioning" of advanced liberalism has led, in part, to technologies of self-government (and a "will to be healthy") for those considered "normal" and responsible and the outright control of those people seen to be deviant.[20] In her articulation of "critical liberalism," however, Courtney Jung points to another, more *self*-critical and in some ways more hopeful aspect of this eternal questioning: "The intuition that lies at the core of critical liberalism is that blindness to injustices, in which even people fighting to right wrongs fail to recognize patterns of unfairness all around them, is a permanent feature of social and political life."[21] With intuitions and obscured vision at its center, this kind of liberalism must count on both critics from without and inspiration from within to work toward its never-achieved goal of righting structural injustice.

But liberal Protestants are not entirely subsumable within these broader political traditions of liberalism. The historiography of liberal Protestantism is still largely defined by intellectual histories focused on theologians and clergy, although Catherine Albanese's recent delineation of a "metaphysical" tradition within American religion, along with Leigh Schmidt's argument for a tradition of religious liberalism in the United States, have inspired a new wave of research into Protestant practice.[22] Liberals formed only a part of the denominations to which they belonged, interacting as a transnational community of like-minded Christians dedicated to social reform, who were nevertheless based in denominations that were intimately structured by the laws, histories, and cultures of national territories.[23] (In Canada, liberal Protestants should not be confused with the Liberal political party; although the two could overlap, many liberal Protestants were active in the founding of the socialist-inflected Canadian Commonwealth Federation, later the New Democratic Party.) My approach to the category of liberal Protestantism via the two denominations of the Anglican and United Churches in Canada is undertaken in the spirit of religion scholar Charles Long, who argued, "The denomination as a classificatory order that emerged only within the structure of modernity might well be the entrée into the problematic of religion in a postcolonial, post-Protestant, and post-Enlightenment world."[24] Although adopting the denomination-crossing label of "liberal" was clearly of importance to many Christians in the early twentieth century (and earlier), most were still tied to denominations as communities of both creed and liturgical practice.

With the rise of ecumenism as goal of global Christian unity, some came to view the denomination itself a pathology of modernity—how else to explain the passion and triumph that characterized the ecumenical overcoming of denominational differences of Presbyterian, Methodist, and Congregationalist that took place with the creation of the new denomination of the United Church of Canada in 1925? Or, for that matter, the repeated (but as yet unrealized) attempts to draft and implement a "Plan of Union" that would unite the Anglican Church of Canada with the United Church.[25] Ecumenism thus brought a changing terrain of difference. As Jonathan Z. Smith argues, "difference is not a matter of comparison between entities judged to be equivalent, rather difference most frequently entails a hierarchy of prestige and ranking" in which the most fraught lines arise between close neighbors sharing religious kinship. [26] In early twentieth-century North America a Protestant's closest neighbors were usually other Protestants or perhaps Catholics, and the differences between an Anglican and Methodist in terms of class, liturgy, and alcohol consumption were thought to be highly significant. But as Protestants became missionaries working to settle new immigrants and as new movements of Christian healing emerged, the proximate other could include a much wider range of difference—including Chinese herbalists, Jewish seamstresses, and Anglo-Canadian Christian Scientists and Pentecostals.

Their response to these new kinds of difference is partly what made liberal Protestants into a usable category, with multiple effects. As Laurence Moore has convincingly argued in the case of the United States, the prevalent use of what he called "mainline" Protestantism—of which liberals were a subset—has emphasized a consensus view of American religion, characterized by ever-increasing unity, tolerance, and calm mediation of opposing views. Using mainstream Protestantism as a category in which denominations such as Methodists, Episcopalians, Presbyterians, Baptists, and Congregationalists could form a mainline but benign coalition has obscured the significance of fractious religious difference for North American religion, argued Moore. [27] Whereas Moore turned to classic "outsiders" including Mormons, Jews, Christian Scientists, and African Americans to make his point about the power of outsiders to shape the religious landscape, his insights could be applied with great fruitfulness to the insiders themselves. [28] Although liberal Protestants may have been considered as insiders by American historians, and actually were insiders in their connections to American medicine, philanthropy and wealth, they also nurtured a sense of being outsiders to these very same realms, whether in social gospel and even socialist critiques of capitalism, strong commitments to pacifism, or in later critiques of a disembodied, unspiritual biomedicine. [29]

Mainstream Protestantism, perhaps because of its assumed cultural dominance and its often easy fit with its cultural surroundings, as well as the fact that as a category it stands in for a rather diffuse variety of Christian traditions with different liturgical, theological, and ethnic practices, does not necessarily conjure the notion of (or appear to itself as) a discrete tradition. [30] Mainstream is a label, however, that others, especially scholars, have happily used to describe that branch of Protestantism that is "most open to modernity's changes, most experienced with

pluralism, least defensive about secular experiment."[31] The most experimental among the mainstream were liberal Protestants, who have been
an important, if often controversial, current within many mainstream
denominations. An imprecise label without a clarifying statement of
faith to define it, the liberal Protestant was ideally viewed as a Christian
who cultivated doubt while expecting commitment. Holding that "theology should be based on reason and critically interpreted religious experience, not external authority," liberal Protestants also came together
in a network of early twentieth-century ecumenical movements such as
world missions, the quasisocialist social gospel, and in later movements
such as the Canadian Council of Churches (1944), the World Council
of Churches (1948), the National Council of Churches (1950 in the
United States), and the civil rights movement.[32]

This twin focus on experience and reason opened liberal Protestantism to some of the most important modern transformations of what
constituted healing, including biomedicine and psychoanalysis. Richard
Fox has argued that Protestant liberalism gained an ambiguous power
from its intimacy with and influence on many realms of early twentieth-
century culture: "[I]t so enthusiastically embraced the 'world'—
secularity, science, the 'natural,' and the therapeutic—that it is impossi-
ble to distinguish it cleanly."[33] I argue, however, that this embrace was
not uncritical. Liberals experimented with healing techniques that
pushed the boundaries of conventional medical and/or Christian orthodoxies and thereby developed critical approaches to what they eventually viewed as a range of social and political ills, including capitalist
excess, religious bigotry, psychic anxiety, alienation due to technology,
racism, sexism, and stress. The self-described liberal Anglo-Catholics
and social gospelers in early twentieth-century Anglican, Methodist,
and United Church circles share a lineage with the socially conscious,
pluralistic Protestants who followed them, even though the earlier liberals might not recognize their heirs' commitments to same-sex marriage
or interest in the fusion of First Nations spirituality with Christian liturgies. Despite these distinctions, I persist in using the term liberal across
the twentieth century not to denote a classic liberalism of the free market or a fuzzy-bordering-on-heretical Christianity, but a kind of Protestantism with a disposition of critical openness to change and science,
optimism about religious interrelations, and commitment to social, political, and economic justice rooted in biblical texts.[34]

THE LAMENT OF PROTESTANT HEALING

Just what kinds of healing Christians should embrace and practice has been a contentious subject both within and without the faith, especially as biomedicine grew in interpretive, legal, and therapeutic power over the course of the twentieth century.[35] Within Christian communities, healing, as the art and science of mending, or at least alleviating physical suffering, has long been considered the responsibility of both religious and medical specialists. Loosely defined as the restoring of physical or emotional wellbeing with recourse to medical, symbolic, or religious means, anthropologists have usually distinguished healing from curing as a therapeutic approach with broader goals than the cessation of particular physical ailments.[36] In Christianity the distinction between medical technique and miraculous healing has been especially blurred, as the earliest Christians combined curing and exorcising by means of relics and charismatic authority with the techniques of hospitals and Galenic medicine. Depicting the gospel writer Luke as a medical doctor and describing Jesus himself as a spiritual healer of mind and body ahead of his time, many Christian traditions of interpretation have portrayed Christianity as a religion with healing at its core.[37]

Protestant rhetorics of healing have emerged not only as discourses internal to specific denominations or to Protestantism more widely, but have also been formed through interactions with a variety of "others." Whether encountering the difference of the neighbor such as the Christian Scientist, the Pentecostal, or even the fellow churchgoer who believed in faith healing, or the difference of the more distant other—the First Nations healer, the Chinese Buddhist or the Indian Hindu—Protestants have contended with anxieties and convictions about morality, truth, divinity, and embodiment through the medium of healing. Protestants have also vacillated between identifying with and differentiating from the medical profession in its broadest sense, including doctors and nurses and the growing sector of professional experts trained in the sciences and social sciences who laid the informational groundwork for an increasingly medicalized society. Although one could easily argue that twentieth-century Protestantism has been medicalized, conversely, one could also contend that the cultural weight of Protestantism in early twentieth-century North America, and its willingness to throw that weight behind scientific medicine, played an important role in generating the cultural authority of early twentieth-century biomedicine.

These anxieties and vacillations have fed into a longstanding lament repeatedly voiced by those who consider themselves healing innovators: the church and the wider culture have lost the knowledge of spiritual healing. I show here, however, that spiritual healing and its lamentation have been a persistent concern of Christianity (and liberal Protestants) throughout the twentieth century. In fact, the lament that the church has forgotten, ignored, or despised its inheritance of spiritual healing has been the clarion call of virtually every new defender of Christian healing in every decade of the century. As a recent example, consider the conspiratorial title of Francis MacNutt's latest book, *The Nearly Perfect Crime: How the Church Almost Killed the Ministry of Healing*. MacNutt, a former Roman Catholic priest who now runs Christian Healing Ministries, a charismatic, ecumenical center of faith healing workshops with a strong focus on deliverance and exorcism, has received extensive support from charismatic wings of the Episcopal Church.

The groups and individuals who frequent the following pages—including medical missionaries, nursing deaconesses, Christian Scientists, the Emmanuel Movement, psychic healers, faith healing revivalists, Christian psychotherapy pioneers, advocates of socialized medicine, parish nurses, Christian yoga practitioners, and labyrinth walkers—have all vigorously claimed to be restoring healing to its rightful but forgotten place at the center of Christianity. Combining goals that have included making a Christian claim to the alluring power to heal in an age of medicalization, differentiating themselves over and against other competing Christian groups, or offering a way that they truly considered to be healing and restoring, all of these Christian groups have tried to root themselves in a tradition that they thought other Christians had misinterpreted, perverted, or forgotten.

The appeal to healing as the birthright of Christianity, or the legacy of Jesus Christ the healer, has heavily depended on history, or perhaps more properly, historicity—the way the past is made use of in a particular present. The past is turned to both as a source of legitimacy and a weapon of critique: Jesus, the most authoritative of historical and theological figures for Christians, was a healer, so too are Christian doctors (or exorcists, or Christian Science practitioners, etc.). Twenty-first-century liberal Christian experiments in pluralistic healing depend on twin histories of Christian tradition and medical orthodoxy: they use traditional liturgy to house non-Christian symbols and rituals in what could be called a disposition of medicalized enchantment. By this last phrase I mean that early twenty-first century liberal Christians are experimenting with healing through faith, prayer, and ritual in order to be opened up to divine presence and agency in a way that does not require that they abandon their recourse to biomedical forms of care. Living in what I have elsewhere called "postbiomedical bodies," they can be heirs and benefactors of scientific method while they simultaneously dwell in a universe permeated with divinity.[38] Medicalized enchantment, as a disposition that gives the body both to scientific readings and to divine illumination, has a long history in Christianity. For liberal Protestants in particular, the beginning of the century would perhaps better be described as a time of enchantment with medicalization, which only later in the century became a critical approach to the hegemony of a scientific, biomedical model of the body that gave little space to the soul. Keeping the oft-heard lament of the lost tradition of Christian healing in mind, then, throughout this book, I consider how Christians claim history (or how they historicize) in their healing innovations.

A related lament focuses on a narrative of the sacralization of medicine, and the concomitant decline of Christian authority. English-speaking Protestants held elite status as culture brokers in early twentieth-century Canada, with the leading laymen in both the Methodist and Anglican churches among the most prominent businessmen and politicians (not to mention doctors) and both denominations playing an important role in developing postsecondary medical education and hospital building.[39] Methodists and Anglicans established some of the earliest medical schools in Canada, only giving them up when they affiliated with state-funded universities in the nineteenth century. After early twentieth-century projects to establish hospitals and to initiate innovative public health programs such as deaconess nursing, Protestants also subsequently bequeathed these programs to medical professionalization and government implementation. In the view of most Protestants, this bequest, while rendering some Protestant medical practitioners outmoded (such as deaconesses), was not primarily a gesture of defeat but instead was a vote of confidence in the state's ability to take on the Christian obligation to care for one's neighbor. Tommy Douglas, the socialist Baptist minister-turned-politician from Saskatchewan, and widely hailed as the architect of the state-funded Canadian health care system, was perhaps the most effective of those who sought to translate Christian convictions into state policy via the field of biomedicine. Though this process of giving up Christian-supported hospitals to the "welfare state" is sometimes considered a prime example of secularization, it could also be viewed as a site of Protestant saturation.

Over the course of the first quarter of the century, however, some Protestants in Canada and the United States were not so sure of their continued relevance, and worried that medicine and science more generally were divesting themselves of their historical and practical links with churches. Consider Reinhold Niebuhr's comment after a pastoral visit to a hospital in 1919: "Sometimes when I compare myself with these efficient doctors and nurses hustling about I feel like an ancient medicine man dumped in the twentieth century. I think they have about the same feeling toward me that I have about myself."[40] And as the psychological notion of the psyche came to rival the Christian notion of the soul (and later on, the cognitivists' neural circuitries of the brain rivaled that of the psyche), Christian epistemologies and embodiments were transformed, if not marginalized.

This marginalization fits with a larger narrative of decline, or secularization, that posits a mainstream Protestantism in freefall, losing out to science, or to other competitors such as liberal unbelief, conservative Christianity, American adaptations of Buddhism, or less institutionally organized New Age religiosity.[41] Although the shrinking numbers of mainstream and liberal Protestants—and Anglican and United Church members more specifically—support this tale of decline, it is not the whole story. As Alison Falby has shown in her research on how Protestants developed practices of group psychotherapy, "secularization can be reconceptualized as a process of increasing intersection between religious and scientific ideas and language."[42] Interpretations of secularization as the decline of liberal Protestantism are often themselves predicated on unarticulated notions of what counts as "pure" Christianity.

The puzzle of liberal Protestant healing, to paraphrase historian Nathan Hatch, is why a movement with such a protean effect on medicalization—one of the twentieth-century's most important transitions—has been given so little attention by scholars of Christianity and of medicine.[43] One answer may be extrapolated from Hatch's contention about historians' appraisals of Methodism—the presumption that liberal Protestant healing is "far too bland."[44] Many of the texts and ideas I encountered in this research, including the Chinese missionary diaries of the controversial and introspective Methodist doctor William E. Smith and the eclectic theory of healing via "spiritual radio" developed by Frederick Du Vernet, have led me to think of these healers as anything but bland. Although a lot went on under the guise of Christian healing that could be considered routine within a biomedically shaped culture, there were also many liberal Protestant characters and movements whose inventive approaches to healing the body and spirit challenged both Christian and medical orthodoxies while they "spoke to" the political, religious, technological, and economic concerns of their day. [45]

Where some scholars and theologians have mocked those liberal Protestants who practice a "cafeteria-style" therapeutic religion for their seemingly indiscriminate borrowing from multiple religious and thera-peutic traditions, and their implied lack of fidelity to particular denomi-nations or to particularly Christian "difference," others recognize this borrowing and bricolage as an attempt to come to terms with the lega-cies of male-dominated, heterosexist, and racist strains of Christianity.[46] These North American forms of bricolage are parallel to what other anthropologists and historians of Christianity have found in situations of indigenous adaptations of missionary Christianity—in the case of liberal Protestants, however, the borrowing flows from those formerly missionized traditions to their own.[47] Attitudes to the ambiguity of syncretism—the blending of various religious traditions—are deeply shaped by what people have to gain or lose with the waning of distinct institutional identities. The ecumenical experiment of the United Church of Canada, formed in 1925 by the merger of Methodists, Congregationalists, and some Presbyterians, was in many ways a step into intra-Christian syncretism that has grown to include relations with religions outside Christianity. Central to this trans-formation have been changing reflections on privilege—where Mabel Cart-wright could once argue that privilege demanded mission, contemporary liberal Protestants claim that privilege demands atonement and redress for injustices done in the name of mission, such as First Nations residential schools. Healing has been a dominant metaphor shaping both versions of the demands of privilege.

Practices of healing became one means through which liberal Protes-tants sought to live out their dawning vision of a cosmopolitan world—a world in which they sought connections beyond their local communities that would tie them to others not necessarily as Christians, but instead as human beings participating in a universal collectivity of "spirit."[48] Many of these liberals sought to build what Leela Gandhi has called "affective communities," in which members of a colonizing nation re-nounce, or at least question, their colonial privilege and choose to affili-ate themselves, partly via relationships of friendship, with the colo-nized.[49] Not an effort to uncritically rehabilitate the battered reputation of Protestant liberalism or to further caricature it, this book is meant as a careful consideration of the ways liberal Protestants have used healing as a set of discourses and practices in which they could build communities and relationships that were grounded within this world but charged by divine forces from without.

SPIRITUAL BODIES IN ANGLICAN AND METHODIST TRADITIONS OF HEALING

Anglicans and Methodists are related yet distinct Christian denominations that have both nurtured traditions of spiritual healing, albeit in quite different ways. Whereas Anglicans have long attended to healing in their liturgy, Methodists—somewhat anti-Catholic in their ritual sensibilities—did not explicitly develop liturgical approaches to healing within the United Church of Canada until very recently. However, both churches have long grappled with the intersection between Christianity and medicine, whether in the case of the Anglican Sir Thomas Browne's *Religio Medici* or in the warnings of Methodist founder John Wesley regarding the health and spiritual risks of tea, tobacco, and sugar in *Primitive Physick*.[50] In the Canadian context, Anglicans and Methodists comprised approximately thirty percent of Canadians in 1911 and were two of the three largest Protestant denominations, along with the Presbyterians. (It is useful to remember, however, that Roman Catholics—with their long traditions of Christian healing—almost equaled the numbers of Anglicans, Methodists, and Presbyterians combined, and overtook them soon after 1911.) In Ontario, where Anglicans and Methodists were most concentrated, they made up approximately fifty-eight percent of the Protestant population.[51] In 1961, Anglicans and United Church members still totaled about one-third of the Canadian population, with Anglicans at about thirteen percent and the United Church members at twenty percent. By 2001 the actual numbers of Anglican and United Church members had declined somewhat, but their percentage of the population had dropped substantially, to approximately seven and ten percent, respectively. The increasing religious diversity of post-1960s immigrants to Canada partly explains these figures, as do the lower birth rates of largely middle-to-upper-class Anglicans and United Church members, and the growing number of people who declared "no religion" to Canadian census-takers.[52] Whether these numbers tell a story of liberal Protestant "decline," as most scholars have concluded, is a question that I leave open for now.

Anglicans, with their roots in the ancient Christian missions to the British Isles, formed in opposition to both the Lutheran Protestant Reformation and the Roman Catholic Church. In the midst of the tumultuous reign of Henry VIII during the sixteenth century, the Church of England gradually emerged partly as a way to grant Henry the authority to divorce his wife Catherine without permission of the Pope and partly as a result of more widespread English dissatisfaction with the conservatism of Catholicism in an era of increasing questioning of traditional authorities and practices. This questioning was especially embodied in new vernacular Bible translations, such as the English translation by William Tyndale, who was put to death as a heretic in 1536. A complicated mix of attachment to a Catholic past and openness to a Protestant future, Anglicanism at once insisted that it remained in the line of apostolic succession from Peter, the first Bishop of Rome, but that it was its own liturgical, theological, and legal authority. Its self-regulation was most clearly represented by Thomas Cranmer's 1549 *Book of Common Prayer*, written in English, which laid out partly "de-Catholicized" ritual formulas for church life and stressed, in a Protestant vein, the reading of the Bible. Although some Anglicans insist that their history means that they are neither Protestant nor Catholic, for practical purposes they are often classed as Protestants, a categorization that makes sense in light of the fact that Anglicans and Episcopalians (their U.S. denomination) have long participated in Protestant ecumenical coalitions such as the Canadian Council of Churches and the World Council of Churches, an organization to which the Roman Catholic Church does not belong.

Anglicanism's mixed heritage of Roman Catholic and Protestant influences has led to deep tensions in the communion that are particularly important for practices of healing and its anthropology of the spiritual body. Some Anglicans have felt deeply connected to a Catholic ritual aesthetic and value such traditions as Saints' Days and the theology of the "real presence" of Jesus Christ in the Eucharistic ritual (known as transubstantiation, or the transformation of the bread and wine of the Eucharist into the body and blood of Christ). As sacramentalists, these Anglicans traditionally attributed heightened importance to sacraments—rituals that function as a sign of and channel for divine grace—when compared to Evangelical, or "Low-Church" Anglicans. (One such sacrament, anointing with blessed oil, was a ritual of healing that gained new popularity, and urgency, at the turn of the twentieth century, with the rise of Christian Science.) These Anglicans, sometimes called Anglo-Catholics or "High-Church", have cultivated an Anglican ritual life that consciously draws from a Catholic past while remaining Anglican—except in the case of those controversial Anglo-Catholics who eventually converted to Roman Catholicism, such as a leader of the Oxford Movement, John Henry Newman. The nineteenth-century Oxford Movement was a clergy- and theologian-led movement that among other things, reestablished monasteries and convents under Anglican episcopal oversight, revived traditions of unction for the sick, and tried to reform the ritual, architectural, and artistic life of Anglicanism via both the heritage of Celtic Christianity and Roman Catholicism. Some Anglo-Catholics, such as clerics Percy Dearmer and Conrad Noel—the founders of the Guild of Health in 1904—were also deeply involved in socialist politics.

The Oxford Movement met with harsh Evangelical opponents within Anglicanism. More influenced by the Calvinist and Puritan traditions within Anglicanism than the Catholic strands, Evangelicals decried Oxford Movement innovations as "Popery," and considered themselves to be more rational and more orthodox than their Anglo-Catholic counterparts. They committed themselves to healing by founding hospitals, commissioning medical missionaries and deaconesses, and largely placing healing in the hands of medical professionals thought to be guided by God. In the twentieth century, however, some Evangelicals came to find their own approach to reviving liturgical traditions of healing by drawing from the charismatic movement. There are several examples within Anglican history of clergy and laypeople who have developed modes of Christian healing informed by both Anglo-Catholic and charismatic Evangelical approaches, such as James Hickson and Dorothy Kerin. The Anglican Church is more generally known for its "via media" of a "broad church" in which space is made for a range of different liturgical and theological commitments, and this mediating stance has also been employed in the case of healing.

Strains of Anglo-Catholicism and Evangelicalism have carried over into the contexts of Canada and the United States, where the Church of England became the Anglican Church of Canada in 1893 and the Episcopal Church with the American Revolution. Still maintaining important links with the English roots of Anglicanism (the Archbishop of Canterbury is the official leader of the worldwide communion of Anglicans), the Canadian Anglican and American Episcopal churches are their own jurisdictions. Although their autonomy has been seriously tested of late due to criticism of the North American churches' growing openness to full participation of gays and lesbians, Anglicans and Episcopalians in North

America have developed their own cultures of Christian community. In the Canadian church, another divisive issue of importance for a discussion of healing has been the process of coming to terms with the legacy of Indian residential schools administered by the Anglican Church, in which First Nations children were schooled far from home, not allowed to speak their own languages, and often abused physically, emotionally, and sexually. Whereas both First Nations and Euro-American Anglicans have turned to the notion of healing as a common rubric for coping with this history, the crisis proved to be also a financial and legal one in which the Church had to pay monetary compensation to redress its wrongs.[53]

Although the dominant voices in the clerical and bureaucratic organization of Canadian Anglicanism and American Episcopalianism have been ones of liberal Protestants deeply concerned with social justice, there have also been splinter groups formed largely in opposition to such liberalism, especially in its acceptance of women priests and gay and lesbian Anglicans.[54] Several healing-related currents within Anglicanism have stayed in the mainstream communion, such as the Guild of Health, but others have edged over to the charismatic side of the via media, such as the Order of St. Luke, a movement led largely by North American Anglican clergy, although it is technically interdenominational and "worldwide." Based on the belief "that the healing of the body, mind and spirit is a vital part of the total ministry of Jesus Christ," the Order of St. Luke had its beginnings in the 1930s, a fruitful time for the rise of healing evangelists from many Christian backgrounds, who were almost never the kinds of Christians who would be characterized as liberal, a trait shared by the Order of St. Luke.[55] Distinctions of Evangelical and High Church still have their institutional embodiments within Canadian Anglicanism, but fiscal and cultural realities have also seen their lessening, as the Church struggles to stay financially solvent in the wake of legal claims related to residential schools.

The Methodists also have their roots in the Anglican Communion, but were a much earlier, and to date more successful, breakaway group than the twentieth-century conservative Anglican dissenters. Founded in the eighteenth century by English Anglican priest John Wesley, and with simultaneous American and English origins, the Methodists did not initially want to leave the Anglican Church, but their commitment to personal religious conviction through revival instead of solely through liturgical tradition brought them to the breach. Wesley's organizational genius was the formation of "classes" of Methodists who would meet at regular weeknight gatherings led by a class leader (not a priest), in which they could discuss the state of their souls and pursue group Bible studies. A kind of Christian protogroup therapy, class meetings were places where men and women could scrutinize their selves and their neighbors, in the search for a perfectible life. Wesley, a prodigious writer, was also deeply interested in questions of healing and medicine, and wrote a book of remedies that was indebted both to folk traditions and to the increasingly authoritative medical profession. Through his experiments with "divine electricity," Wesley also developed what could be called one of the first versions of shock therapy.[56]

In Canada and the United States, the Methodist Church was largely built by itinerant preachers and laypeople often living at far-flung distances and was a mixture of democratic participation and clerical hierarchy.[57] Although some women with the desire to preach benefited from the Methodist openness to women's exhortations, the episcopal structure of the Church (hearkening back with a little less insistence than the Anglicans to that historically virile line of male bishops stretching all the way to first-century Rome) ensured that conservative forces could keep such innovations as women ministers at bay, at least until the twentieth century.[58] But the force of another movement, the Holiness movement, itself with significant female leadership, could not be quelled by the Methodist hierarchy. By the mid-nineteenth century in Canada and the United States, Methodism had grown much more respectable than its circuit-riding itinerant founders, and Holiness movements started to "shake things up." Holiness drew its patrimony from Wesley's doctrine of perfectionism—namely that one could reach a state of Christian perfection in this life if one fully gave oneself to God—but went further to articulate the exact stages of such an achievement. Deeply influenced by German pietism, and also by African-American traditions of enthusiastic worship, Holiness advocates stressed a two-step, highly emotional and even mystical process in which a Christian was first converted and then sanctified. After sanctification, the perfected Christian should live a life of righteousness experienced in the internal soul and displayed in the external self. Although some Holiness supporters managed to stay within the bounds of traditional Methodism, many did not, with some becoming members of newly founded churches, and others setting up Christian homes of divine healing in which the power of prayer could not only sanctify but heal.[59]

In the early twentieth century, Anglicans were not as anxious as Methodists when it came to spirit-filled religion, perhaps because of their intense grounding in textually mediated ritual via the Bible and the Book of Common Prayer but also because they had already rid themselves of their revivalist spin-offs a century earlier, with the formation of the Methodists. Although approaches to ritual and evangelism divided Anglicans in complicated ways, setting Broad Churchmen, Anglo-Catholics, and Evangelicals in tension, in the early twentieth century they did not grapple over issues of charismatic authority as persistently as did the Methodists.[60] Although the world-travelling healer James Moore Hickson prompted controversy among English Anglicans because of his charismatic leadership, his version of faith healing was mostly viewed as within the sacramental tradition of Anglicanism, especially among "overseas" Bishops.[61] With church sanctuaries as his stage and official liturgies such as anointing with oil as his rituals, Hickson moved within the stability of traditional places and gestures that downplayed his personal attributes. As one observer put it, instead of Hickson the faith healer, "It was the mighty working of the Spirit of God, it was the healing power of our Blessed Saviour that brooded over that great throng."[62]

With the most committed devotees of Holiness, and its daughter movement, Pentecostalism, having left Methodism, the liberal Methodists of the early twentieth century were largely in control of the agenda of the church, which was increasingly social gospel focused, concerned more with social service work than evangelizing through revival meetings.[63] The early twentieth century was also the era of increasing ecumenism, as liberal Protestants began to think hopefully of a united Christianity. Increasingly embarrassed by the ironies of Protestant disunity in the mission field, Protestants came to see the virtues of giving institutional structure to the category of Protestantism itself. While ecumenism had one of its greatest and earliest successes at the Edinburgh World Conference of Missions in 1910—whose motto was "The Evangelization of the World in This Generation"—another of its celebrated accomplishments was the establishment of the United Church of Canada in 1925.

Like all early twentieth-century Protestants, Canadian Anglicans and United Church members were deeply enmeshed in global networks first formed by late nineteenth-century missionary ventures throughout the British Empire and beyond, spreading through China, India, Japan, Southeast Asia, and Africa. Living themselves in a settler colony, early twentieth-century Canadian Protestants also saw their own country, and its cities, countryside, and wilderness, as a mission field, with First Nations peoples and new immigrants as their primary targets. Medical missions were a specific vocation that required professional credentials and an evangelical call. Prospective Anglican, Presbyterian, and Methodist missionaries trained as doctors and nurses at medical schools—often at the University of Toronto—and then interned at city hospitals around North America. Most found this training not quite adequate to the conditions they would encounter in the villages of India and China. The eventual liberals among them—such as Belle Oliver—at first embraced, and then critically rethought medical missions, as they came to question the confident Christian triumphalism that undergirded early mission efforts. Their professionalization as doctors often gave them a space of authority in which to continue what they saw as a life of Christian service while they questioned the raw pursuit of conversion.

Belle Oliver's decision to leave the Presbyterian Church to become a member of (and missionary for) the new United Church was its own kind of conversion. Canadian Protestants of many stripes had been working toward "church union" for many years when finally in 1925 Methodists, Congregationalists, about two-thirds of the Presbyterians, and a group of early unionists known as the Council of Local Union Churches came together to form the United Church of Canada. The United Church achieved a remarkable, although not total, dissolution of denominational identities, resources, institutions, and properties to establish what was to be the de facto national church of Canada. The Evangelical United Brethren joined in 1968, but despite several rounds of negotiations, there has yet to be a union of Anglicans with the United Church, with apostolic succession and the role of the episcopate as prominent obstacles. Carrying on the tradition of the social gospel, in the 1970s and onward the United Church launched campaigns for economic divestment from the apartheid government of South Africa and engaged in environmental and antiwar activism.

Today, the United Church of Canada is known as a remarkably liberal church liturgically and politically, in which hard-fought battles—especially over women's ordination and openness to gays and lesbians—have been won by those in favor of change. Along with concerns about the declining size of congregations, the United Church also shares with the Anglican Church the issue of responsibility for Indian residential schooling. The United Church initiated a "Healing Fund" in 1994 to address the needs of First Nations communities dealing with the legacies of abuse and mistreatment at the schools. No stranger to controversy, the United Church also made the news in 1997 when its then-moderator, Rev. Bill Phipps, suggested to journalists that the divinity of Jesus was an open question.

The recent embrace of healing services, therapeutic touch workshops, and labyrinth walks on the part of many United Church laypeople and clergy is entirely in keeping with this experimentalist approach to ritual and change. Although the United Church does not have the same history of healing practices as found among Anglicans—namely such organizations as the Guild of Health and prayer book rituals of anointing with oil—its current eclectic approach to healing is in the tradition of John Wesley, Methodism's founder. Pairing eclecticism with more political approaches to health care, such as funding street nurses for the homeless and parish nurses to stop up the gaps left by the state health care system, as well as making depositions to the government on the importance of health care funding for the nation, the United Church is keeping up its traditions of healing at the intersection of medicine, politics, and the spirit.[64]

METHODS AND MEDIATIONS

It was by turning to church newspapers—the *Canadian Churchman* and the *Christian Guardian* to start with—that I realized that a very different kind of story could be told about the relationship between liberal Protestantism and healing, a story that included not only biomedical champions but also experimentalist advocates of radio mind. Especially in the case of the Methodists, known as pioneers of print journalism in North America, newspapers played a large role in constituting their early, far-flung communities. Newspapers were vessels of community and forums for debate that reveal much about self-representation as well as perceptions of the other, while they also provided a place for building community identity. Editors often had a great deal of independence in these church newspapers, sometimes being private owners with no denominational oversight. Both the Anglican and Methodist/United Church papers were based in Toronto, and despite efforts to be broad in scope, they have reflected the partiality of specific theological traditions, and to a lesser degree, specific regions.

First published as the *Dominion Churchman* in 1875, by the beginning of the twentieth century the Anglican *Canadian Churchman* was owned by a layman, Frank Wootten, and was under the editorship of High Churchmen, including a Trinity College professor, Rev. William Clarke, until Wootten's death in 1912. At this point, a group of Evangelical Anglican businessmen bought the paper, and a varied group of Evangelicals continued to publish what they hoped would be a national church paper until the Anglican Church took it over in 1948. It became the *Anglican Journal* in 1989 and has editorial independence from church authorities. Founded in 1829 by Methodist educator Egerton Ryerson, the *Christian Guardian* was edited by W. B. Creighton from 1906–1925 (and unofficially even earlier), who developed as a progressive social gospeler during his tenure. In 1925 with the establishment of the United Church of Canada, the *Guardian* became *The New Outlook*, still under Creighton's editorship. In 1939 it was renamed the *United Church Observer*, and in 1986 it was independently incorporated, receiving only a small percentage of its funding from the United Church. Five different editors have served the paper since 1939, and the paper now has a sophisticated online presence, while it proudly describes itself as "the oldest continuously published magazine in North America and the second oldest in the English speaking world."[65]

Church newspapers were central to the "text-based cosmologies" of early twentieth-century Anglicans and Methodists, in which reading and writing texts were major ways of establishing one's religious identity.[66] The church newspaper, the Sunday sermon, the missionary's letter to home—all these texts worked together to establish a print culture specific to particular denominations, while they also inscribed identities based in being Protestant, Christian, or Canadian.[67] As Benedict Anderson has argued, print-capitalism—with newspapers as its greatest harbinger—was central to nineteenth- and twentieth-century projects of imagining the new form of modern community, the nation. Newspapers, as daily or weekly compendiums of "current events" consumed by many readers simultaneously, provided a shared identity of readership along with the reassurance "that the imagined world is visibly rooted in everyday life."[68] Anderson's heralding of the newspaper reader as the most "vivid figure for the secular, historically clocked, imagined community,"[69] however, ignores the significance of nineteenth- and early twentieth-century church newspapers as media for the cultivation of religiously imagined communities.[70] Media—newspapers, radio, television— have been deeply formative of Christian identity by including clerical and lay religious actors within networks of knowledge, and inculcating within them certain habits of devotional practice as consumption. But some Protestants understood media as not only a means to imagine communities but also a means to communicate energies both healing and poisonous.[71]

In addition to the systematic gathering of healing-related texts from these two Canadian church newspapers, I also visited the archives of the

Mary Baker Eddy Library for the Betterment of Humanity, a treasure trove of early twentieth-century Protestant invective about Christian Science. Together with several research assistants, I went through the newspaper cutting files of the Christian Science Committee on Publication, to which Christian Scientists around the world would send any reference, positive or negative, to Mary Baker Eddy or Christian Science. The files were full of articles from Protestant newspapers around North America debating and detailing healing practices, which always included at least one, usually uncharitable, comment on Christian Science.

Coming to approach newspapers and other texts as ritual artifacts as well as modes of communication has led me to step back and consider the significance of media for healing in other contexts. Although texts continued to play a central role in Protestant practices of healing, radio also channeled intriguing connections, such as DuVernet's notion of spiritual radio. At the beginning of a media innovation, when a particular technology is most unfamiliar and seemingly wondrous, the words printed on a page or the voices traveling through the air or wires help to constitute religious imaginations. Once radio became more conventional, liberal Protestants quickly made new use of it. James Ward, an Anglican priest with a particular interest in spiritual healing, was one of the first ministers to broadcast his sermons live on Sundays, and he later went on to design and host "The Way of the Spirit" on the state-funded Canadian Broadcasting Corporation (CBC). Whereas liberal Protestants were at the cutting edge of media technologies when it came to newspapers, lantern slides, and radio, their impact on television was harder to detect. Where evangelicals or fundamentalists produced dramatic mass healing revivals on television, liberal Protestants had a more subtle influence, as when Patrick Watson moved from the United Church production company to host the CBC's "human affairs" program, "This Hour has Seven Days." Working in the shadows without direct media attention has perhaps given liberal Protestants more latitude in their healing innovations. Although the vision of the televangelist laying hands on a supplicant's forehead and declaring "you are *healed*!" is a much more common cultural trope than that of an Anglican priest teaching a particularly tricky yoga pose, both are examples of healing Christians in a therapeutic age.

At the same time that I was pursuing the question of liberal Protestant healing in newspapers, autobiographies, and archival records, I was also considering its contemporary forms. From 2000 through 2004, I attended healing services, meditation/Bible studies, yoga classes, Taizé prayer evenings, drop-in Reiki clinics, Sunday services, and meetings at two Toronto churches, which I have called St. Luke's (Anglican) and Confederation Street (United). I also engaged in in-depth interviews and discussions with the ministers and some laypeople in the two churches, and from these conversations I was led to other Anglican and United Church people and places where questions of healing were central.[72] In the process I was directed by Father Patrick of St. Luke's to the Episcopalian monastery of the Society of St. John the Evangelist in Cambridge, Massachusetts, which had its roots in England and once had a location in the cottage-country region of Muskoka. I also traveled to Burrswood Christian Hospital in southern England, founded by the Anglo-Catholic spiritual healer Dorothy Kerin and used as a model for a similar, but ultimately aborted, Anglican healing center in Toronto.

In the course of this research, I have often felt won over by people like Belle Oliver and Frederick Du Vernet. With my skeptical disposition as a scholar without liberal Protestant roots, I have often found their missionary rhetoric hard to swallow, but I remain impressed by their willingness to relinquish a comfortable professional life in the growing city of Toronto to throw themselves into the give and take of colonial encounters with people who were not family and in places that were not home. This version of cosmopolitanism is still alive and well in our world, and to caricature or disdain it as only the misguided ploys of colonizers is to misrecognize some of the most potent rhetoric of change and hope that continues to orient much anthropological and political discourse. *Spirits of Protestantism*, then, brings together the present and the past in a sustained encounter that explores the dead ends of liberal experiments with healing as well as the more enduring practices of supernatural liberalism that continue to shape liberal Protestant engagements with bodily suffering in what they have long hoped is a cosmopolitan—and cosmically charged—world.

CHAPTER I

Anthropologies of the Spiritual Body

There is a natural body, and there is a spiritual body.
And so it is written, The first man Adam was made a living
soul; the last Adam was made a quickening spirit.

—1 Corinthians 15:44–45, King James Version

The joy of Easter is the joy of a progressive life, ever adapting
itself to its new environment in a more spiritual body.

—Frederick Du Vernet, *Out of a Scribe's Treasure*, 1927

The most famous Canadian medical missionary, one might argue, was
not ultimately filled with the spirit of Jesus, but was instead emboldened
by the spirit of communism. Dr. Norman Bethune, the son of an Ontario Presbyterian minister, met with international renown for his front-
line medical work in two twentieth-century revolutionary hotspots—the
Spanish Civil War and the Chinese communist battle against the Japanese occupation. Bethune became truly legendary after his 1939 death
on the front in war-torn China, when Mao Tse-Tung lionized him as a
communist martyr, praising him for his selfless embodiment of "the spirit
of internationalism, the spirit of communism, from which every Chinese
Communist must learn." In the end, Mao argued (at least in English
translation), it was spirit that counted: "A man's ability may be great or
small, but if he has this spirit, he is already noble-minded and pure, a man
of moral integrity and above vulgar interests, a man who is of value to
the people."[1] Although Bethune held the Christian elements of his spirit
at some ironic distance, it is clear that something of the spirit of Jesus—
the Jesus construed as a laboring man of the people, if not an outright

revolutionary—was an early spark for his activism. As a nineteen-year-old medical student Bethune spent 1911 working with the Protestant-based Reading Camp Association, during which he taught immigrant lumberjacks to read by evening while working with them by day.[2] Between this early Christian-inflected mission and his later communist one, medicine remained at the heart of his public witness: after struggling with tuberculosis in a sanatorium in his hometown of Gravenhurst, in Muskoka's cottage country, Bethune became a champion of publicly funded Canadian health care.

But Bethune's spirit was not necessarily so far from that of some of his countrymen who stayed in the church, such as Salem Bland (1859–1950), the renowned Methodist (and later United Church) minister who argued in 1920 that public ownership of state infrastructure was the most "divine" of all movements in the modern world: "To discredit and attack the principle of public ownership is to discredit and attack Christianity. It would seem to be the special sin against the Holy Ghost of our age. He who doubts the practicability of public ownership is really doubting human nature and Christianity and God."[3] Bland's colleague Grover Livingstone (1887–1966), offered a less fervent, but no less spirited anthropology, as a United Church minister and chaplain. In 1926, the same year that Bethune had journeyed to the curative climate of Muskoka to relieve his TB, Livingston became chaplain to another Gravenhurst tuberculosis sanatorium, where he had once been a TB patient himself. Blind and deaf in one ear due to a childhood illness, Livingstone took an approach to the spirit not marked by the same fiery decisionism and internationalism as Bethune's communism.

In 1954 Livingstone wrote a little book called *Through Sickness to Life* based on the sermons he delivered over the loudspeaker of the Muskoka hospital, housed in a region where wealthy Canadians and Americans built their summer homes on the rocky outcrops of the Canadian Shield. With the tonic of Muskoka's sparkling waters as his backdrop, Livingstone offered "techniques of devotion" that would bring spiritual equilibrium: ministers and the patients under their care should cooperate with medical doctors and accept the inevitability of suffering and the finitude of human embodiment, while also cultivating an active faith. Livingstone's book offered an anthropology of the spiritual body inspired by the Bible, Shakespeare, Thomas Mann, Adam Smith, Marcus Aurelius, Aldous Huxley, Rabindranath Tagore and deeply indebted to liberal Protestant ministers such as Harry Emerson Fosdick and

Elwood Worcester.[4] His cosmopolitan citations helped him to counsel that with the right techniques of devotion—such as Bible reading and memorization, reading of good literature, meditation, and prayer—sickness could be the "bearer of life" even in the absence of bodily healing. Such techniques could effect the "secret processes of the spirit" without crossing over into what he considered questionable modes such as "sacramentalism," "faith healing," or "magic." Fully committed to biomedical care, Livingstone, like many liberal Protestants, tacked between asserting that illness was an inevitable part of human experience that could bring one to greater empathy with others and cautiously suggesting that sickness itself carried the fertile potential for a kind of healing that could lead to "strange places of the spirit."[5]

Livingstone's therapeutic loudspeakers, remedial Bible reading, and restorative meditation were devotional techniques that put a great deal of faith in the written, spoken, and read word. His cultivation of language practices was part of what anthropologist Webb Keane has called a "semiotic ideology," or a set of historically particular convictions about what counts as a sign and what effects such signs can have in the world—about how spoken or written words, bodily gestures, images, and material things communicate across both distance and difference. The concept of semiotic ideologies is so powerful precisely because everybody participates in (at least) one—even anthropologists. Rooted in convictions about and practices of the body, semiotic ideologies have everything to do with how people understand the interactive power of particular forms of communication to transform, harm, and heal. Livingstone's citations showed him to be a citizen of the world grounded in the Christian Bible, who thought that reading could clarify the mind and heal the body; he was an experimentalist mystic with faith both in biomedical and spiritual explanations for human embodiment. Liberal Protestants, with their faith in the word, are often described by anthropologists, their evangelical and Pentecostal critics, and even by themselves, as wooden in their ritual practice (if considered to have "ritual" at all), or as hopelessly rational in their approach to the workings of the spirit. With the tool of semiotic ideologies, the study of healing provides a lens through which to see how liberal Protestants, revolutionary doctors, and even anthropologists of Christianity have participated in ideologies of the spiritual body deeply infused by assumptions and convictions about what counts as the spirit and what we can know of the body.

ANTHROPOLOGIES OF THE BODY

Events of sickness and healing were experiences in which liberal Protestants contended directly with how they understood the "spirit" of God to be felt, sensed, and adjudicated in modern bodies. Questions of healing brought liberal Protestants face to face with what anthropologist Matthew Engelke has described as the "problem of presence," or the discernment of how "certain words and certain things—defined as such according to specific semiotic ideologies—become privileged channels of divine apprehension."[6] How could bodily sickness or its resolution bring one closer to God? To use another conceptual frame, healing forced the consideration of what anthropologist Birgit Meyer has called sensational forms: the rituals, material culture, and media by which "religious practitioners are made to experience the presence and power of the transcendental." Sensational forms, Meyer writes, work by "invoking, framing and rendering accessible the transcendental," thus both producing the very notion of the transcendent *and* enabling religious practitioners to experience it.[7] Livingstone recommended his techniques of devotion as pragmatic ways to make intellectual sense of illness, but at the same time he advocated Bible reading and prayer as sensational forms by which one could experience the "unseen presence" while also leaving oneself in the hands of medical (and ministerial) professionals.

The problem of presence and the concept of sensational forms are framing devices developed by anthropologists to make sense of contemporary religious practice. Not surprisingly, looking around, or behind, these frames reveals a background of older convictions about human nature and intercourse with the spirits. The anthropological act of framing the spirit, the unseen presence, or the transcendent has a long past that dips into the less well-known, theological version of the term anthropology. All versions of Christian healing— Frederick Du Vernet's vibrational prayers of "radio mind," faith cure, pastoral counseling, exorcism—have based their therapeutic approaches on particular understandings of what it is to be a human being in relationship to God, or what could be called anthropologies of the spiritual body. These anthropologies are intimately tied to ontologies—theories and convictions about what "being" is in and of itself. Ontologically rooted, theological anthropology has provided a language, whether implicit or explicit, for Christians to articulate how they understood spiritual forces to have physical, and sometimes healing, effects on human beings.[8]

Theological anthropology is a field of study that dates back at least formally to the seventeenth century, but reflection on Christian understandings of how God relates to different aspects of human personhood, whether body, soul, spirit, or mind has always been part of Christian thought (as well as that of its contributors, such as Hellenistic philosophy and Hebrew scripture). Whether Platonic-influenced dualisms of body and soul still at play in the nineteenth-century Protestant health movements described by Marie Griffith, or what Dale Martin has called early Christian and Greco-Roman "hierarchies of essence" distinguishing psyche, soma, and pneuma, Christian anthropological speculation has long grappled with the question of how best to understand embodied being in relation to divine agency.[9] As a technical theological term, anthropology is distinct from the current reigning understanding of the word as "intrinsically a secular discipline" that is focused on the study of "culture" and not tied to theology—this distinction, however, is less clear-cut than most anthropologists of religion have usually assumed.[10] Several anthropologists have recently demonstrated the complicated indebtedness of many anthropological and theoretical categories to Christian theology—including Fenella Cannell's discussion of "genealogical ontology," Joel Robbins's provocative critique of the "social ontology" of power and conflict that lies at the heart of much anthropological analysis, or Talal Asad's account of the Christian grounds for the formation of secular liberalism itself.[11] These recent critiques, however, have not gone so far as to interrogate the implications of the Christian theological lineage of the concept of anthropology itself, or, for that matter, how "theological anthropology" continues as a core aspect of Christian theological practice today. Taking Kevin O'Neill and William Garriott's suggestion that anthropologists take a dialogical approach when asking "Who is a Christian?" I ask in turn, who is an anthropologist?[12] Acknowledging how the category of anthropology has contained, if repressed, the overlap of theological and secular ontologies is particularly important for the study of liberal Protestants, who share with cultural anthropologists the realization that their mid-twentieth-century cosmopolitan ideals were partly formed in complicity with colonial power.

ANTHROPOLOGY'S THEOLOGICAL AFFINITIES

According to the Oxford English Dictionary, the earliest English uses of "anthropology" in the sixteenth and seventeenth centuries denoted the consideration or study of the human "body and soul."[13] In the eighteenth century Immanuel Kant, renowned for his critiques of metaphysical ontologies, also pioneered the vision of anthropology as an academic discipline separate from theology by publishing his *Anthropology from a Pragmatic Point of View*. Based on his popular lectures to university students, Kant's *Anthropology* remained in part a prescriptive, if not conventionally theological, project both as a study of the empirical principles of human nature as a universal condition and as a pragmatic disquisition on how best to cultivate a universally grounded cosmopolitan "virtue ethics" in the young men who were his audience.[14] By the nineteenth century theological anthropology was aware of its enlightened competition but still considered itself as part of the conversation: an 1883 biblical encyclopedia described anthropology as a "scientific theology" that "distinguishes itself from physiological anthropology by viewing man not as a natural being, but in his relation *to God*."[15] Confident in the necessary and close relationship of theological and physiological anthropology, the entry fit the study of "body and soul (or according to the Trichotomists, body, soul, and spirit)" firmly within the task of anthropology.

The overlap between anthropology as an academic discipline and as a space of theological inquiry into human nature is not as seamless today, of course. Whereas academic anthropology has come to understand its task to be "denaturalizing" what is taken as natural by questioning cultural categories and norms, theological anthropology denaturalizes the empiricism of secularity itself, insisting on the (Christian) *super*natural as a matter of course. These twin versions of anthropology, however, are closer than they may appear. Theological anthropology's task of investigating the relationship of human nature to God, and the task of anthropologists of Christianity who study the ways human beings experience and assess "God's simultaneous presence and absence" are distinguished largely by their intended audiences and by the differently normative repercussions of their work.[16] Whereas theologians often advise how Christians should best *encounter* the spirit of God, anthropologists make arguments for how other anthropologists should best *interpret* Christian claims of encountering the spirit of God. Although this normative difference matters, it becomes less stark when anthropological critique is compared to the "prophetic" critique of power endorsed by liberal Protestants, those Christians most closely aligned with paradigms and ontologies of scientific modernity and most affected by the same kind of chastened postcolonial awareness that has shaped cultural anthropology.[17]

As several scholars of religion have shown, liberal Protestant categories of analysis have shaped, consciously or not, the academic disciplines that have sought to explain religion, including anthropology. Partly because of their influential positions in higher education in North America, in which many universities have Protestant roots, liberal Protestants—including Paul Tillich and many others whom I discuss in the following chapters—played a disproportionate role in setting the terms for the social scientific study of religion.[18] Protestant categories of human nature and Nature writ large, along with, in Murray Murphey's words, "the sharp distinctions we make between 'science' and 'religion,' 'normative' and 'empirical,' 'verifiable' and 'metaphysical,' " have been unwittingly applied as universal categories in the "scientific" study of religion, when they are in reality a "particular, highly parochial way" of dividing up the world.[19] Liberal Protestant projects of theological anthropology are still embedded and often unmarked in the methods and theories of "academic" anthropology, especially when it comes to the study of Christianity.

Consider the example of Anthony F. C. Wallace's 1966 book, *Religion An Anthropological View*. An eminent ethnohistorian of First Nations peoples in Canada and the United States, who often testified as an expert witness for Iroquois and Sioux land claims, Wallace is best known for his work on "revitalization" movements in which he combined his interests in psychiatry, native peoples, and religion. Wallace declared that religion was on the path to "extinction" both because science was making "supernatural beings and forces" unbelievable and because ritual, as the real active force of religion, was being successfully secularized. In the wake of the loss of supernaturalism, Wallace argued, came the risk of fascism, in which people would transfer their "masochistic longings" from religious figures to political leaders. To avoid this Wallace argued, a "secular faith" was required, "a non-theistic theology" that, like that found in "desupernaturalized" and "liberal" religious groups, would not abide supernatural forces or contradict science but would carry on with psychoanalytically appropriate rites of passage and ecclesiastical organizations. A secular faith "must include the accomplishment of these ideological, salvational, and revitalizational transformations which are deemed to be essential for the creation and maintenance of healthy personalities in a healthy society." Although Wallace did not fully explicate it, he emphasized the need for "a fairly specific theory of what constitutes a healthy personality in our society."[20] Wallace's theory of health would have not been far from that of many liberal Protestants in

1966, who themselves valued science, were supporters of First Nations land claims, and engaged with psychiatry to question the pathologizing of homosexuality (as did Wallace). Whether either Wallace or liberal Protestants had successfully de-supernaturalized—or secularized in Wallace's terms—was debatable. In the same issue of *Zygon* in which a short version of Wallace's book appeared was an article by a Unitarian minister, Donald Harrington, who made an appeal to "modern man" that was quite parallel to Wallace's:

> . . . he wanders a wasteland, waiting a spiritual summons worthy his reasoning spirit—in tune with the present, unsundered from the past. That call, when it comes, will reach out to the world's wide circle and bring all men at last to freedom and brotherhood and peace with justice under God's universal law. Those who call themselves liberal religionists, have, I believe, the possibility of becoming a channel for such a call, to make a scientifically renewed and reinforced religion a redemptive power once again in this rapidly changing contemporary world.[21]

If they were to be channels for the call of redemption, Harrington argued, liberal Christians needed to keep their own version of a "healthy" supernaturalism charged up and in tune, via their own anthropology of the science-friendly, spiritual body.

To borrow from William James—an excellent example of the fuzzy line between liberal Protestant and social scientist—anthropology as a term often functions as a "*denkmittel*" of its own, that is, it functions as an often unmarked category by which we cope with the multiplicity of the world.[22] Now relatively obscure in relation to the anthropology that counts Franz Boas and Margaret Mead among its founding figures—and having even lost its standing in contemporary dictionaries of the Bible—theological anthropology nonetheless continues to lay confident claim to the "comprehensive science of man" in a vein similar to one of its most renowned practitioners, the midcentury German theologian Karl Barth.[23] Boldly taking on the rival secular discipline, Barth claimed that insofar as nontheological anthropology "conceives its aim atheistically, it rests on a plain error."[24] Taking their cues both from Barth and Margaret Mead, liberal Protestants did not always explicitly frame their arguments as theological anthropology, but they were its practitioners; theological conceptions of body, mind, and spirit allowed them to translate their own experiences of and convictions about the supernatural into medical and psychological models of healing.

As liberal Protestants went about dividing up human nature into such sectors as "brain," "mind," "body," and "soul," the analytical work they did was akin to Barth's version of anthropology. At its core, Barth professed, the "basic anthropological insight" was the following: "Man exists because he has spirit. That he has spirit means that he is grounded, constituted and maintained by God as the soul of his body."[25] Despite the appearance of empiricist universalism, which he clearly sought to cultivate, Barth's anthropology of a human nature made up of soul, spirit, and body itself had a history, with its own set of contested practices shaped by influences outside of Barth's neo-orthodox theology, including psychoanalysis and varieties of Christian healing. The very notion of human nature was itself in question in academic spheres, as Jewish philosopher Hannah Arendt, Barth's contemporary, argued.[26] Reading Barth and Arendt at the same time as they were imbibing the teachings of "dynamic" psychologist Carl Rogers (who studied first at the liberal Protestant hub, Union Theological Seminary), mid-twentieth-century liberal Protestants were also encountering the writings of anthropologist Margaret Mead, who, as a committed Episcopalian and an expert on "human nature," wrote for Protestant publications.[27] With all these versions of the anthropological at play, liberal Protestants developed their own anthropology of the spiritual body while doing their jobs as pastors, doctors, hospital chaplains, and pastoral psychologists, and later on, as parish nurses and yoga instructors.

SPIRITUAL EQUILIBRIUM AND SPIRITUAL INTERVENTION

What constituted a liberal Protestant anthropology of the spiritual body? Although a hierarchical dualism privileging spirit over matter has been indicted as the source of Christian misogyny, environmental degradation, or Protestants' alienation from their bodies, such a neat dualism does not actually characterize the ways that Protestants were imagining what it was to be an embodied person in the twentieth century.[28] Judging from its repeated invocation across a wide swath of texts and times, liberal Protestants most commonly adhered to—while of course not always practicing—a tripartite anthropology of body, mind, and spirit. Simultaneously, they insisted on a social ontology in which humans needed both each other and God. Hardly the atomistic individual attributed to liberalism writ large, the *self* of Protestant liberalism was supposed to be both self-critical and socially aware, living in the conditions of sociability that Arendt termed "plurality."[29]

Anthropological renderings of being—whether the triad of body, mind, and spirit, Frederick Du Vernet's hypothesis of the fourfold self animated by divine radio waves, or the Chinese notion of *qi*—are the metaphors that ground convictions about how spiritual forces connect with physical, embodied people. As metaphors, anthropologies of being are expansive, if not engulfing; as historian of medicine Anne Harrington puts its, metaphor's "capacity to connect different orders of reality simultaneously" largely constitutes its appeal.[30] Drawing explicitly from ancient traditions and terminologies while also engaging newer views of psychology, liberal Protestants embraced a trinity of body, mind, and spirit as a cultural and religious trope that licensed them to carve out new territory as healers—territory that encompassed the growing cultural presence of psychology, burgeoning charismatic movements, and a dawning awareness of the importance of sexuality to both self and society. For example a few years before writing her sexual education manual, Belle Oliver found the anthropology of body, mind, and spirit an appealing way to understand both the self and social obligation. She quoted in her Indian diary from the 1917 "Statement of Social Duty" passed by the Society of Friends, in which the Quakers urged "the fullest development of the physical, mental, and spiritual possibilities of every member of the community."[31] Nurturing the equal development of these three aspects of being within the person and within the community would meet the demands of both self and society.

Oliver's repeated invocations of the triad of body, mind, and spirit in her later writing reflected the increasing ubiquity of an anthropology that was not limited to Christianity—it was "vague" in the philosophical sense, meaning that it at once pointed to a kind of common sense but also held within it the possibility of deep contradictions.[32] Put another way, body–mind–spirit served as what William James, himself referring to the concepts of "'Self,' [and] 'body' in the substantial or metaphysical sense," called a "common-sense *denkmittel*," or a "form of thought" from which "no one escapes subjection." What I am calling the holistic trinity of body, mind, and spirit seems to have become, to use James's words, "uniformly victorious": invoked in the early twenty-first century in such diverse contexts as the mottos of a downtown Toronto liberal Anglican church, the Pentecostal Oral Roberts University, a plethora of New Age healing websites, and in the peddling of spa services, yoga classes, and even breakfast cereal.[33] Underneath this wide serviceability, however, lie very different understandings of just what counts as body, mind, or spirit and just what fits within the optimistically expansive notion of holistic.

The trinity, a theological "mystery" making the three persons of God, Christ, and the Holy Spirit into one, was a peculiar yet popular metaphor that mid-twentieth-century Protestants transposed onto the self as they sought to bring together psychology and religion in the work of healing. Almost always paired with a declaration that healing equaled "wholeness" in etymological, metaphorical, and therapeutic terms, the "holistic trinity" of body, mind, and spirit resonated with liberal Protestant champions of pastoral counseling such as Paul Tillich, as well as with conservative, charismatic Anglican healers, such as Agnes Sanford.[34] Crossing lines of professional identity, the ideology of the holistic trinity encompassed doctors and psychiatrists such as the University of Toronto professor Daniel Cappon, as well as clergy such as the Canadian Anglican priest who made the following optimistic pronouncement: "Today the physician knows that to be well one must have a healthy body and an adequately functioning mind, the whole sustained by a strong and mature spirit."[35]

A ubiquitous but not always explicit anthropology, the holistic trinity emerged within the spate of books, reports, and articles on "religion and health" written by liberal Protestants before, and especially after, World War II.[36] These midcentury authors gravitated to one of two paths when articulating their views of healing as wholeness: (1) many theologians, seminary professors, and chaplains adopted a discourse of what I call "spiritual equilibrium" that, largely within the emerging movement of pastoral counseling, sought a blend of Christian theology and psychological and psychoanalytic theories that would allow people to work toward a healthy balance among body, mind, and spirit; (2) other clergy and lay people favored a discourse of "spiritual intervention" that considered healing to come primarily from a divine spirit, whether through psychic healing, charismatic gifts, or the sacraments (or sometimes all three) and that understood sickness through a spiritual etiology that considered illness to enter the body via sin or demonic spirits. Proponents of a spiritual equilibrium focused less on what were called "organic" or physiological diseases and more on therapies for "functional" or psychological illness: the healing of the psyche, or the inner self, was their preoccupation, even if this only meant Christians finding a way to "adjust" properly to the suffering of illness. Spiritual interventionists placed less emphasis on the powers of the psyche and more on the powers of the spirit, making bold claims for organic, bodily healing via spiritual means, whether in curing anxiety, cancer, or blindness.[37]

In its blend of traditional and modern categories, the holistic trinity of body, mind, and spirit served as a religious language ideology, in Webb Keane's sense of "the peculiar or marked forms and uses of language . . . [that] are constructed in such a way as to suggest, often in only the most implicit ways, that they involve entities or modes of agency which are considered by those practitioners to be consequentially distinct from more 'ordinary' experience."[38] Keane goes on to suggest that religious language ideologies are also defined by being "situated across some sort of ontological divide from something understood as a more everyday 'here and now.'" The holistic trinity, however, has not functioned by way of an ontological divide but, instead, has depended on an ontological continuity in which body, mind, and spirit are distinct yet supernaturally infused entities that can be differently weighted in different contexts. The holistic ideologies of spiritual equilibrium and spiritual intervention, both sharing an anthropology of body, mind, and spirit, are thus able to coexist within Protestant communities such as the Anglican and United Churches, albeit with considerable tension.

Why have so many different twentieth-century Protestants found the frequent incantation that healing was about the wholeness of body, mind, and spirit such an uncomplicated and essential repetition?[39] Commandeering wholeness as their raison d'être, the partiality—and competition—of these holistic ideologies is visible in retrospect. As Robert Thornton has felicitously phrased it within his own analysis of the holism of anthropological thinking itself, "reference to some ulterior entity is always implicit in holism. . . . these ulterior images of wholes are not directly accessible to either the author's nor his subject's experience."[40] An idiom that could be enjoined by psychologists, charismatics, and experimentalists alike, the holistic trinity of body, mind, and spirit at once allayed and disguised multiple anxieties about Christian healing. First, although Protestants—whether doctors, clergy, or laypeople—granted authority to medical and psychological views of the person, they also insisted that the "spirit" was central to any such anthropology, thus proclaiming the relevance of Christianity to the medical task of healing. Second, having claimed a space for the spirit in psychological anthropologies of the self, liberal Protestants then turned within Christianity to invoke their authoritative knowledge of psychology to delineate what qualified as a "mature" spirit, as opposed to the "spirit-filled" exuberance of faith healers or the "fraudulent" and "occult" performances of spirit mediums, who were both enjoying a post–World War II renaissance (as they also had after World War I). It was a tricky task to discern the mature spirit at a time when liberal North American Protestants were entering into an age of intensified religious hybridity that saw the flourishing of a wide range of blended movements, such as charismatic "renewal," Christian ashrams, Christian yoga, and Christian psychotherapy. In the midst of this blending, the holistic trinity of body, mind, and spirit could both travel and stay rooted in the textual sources of the Christian tradition.

THE HOLISTIC TRINITY

Keeping in mind Arjun Appadurai's comment that genealogy "is an argument in the guise of a discovery," a short genealogy of the "holistic trinity" will help to situate the multiplicity of spirits in supernatural liberalism.[41] Tracing the roots of the holistic trinity requires considering a nagging tension that has long beset the encounter between Christianity and scientific medicine, produced in part by the overlap between biomedical and Christian epistemologies of personhood: whereas both agree on the material reality of fleshly existence (for the most part, setting aside the idealism of Christian Science), they do not agree on how to think of other aspects of personhood, whether soul, mind, spirit, or conscience. A contrast between dualistic and monistic thinking has long characterized this disagreement. Where dualism splits the human into body and soul, or spirit and matter, monistic thinking understands the human being to be a unity of mind and body, leaving no room for an impalpable spirit that could channel divine communication or energy to human beings.[42] Monistic thinking, dubbed "medical materialism" by William James, has typified many scientific views of the self.

More recently, Mark Johnson has advanced a philosophical version of monism that he calls the "embodied mind," drawing on such thinkers as John Dewey and Maurice Merleau-Ponty. For Johnson, religious traditions—exemplified in his book by a loose reference to Paul Tillich—have obscured the visceral realities of mind in body in their concern to escape what they mistakenly view as the "finiteness" of the human body in relation to the "vertical transcendence" of the infinite divine.[43] Arguing for an "embodied spirituality" based in "horizontal transcendence," Johnson redefines Christian concepts (implicitly read through their Protestant versions) of faith, grace, and love such that our "body–minds" require no transcendent spirit to lead the way to truth or ethical engagement. Johnson has precursors in this act of translation, such as Thomas Harris, whose 1969 pop psychology bestseller *I'm OK—You're OK* also found the Christian concept of "grace," as mediated through Paul Tillich's writing, a helpful secular correlate for the ideal of unconditional acceptance that he considered necessary for both health and truth.[44]

Whereas Johnson lays much of the blame for a dualistic severing of mind from body on implicitly Protestant theologies of human nature, James Opp, in his ground-breaking work on Protestant faith healing in Canada, critiques liberal Protestant anthropologies from a different perspective. Arguing for the holism of Pentecostal therapeutic approaches in contrast to their liberal Protestant and medical opponents, Opp considers that conflicts over appropriate modes of healing among early twentieth-century Pentecostal faith healers, their liberal Protestant detractors, and medical authorities were largely rooted in "epistemological gaps" among these groups. According to Opp, liberal Protestants allied themselves with medical authorities by viewing the suffering body with a compartmentalizing biomedical gaze that saw discrete organs in the place of a whole person. In contrast, Opp argued, "divine healing relied upon whole bodies to narrate their experience to the glory of God, and these stories constituted an extension of the self."[45]

Altough not using the terminology of theological anthropology, Opp shows that in cultivating faith healing, early twentieth-century Pentecostals adopted their own "tripartite" holistic anthropology of the self—drawing from Pauline demarcations of the soul (psyche), spirit (pneuma), and body (soma) as well as from nineteenth-century Christian perfectionism and sectarian medicine. Both Pentecostals and liberal Protestants, however, shared the challenge of the "rewriting of the soul" undertaken by the new science of the mind that was psychology.[46] For many late nineteenth-century Protestants, Opp argued, this challenge was costly: "The ascendancy of the mind as the arbiter of experience and evidence for the reality of the divine met the needs of both evangelicals concerned with religious experience and other Victorians intent on reconciling religion with science. However, this accommodation came at the cost of severing the mind from the body and physical matter, territory that was increasingly conceded to science alone."[47] For Opp, then, a holistic Pentecostal epistemology of the body rooted in spiritual intervention challenged this scientific severing of mind from body, while liberal Protestants—or what their faith-healing foes called "sad Christians"—actively conceded to biomedical alienation of the embodied soul.[48]

But did sad Christians really yield so readily to medical science in its "sheering off" of the spirit? The liberal Protestant rewriting of the soul has not so much abandoned the mind to science, as transposed the concept of the soul into both psyche and spirit, with the latter being an ambiguous term that can imply a divine agent as much as a quality of inner vitality, useful to describe both Norman Bethune and Pentecostal healers. The holistic bonding of body, mind, and spirit is a cultural act. Claimed by charismatic Christians, pastoral psychologists, eco-feminists, and philosophers such as Johnson, the virtues of a "redemptive" holism bear consideration and even dissection.[49]

A neologism of the twentieth century, "holistic" is first found as an English adjective in Jan Smuts 1926 book, *Holism and Evolution*.[50] Smuts, an Afrikaner who was twice the Prime Minister of South Africa (first from 1919–1924), had both political and philosophical interests. As a politician Smuts worked for a racist "holism" that would unify only white colonists in Southern Africa; as a philosopher Smuts argued for holistic evolution as a creative process that included scientific, metaphysical, and spiritual development. Although Smuts's book is now remembered more for coining the terms "holism" and "holistic" than for its argument, it is worth considering his anthropology:

> The view which degrades the body as unworthy of the Soul or Spirit is unnatural and owes its origin to morbid religious sentiments. Science has come to the rescue of the body and thereby rendered magnificent service to human welfare. The ideal Personality only arises where Mind irradiates Body and Body nourishes Mind, and the two are one in their mutual transfigurement.[51]

Casting aside the soul or spirit while still depending on them to make his point, Smuts's confidence in the rescue by science did not make his particular notion of holism successful among scientists, nor did it rescue him from the racist partiality of his thought. A wider notion of holism, however, was at play in medical contexts in early twentieth-century Europe and North America, "as a vehicle for both political anxiety and social reformist zeal."[52] Developed in colonial and postwar contexts characterized by fragmentation, difference, and brokenness, holistic thinking has often idealized wholeness while obscuring religious, economic, gendered, and racialized difference. As anthropologist Louis Dumont has shown in his work on early Christianity and elsewhere, holism is both a crucial concept for thinking anthropologically about societies and their members as well as a pathway for creating and maintaining hierarchy and difference.[53]

The metaphysical current in accounts of holism was shared by Christian modernists such as British Anglican cleric Percy Dearmer who argued against the reductionism of materialist monism and for "good dualism."[54] Dearmer's friend and colleague, Canadian Anglican Lily Dougall, argued for dualism against another foe, the tripartite schemas of human nature emerging among Pentecostals.[55] Broadminded in her cautious acceptance of many forms of Protestant spiritual healing, including accounts of the miraculously healed Anglican Dorothy Kerin and those of Pentecostals, Dougall drew the line at a three-fold anthropology: "The tripartite division of man into body, soul and spirit is not found in the Gospels, and is foreign to modern thought." Suggesting that Paul's tripartite anthropology was not in keeping with that of Jesus, Dougall drew upon biblical scholar R. H. Charles to argue that a neat dualism of body and spirit was better equipped to convey the "more noble and godly activities of the mind." [56] Her biblical evidences notwithstanding, even Dougall was consigned to shift among the terms body, mind, spirit, and soul as she argued for the reality of spiritual healing.

Many evocations of a body and spirit dualism were couched in a less argumentative and more prosaic manner than Dougall's, such as the *Canadian Churchman's* celebration of medical missionary Albert Schweitzer as a missionary to souls and a doctor to bodies.[57] This casual dualism, however, became less common as liberal Protestants increasingly found a reservoir for the anthropology of body, mind, and spirit not only in biblical texts but also in psychological discourses. The ministers Elwood Worcester and Samuel McComb, Anglican pioneers of Christian psychotherapy in the Emmanuel Movement, proclaimed a therapeutic union of Freud and Jesus in their 1932 book, *Body, Mind, and Spirit*, written long after the prime of their movement. Emphatically criticizing doctors who held "physiological" views of healing that smacked of medical materialism, Worcester wrote his chapters while at his cottage "in the wilds of New Brunswick, Canada, with access to very few books." Based on his memories of the "outstanding thoughts" of luminaries such as Freud, Jung, Adler, and many others, Worcester also drew his evidence from his reminiscences of healing encounters with patients who sought him out in his church clinics in Boston and New Brunswick.[58]

Arguing for an anthropology that saw mind, body, and spirit as mutually influential in deeply intimate and often subconscious ways, Worcester gratefully appropriated Freud's theories of repression and "hidden associations" while he remained critical of Freud's approach to religion and overtly hostile to "Freudians."[59] Distancing himself from Freud's "exaggeration" of the "power of the sex instinct," Worcester simultaneously argued against punitive laws or hostile attitudes toward male and female homosexuality and considered male and female masturbation—after puberty—a normal practice.[60] Worcester most explicitly distinguished himself from Freud, however, in his interpretation of the subconscious as a site of the spirit. As Andrew Heinze has observed, Jewish popularizers of psychology in North America, including the psychiatrist Isador Coriat, who worked with Worcester early on, understood the subconscious as a site of inner conflict, not of cosmic spiritual connection. Just as Coriat "warned about mystifications of the psyche" in his work with the Emmanuel Movement, in the 1940s Joshua Roth Liebman, author of the bestselling *Peace of Mind*, would caution against a "spiritualized psyche" that held "hidden reserves of power."[61] For Worcester and many other liberal Protestants, however, the subconscious was such a useful concept precisely because they could bestow on it so many different kinds of spirits and energies.[62] Like most early-twentieth-century liberal Protestants, the "religion" that Worcester sought to unify with medicine would have been more accurately called Protestantism in a New Thought key.

Throughout his writings Worcester turned to New Testament texts, approvingly quoting Paul's advice to the Thessalonians to "Quench not the Spirit" and endorsing Paul's prayer that "Your whole spirit and soul and body be preserved blameless unto the coming of our Lord Jesus Christ" (1 Thessalonians 5:19–23, KJV). Worcester's prolonged discussions of the spiritual, however, often had little to do with the Holy Spirit.[63] Armed with a PhD in psychology from the German lab of Wilhelm Wundt, and with William James and Immanuel Kant as his authorities, Worcester recounted his successful attempts to heal paranoid patients using an etiology of "extra-organic" spirit possession: "Granting that discarnate spirits exist and that communication between them and us is possible, it would not be unthinkable if this invitation were sometimes accepted and if these strange and frequently sudden changes of personality, these apparitions, these disturbing voices, should proceed from a cause outside ourselves."[64] Employing mediums to channel the voices of the spirits, Worcester claimed to cure several men and women of their bodily and mental ailments through calmly persuading spirits to cease their antics and then counseling his patients to quit spiritualist practices, such as automatic writing, that would expose them to spirit possession.[65]

Dreams served as another pathway for the spirit, according to Worcester, who considered sleep a "healing" and "spiritual experience" by which "we touch a source of spiritual renewal and refreshment which no drug can bestow upon us."[66] Worcester recounted the story of his friend, the "Dean of a Canadian cathedral" who summered with Worcester in rural New Brunswick, as evidence of the power of revelation from "He who sendeth dreams and visions."[67] The Dean's son, who lost his father's highly valued pearl shirt stud, found it again via a dream that told him exactly where to look. Proffering this story as evidence for the "delicacy of perception" of the subconscious mind, Worcester blended subconscious, embodied memory—the son's bodily but unknowing memory of dropping the pearl—with divine revelation from the sender of dreams, embracing both Freud's analysis of dreams and a longer tradition of Christian dream interpretation. Worcester's anecdotal evidences of his own healing abilities and his confident citations of psychoanalytic theorists and psychic researchers alike made for an entertaining anthropology of body, mind, and spirit, only partly acknowledged by those in his wake.

A notably different approach to Christian healing was voiced by fellow Bostonian and early supporter of the Emmanuel Movement, Dr. Richard Cabot of Massachusetts General Hospital, whom Worcester declared to be "noble and chivalrous" even though he had counseled Worcester against taking on psychiatric cases because of his lack of medical training.[68] *The Art of Ministering to the Sick*, a best-selling and oft-reprinted book first published in the United States in 1936, was co-authored by Cabot and Russell Dicks, a Presbyterian minister and hospital chaplain. Perhaps in response to Worcester's refusal to stay off their turf, Cabot and Dicks set out to answer the following question: "The Catholic priest hears confessions, gives absolution, and administers extreme unction. But can the Protestant minister be anything but a nuisance [in the hospital]?" These pioneers of what became "clinical pastoral education" argued strenuously in favor of the usefulness of Protestant ministers who could "counteract the evils of [medical] specialism" by offering "glimpses of the whole"—albeit not a whole that included spirit possession within its bounds.[69]

Cabot and Dicks's pragmatic guide was a model for Grover Livingstone's *Through Sickness to Life*, in which biomedicine, psychology, and spiritual care were interdependent and not, in his view, magical: "What we here offer is not new. We prescribe nothing mechanical: 'Recite this formula, and the charm will work.' 'Say that ten times and you will get what you want.' That is what we do not offer." [70] The experience of illness itself could furnish spiritual experience through bodily knowing: "In experiencing physical pain we are having in our bodies a feeling of what He knew on the cross. Can it be that this also is to know the fellowship of His sufferings?"[71] For Livingstone, and most liberal Protestants, to have faith did not necessarily mean to be healed. Despite his hardly veiled allusion to the "mechanical" magic of Catholic (or even Anglican) techniques of prayer, Livingstone went on to recommend the therapeutic benefits of Sulpician prayer and meditation. In another encompassing gesture, he declared: "modern psychology is a blessed discovery and belongs to the best of the pastor's equipment."[72]

The blend of optimism and pragmatism found in advice books such as *The Art of Ministering to the Sick* and *Through Sickness to Life* tried to clear a space for a kind of "spirit" that was neither "occult" nor "magical"—a spirit that could easily mingle with psychological views of the self without getting in the way of the work of the doctor. The liberal Protestant acceptance of psychological views of the self—merged with those of Shakespeare and Stoic philosophers such as Marcus Aurelius—demonstrated the openness of the Protestant minister to multiple ways of understanding human identity in collaboration with biomedical anthropologies. Especially in the temporal world of the here and now, an anthropology of body, mind, and spirit provided both doctors and liberal Protestant ministers with their own realms in the common task of healing.[73]

In a cultural context where tripartite divisions of the human were finding growing currency—whether that of Pauline Pentecostalism or the id, ego, and superego of Freudian psychoanalysis—liberal Protestants eventually came to accept, or at least imbibe, such a tripartite division. By the time they were fully "holistic" in the 1960s, they had abandoned the dualistic pair of body and soul for the trinitarian "balance" of body, mind, and spirit.[74] Leslie Weatherhead (1893–1976), a well-known liberal British Methodist clergyman considered an expert on spiritual healing, often cited in the *Churchman* and the *Observer*, put it this way in 1969:

> . . . man is a trinity in unity. He is body, mind, and spirit. Now the body clearly is that physical part of ourselves through which we make contact with the outside world. The mind is that unseen immaterial part of man by which he expresses thoughts. . . . Now the spirit (the soul and the spirit I take to be the same) I regard as that part of the mind with which I can worship, that part of my immaterial being that is capable of communion with God.[75]

Weatherhead was an experimental modernist with a very liberal approach to healing and physicality generally. Even bolder than Belle Oliver, he wrote advice texts pleading for a Christian embrace of male and female sexual energy, properly channeled: ". . . whatever we have suffered, our children may grow up with real chances of attaining a normal and harmonious sex life, with healthy minds in healthy bodies, minds to which nothing is unclean except sin, and bodies which are temples of the living God."[76] Weatherhead wove together psychoanalytic perspectives with theories of the healing magnetism of "odic energy" (from the Norse god Odin), and with a strong, spiritualist belief that life continued after death in an "etheric body."[77] Weatherhead's therapeutic authority, like that of Worcester, derived more from experience than formal training, and both men were important precursors to the more institutionalized version of psychiatrically grounded spiritual equilibrium. Their eclectic theories of odic energy or spirit possession, however, made them simultaneously proponents of spiritual intervention. Whereas an anthropology of body, mind, and spirit could make room for such overlapping views, as liberal Protestants became more invested in psychiatric and psychological approaches such overlaps became less viable.

TILLICH'S DEMONIC AND THE SYNTHETIC UNITY OF THE SPIRIT

Weatherhead, while achieving notable status in his day, enjoyed nothing close to the influence of the dominant theologian of liberal Protestant modernity, Paul Tillich. Harvard professor and author of the immensely popular *Courage to Be* (1952), Tillich urged his readers to overcome the modern curse of anxious dread "aroused by the loss of a spiritual center" by grounding themselves in "ultimate" being. Healing, Tillich argued, could be a cosmic blend of the temporal and eternal leading to such ontological grounding.[78] An émigré from 1930s Germany who started out at Union Theological Seminary in New York City in the company of Reinhold Niebuhr and colleagues in psychology at Columbia University, Tillich had a particular—and psychoanalytic—anthropology of the spiritual body. Over the course of his writings, which had a profound effect on both liberal Protestants and more "secular" readers throughout North America, Tillich developed a theological anthropology based on his concept of the demonic, first articulated while he was still in Germany in 1926:

The demonic appears as a breaking into the center of personality, as an attack on the synthetic unity of the spirit, as a superindividual and yet not natural power. Its dwelling is in the subconscious level of the human soul. The peculiar disunity between the natural-character and the strange-character of frenzy results from the observation that in the possessed state elements of the subconscious arise which, to be sure, constantly give the personality its vital impulse, its immediate fullness of life, but which in a normal state are prevented from entering into consciousness. What we name these elements depends on the symbols by which the subconscious is interpreted. The symbols can be poetic, metaphysical, psychological, but always remain symbols, that is, indications rather than concepts. Whether one speaks of the "will to power" or of the "chaos" or of the "ego-instinct" or of the "libido"—in each instance feelings or events of the formed consciousness are used as symbols of unformed psychic depth.

In a 1965 interview with the popular psychologist Carl Rogers, Tillich reflected on why he turned to the New Testament to find his own "symbol" of the demonic to frame his "interpretation of history."[79] He sought to account for the two kinds of structural forces illuminated by Freud and Marx: what he called the "neuro-psychotic structure" and the "analysis of the conflicts of society." Finding the Christian notion of "sinful" man not enough to account for these structural forces, but yet wanting to root his analysis in Christian symbols, he stated: "The only sufficient term I found was in the New Testament use of the term 'demonic,' which is in the stories about Jesus: similar to being possessed. That means a force, under a force, which is stronger than the individual good will."[80] Translating both the psychic and the social into the concept of the demonic, Tillich tried to voice what he called the "Protestant principle"—the notion of a prophetic critique of both religious and political power—in such a language that it could engage with multiple universalizing theories: the inner "drives" of psychology, the historical materialism of socialist critique, and the symbolic analyses that characterized the burgeoning field of comparative history of religions.

Tillich began his "little pamphlet," *The Demonic: An Interpretation of History* (1926), with a classic history of religions comparative approach—a swift cataloguing of a "picture of the demonic" through the centuries and across religious traditions. He listed the "holy demonries" of "vital-orgiastic nature cults" and "ritual prostitution" found among "primitive peoples and Asiatics," those of Canaanite "war gods" of the Hebrew Bible, and the demonry of any religious institution that makes itself absolute (i.e., for Tillich, Roman Catholicism).[81] The plenitude of Tillich's examples of demonic creativity and destruction led him to a singular, universal conclusion: the plurality of the demonic could only be "fulfilled in the spirit, not in 'spirits.' "[82] Without this fulfillment in the mature spirit in the singular, the demonic would lead to "demonry" and possession, fragmenting the "synthetic unity of the spirit" and the self.

As his simultaneous engagement with both psychoanalytic and socialist theories showed, Tillich understood demonry as not limited to the level of the personality. In a new version of an old social gospel argument about social evils, Tillich transposed the demonic possession of the self to the demonic possession of the social, declaring nationalism and capitalism to be the two most lethal "demonries of the present."[83] At both the individual and the social level, Tillich's solution for the demonic was a monotheistic, theological answer rooted in the unified spirit: "Demonry breaks down only before divinity, the possessed state before the state of grace, the destructive before redeeming fate."

In a 1945 discussion of religion and healing at a Columbia University seminar that included psychoanalysts Karen Horney and Rollo May (another Union Theological Seminary graduate), Tillich brought together his notion of the divine as "the Ultimate" with his tripartite view of the self as holistically integrated body, psyche, and spirit. To make his point, he sharply distinguished between "magic" and religion, in a manner not unlike many anthropological definitions, and that was parallel to his distinction between the demonic and grace: "Magic is a special kind of interrelation between finite powers; religion is the human relation to the infinite power and value. Magic can be creative and destructive, while religion stands essentially against the destructive powers."[84] He went on to argue that the multiple gods and spirits of polytheism are necessarily magical (if not demonic) because their "plurality indicates that none of them is really ultimate." The only way to overcome the problem of possession, in Tillich's understanding, was to house—or contain—the spirits in the psyche: "The idea of spirits as things or persons is a superstition. But spirits as psychic forces are a reality, or at least a potentiality." The healing potentiality of these "vital" life forces, however, could only be realized with the right kind of faith, liberated from all "inferior connotations (e.g., as opinion without much evidence, or acceptance of authorities on irrational grounds, or subjection to foreign or auto-suggestion), and restore[d] it to its true religious sense, in which faith is the state of being grasped by the Ultimate."[85] Where Worcester accepted the existence of "discarnate" spirits and humans' ability to communicate with them, Tillich internalized such "superstition" within the psyche. As we will see in Chapter 4, Tillich's ontology of the modern self circulated beyond the arena of theological debates and into practical sites of healing, including, most importantly, pastoral counseling.

SPIRITUAL EQUILIBRIUM, SPIRITUAL INTERVENTION, AND GLOBAL CHRISTIANITY

Different anthropologies of the spiritual body lead to different techniques of devotion in the service of healing. The holistic trinity of body, mind, and spirit has contained both anthropologies of spiritual equilibrium and spiritual intervention, but not without a history of contestation within Protestantism more generally, and among Anglican, Methodist, and United Church communities more particularly. Debates over faith healing, medical missions, spiritualism, and other movements of Christian healing have often hinged on what kind of evidence can be marshaled for the bodily effectiveness of a given therapy—when the active agent is the spirit, such "evidence-based" healing is particularly controversial. As these debates occurred in the global context of the post–World War II World Council of Churches (WCC), the question of the spirit remained heavily inflected by Tillich's anthropology.

By the end of the twentieth century, liberal Protestant medical practitioners were less likely than their precursors to be setting up "Christian" hospitals or to view their work as "medical missions." Many doctors and nurses found secular agencies better fitted to their task, although some continued to think of their biomedical practices as part of their Christian witness, and as a service not only to Christians, but also to humanity writ large. At a global level, many of the doctors, policy analysts, and activists who engaged in biomedical health care as Christians did so with the support of the Geneva-based WCC. In the mid-1960s the WCC lent its support to a pair of consultations that brought together medical missionaries, health care professionals, and theologians in Tübingen, Germany. The consultations occurred at time when newly independent colonial states were nationalizing Christian hospitals and establishing their own health care networks based on, and sometimes literally in, missionary hospitals.

In the face of this transformation the Tübingen participants wondered if the "secularizing" of medicine was not in itself a sign of the success of medical missions and part of their necessary evolution. The WCC Director of World Mission and Evangelism, Lesslie Newbigin, a British Presbyterian and founder and Bishop in the ecumenical Church of South India, wondered "whether we have reached a point in world history where the Gospel has to be reinterpreted in secular terms." Insisting that the "Welfare State" and secular medicine were themselves "obviously a by-product of the Gospel," Newbigin posed the question: "Given the fact that we now possess technical means for the mastery of disease undreamed of when the Gospels were written, what is today the relationship between the work of healing and the announcement of Christ's victory over the powers of evil?"[86]

Newbigin's bold claim that secularity was itself inherently Christian— a different take on more recent arguments about the mutual embeddedness of Christianity and the secular—was echoed in the approaches of his colleagues in Tübingen.[87] Together, they emphasized the need to work with scientific medicine and to be suspicious of sensationalist faith healing, while they also repeatedly asserted that all healing came from God and was a "dethroning of the powers of evil."[88] Deployed in tandem with psychological concepts such as anxiety ("a red light testifying to the abyss") and medical approaches such as psychosomatic medicine, the diabolical tenor of the Tübingen consultation's definition of healing drew from the discourses of both spiritual equilibrium and spiritual intervention.[89] Norwegian missionary Erling Kayser, the organizer of the meetings, urged caution in this blending, voicing an unusually harsh skepticism of the merger of healing and wholeness: "Man is not whole, and man cannot be whole. Man is in the everlasting fight between the negative and the positive, the destructive and the creative, the diabolic and the symbolic, the urge to death and the urge to life, and in theological terms: crucifixion and resurrection." Asserting that illness was a "symbol of the meeting with the ultimate dualism," Kayser drew from Tillich to argue that the only way to deal with illness was to encounter the anxiety provoked by it, and to understand that "man is not a static whole."[90]

In his contribution to the papers of the first consultation, Martin Scheel, the Director of the German Institute for Medical Missions, pointed to the significance of another dualism, the scientific methods of the "West" versus the supernatural diagnoses of the "East." Suggesting that "maybe the thought of Asia and Africa has something to teach us," Scheel drew on his experience as a medical missionary to question the limits of scientific approaches to healing but concluded that "the profoundest expression of pre-scientific healing is to be found in the Christian religion."[91] The last word was given to U.S. Presbyterian James McGilvray, who argued for what Tillich called the "multidimensional" approach to health in terms that were discordant with those of Kayser,

yet deeply familiar: "As Christians it is imperative that we again empha-
size the Biblical view of man as a whole—the creation of God in body,
mind, and soul who can never be separated into distinct parts and who
must be seen in terms of the redemption which awaits him."[92]

Out of the Tübingen consultations came a new WCC organization,
the Christian Medical Commission, established in Geneva in 1968 and
directed by James McGilvray. The Christian Medical Commission attempted to coordinate the work of Christian hospitals, especially in
newly independent colonial states, within an ecumenical network. In the
1970s the Commission sought to transform the legacy of medical missions via an innovative and explicitly holistic and postcolonial model of
what they called "primary health care." Inspired by "barefoot doctors"
of the People's Republic of China (who themselves had antecedents in
medical missions), and drawing on the skills of the "traditional healers"
formerly spurned by some medical missionaries, primary health care
sought to turn the focus from funding large-scale hospitals in national
capitals to empowering local health care workers to offer a blend of
biomedical and traditional care in local contexts.[93] According to Christian doctors Christoph Benn and Erlinda Senturias, medical missions in
this postcolonial era were newly open to traditional healing techniques
exactly because missionaries had come to adopt a model of healing that
emphasized not "charity" but "holistic" care, that understood that "the
human person represents a unity of body and soul so that all healing
methods have to be multidimensional."[94]

Primary health care was yet another Christian healing innovation
adopted by a "secular" biomedical organization. It soon captured the
attention of the neighbor of the Christian Medical Commission in
Geneva, the World Health Organization (WHO) of the United Nations,
and in 1974 WHO partnered with the Commission to formulate a program for primary health care. Other popular movements spurred by the
Christian Medical Commission in coordination with WHO included the
breast-feeding revival that saw North American and European Christians
(among others) organize a boycott of Nestlé to protest the company's
practice of giving out free baby formula to new mothers in poor countries, where these women had neither the money nor the clean water to
continue using formula to safely nourish their children.[95] In the wake of
these global movements, the formula of healing and wholeness was expressed in increasingly political language. Defining health as an issue of
justice, peace, the integrity of creation, and spirituality, a 1990 Christian
Medical Commission report stated: "Health is a dynamic state of well-

being of the individual and society; of physical, mental, spiritual, economic, political and social well-being; of being in harmony with each other, with the material environment, and with God."[96] Based on regional consultations held around the world, the report included accounts from Christians from disparate places who advocated a gospel of holism, such as the Bethel Baptist Healing Ministry in Kingston, Jamaica, with its ambitious motto of "Total healing to the Whole Person."[97]

At the same time, the report offered many examples in which "basic medical care" still meant biomedical interventions: collaboration between church groups and the Sandinista government in Nicaragua to increase immunizations; health seminars in which the Christian Health Association of Liberia introduced home-made rehydration solutions for children with diarrhea; and health-promotion volunteers recruited from North Carolina congregations who were trained to teach their fellow parishioners about stress management, smoking cessation, and weight reduction. Across this wide range of health issues found in countries with vastly different wealth and resources, biomedical diagnoses and treatments were clearly still of great utility. As the Honduras consultation put it, "We cannot exempt ourselves from the responsibility of using the resources of medical science or from political participation simply because we are praying for the sick!"[98] The epistemological basis of Christian healing articulated by the report's authors, however, was increasingly critical of its biomedical grounding. But instead of tying itself to a discourse of charismatic spiritual intervention, it claimed a cautious affinity with "traditional healing practices." The report suggested that "[t]hese traditional societies view health as complete harmony within an individual, family, community, and environment, and may thus be closer to a Christian view of health (wholeness) than that of Western medicine."[99] Earlier versions of missionary hostility toward traditional healing practices were thus inverted, as Christians who were engaged in the postcolonial version of medical mission increasingly considered biomedical anthropologies of the healing process to lack a kind of spirituality that could only be restored by traditional means.

The rise of HIV/AIDS, among other factors, thwarted the optimistic goals of the primary health care movement—with its 1978 slogan of "Health for All by the Year 2000"—but the influence of the Christian Medical Commission on the World Health Organization took other forms. In 1997, WHO's constitutional review board took a page from the Commission when it advocated for the inclusion of "spiritual well-being" in the WHO's definition of health. In 2005 the Canadian Nurses'

Association passed a resolution, brought forward by its own Parish Nursing Interest Group, to include spiritual well-being in its definition of health in 2005, and further resolved that it would take on a "leadership role" in trying to convince WHO to do the same.[100] To date, however, WHO has resisted the pressure to join the refrain that, as Winnifred Fallers Sullivan puts it, "we are all spiritual now."[101] The Christian Medical Commission is now defunct—in its wake, the notion of spiritual well-being in the WCC has become increasingly shaped by a discourse of spiritual intervention.[102]

SECULAR SPIRITS

Given its proximity to institutions of "secular" culture, such as the WHO, it is not surprising that liberal Protestantism has been particularly concerned to speak to "the cultured despisers of religion."[103] Addressing themselves to a science-loving, religion-doubting audience, of which they were themselves a part, throughout the twentieth century liberal Protestants struggled to make a case for the efficacy of prayer and the related benefits of a disposition of faithful Christianity, especially in the realm of healing. Competing with other groups, Christian and not, in conveying their message, some liberal Protestants' proximity to and preference for a secular audience shaped their message in ways that were not always biomedically or religiously orthodox, as when leaders such as Frederick Du Vernet and Sherwood Eddy embraced forms of psychic healing in the guise of a scientific Christianity. Their allegiance to science also led liberal Protestants to argue against "heretical" groups that they did not consider to be Protestant, let alone Christian, such as Christian Science, and to debate Pentecostal approaches to healing. For their part, Pentecostals, embodying a complex mix of faith healing, suspicion of scientific and medical approaches, including psychoanalysis, and their own version of medicalized enchantment, have grown from being easy prey for science-literate liberal Protestants to being sophisticated defenders of their own versions of Christian healing backed up by their own scientific experts.[104]

Although there are many examples of a rapprochement, especially between Pentecostal and liberal Christians—as in their cooperation over parish nursing, their shared valuing of the "spirit," and conjunctions of Anglo-Catholic and charismatic approaches to healing in the Anglican Church—the divisions between conservative and liberal Christianity are still deep and powerful. Acceptance of women clergy and full rights for gays and lesbians have been some of the most recent and prominent issues over which liberal Protestants have battled with their conservative counterparts, even within Anglican and United Churches in Canada. The metaphor of healing, in its relation to Christian anthropologies of the spiritual body, has sometimes played a role in mediating these divides and sometimes exacerbated them further.

The portrayal of liberal Protestantism as hyperrational and liturgically stilted—or even "spiritually dead"—is a refrain that has been invoked by many, whether Pentecostals declaring "sad Christians" to have lost the spirit, or secular critics mocking the pew-bound predictability of a Protestant congregation's responsive readings. Even liberal Protestants themselves have joined the chorus, lamenting the stodgy, cerebral fixity of Protestant ritual.[105] Contrasted with the lively Pentecostal and charismatic "direct experience" of bodies filled up by God's spirit, the "appeal to experience" in the clinical encounter of the pastoral counselor and his client seems tame in comparison. A diagnosis of spiritual deadness, however, misses the energy of liberal Protestant experiments with channeling the spirit whether through pastoral counseling, radio mind, yogic Christianity, or psychic healing. Even the early twentieth century Anglican movement for renewing the rite of healing with holy oil was a move to reestablish a channel for directing the spirit into the body. Inventing and reinventing experiential ritual modes built upon anthropologies of bodies infused with God's spirit, Protestants of all sorts have been going to "strange places of the spirit" in the search for healing for quite some time.[106]

CHAPTER 2

The Gospel of Health and the Scientific Spirit

Few scientific men can pray, I imagine. Few can carry on any living commerce with 'God.' Yet many of us are well aware how much freer in many directions and abler our lives would be, were such important forms of energizing not sealed up.

—William James, *The Energies of Men*, 1907

This baptism of the holy, scientific spirit, descending like a golden shower on both wings of the advancing army, will bring to [scientific social service] the energizing power of sacrificial love, and to [Christian social work] the inspiring power of great deeds, greatly conceived and greatly accomplished.

—Robert Milliken, *Christian Guardian*, 1923

Anna Henry was a scientific woman who could pray. A doctor with the Canadian Methodist Women's Missionary Society in China, Henry penned a short pamphlet in the early 1900s called *Life from the Dead*, describing to her readers her experience with opium addicts: "As they go through the terrible throes of the unbearable craving for the cursed opium, they cling to you so, beseeching help, while their abject, pain-distorted features, attitudes and motions remind one of Dante's Inferno."[1] Although Henry's readers may not have had Dante's epic poem to hand, there is a better chance that they would have caught the biblical reference of her title: "Neither yield ye your members as instruments of unrighteousness unto sin: but yield yourselves unto God, as those that are alive from the dead, and your members as instruments of righteousness unto God" (Romans 6:13, KJV). For Henry, prayerful famil-

FIGURE 4. Portrait of Dr. Anna Henry, "pioneer doctor to West China," 1899. Courtesy of United Church of Canada Archives, Toronto, Portraits Collection, P2639.

iarity with the words of the Apostle Paul was a powerful medicine well fitted to the agony of withdrawal; she prescribed both prayer and Bible reading to all her patients and literacy lessons to those who could not read.

Anna Henry was not alone among missionaries, or even among Canadians more generally, in thinking that reading could be a transformative act capable of freeing a person from addictions and tyrannies of physical, social, and economic origin—as a medical student Norman Bethune thought so too when he taught immigrant laborers to read using Bibles and hymn books in northern Ontario.[2] Missionaries gave a particular spiritual importance to both reading and writing: reading could educate the illiterate and make Christians of the heathen, and writing, in the words of Belle Oliver, was a "ministry," inscribed in letters, tracts, and booklets.[3] In the back of every pew and on the shelf of every library, texts intimately marked the lives of Protestants in North America as sensational forms that channeled the "energizing power" of "the holy scientific spirit," freeing the lives of its recipients for sacrificial love and scientific accomplishment.

This early-twentieth-century Protestant gospel of health was an overlay of Christian and biomedical convictions in which a role for the "spirit" was both expected and debated. The strongest example of this blend was the medical missionary, whose "ministry of letter-writing" was meant to document the therapeutic effects of evangelism. Within a print culture of tracts, newspapers, and holy writ, Protestants created an "imagined community" that drew boundaries differentiating the healthy Protestant from the non-Christian, the colonial convert, or the wayward fellow Christian, while also providing a scientific warrant for new openness to frank education about the body and sexuality.[4] Sometimes, as in Belle Oliver's *Anandi's Question,* the mission provided the narrative setting for such sexual education, intertwining both kinds of discovery. The gospel of health grew more fractious when new Christian healing movements such as Christian Science and divine healing (later Pentecostalism) competed with considerable success against the biomedically friendly Protestant anthropology of the spiritual body. These new movements premised their healing innovations on very different relations to biblical texts, but for all Protestants the Bible, and the ways it was read and ritualized, served as a standard to judge modes of Christian healing.

Anglicans and Methodists particularly deemed Christian Scientists and Pentecostals to have misread the New Testament in their antibiomedical innovations. Christian Scientists advanced an anthropology that considered the physicality of the body to be "error" or illusion, as articulated in founder Mary Baker Eddy's rereading of the New Testament, *Science and Health with a Key to the Scriptures.*[5] Pentecostalism also proposed new interpretive and ritualized relations to biblical texts by reading New Testament texts describing the gifts of healing bestowed at Pentecost as gifts still available to believing Christians and by embracing ritual practices—whether in divine healing, speaking in tongues, or extemporaneous preaching—that distanced them from the formality of written texts (or even languages), be they read sermons or written prayers. Countering these new Christian healers via a "text-based cosmology" that encompassed Christians and scientists, liberal Protestants contended that healing could not be demonstrated only by testimonies of bodily transformation but also had to be documented via the scientific method.[6] Liberal Protestants built much of their solidarity with biomedicine through their vociferous disagreement with the textual "heresies" of Christian Science and Pentecostalism. This solidarity was partly established on the liberal Protestant commitment to rational, sober processes of reading and recording evidence in print, based on the scientific method, as the best way to adjudicate the effectiveness and authenticity of healing practices. But the scientific spirit was anxious about just what it could prove: liberal Protestants argued that the emotional performances of faith healers were fraudulent by the standards of science, but they were less certain about the claims and practices of psychic research and psychology, as we will see.

Since its beginnings in the Reformation's focus on *sola scriptura,* textuality has been deeply constitutive of Protestantism while it has remained potentially treacherous.[7] In the gradually more literate twentieth century, Bibles, books, newspapers, magazines, and tracts were the relatively democratic grounds on which theologians and biblical scholars essayed their intellectual breakthroughs and missionaries translated their message for non-Christian audiences. Although new technologies of communication such as the telegraph, the phonograph, the lantern slide, and the radio were becoming available, texts were still the dominant medium of the time and had a symbolic import beyond their communicative content that shaped the daily practice and sense of identity of Protestants.[8] For example, at the same time that Protestants grappled at home with the disenchantment—or possibilities—of scholars' higher criticism of the Bible, missionaries abroad relayed narratives of encounter that told of "the heathen" receiving the Bible not as a communicative tool, but as a magical talisman.[9] Native reception of the Bible as talisman, although useful for the purposes of conversion according to some missionaries, also pointed to the "lack" the missionaries considered the Book to illuminate: lack of literacy, lack of knowledge, and lack of ethical religion.[10]

As Homi K. Bhabha wrote of missionary encounters in India, "the discovery of the book installs the signs of appropriate representation: the word of God, truth, art creates the conditions for a beginning, a practice of history and narrative. But the institution of the Word in the wilds is also an *Entstellung,* a process of displacement, distortion, dislocation, repetition—the dazzling light of literature sheds only darkness."[11] Redirecting Bhabha's insights reveals that a Protestant text-based cosmology also had a talismanic—or therapeutic—dimension for Protestants themselves. Inhabiting a "strange world of textual intimacy" in which Bibles were read and analyzed but also nuzzled and heard to speak, Protestants have also granted books ritualized and therapeutic powers, however concealed by the primacy of their use of texts as intellectual or doctrinal tools.[12] Supernatural liberalism was itself premised on a textual intimacy in which the written word was both a source of spiritual revelation and a tool for scientific verification. Taken together, the emotional, material, and intellectual roles of texts in early twentieth century Protestant discourses of healing did not make for an enlightened, lucid mirror to the distortions (*Entstellung*) of colonial readings. Instead, the text-based cosmology of Protestantism bore within itself reflections of its disparaged literate and illiterate others, and of its often agonizing love for both biblical and scientific truths.

MEDICALIZATION AND MORAL THERAPEUTICS

Pursuing their goal of spreading the "duty of good health" around the world, early twentieth-century Protestants did their "preaching, teaching, and healing" in the midst of a wider cultural process of medicalization, through which biomedicine was gaining authoritative knowledge and institutional power within North America (see Figure 5).[13] Exhorting physical fitness, longevity, control of the nerves, and temperance as duties of the Christian citizen in a "strenuous" age beset by the opposing forces of "Bolshevism" and "bloated capitalism," Anglicans and Methodists sought to impart standards and practices of hygiene to new immigrants and First Nations peoples.[14] Only recently schooled in modern norms of hygiene themselves, as doctors, nurses, academics, teachers, clergy, and missionaries, Protestants were at the heart of the middle-class networks that included both the practitioners and the client base of the ascending medical profession.[15] Taking on challenges posed by growing scientific disciplines such as psychology and public health, many Anglicans and Methodists came to see themselves as "modernists" or "liberals" eager to be infused with the scientific spirit. Liberal, social-service-oriented Christianity hoped for a successful and seamless union among state-supported biomedicine and Christian mission that would also help them to discredit their competitors, such as Christian Science and Pentecostalism. Armed with both medical and biblical evidences, Protestants hitched their moral therapeutics to the train of medicalization, gaining from and being transformed by biomedicine's authority, while also structuring and "moralizing" it in turn.[16]

Michel Foucault's analysis of medicalization has shown how the field of biomedicine (including doctors, hospital administrators, and

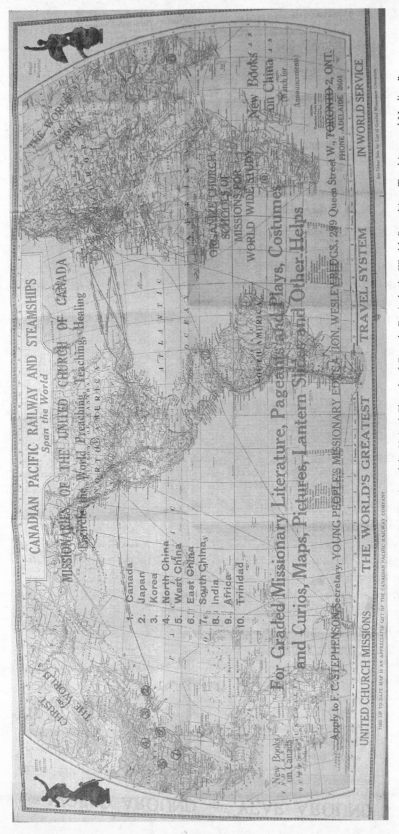

FIGURE 5. Map of United Church Missions, "Missionaries of the United Church of Canada Encircle the World, Preaching, Teaching, and Healing," ca. early 1930s, superimposed on the shipping routes of Canadian Pacific Railway and Steamship Lines, and with mission-related reading suggestions for all ages on the reverse. Courtesy of United Church of Canada Archives, Toronto Sidney Barlow Stokes Fonds, 88.059P/19.

pharmaceutical companies) has produced a normative, naturalized, scientific discourse of the human body while gaining authority over an increasingly wider range of spheres external to its specific, physiological expertise. In Foucault's analysis, the "authoritarian intervention of medicine" has reached into nonmedical spheres, such as when a person's employability is partly based on medical testing, constructing new spheres of knowledge under the combined authority of state and medical "biopower."[17] Drawing from Foucault's critique of biopower, several scholars, such as Bryan Turner and Deborah Gordon, have advanced similar arguments, contending that the process of medicalization enabled biomedicine to assume—or steal—the authority of religion as the ground and regulator of morality and ethics in western societies. Gordon, for example, argued that the twin Enlightenment bases of biomedicine—naturalism and individualism—have cultivated biomedicine as a triple threat of cosmology, ontology, and epistemology that at once declares its objectivity while at the same time it demands obedience of its subjects. In Gordon's words, "The biological reductionism by which modern medicine is frequently characterized is more theoretical than actual; in its effects, biomedicine speaks beyond its explicit reductionist reference through the implicit ways it teaches us to interpret ourselves, our world, and the relationships between humans, nature, self, and society."[18] Put another way, biomedicine has taken on the work of anthropology in its original Christian, theological sense, by prescribing how human beings, as bodies, should relate to others, including spiritual entities.

In a different vein sociologist Malcolm Bull argued that, with medicalization, religious functions were not so much secularized as "reallocated" when new healing-based Christian movements assumed the "supernatural claims of the declining churches" (meaning more established Protestant denominations). Similarly to Bryan Turner, Bull also contended that medicalization transferred "moral domination . . . from established religion to medically orientated secular institutions whose authority extends beyond what is rationally and empirically justifiable."[19] Exploring his hypothesis via the example of Seventh Day Adventism in the United States, Bull convincingly argued that Adventism was both "a product and an agent of medicalization" in the way that it maintained supernatural claims while it embraced scientific concepts and medical regimens of the body.[20] However, Bull's contention that established Protestant denominations had abandoned their moral authority to medicalization, whereas the young, "energetic" sects, such as Adventists, joined the medical wave in a blend of innovative theology and medical technique, miscasts the role of Protestants in medicalization.[21]

The "established" churches enjoyed much more agency and responsibility in the process: they accepted, encouraged, and enacted medical authority through urban, remote, and foreign medical missionaries, denominational hospitals, and combinations of psychotherapeutic and pastoral care. In this embrace of medicalization, liberal Protestants, as deaconesses, doctors, nurses, chaplains and psychologists, were at the heart of the medical profession while they maintained a supernaturalism that led them to pray before surgeries or to recommend Bible reading to a patient. Christian (both Protestant and Catholic) clerical and medical professionals enlisted the category of "religion" to craft the naturalizing power of biomedicine, as well as to set Christianity in a necessary if attenuated relationship to supposedly secular biomedicine. In North America, people acting in the name of "religion"—both Christians and Jews, who were often not allowed to practice as doctors in Christian hospitals, and thus started their own—enthusiastically contributed to the rising cultural authority of biomedicine, sometimes even by way of its critique. [22] The naturalizing power of both religion and biomedicine, then, has been constituted in intimate combination.

Protestant engagement with medicalization also took shape in an era of growing consumption (both the commodified and the tubercular kinds), in which medicines, regimens, and therapies of many kinds were for sale—advertised in church newspapers and secular magazines.[23] Perhaps partly because the market called on them to be such active health consumers, many early-twentieth-century Christians felt a sense of entitlement with respect to medicine, whether to criticize, endorse, or experiment with it. At the same time, many Canadian Christians were increasingly convinced that biomedical care was not best understood as a good to consume but, rather, as an obligation of the state to its citizens—they vigorously advocated for a biomedical health care system backed by state funding, conceiving of it as their movement and their birthright. Through church newspapers, books, secular press, sermons, and a wide variety of clinics, hospitals, and less formal therapeutic sites, Protestants spread the good news of "secular" medicine as in itself a religious calling and counsel.[24]

THE MINISTRY OF READING AND WRITING

The Protestant gospel of health depended on church newspapers to shape the Christian as a virtuous and healthy reader, usually in a denominationally specific way, as weekly editions encouraged regularized rituals of reading in the midst of an increasing variety of religious and secular reading options.[25] The editors of the Methodist *Christian Guardian* and the Anglican *Canadian Churchman* situated their papers as educational tools meant to build Canadian Christian community, within a wider network of U.S., British, and missionary settings. As the *Guardian* editorialized: "The religious newspaper of today in every issue is demonstrating the fact that it has a place and a great mission among men."[26] One Methodist deaconess even proclaimed humorously that the church newspaper was an agent of healing, reporting about a sick man whose subscription had lapsed: "A Methodist without his *Guardian*! No wonder he was ill!"[27] In the years 1900–1925 both newspapers were filled with frequent and varied references to healing, encompassing discussions of medical developments in "Radium as a Cancer Cure," exposés of Christian Science and patent medicine in "An Epidemic of Faith Killings" and "Fakes and Quacks," panicked warnings of the spread of disease in "Moslem Menace," and assertions of the purifying Gospel, in "Christ the Cleanser."[28] Letters to the editor demonstrated that the editorial voice in these papers was not representative of all readers, but it was largely in keeping with the spirit of the public Protestantism of the day: one that was masculine and confident in its Christian citizenship.[29]

Building up the body as a temple in the service of the greater good meant keeping oneself healthy to be a servant of Christ, refraining from questionable therapies such as patent medicines and Christian Science techniques, sacrificing self and resources for the benefit of the ill, whether at home or elsewhere, and living a life of "pure citizenship" unsullied by social disease (i.e., sexually transmitted diseases). For *Christian Guardian* letter-writer R. D. Hare, such purity had to be taught, especially to adolescent boys, faced as they were with a "carnival of nastiness, a miasma of unclean and malign influences, which attenuate the mind, pollute the imagination, and disintegrate the soul—all because they atrophy and paralyze the will." With honest sexual education from church, state, home, and school, Hare urged, a youth could have "his conception of his bodily powers changed from the vulgar to the holy, by sympathetic, scientific instruction, [such that] his craving for the unnatural could be brought under his will."[30] With science in the service of the holy, liberal Protestantism was far from being a disembodied religion. Blending authoritative biomedical, biblical, and ritual knowledge with socially engaged Christian conviction and curiosity regarding "scientific" study of sex, the soul, and the afterlife, liberal Protestants sought to bear forth their dreams of a Christian civilization in the flesh.

Medical missionaries offered a particularly vivid example of the talismanic powers Protestants gave to texts at a time when liberal Protestants were still convinced of their superiority over all other religions and cultures. In accounts from China, India, Africa, and urban and northern Canada, newspapers repeatedly depicted the medical missionary as a powerful tonic since with "the Church ... like the British Army, a little of her goes a long way."[31] Directed at both the mind and the body, medical missions were considered the most effective to convey the scientific spirit, both at home and abroad.[32] Testimonials and letters from the field were read at women's missionary society meetings across North America, sometimes by the visiting missionaries themselves, and were reprinted in church newspapers, forming both lived and virtual Protestant communities centered on narratives of suffering and salvation in distant lands. After recording donations of one and two dollars from several Toronto laywomen in 1901, Anglican recording secretary Caroline Macklem went on to detail the suffering of famine victims in China and India, quoting a fellow churchman's letter to her: "[A]ll this suffering may be God's way of opening the country to Christianity and civilization, the true civilization which only comes with the knowledge of Christ."[33] The Anglican Bishop of Derry was convinced of the portable efficiency and civilizing power of the text: "There is nothing else that our civilization has mastered that you can possibly offer to all the inhabitants of the world. Whether you go to the Eskimo, the African, the cultured and cultivated Indian, the South Sea Islander, or to any of our own islands, they will tell you that our Gospel is what they crave, and what they were made for."[34] If the "natives" somehow failed to feel such cravings, medical missions could help, according to Rev. A. R. MacDuff: "[O]nce those sick are cured, then their hearts are aglow with gratitude, and their minds are opened to receive the Gospel."[35]

Missionary pages of the church newspapers often urged their readers toward a gendered sympathy. The Anglican Toronto Woman's Auxiliary listened as Mrs. Hickman, a CMS missionary working with Chinese women, gave "a vivid description of her experiences among the Chinese. . . . Her account of the cruel practices and superstitions of the

Chinese deeply moved her hearers."[36] The trope of the exploited heathen woman was a feature of books on medical missions, which often
included chapters on the challenges that cultural norms of modesty
posed to medical missions among women.[37] One solution to this challenge was to train women as doctors, nurses, and deaconesses who could
also write about their experiences for popular audiences. Belle Oliver
and Anna Henry, for example, graduated from Toronto's Women's
Medical College in 1898, commencing their careers as doctors and
writers. In *Life from the Dead*, Henry told a story of an opium addict
named Mrs. Wang, brought to the hospital by her "kind-hearted" husband. Despite several near escapes from the hospital, Mrs. Wang emerged
from the torment of withdrawal "like one from the dead or like one
from whom an evil spirit had been cast out, leaving a very helpless
wreck."[38] Joining in daily morning prayers and literacy training at the
hospital allowed Mrs. Wang to overcome this powerlessness, according
to Henry, "and with praiseworthy persistence she applied herself to
studying the little books taught to beginners."

Six months after her return home, Mrs. Wang, having avoided the
common fate of relapsing into addiction, visited the mission hospital,
"bubbling over with appreciative speeches and loving demonstrations,
and told us that every morning at eight o'clock, the hour for hospital
prayers, she and her husband read from the New Testament we had
given her, and then knelt in prayer." Through becoming literate and rit-
ualizing her reading of the Bible at home, argued Henry, Mrs. Wang
was truly healed, "fortified by the strength that God alone provides."[39]
In multiple examples chronicled in the *Christian Guardian*, Henry reit-
erated that the path to lasting healing came through developing twinned
habits of biblical reading and prayer. Surgical interventions and medicines merely prepared the ill for their true healing through the Word,
"as we try to impress upon them that in order to serve the true God
aright and know what He would have them do, they must read His
book."[40]

Missionary accounts varied in casting women as the source of the
deliverance or the destruction of their cultures, but children—young
enough to be educated and given the tools of literacy—consistently appeared as a source of innocent hope among their cultures' supposed ignorance of true religion and science.[41] At a Woman's Auxiliary meeting
in the Niagara region, women learned about the Sarcee Indians from
Anglican missionary Miss Crawford, who "gave a most interesting
address, pointing out how the Indian tribe was being diminished in

numbers, owing largely to their lack of knowledge about their physical requirements, and urging the necessity of bringing the knowledge of salvation to those benighted pagans; she dwelt on the many touching examples of conversion among the Indian children, and read several letters that the children had written to her since she came East."[42] Missionaries often cast First Nations peoples as victims not only of their "superstitions," but also of their supposed ignorance of science and physiological needs, despite the fact that their physical ailments were often the direct result of the violent displacement brought by global trade, missionaries, and colonial governments. Other missionaries, however, such as United Church doctor R. W. Large, remarked on the health benefits of indigenous diets in the Pacific Northwest while his colleague, George Darby, struggled to prove his worth next to the local "shamans."[43] For Miss Crawford and her listeners, however, it was a mark of missionary success for children to learn to read and write in their supposed physical and spiritual deprivation.

Medical missionaries considered their effectiveness to be rooted both in medical techniques and, as Anna Henry's therapeutic approach demonstrated, in the Book. As one optimistic 1914 article entitled "The Medical Missionary and the Redemption of China" put it, the hospital waiting room was the perfect place to dispense texts and/as medicine: "Each patient receives a portion of Scripture and a tract. In this way the Word is distributed far and near, and seed is sown broadcast. A large number of homes are reached, as we have over one hundred patients each dispensary day."[44] Inpatients received an even more "intensive" introduction to the Word, as they sat through prayers, New Testament readings, and morning and evening hymns. Whether or not a largely illiterate population could read these tracts, missionaries were confident that the mere distribution of printed material in native languages would later bear fruit. They were not necessarily mistaken, as demonstrated by Homi Bhabha's quote from "the shrewd view of an unknown [Indian] native, in 1819: 'For instance, I take a book of yours and read it awhile and whether I become a Christian or not, I leave the book in my family: after my death, my son, conceiving that I would leave nothing useless or bad in my house, will look into the book, understand its contents, consider that his father left him the book, and become a Christian.'"[45] Missionaries were keenly aware that the power in the text lay partly in its ability to communicate long after the missionary was gone.

When U.S. Methodist missionary Walter Lambuth ranked the four essential tools of the medical missionary, he placed a book-lined study

FIGURE 6. Dr. George Darby, United Church medical missionary at Rivers Inlet, BC. "Discharging little patients," with First Nations woman and baby, 1930. Photograph by Harvey Doney, from collection of F.C. Stephenson, Secretary, Young People's Missionary Education, United Church. Courtesy of United Church of Canada Archives, Toronto, From Mission to Partnership Collection, 93.049 P/214.

first, ahead of the dispensary where medicine and tracts shared shelves in front of waiting patients, followed by the chapel and hospital. The bookishness of the missionary's study would include medical journals, dictionaries, the Bible translated into the native language, account books, patient files, new remedies, and hanging scrolls with biblical quotations and proverbs from "sages of the country."[46] Medical missionaries also wrote books of their own, especially translations of biblical or medical texts into the language of their host country.

Anna Henry's colleague in the Canadian Methodist mission in West China, Dr. William E. Smith (1864–1944), kept detailed and often introspective diaries of his more than thirty years as a missionary, with many of his earlier entries recounting his afternoons of selling biblical tracts at the city gate. Smith's diary records how he combined his medicalized perspective with diverse Christian anthropologies of the spiritual body and an ambivalent exploration of Chinese culture. At the beginning of his mission in 1898 he wrote: "In Kiating, when I saw the filthy gutter teaming with microbe life ready to destroy human life I wondered how long we could survive in China." One month later he reflected: "We visited the Dawost [sic] temple (erected in honor of the man who started the system of negation) and his second son. There [sic] statues are there & worshippers every day & burn incense to them. It is the most beautiful temple I have yet seen. Supposed to be the best in China." Smith agonized over his slow progress in learning Chinese, partly because he wanted to be able to preach and convert his patients but also because he wanted to learn all he could about Chinese culture. His entries dwelt on the successes and failures of the tract business and on his progress in learning Chinese with a variety of teachers, including Buddhist monks. In comparison, he gave less attention to surgeries or health concerns; in 1903 he even informed an unwilling colleague that he had to move to another town so that his house could be converted into a print shop.[47] Clearly a lover of books, Smith's list of texts loaned out to a colleague included works by Emerson, Ruskin, Adam Smith, Rudyard Kipling, as well as James Legge's translations of Mencius, and a book on cholera. The same Sunday that he proudly related achieving his goal of reading aloud publicly in Chinese, he also told of reading Baptist medical missionary Adoniram Judson's discussion of the spirit-filled life: "His arguments are plain & convincing on the importance and benefits of the second blessing or the filling of the Spirit."[48] A few months earlier, he quoted the liberal Methodist minister S. D. Chown: "Truth is that moral quality in knowledge which is creative of character."

Missionaries and their supporters considered the performance of the gospel— reading the Bible but also displaying and purveying it—to have healing and redemptive powers at the same time that it had the power to civilize. As Jean Comaroff has argued in the South African context, British missionaries who brought the Bible and, perhaps more importantly, literacy, also brought about a cosmological shift, as "perhaps the most palpable effect of literacy is that it transforms the consciousness of those who acquire it, setting it off, in unprecedented ways, from the world view of their illiterate fellows."[49] The improving qualities of the Bible were at times clearly more ceremonial than effective, however, as reported in the *Christian Guardian*: "the Basuto chiefs of South Africa visited England to stop the importation of liquor. . . . No definite answer to their plea was given, though they were presented by the British and Foreign Bible Society with handsomely bound Suto Bibles."[50] The Bible as an artifact ceremonially bestowed held a larger symbolic significance than simply that of a tool of rational communication—in the Basuto case, the bestowing of the Bible was also the deferral of a pressing question of political, religious, and medical import.[51]

BIBLE-BASED HEALING: CHRISTIAN SCIENCE AND THE EMMANUEL MOVEMENT

In 1901, the *Christian Guardian* told a story of a famous physician who, instead of prescribing drugs, prescribed Bible reading to his anxious female patient. When the prescription worked, he told her "with deep earnestness, 'If I were to omit my daily reading of this book, I should lose my greatest source of strength and skill. I never go to an operation without reading my Bible. I never attend a distressing case without finding help in its pages. Your case called, not for medicine, but for sources of peace and strength outside your own mind, and I showed you my own prescription and I knew it would cure.' "[52] At a time when the healing movements of Pentecostalism and Christian Science were attracting growing numbers of Protestant women—including Methodists and Anglicans—as patients and healers, the Bible as a basis for healing became newly contentious. As James Opp argued, when women established themselves as healers on the basis of firsthand experience of divine healing, they found themselves "arraigned by a masculine professionalism that came in a variety of forms: the cleric, the doctor, and the scientific knowledge within . . . books."[53] The famous physician in the *Guardian* merged bookish masculine professionalism with more feminized and experientially based approaches to healing in his version of a Bible mind cure, but his medical authority and the textual orthodoxy of his (biblical) prescription shielded him from the condemnation the *Guardian* often gave to his female mental-healing counterparts.

The *Guardian's* support for the biblical strategy of the famous doctor led to a difficult tension for liberal Protestants as they sought their role in the midst of the rising authority of biomedicine. The doctor prescribed Bible reading because he understood that some kinds of ailments could be cured through a change in mood and mind—the power of suggestion could effect such change, and the best source of suggestion, in his view, was the Bible. Liberal Protestants were united in their conviction of the truth that the mind (or sometimes the soul) could have a powerful influence over the body. In this small window there was room for a kind of faith healing akin to William James's healthy-minded religion.[54] However, they were also convinced one could go too far in making claims for the power of suggestion and considered a gross overstep Mary Baker Eddy's recommendation to read *Science and Health* alongside the Bible, in order to attune the mind (and the illusory body) to God. Eddy's Protestant detractors lambasted her writerly "self-delusion," etched as it was even into the walls of the new Christian Science mother church, opened in Boston in 1906:

> They dare to parallel (engraven everywhere on the walls of their building and read as the substance of every service) the sublimest utterances of Holy Writ, the choice words of Jesus Christ and St. Paul, with lucubrations and vaporizations, the platitudes, obscurities, absurdities, inanities, and mock profundities, of the one who is to them evidently greater than all the prophets and apostles, if not a little superior to the Lord himself. Had we space to give quotations from Mrs. Eddy's words, even those read at this service, or those cut deep into the stone . . . no unbiased person could rank them for a moment with those by whose side they are flauntingly displayed.[55]

At the same time that Protestants were attacking Christian Science for their epigraphic and lectionary sins, however, some within their fold argued that Christian Science was not all quackery. As Yale professor George Ladd suggested in an article reprinted in the *Christian Guardian*, there was some truth to the claims of Christian Science: "Among these truths the most precious and important is the truth of the indwelling divine presence in the whole world of matter and mind. Theology and philosophy are more and more elaborating this truth in sane and rational ways." Although Christian Science distorted these truths, he argued, Protestant ministers failed in their responsibility to present a sane version of the connection among God, mind, and matter: "The multitudes of the people have long been hungry, have been almost starving for the clear, authoritative and convincing presentation of these truths. And the clergy of all the different sects have been, and still are—either through lack of training or of courageous manliness, or of spiritual insight or of a powerful sense of their mission—incapable and ineffective, as a body of men, in respect of the teaching of these truths."[56]

The liberal Protestant dispute with Christian Scientists' anthropology of the spiritual body was literally a war of words in which courageous manliness was at stake. Protestant clergy condemned Christian Science not only for its misreading of the Bible, but also for what they viewed as its theological syncretisms, blending pseudoscience, psychology, and Eastern mysticism in a female-dominated religion with a great potential for inducing moral licentiousness. In 1900 Methodist minister S. D. Chown lectured to Anglican and Methodist audiences about the dangers of an approach of "hazy optimism" toward Christian Science teachings. Although "men and women of well balanced moral nature" might be able to profit from some aspects of Christian Science, Chown insisted that its matter-denying creed "when interpreted in hours of temptation by devotees of very imperfect character shall yield to their morally jaundiced vision, a license to commit most heinous sins."[57] Chown turned to etymology for his critique: "Gnosticism was the Christian Scientism of the early Church. Gnostic and Scientist mean the same thing, as you know, one word being Greek and the other Latin."

Walking a line between loyalty to science and fidelity to God's incarnated spirit, Protestants took on the Christian Science anthropology of matter as "error" not only as an heretical affront to Christian doctrines of the incarnation, in which Jesus was the human embodiment of God, but also to biomedical explanations of the human body.[58] They devoted such attention to Christian Science precisely because of their commitment to modern medicine as a realm in which Christians could exercise virtue and God could act. Protestant attacks, however, were also shaped by their growing awareness of medicine's indifference if not hostility to Christianity; Professor A. B. Macallum, for example, lectured to Mc-Gill's Medical Faculty in 1907 on the necessity of the "scientific spirit" to ward off the "semi-paranoiac creeds" that cultivated a "dangerous cult of mysticism in which people intoxicate themselves with the maunderings and moonings of Christian Science."[59] S. D. Chown also joined the cause of the scientific spirit, albeit with appropriate divine guidance: "There is no room to doubt but that in the kind providence of God genuine science will be led to clear up much that is not mysterious in the relations between mental and physical states, and as astrology passed into astronomy so Eddyism and kindred isms, passing through the clear, white light of science, truly so called, shall be freed from the contamination and injury of morally unsafe beliefs and transmuted into unmixed blessings to the race."[60]

Among Anglicans and Methodists, gender was a persistent subtext to the lament that Christian Science was "attracting large numbers of the best and most intelligent members of the churches," especially middle-class women, the core group providing the voluntary labor so vital to the social service-focused church. Although the notice of Mary Baker Eddy's death in the *Canadian Churchman* acknowledged that she was "one of the most remarkable women of history," most references to her were not so kind and were often expressed in quite violent language.

That said, one 1924 commentator did presciently note that the "whole question of what might be called 'female theology' awaits the investigations of the critics."[61] Given that Eddy's movement attracted women and gave them a source of income if they became practitioners, it is not surprising that some of the most vociferous critiques of Christian Science centered on accusations that struck at the supposed vulnerabilities of middle-class women: vanity and selfishness. Not only did Protestant clerics lambast Christian Science as incoherent ramblings from "the weak, undisciplined mind of a vain woman," but they also considered it to be "the greatest home destroyer of the present age": women neglected their wifely and motherly duties by going to Christian Science services and setting up shop as practitioners, "teaching a great and wonderful selfishness."[62] The Christian Science practitioner was considered to be caught by a "seductive heresy" masquerading as the "faith of the fathers," who could create serious problems: "[O]ne sweet-faced deaconess will do more good in a day than these people in a year."[63]

Protestants also employed racial and religious difference in their strategies of feminization as condemnation: they criticized Christian Science as a gospel of comfort, while assailing it for its syncretism of religious traditions also feminized in Protestant accounts, including Roman Catholicism, Judaism, "Mohammedism," Bahaism, and traditions of the "Oriental."[64] As the *Canadian Churchman* editorialized on Eddy's death: "The essence of religion is forgetfulness of self, and the essence of Christian Science is to make oneself comfortable."[65] *Christian Guardian* editors turned to biblical referents: "[T]here was no trail of mammon over Christ's method of healing; surely this cannot be said of Christian Science!"[66] This syncretistic gospel of comfort was even worse for its ignorance of the impoverished "heathens"; Episcopalian Reverend McGann decried, "Christian Science supports not missionaries, hospitals, orphanages, reformatories, yet seeks money from congregants."[67] Another Episcopalian pointed out that among the "horrors of plague and healing fakirs" in China, India, and Africa, hospitals all had the "sign of the cross" above them, and he challenged Christian Scientists and other "jugglers with psychological power" to try their skills in these foreign lands.[68] Not drained by the massive expenditures of missions—especially medical missions that were financially supported in Protestant churches largely by women's missionary associations—the North American expansion of Christian Science must have been enviable to established Protestant churches.

Although Christian Science was not bringing Christianity to the "heathen," it was bringing heathen texts to North America, according to Methodist minister T. C. Martin who accused Christian Science of contributing to "race suicide" by "planting in the western continent the mysticism of India."[69] Frustrated with Christian Science's wide appeal, one *Canadian Churchman* critic condemned it as a "religion so thoroughly adaptable one can be a Jew, Mohammedan, Buddhist or almost anything, and still be a Christian Scientist."[70] The homegrown "heresy" of Christian Science thus became a cipher for Protestants to assert their racialized supremacy over all the world's religions. Protestant attacks on Christian Science, compared to those against Pentecostalism, cast it as non-Christian, unleashing some of the ugliest of vitriol. For example, some Protestants considered Jews to be particularly susceptible to Christian Science due to their supposed "weakness and materialism"; others thought Christian Science appealed especially to "Brahmanists" because of Eddy's denial of the "reality of sin." Paralleled to Islam, Christian Science was found to have "no more real Christianity in it than the Koran," and thus to be following the "shady business practice of taking on the name of a competitor."[71] For these alarmists, Eddy's "shadiness" extended to another textual sin, in the accusation that she plagiarized her "new" revelation from "ancient Hindu philosophy." With Pundita Ramabai, an Indian convert to Christianity, as his expert witness, Rev. William Washburn proclaimed in 1903 that "the baseless assumptions of Christian Science are identical with those of one of the airy, grotesque philosophies of India," by which he meant the Christian Science belief that matter is error.[72] Other critics accused Mary Baker Eddy of plagiarizing from Plato, Hegel, Anton Mesmer, and Phineas Quimby.[73] In an anti-Catholic turn, Canadian Methodist Byron Stauffer cited John Wesley when comparing Christian Science to Roman Catholicism in their shared "queen-of-heaven perversion" (venerating the Virgin Mary and "deifying" Mary Baker Eddy) and their shared "lack of faith and fear of death."[74]

Heathenizing Christian Science depended on a strategy of "discrediting by analogy" that drew comparators from the mission fields, philosophy, and early Christian history.[75] Even these strategies, however, could lead to reluctant acknowledgment of the glimpses of truth in Christian Science. Rev. J. N. Carpenter, principal of an Anglican seminary in Saskatoon, pointed out that because of the "elements of Truth" in Islam, "it is more difficult to present the Gospel successfully to the Monotheistic Muhammedan, than to the polytheistic and idolatrous Hindu. . . . The home worker finds the same difficulty in approaching members of the Christian Science Churches." The best approach, according to Carpenter, was to "acknowledge first of all those good things in that system which make for strength, and on this basis of common ground to build up a structure which will cause the false to be abandoned."[76]

Crediting Christian Science with having "directed the attention of the public mind to the marvelous influence of mind over matter" and with having appealed to a "large class who have ceased to feel religion as a vital force," Protestant clergy demonstrated that Christian Science had not only raised their orthodox ire but that it had also worked a transformation of their thinking. By emphasizing the "supremacy of the spiritual," one Methodist minister suggested, Christian Science had "met a deep want in human experiences," but it had also "snatched our birthright and appropriated our heritage." He went on to argue that in Christian Science's emphasis on spirit it mistakenly denied the reality of matter and disease, whereas "the Christian churches have rightly held to the reality of disease, but have shackled the Spirit in the healing of disease."[77] Although for some Methodists and other Protestants unshackling the spirit came to mean embracing Pentecostal faith healing, many Anglicans turned to a sacramental resource, namely holy unction, or anointing the forehead or other bodily parts with oil blessed by a bishop, a ritual traditionally associated with healing (and most commonly with extreme unction, or the last rites) in the Roman Catholic and early Anglican church.

Some High Church Anglicans recommended holy unction as a sacramental tactic that could repudiate Christian Science by insisting that the healing legacy of Jesus resided in the historic rituals of the church, whose authenticity was maintained through the Anglican version of apostolic succession. Christian Science, which Anglicans criticized for its "spiritualizing of the sacraments," defended its rejection of even the central Christian sacrament of the Eucharist, or communion, arguing that "no memorials are necessary" for communion with God through prayer. Anglicans pounced on these "spiritual conceptions of Jesus" with proof texts, as when C. E. Luce insisted that Paul, when discussing the body as a temple, did not refer to merely "spiritual fornication." Luce charged Christian Science with offering a "phantom Christ" and a "cold message that chills the heart," for its rejection of sacramental embodiments of the crucifixion.[78]

Seeking middle ground between idealist Christian Science and materialist biomedicine, Protestants depended on texts not only as paths to devotion but also as the grounds for truth claims about Christianity's essential role in the new age of medical and scientific progress.[79] For Methodist and Anglican writers to forswear the principles behind Christian Science altogether would be to deny God's effectiveness in the world. British Anglican priest Percy Dearmer—a combination of Ruskinesque reviver of old English liturgy, hymn-writer, and Christian socialist—wrote in his 1909 text, *Body and Soul*: "All things indeed come of God, both high and humble, for spirit, soul, and body; all means of health and healing, spiritual, psychic, material, may be used under God and with his blessing. But mighty works may be done by spiritual means when all others have failed."[80] Charting a course between the "bald materialism" of scientific detractors of religion and the "mentally defective" idealism of Christian Science, a *Canadian Churchman* reviewer argued that "science, really science, is tending to corroborate revealed religion."[81] A coalition with science would thus lay the grounds for liberal Protestant relevance, and the grounds of its verifiability, in a modernizing world.

Anglicans such as Dearmer were in the lead among Protestants in their attempts to combat Christian Science through practical means, as demonstrated by his 1904 founding of the interdenominational Guild of Health in London. A couple of years later in Boston, the heartland of Christian Science, Episcopalian minister Elwood Worcester's Emmanuel Movement turned not to holy unction but to the modernization of another castoff Catholic sacrament, that of confession.[82] A "clinic" formed in 1906 at Boston's Emmanuel Episcopal Church by Worcester and his assistant minister Samuel McComb, along with a Jewish psychiatrist Isador Coriat, the movement sought to relieve those suffering from nervous disorders by utilizing resources of clergy and the medical profession.[83] Versions of the Emmanuel Movement (as it was dubbed by the press) spread through urban centers in Canada and the United States, and Worcester also established an Emmanuel-style clinic at his Canadian summer home in New Brunswick.[84]

It did not take long for the Emmanuel Movement to provoke a response among Canadian Anglicans. At a session of papers on the Ministry of Healing at the 1910 Canadian Anglican Bicentenary and Church Congress held in Toronto, clergy endorsed the movement's medical and theological credentials, as did Episcopalian visitor Lyman Powell, whose enthusiastic speech had to be cut short.[85] Doctors attending the congress, however, were not so supportive, cautioning that the "medical profession maintained the Christian religion, and endeavored to do everything to set it forward" but that clergy could do little more to aid healing than to offer prayers, in the manner of any pious person. Any sanctioning of "spiritual healing" or cooperation between doctors and clergy would only lead to "confusion of spheres of influence, and lead to many needless deaths." Dr. Charles Kirk Clarke, a leader in Toronto's newly institutionalizing field of psychiatry rose from the audience to insist that "he had heard enough to convince him that the clergy were meddling with something of which their knowledge was practically nil." Anecdotal evidence mustered in support of faith cures was useless in his view, and the only appropriate partner of the doctor in the cause of healing were the "forces of Nature."[86]

Despite the scorn of medical professionals, the Emmanuel Movement was an overnight sensation, both in terms of lay popularity and press attention, as one Boston paper trumpeted: "Hundreds of Neurotics Join Emmanuel's New Healing Movement."[87] The avid press coverage often focused on the Movement's opposition of Christian Science and its bid for the attention of the "well-heeled" women of Boston.[88] Pegged by one Protestant critic as "Christian Science set to organ music," in actuality, the Emmanuel Movement was not particularly concerned with the musical or sacramental qualities of Anglicanism.[89] Although Worcester acknowledged John Henry Newman and John Keble, leaders of the highly sacramentalist Oxford Movement, as exemplars of Christian men who had revealed Jesus' relevance for modern life, he devoted little attention to the power of the sacraments to heal. The Jesus revealed by Worcester was more indebted to German historical-critical biblical scholarship that Worcester had encountered during his PhD studies in Germany—scholarship that he thought displayed the "historical trustworthiness" of the gospel accounts of the healing miracles of Jesus.

Worcester's Jesus was a man/God who recognized the moral causes behind disease and who healed through the "psychological medium and spiritual condition" of faith. Insisting that "the Church has mutilated the Christian religion, retaining with some degree of faith Christ's message to the soul, but rejecting with unbelief His ministry to the body," Worcester sought to "visibly reproduce" Jesus's healing in his own parish through the insights of psychology.[90] Via the two "therapeutic agencies" of (1) appealing to the moral and religious nature to consciously stimulate the will and (2) waking suggestion to the subconscious, Worcester and McComb claimed to be able to cure a range of "functional" nervous disorders and "bad habits" in both adults and children, including neurasthenia, alcoholism, sexual vice, constipation, regulation of menstruation, bed-wetting, morbid fears, nocturnal emissions, and a disposition to lying.[91]

The Emmanuel clinic was most noted for its individual counseling, in which Worcester, McComb, and their male staff met with "patients" free of charge (unlike Christian Science practitioners).[92] After settling the patient in a reclining chair, Worcester stood behind him to "gently stroke his forehead and temples, which has a soothing and a distracting effect." (Despite women comprising the majority of the patients, Worcester always used the male pronoun when describing the typical patient.) Telling the patient that he was now relaxed, Worcester gave "curative suggestions" that the patient repeated for anywhere from fifteen minutes to one hour. Worcester proffered many anecdotes of the physical efficacy of his treatment—such as the constipated man who returned to request that Worcester reduce his suggestion of twice-daily evacuations to only one—but he clearly felt that the main purpose of bringing people into this "religious state of mind" was to foster "moral regeneration." When in the peaceful state of therapeutic relaxation, Worcester argued, "the Spirit of God enters into us and a power not our own takes possession of us." Alcoholics, paralytics, and those suffering from sexual vice were all amazed at the power of this "new spiritual energy," which could heal without requiring any effort on their part. Far from a mystical struggle on the path to ecstasy, for "the instrumentality of a higher power" to succeed, the patient needed only to relax under the gentle voice and hands of the minister.[93]

Not surprisingly Worcester insisted that his method was not the same as hypnotism, a morally dubious technique for many Christians. Worcester's method, in which men and women needed to "unburden their troubles" to the minister before the appropriate curative suggestion could be given, was dubbed the "modern confessional" by some, but Worcester and McComb preferred the "moral clinic." They repeatedly insisted that their work was always "under strict medical control": no patients could be seen by ministers until they had been assessed by medical doctors, and the clinic only accepted functional nervous disorders and not "organic" diseases such as cancer.[94] This medical affiliation was crucial to differentiating the Emmanuel Movement from Christian Science and was necessary for Worcester's hopes for legitimacy as a psychotherapist. To this end, in newspaper interviews he emphasized his psychological training at Leipzig University under Wilhelm Wundt.[95] In *Religion and Medicine* Worcester frequently quoted Wundt's rival, William James. Drawing from James to argue that the "universe was a great storehouse of invisible energy," Worcester tried to bring together a mode of healing that was modern, Christian, and scientific.[96]

Proclaiming that psychology had ensured that people would no longer settle for being "disembodied spirits" in a disembodied Christianity, while also rooting the "motive force of religion" and healing in the subconscious mind, Worcester's union of mind, body, and spirit—although most attractive to women—was focused on middle-class men. Worcester portrayed himself as an outdoorsman tested in the Canadian wilds, traipsing through the Newfoundland wilderness with a First Nations guide, hunting in the Rockies on horseback, and canoeing over raging rapids.[97] The branding worked, with one interviewer commenting that as "a strong outdoorsy man with psychological training" Worcester was the "perfect man for giving the mental cure theory a thorough test."[98] These portrayals served the dual purpose of demonstrating how the resources of the subconscious mind could manifest themselves in amazing bodily abilities, as well as bestow virility on a therapeutic method based on submission, relaxation, and lack of effort. According to Worcester: "Our fathers wrestled against flesh and blood and to virile men this struggle is the easiest. We must wrestle against effeminating luxury, against corrupting materialism, against our own debilitated nervous systems, against the vastest doubts which have ever dismayed the minds of men, against the very richness and complexity of the life we have inherited."[99] Decisive affirmation, he felt, could thus counter the wasting effect of liberal Protestant doubts about modern life under capitalism.

With the pressures of medicalization and the market, the Emmanuel Movement's dedication to being Christian and scientific was its downfall.[100] Not long after its beginnings, medical doctors—including Sigmund Freud, during his 1909 visit to the United States—began their attack on its medical pretensions, and the core of what distinguished the Emmanuel Movement from Christian Science was seriously damaged.[101] Despite several ministers setting up moral clinics in other North American cities, eventually even clergy joined in to chide the Emmanuel Movement for being faddish, morally irresponsible, and unscientific.[102] Worcester toned down his notoriety, refusing any press coverage after 1912 and scaling back the movement. Worcester and McComb continued their version of lay psychotherapy at Emmanuel Church until 1929 when Worcester retired, his hopes for the widespread embrace of his blend of "religion" and medicine significantly dampened and his approach increasingly influenced by the psychic research he described in *Body, Mind, and Spirit*.[103] His articulation of "religion and medicine," however, had a lasting influence both inside and outside Christianity. Under the category of "religion," he provided a model for Christian engagement with psychology in pastoral care, his work prompting the British Medical Association to initiate a study of spiritual healing, and he inspired later movements of group "therapy" such as Frank Buchman's transnational Oxford Group in the 1930s, Henry Burton Sharman's Student Christian Movement Bible study retreats in Canada's Algonquin Park, and the better known Alcoholics Anonymous.[104]

PROOF TEXTS: SCIENTIFIC METHOD AND SCRIPTURAL ECONOMIES

Many of Worcester's fellow Anglicans agreed with his conviction that religion—which in effect meant Christianity—had an important role to play within the sphere of medicine and psychology, as did W. G. Nicholson, who exhorted a Winnipeg audience in 1916 that "the church must not leave healing to Medicine." Some Methodists also cautiously supported the efforts of the Emmanuel Movement in "this soul-cure business," claiming that the Church had neglected its purpose as a source of healing while also emphasizing that souls were always more important than bodies.[105] How the Christian claim to healing was to engage with scientific medicine, however, was not agreed on. Whereas some commentators contended that psychoanalysis could render Christian healing "sane and scientific" and that Christianity could bestow on psychology a spiritually informed vision of the "world of psycho-physical facts," those with "New Thought" or Pentecostal leanings were not as dedicated to a biomedical worldview.[106]

Their different relationships to biomedical authority led to bitter division between Protestants committed to a supernatural liberalism that valued an equilibrium between science and the spirit and those who were sceptical of biomedicine and thought the spirit trumped science—a division that would continue to shape Anglican and United Church communities throughout the century. For proponents of divine healing in particular, science-friendly Christians had lost their ability to see the hand of God at work in the body and had become trapped in "naturalistic empiricism."[107] Supporters of the scientific spirit, however, found the claims of divine healing profoundly suspicious exactly because their proof lay in personal stories and not in scientifically documented testimony.[108]

In the early twentieth century biomedicine was steadily moving toward a less patient-focused and more disease-specific approach, which, as several scholars have suggested, sought to depersonalize and despiritualize healing while cultivating a biomedical account (or perhaps cosmology) of the "real" body.[109] Aligning Christianity with evidence-based biomedicine, liberal Protestants fused the spiritually edifying practices of reading and writing with the legitimacy borne of scientific methods and documentation. As historian Timothy Lenoir argues, science itself emerged as a discourse authorized by the "constitutive powers of inscription" in which inscribed texts—whether those of scientific articles, telegraphy, or even x-rays—were thought to transparently convey truth.[110] Scientific documentation made ineffable things real—whether energies or microbes—while it also contributed to what Michel de Certeau called a "scriptural economy" in which modern practices of medical inscription literally rewrote the body as a mechanized individual: "After having long been only a 'member'—arm, leg, or head—of the social unit or a place in which cosmic forces or 'spirits' intersected, [the body] has slowly emerged as a whole, with its own illnesses, equilibriums, deviations and abnormalities."[111] In the late nineteenth and early twentieth centuries, both Anglicans and Methodists argued that correct practices of reading and writing, in concert with a kind of "Baconian" scientific method based on the accumulation of facts, could establish proof for properly scientific claims about the blend of religion and healing.[112] At the same time, scientific documentation could contradict unscientific and false claims about Christian healing—Christian Science healings were made suspect because of their lack of proper documentation according to the format of scientific experimentation, while x-rays were used to prove the ineffectiveness of Pentecostal healings.[113]

For liberals, even the Bible itself was open to principles of verifiability, as a *Christian Guardian* article critical of Christian Science declared: "Either in science, religion, or finance, when a person adopts a principle which contradicts reason, philosophy and the laws of nature, and then, if it happens to touch the subject of religion, distorts every passage of Scripture to make it agree with his irrational theory, he can believe anything."[114] Percy Dearmer dramatically underscored the symbolic power of books in this marriage of science and religion.[115] In

Body and Soul, he made the following vow: "I do not in this humble work propose to prove the truth of religion; it is one of my postulates, and the truth of natural science another. If natural science should change again, I shall have to rewrite this book; if religion should be disproved, I would burn it."[116] Whether Dearmer's book-burning vow suggested that he would abandon his faith or protect it in the face of scientific invalidation, it was an extreme promise, with scriptural warrants, coming from a man who loved the texts of his tradition and who wrote "the Bible is given a place supreme, as the sacred library of the Christian revelation. It is the greatest book in the world; but next to it, among English books, the English-speaking nations of the world would place the Book of Common Prayer."[117] "Scientific Christianity" necessarily expected its own transformation or even destruction in the wake of experimentation.

Despite condemnation of what they proclaimed the "wrong" kinds of divine healing, whether John Dowie's faith healing in Zion City near Chicago, the Catholic healing shrines at Lourdes and Québec's St. Anne de Beaupré, or the communication with the dead in spiritualist healing, liberal Protestant commentators could also easily claim that the "universe is crowded with the healing forces of God" and that the "natural tendency of all physical organisms [is] to cast off disease."[118] The desire to be scientists who could pray while succumbing neither to a Pentecostalist nor a spiritualist understanding of spiritual intervention posed a theological challenge for both Anglicans and Methodists. For example the *Churchman* strongly condemned Rev. J. M. Thompson, the Dean of Divinity of Magdalen College, Oxford, for his booklet questioning the miracles of the New Testament—including the resurrection of Jesus— while it directed equally censorious editorials at the unwise "speculations" of Bishop Welldon, the Dean of Manchester Cathedral, and those of English cleric J. H. Skrine. Welldon had given a sermon that spoke hopefully about possibilities of miraculous cures in the present, while Skrine, in his 1911 Bampton Lectures (an Oxford lecture series originally designed to root out heresy), detailed his experience with "vibrations" from the dead. Whereas the *Churchman's* criticism of Welldon was muted by a guarded account of the "apparently trustworthy" miraculous and visionary healing of "a Miss Dorothy Kerin, of Herne Hill, aged 21" (of whom we will hear more in later chapters), Skrine's spiritualist leanings were clearly condemned as contrary to the purpose of the Bampton Lectures.[119]

The editorial tone in the *Christian Guardian* was more uniformly suspicious of divine healing, perhaps because Methodists were not as distracted by in-house "faith healing" approaches such as the Emmanuel Movement or the campaign to reintroduce the sacrament of unction for the sick. Methodist arguments that a faith dependent on miraculous cures was "childish, if not irrational," however, did provoke dissenting letters asking, "if the religion which has healing associated with it today is 'insane' why was it not so in the apostle's time?"[120] The dominant opinion in both Methodist and Anglican papers was that if divine healing were ever to occur, the seeker would have to be entirely unselfish, and not beholden to the "mistaken doctrine" that God never allows bodily suffering or that God always responds to prayer with "automatic cures."[121] Reading biblical miracles as limited to the apostolic age, many early twentieth-century Protestants directly refuted Holiness and emergent Pentecostal claims to gifts of healing by arguing that, yes, Jesus was a healer, but that, no, Christians could no longer directly access and transmit his healing gifts.[122] In a letter critical of a book that argued for the ability to speak in tongues, L. M. England posed and answered the question this way: "Do we today have the gifts Paul mentions [in Acts and First Corinthians]? Yes, in God-given ability, the ability of the linguist in his patience and delight, in the ability of the consecrated physician and nurse. . . ."[123] Liberal Protestants did not deny that Jesus and/or God could heal, but they argued that people could not channel this spiritual healing in the twentieth century without the medical authority to do so.[124]

Nevertheless, some Methodists endorsed divine healing and rejected medical approaches without hesitation, as one letter writer who signed himself J.T.P. urged: "We cannot pretend to trust him [the Lord] and still be clinging to something else, for fear he might fail us, for the healing of our bodies any more than we can for our spiritual bodies—it is Jesus Christ wholly—or nothing."[125] Editorial comments, however, revealed the discomfort that leading Methodists had with embracing Pentecostal-style faith healing while Methodism was moving toward a social gospel-based, "respectable" style that considered itself in partnership with the natural and social sciences.[126] The editors appended this cautionary and tepid endorsement to J.T.P.'s healing testimony: "While we might hesitate to make too many generalizations from his experience, there can be no doubt that that experience was just as he has represented it to be."

The letter directly following J.T.P.'s shed further light on growing Methodist discomfort with convictions about divine healing gained from personal experience. W. M. Bielby praised Ann Preston, or "Holy Ann" as an Old-Time Methodist tempted but not swayed by Holiness revivalists such as Nelson Burns, deposed by the Methodist Church in the 1890s.[127] Holy Ann, an inspirational prayer leader, was saved from the excesses of "Burnsism" when "she opened her eyes to the pretence that a man could be so holy as not to need the written Word." Indeed, Bielby added in a metaphor fit for a text-based cosmology, "She was a living concordance."[128] A particularly compelling example of the admixture of text and healing, Holy Ann was an unschooled Irish immigrant who came to Ontario in the 1830s as a young servant to the family of a Methodist doctor. By the time of her death in 1906, she was widely known as a pious Methodist with a power for prevailing—and noisy—prayer, which included the power of healing prayer, which she often undertook from her wooden prayer hut built by her employer at some distance from the house. Ranking high among the amazing feats attributed to Ann was her divinely granted ability to read only one book, the Bible: "A newspaper was like a foreign language to her."[129] Although said to be unable to memorize passages of scripture, she could, through "heavenly mnemonics," recite word for word the most appropriate scripture for any occasion by asking God to bestow it upon her.[130] Pentecostalism began luring Methodists less loyal than Holy Ann from the fold by cultivating the intervention of the Holy Spirit in ways that, for Methodists, disrupted the delicate equilibrium of the biblical text as an anchor for both Christian experience and for medical science.[131]

World War I further cemented the liberal Protestant sense of oneness with medicine. In June 1915, almost a year into the war, the *Christian Guardian* ran a front page graphic headlined "The Healer of Men," which described Jesus as a "healer of sorrows and maladies" whose "redeeming power" knew no limits.[132] Many stories of soldiers brought to Christian faith through their brushes with death, as well as through the caring ministrations of Christian nurses, emphasized both the terrors of war, and the importance of Christianity to soldiers' healing, via medical means.[133] In addition, the phenomenon and treatment of shell shock prompted considered discussions of the power of suggestion and psychotherapy in alleviating physical disorders.[134] After the war, however, both divine healing and spiritualism enjoyed a revival, prompting some Protestants to choose sides in their commitment to medicine. The 1920s healing campaigns of the British-born evangelists James Moore

Hickson, an Anglican layman, and Charles S. Price, a Methodist minister turned Pentecostal faith-healer, intensified the bitterness of the dispute between those who supported revivalist divine healing and those who did not. Although Protestant reception of Hickson was much more irenic than that of Price, both of these healing impresarios, with their international campaigns, sensational press coverage, and phenomenally large crowds instigated a searching critique of Christian healing within Anglican and Methodist denominations that brought these churches into closer identification with medicine and its modes of scientific documentation.[135]

The church newspapers, even if they were less sensational than secular papers, were not immune to the allure of such healers. Anglican James Moore Hickson's 1919 visit to the U.S.–Canadian border cities of Buffalo and Detroit prompted mixed reviews in the Methodist *Christian Guardian*. One commentator distinguished Hickson from Christian Scientists and praised him for "wonderful cures effected," whereas an editorial more skeptically compared him to John Dowie, Catholic healing shrines, and Christian Science, and it cautioned readers not to "expect God to cook your meals or heal your body" and not to "abandon God's own healer, the well-educated physician."[136] Hickson's June 1920 visit to Toronto drew crowds to the Anglican St. James' Cathedral and University of Toronto's Convocation Hall—one year later, in a building across the street from Convocation Hall, Frederick Banting and Charles Best would begin the experiments that led to the discovery of insulin. Hickson garnered a cautiously positive *Guardian* editorial, appreciative of his stress on the mere possibility of a "gradual cure" and his cooperation with medical doctors. However, Hickson's claims during his Australian tour to be able to cure both functional and organic diseases reversed this guarded endorsement, leading the editor to recommend a combination of Christianity, intelligence, and scientific means of healing and to pose the question, "would the proper place of the faith healer not be the hospital?"[137]

The Anglican response to one of their own was more accepting, occasional references to "scoffers" aside.[138] Hickson's 1919 visit to Detroit, coincident with the Episcopalian General Convention, was considered a historical first twice over, according to one writer, because first, Hickson, as a layman with no approval from a bishop, managed to claim the attention of "the members of the episcopate and priesthood on a purely religious subject and was even questioned by them." Second, during his healing services at Christ Church, "an exclusive and rich man's church became for a brief period the centre of suffering humanity. . . . It was indeed an unusual experience to witness the mingling of all classes at the altar, rich and poor, young and old, black and white, and to feel that here, for once at any rate, all hearts were in tune with the Infinite and mindful of the Divine aid."[139] This theme that the desire for healing equalized social and economic divisions reverberated throughout discussions of Hickson's services whether in Canada or in India, where he was said to have successfully crossed even the lines of religious difference, attracting Muslims, Hindus, and Parsis to his rites.[140] Following the paths of British colonial domination, Hickson's world tour through Canada, the United States, Egypt, Ceylon, India, China, Japan, Palestine, South Africa, Australia, and New Zealand was likened to a "spiritual earthquake" and was more ambitiously international than that of any other 1920s Christian faith healer.[141]

Hickson's method was a careful blend of Anglican sacramentalism and medical appeasement.[142] He usually led open services of laying on of hands and hymn singing in large cathedrals, as opposed to the unconsecrated arenas and stadiums often favored by evangelists such as Charles Price. In addition, he always insisted that he was a mere channel for God's grace and, perhaps more importantly, that penitents should also consult their doctors.[143] Insisting that healing could only come with the requisite faith, Hickson required no outward displays of such faith, preferring a calm, controlled, unemotional style. An initially "resistant" Australian bishop described one service thus: "The least sign of emotionalism he crushes instantly. He will not have sensation, nor the working up of emotion. You catch his sharp command, 'Be quiet, woman!' as a patient indulges in some obviously forced expression. Yet he has an infinite gift of sympathy."[144] Although both Hickson and Worcester attracted mostly women to their cures, Hickson's "sharp" and commanding approach was quite distinct from the self-scrutiny and the expression of emotion and sensation cultivated in the Emmanuel Movement.

Hickson's method depended on his authority as a charismatic commander, despite his humble insistence to the contrary. Controversy—along with his layman's status—brought the Church of England to establish an "expert" committee of clergy and medical personnel to evaluate Hickson's healing claims in 1924. The committee report cautiously endorsed Hickson, but it also insisted that medical treatment was the first recourse for disease and that faith was more important than cures.[145] The flurry of publicity around Hickson eventually died down, although he continued his mission throughout the 1920s, remaining a layman, and his work was eventually taken over by a sympathetic priest on his death in 1932.[146]

Methodists reacted to Hickson with reserve, but their response to Charles Price was much more divisive.[147] Charles S. Price lived in England before moving to Canada, and then to California, where he was a Congregationalist minister. According to Price, he embraced Pentecostalism when on a skeptic's visit to the church of Pentecostal healer Aimee Semple McPherson. Finding that he too had the gift of healing, Price toured up the West Coast, hosting large healing revivals in Victoria and Vancouver, two staunchly British cities at the time. Price's British sensibilities smoothed the way for his American-style revivals, and like Hickson, some commentators appreciated his articulate, gentlemanly style.[148] By contrast, H. R. Trumpour, professor at Vancouver's Anglican Theological College, depicted Price's spectacle more ironically, calling Vancouver the "happy hunting ground of the cults" and commenting that "at times the platform looked more like a morgue than a gospel scene, with twenty to thirty women laid out on pillows." Criticizing the way Price's seekers "fairly slipped into salvation" with little effort on their part, Trumpour called for government regulation of nonmedical healing, asserted the medical tenor of the Gospels, emphasized that many doctors appreciated "sensible clergymen in the sickroom," and contested what he considered to be the magical view of Christianity as "charm." Instead, Trumpour asserted, Christianity "supplies surrender and confidence for psychotherapeutic treatments and courage and triumph for incurable ailments."[149]

Trumpour's article attracted some critical, pro-Price responses that charged Christianity with surrendering too much authority to medical science and cast aspersions on the professor's ability to withstand the "strenuous work of the healing mission." The debate in the *Canadian Churchman*, however, was nothing compared to the wrangling that went on in the *Christian Guardian*. W. B. Creighton, the *Guardian*'s generally anti-divine-healing editor, made what was probably an unwise decision for the editor of a church-sponsored newspaper when, after publishing a critical report on Price's campaign, he refused to publish the resulting pro-Price letters from ministers. The critical report written by the pseudonymous Edward Trelawney (Ernest Thomas), labeled Price's technique as suggestion clothed in "spectacular psychotherapeutics." He described the "elaborate stages of ritual preparation for healing over a course of days" that included "sweetly reasonable" sermons about "saving energy," singing with raised arms, and an elaborate selection process whereby Price's female assistants provided white information cards to a chosen few among the supplicants, and then Price anointed an even more select group of these with oil and proclaimed them to be healed. Claiming cures of everything from tuberculosis to shortened legs to brain cancer, Price was especially criticized by Trelawney for thinking solely in "religious terms, and not scientifically."[150] Writing in response, the Victoria and Vancouver supporters of Price were dismayed by the "grave discourtesy" of having their letters censored.[151] Despite this controversy, the next week Creighton satirized those letter writers who had admonished him that "not to believe in faith healing in the orthodox way is very wicked indeed," and then used his editorial prerogative to conclude that faith healing operated through a divine law of suggestion that was best understood through scientific and psychological perspectives.[152]

The discussion of Price's revival persisted in the Guardian until well into 1924, with the publication of the Vancouver clerical association's Special Committee report, composed by a committee of clergy, doctors, and one lawyer, which condemned the Price campaign as harmful and misguided. The report detailed many cases of healing considered by the Special Committee, tabulating that of these 350 cases there were only 5 cures of functional, not organic diseases, 38 cases of improvement, 212 cases of no change, 17 cases of worsened suffering, 5 subsequent cases of insanity, and 39 deaths. Once again the pro-Price ministers claimed censorship when the minority report in favor of Price was not printed in full with the report.

As Protestants grappled with the significance of divine healing within their midst, most liberals decided that to embrace divine healing was to abandon science as well as to "hinder the Church's work" in healing the structural pathologies of modern society, not simply the diseases found in individual bodies. Miraculous healing would distract Christians from the pressing needs of others in their society and would foster an enthusiasm that would lead to disappointment, if not dissipation, when promised healings did not materialize.[153] The choice for a medically mediated Christianity became even clearer when, in the wake of Hickson and Price, both the Christian Guardian and the Canadian Churchman began publishing a series of articles on science, medicine, and health authored by medical doctors and sponsored by the Canadian Medical Association. Covering topics such as specific diseases, industrial accidents, nutrition, preventive medicine, healthy holidaying, and environmental dangers, the Canadian Health Service articles also profiled famous doctors and ran the occasional anxiety-provoking headline, such as: "Do you know how to feed your child?"[154] The series comprised over fifty articles appearing weekly in 1924–1925, and was one of the clearest indications of Protestants' allegiance to a science that would save.[155]

That Anglicans and Methodists turned to committees of doctors and clergy to write reports evaluating these new inflowings of the holy, healing spirit, says a great deal about the faith they placed in scientific standards of documentation and adjudication. Depending on scientific standards of proof to support Christian healing had already been shown to be risky by British physicist and skeptic John Tyndall's nineteenth-century call for a "prayer gauge" as a scientifically controlled test for the efficacy of healing prayer.[156] Nevertheless, liberal Protestants were optimistic: "As time goes on it will be ever more and more clearly established that the art of healing is essentially a diverse one and that the work of the physician of men's souls and that of the physician of men's bodies is most intimately correlated."[157] Again, medical missions were brandished as a prime example of this alliance, as British missionary R. Fletcher Moorshead contended that medical missions "stand essentially for that union between Science and Religion which can provide the antidote to the ravages of materialistic science as well as to non-Christian superstitions."[158] With a text-based cosmology that rooted proof in textual documentation, liberal Protestants sought to align their supernaturalism as complementary to the nascent biomedical world view.

Psychic research became a curiously attractive forum for liberal Protestants to enact such complementarity. After establishing himself as something of an expert on Christian healing, Anglican Percy Dearmer found his way into the Society for Psychical Research, eventually editing his second wife's book of "automatic writing." The Fellowship of the Picture cast Nancy Dearmer as the entranced scribe for musings from the afterlife of a soldier killed in World War I, and demonstrated Dearmer's eclectic commitment to textuality as proof of the divine, or at least as proof of messages from beyond.[159] The controversy prompted by Dearmer's colleague in the Society for Psychical Research, Sir Oliver Lodge, also revealed the profound Methodist dedication to textual proofs. Lodge, esteemed scientist and pioneer of radio and wireless telegraphy, had embarked on controversial investigations of spiritualist phenomena, buttressing his psychic research through both his scientific competence and his Christian orthodoxy.[160] Treading a middle path similar to the one that tried to critique Christian Science without giving up the God-infused body, a *Christian Guardian* editorial cautiously praised Lodge's psychic research into telepathy, automatic writing, and the admittedly "Christian belief in man's survival of bodily death." Openly impressed by Lodge's many titles, inventions, and publications, the editorial closed with a reassuring tone: "At least, it is a source of satisfaction to know that this whole question of spirit communication is not to be left entirely in the hands of charlatans, but that men of the scientific temperament and undoubted honesty are giving careful and painstaking attention to it."[161] A flurry of letters responded with outrage, calling Lodge "Christless and Godless" and demanding that the "*Christian Guardian* will be true to its name, and sound an alarm" or the influence of its article would be "deadly."[162] Invoking the biblical proof of Deuteronomy 18:10–12, which forbids those loyal to God from obtaining the services of one "who consults ghosts or spirits, or who seeks oracles from the dead," C. L. Bedson insisted: "Nothing should come from a church paper which in the least would seem to support or give color to those ideas."[163]

Another letter writer, George A. Bainborough of Toronto, defended Lodge by citing his 1907 *The Substance of Faith Allied with the Sciences* as an example of Lodge's orthodox Christian creed and by arguing that Christian faith would only be strengthened were "respectable science" to "succeed in establishing a communication between the seen and the unseen worlds."[164] In another exchange of letters, one pro-Lodge writer took care to mention that he "receives communications in writing from many of his old friends who have passed away." Critics of Lodge, however, also turned to texts as proof. The unreplicable vagaries of Lodge's messages from the spirit world rendered them suspect: "The puerility . . . of these messages has been admitted by its best friends. The investigator in this field will not go far until he reaches the ridiculous as well as the mysterious."[165] Despite such vociferous critics, the editors of the *Christian Guardian* responded with brief and cheeky assertions that to view their editorial as supportive of spiritualism instead of science was a gross misinterpretation. Trying to forestall the twin attack from biblical proof-texts and scientific proofs, they offered this nod to the vexed and unpredictable power of writing: "Our words must have had some occult meaning altogether unsuspected by us."[166] The debate about the soundness of Lodge's psychical research—both from a Christian and a scientific perspective—fit within a long tradition of Christians who turned to science and scripture to discount oracular spirit voices of all kinds, while still hoping to preserve the scriptural voice of the Christian God.[167]

Turning to scientific modes of documentation—surveys, reports, and curricula—Protestant leaders hoped to transform their denominations into centralized, efficient bureaucracies engaged with the burgeoning social and natural sciences, and with fields such as public health and hygiene.[168] This "fact-based" turn came partly in response to a wider anxiety over the feminization of religion in terms of leadership—including female medical missionaries and nurses—and lay participation. One *Canadian Churchman* writer longingly remembered the time before nurses had broken up the close friendship between ministers and doctors, "when doctor and parson 'hunted in couples' and where one went the other as a matter of course followed."[169] The author was not without hope, however, that a new relationship of medicine and religion would restore proper relations: "The immense importance of the mental and spiritual factor in the treatment of disease will, we believe, be eventually accepted by the medical profession as a whole, and the clergyman will come into his own again as the recognized ally of the physician."[170] At the same time, however, utilizing surveys, statistics, and medical reports, social gospel Methodists and Anglicans carefully documented the social situation of early-twentieth-century urban and rural Canadians, both for the purposes of planning revivals and for lobbying governments to develop woman-friendly policy innovations such as mothers' allowance, education regarding social purity (including sexually transmitted diseases), and child welfare reform.[171] The power of the scientific text to forward the goal of "Christianizing the social order" lay not only in its effects on others, but also in its disciplining of Anglicans and Methodists themselves, both lay and clerical.[172]

The effects of the scientific spirit on women's participation in Christian social service are clearly seen in the fate of Anglican and Methodist Sisterhood and Deaconess movements, which encouraged techniques of nursing and personal hygiene in both hospital and home and which were tacitly based on Catholic models of nursing convents. Sisters and Deaconesses claimed the emerging field of medicine as a Christian realm in the service of the nation, enacting the medicalization of the urban poor while contributing to the medicalization of Christianity itself. For example, in Canada, the Sisterhood of St. John the Divine opened their first hospital in Moose Jaw in 1884, caring for soldiers injured in the Northwest Rebellion, and in 1885 they opened Toronto's first surgical hospital for women. In 1922, the Sisters opened the St. John's Medical

Mission at St. John's Garrison Church in Toronto, "as a free clinic for men, women, and children of all denominations."[173] By 1936 this mission had become the first hospital focused on convalescent care in Canada, the St. John's Rehabilitation Hospital.

In their role as harbingers of medicine and hygiene, Sisterhoods presaged their Evangelical counterparts (or competitors), Deaconess Orders. Evangelical Anglicans, as well as Methodists, soon realized that Sisterhoods were opening vocations that women within their own ranks also desired and that they needed to act. Secure in a New Testament justification for the office of Deaconess that predated Catholic convents, late-nineteenth-century Canadian Protestants forged ahead with Deaconess Orders and training schools, with a hybrid of seminary and science courses.[174] In their working lives (which were virtually constant, as these women made a lifelong commitment and would have to leave the order if they were to marry), sisters and deaconesses wrote about their work in ways that both underlined and traversed boundaries of class, depicting for their middle- and upper-class readers the devastating poverty and dire circumstances of many of their patients. As one *Christian Guardian* writer put it, "Sometimes I think deaconesses do their best work in simply letting the rich folk know the needs of the poor folk."[175] The "Deaconess World" column featured agonizing tales such as that of an impoverished, abused woman, beaten to unconsciousness by her drunken husband. The woman was found by a deaconess on a home visit and then "nursed . . . back to consciousness and salvation."[176] From the many "anecdotes of squalid poverty in homes of Jew and Gentile alike," it is clear that deaconesses entered into social situations that their middle-class lay counterparts probably rarely saw.[177] Filters between what was considered the dirty contagion of slum-dwellers and the well-ventilated (and fumigated) Christian gentility, deaconesses also put faith in Anna Henry's methods of textual persuasion by reading at the bedside of "sin-sick souls, bringing them glimpses of salvation."[178] At the front lines of the social gospel, deaconesses became impassioned advocates for revision of labor conditions for factory workers, establishment of public health and sanitation services, and improvement of social and state support for mothers and children.[179]

In their work as intermediaries between new immigrants and established Canadians, deaconesses occasionally reported on their failures, such as when the Anglican Deaconess House announced that "story hour has been discontinued due to the trouble we had with the boys"; cross-cultural successes were often marked, as when "the reappearance of our little Hindu woman" at Mothers' Meetings was happily noted.[180] Deaconesses could be defenders of immigrants—at the expense of the native-born poor—arguing that "foreigners are often cleaner and more courteous," while they also commented on the challenges of their version of cross-cultural exchange. Anglican Hilda Hellaby frankly noted the hostility she encountered when attempting to do "sick-visiting" among the Chinese population of Vancouver, despite her unusual ability to speak their language.[181] Hellaby's self-reflective description of her cold reception was in contrast to the puzzlement of some of her male medical missionary colleagues, who appeared completely perplexed at why the various First Nations peoples they encountered wished to keep their religious and healing traditions from the missionary's gaze.[182]

The deaconess, a combination of nurse, social worker, and missionary, became an increasingly untenable mix in an era of professionalization, largely because she was thought to have not quite enough of the scientific spirit. Despite the careful monthly documentation of obstetrical cases, appendectomies, home visits, and clinics detailed in the *Canadian Churchman* by the Anglican Deaconess House in Toronto, and the extensive curriculum in subjects such as "scientific temperance" described by its Methodist counterpart, the nurse eventually triumphed over the deaconess as the scientific, feminine side of medicine in the consciousness of Anglo-Protestants and their papers.[183] In 1911 *Christian Guardian* journalist and women's labor activist Alice Chown was accused of "flagellating" the church for her harsh accusations that deaconess education was lacking rigor and that the self-sacrificing mode of deaconess life was unprofessional and denigrating to women.[184] Deeply shaped by her experiences in U.S. settlement houses, Chown argued strongly against the unscientific qualifications and unprofessional terms of employment for deaconess training and work, proclaiming that "the skilled nurse who saves one baby from blindness is worth more than twenty deaconesses with their pious platitudes of indignation." Chown condemned the "sentimental sops" that Methodist deaconesses sent in as reports to the *Christian Guardian*, "which arouse feeling and sympathy for the unfortunate poor, but do not lead the readers to delve below the surface of the misery to find a remedy, or preventive to future misfortunes." With a socialist tenor, Chown argued that the Methodist Church more generally was unaware of the new "cosmic consciousness" that called for revolutionizing the social and economic causes of poverty and disease, not "distributing Christmas baskets nor writing nice little sentimental stories."[185] Even though Chown's articles drew a great deal of indignant critique at the time, fourteen years later, Janet McGillivray wrote of women's work in the newly formed United Church, arguing that "the deaconess' 'personal touch' was important, but now we need new methods and systems with the modern era."[186]

In 1916 the *Christian Guardian* celebrated the Manitoba government's venture to send out four nurses as what the *Guardian* called "Apostles of Health" who would "blend the ideals of the Saviour of man with the practical application on earth of this teaching." One of the important benefits of such apostles, the *Christian Guardian* argued, would be to remedy the condition of "below par children found due to bloated capitalism on the grain exchange, closed windows and indifferent cooking."[187] No longer would deaconesses be the main link between new immigrants and Canadians, instead the public health nurse—assumedly Christian—would take her place: "rural Manitobans and many 'new Canadians' will now be reached by the 'long arm' of the provincial health board paid for by the municipalities and provincial government."[188] Nursing, having the added advantage of being supported by the reliable funds of the government and not being beholden to church-based charity as were deaconesses, was considered to be more systematic in addressing public health concerns.

Protestant calls for financial support for Canadian medical care increasingly turned to governments, and no longer to congregations, as the *Christian Guardian* showed in its endorsement of Mrs. McNaughton of the Women's Grain Growers Association, when she declared in 1916: "The government must fund health care on par with road building."[189] Although deaconesses, sisters, and nurses were all pioneers in establishing networks of public health in Canada, it is clear that they were not considered sufficient: a "medical man" was always the most desirable in the view of the churches and medical authorities, except in the case of the foreign or urban mission field when women were the only Christians welcome in the home.[190] Deaconesses did not relinquish their Christian path to medicalization without a struggle. They attempted to start Bible study groups for secular nurses working in hospitals, encouraging nurses to wear buttons while working that declared them to be "King's nurses doing the King's business."[191] The Sisterhood of St. John the Divine enjoyed more long-lasting success than its deaconess counterparts, as it is still active in Canada, especially in Toronto where the Sisters' new convent was recently built on the grounds of the thriving St. John's Rehabilitation Hospital. Anglican deaconesses eventually gave up their medical functions and became "deacons" on par with their male colleagues in the Anglican Church, while within the United Church, a new dual position emerged to deal with all the paper records flooding the modern, bureaucratic church, namely the "secretary-deaconess."[192]

At the dawn of what many Christians considered to be the morally ambiguous media of moving pictures and radio, the ambivalent power of texts themselves to purify or defile souls was keenly felt by Christians. As one Methodist asserted in 1910, "Few things are more mightily effective in giving character and stamina to a people than good reading and, on the other hand, few things will sooner and more surely devitalize and vitiate and coarsen a people than the constant reading of trash."[193] In the Protestant text-based cosmology the morality of literature was a prominent factor in determining what constituted good reading, but so too was the imprimatur of scientific legitimacy. The respect and prominence given to documentation and inscription within the scientific method emphasized textuality as a means to truth.[194] The kind of healing that could be tested, written up, and therefore proven, was much more intelligible than that which seemed to defy both nature and scripture in its unverifiable personal testimony.[195] Scientific proofs displayed through textual recordation were considered a mirror—however warped—of the divine proof proclaimed through holy writ.

CONCLUSION: A HAPPY MEDIUM

Early-twentieth-century Protestant arguments for merging Christianity and medicine were formed in relation not only to scientific or secular critics but also by the threats posed from within by those who left for Pentecostal and Christian Science churches, and the challenges posed on the mission field by curious, but often unyielding non-Christians. Whether attacking such rivals with racialized and gendered vitriol or attempting to transform them into Christians, Protestants used texts as the most important of weapons and medicines, as texts connected magical, rhetorical, and cultural forms of power. Texts served as manuals for how to live a healthy Christian life as well as sensational forms for channeling the power of the divine. In an era of nonstop invention in communication technologies, however, a text-based cosmology had numerous competitors. Even among mainstream Protestants, theologians and clerics were adopting a spiritual language oriented by concepts such as "energy," "vitality," and "currents."

For their part, doctors, demonstrating a Christian sympathy, encouraged ministers to preach the "gospel of health" and hygiene during medicalized church services such as "TB Sunday" and "Sanitary Sunday." Although these newfangled devotions had their detractors, such as the critic who complained that "Insanity Sunday" would be next, they were evidence of the deep sense of shared purpose between doctors and ministers.[196] By the 1920s this shared vision of medicalized Christianity (or Christianized medicine) was heralded by Methodist Robert Milliken as a "baptism of the holy scientific spirit and method" that would bring socialistic and systematic solutions to problems of public health.[197]

The relations of Protestantism and medicine were often so intertwined and naturalized as to be almost invisible—for example, Canadian-born Anglican William Osler, one of the most esteemed doctors of the early twentieth century, employed Lyman Powell, then a graduate student at Johns Hopkins, to revise his "magnum opus," *The Principles and Practice of Medicine*.[198] Powell went on to become a clergyman with an investigative yen for Christian healing, as his paper on the ministry of healing at the 1910 Anglican Congress in Toronto showed. His medically informed criticism of Christian Science became more sympathetic by the time he wrote his biography of Mary Baker Eddy—the writing of which meant that he had provided literary mediations of both Osler, the consummate medical man, and Eddy, Osler's female antithesis. This textual mediation of biomedicine and spiritual healing is aptly symbolic of the position of liberal Protestants more generally, as they sought a happy medium by defending and enacting the moral and practical necessity of biomedicine while simultaneously making space for the "spirit."

When Protestants invested biomedicine with nobility, authority, and sanctity, they did so with an assurance that could allow them to ask: "What would the world do without its MDs and DDs to look after the bodies and souls of its bilious and sinful mortals and fellow-citizens?"[199] Reading the body through techniques and terminology of biomedicine—such as x-rays and hygiene—could be a sensational form by which to access God's will and God's grace, they argued. Murmurings of dis-ease with the growing power of medicine occasionally arose (or exploded in the case of healing revivals), but Christians could still take heart that doctors needed them. In 1925 the *Christian Guardian* happily reported that when the University of Minnesota inaugurated a new medical institute for the study of cancer, the medical staff asked the churches of

Minneapolis to beseech God on their behalf with the following prayer on Sunday morning: "[E]nable with Thy grace, we pray Thee, the dullness of our blinded sight, and grant a new vision to all those who serve Thee in their search for the cause of cancer and its cure."[200] Even if they had to delegate the work of prayer to local churchgoers, medical personnel thought being in commerce with God was worth it.

CHAPTER 3

Protestant Experimentalists and the Energy of Love

We cannot use electric lights and radios and, in the event of illness, avail ourselves of modern medical and clinical means and at the same time believe in the spirit and wonder world of the New Testament.

—Rudolf Bultmann, "New Testament and Mythology" 1941

The prayer of faith shall save him that is sick.

—James 5:15, quoted by Dr. Belle Choné Oliver in *Tales from the Inns of Healing*, 1942

German Protestant Rudolf Bultmann was a leading biblical scholar much beloved by North American liberal Protestants both for his early condemnation of Nazism and for his attempt to unearth the core Christian message, fit for a scientific age, from within the "mythologies" of the New Testament. In 1941 he put the matter starkly: to be modern was to leave behind the gospel promises of bodily healing through the spirit. Articulating a theological anthropology indebted both to his existentialist colleague Martin Heidegger and to his own deep knowledge of Hellenistic and biblical traditions, Bultmann sought a conception of "man" that could withstand empiricism, endorse freedom of the will, and leave room for grace. His rebuke of supernaturalism depended on a sense of faith profoundly conditioned by—and committed to—the responsibility that comes with historicity: "Faith is faith in God 'who gives life to the dead and calls into existence the things that do not exist' (Rom. iv. 17). Faith is therefore faith in the future which God bestows on man, in the coming God. And this means that in the Bible man is understood in his historicity, *as qualified by his past and required by his future.*"[1]

With faith in a God who gives life to the dead alongside disbelief in the wonder world of the New Testament, Bultmann walked a paradoxical line along which he had many Protestant companions. Leaving behind the uncanny wonder of miraculous healings did not mean that all liberal Protestants turned their backs on the possibilities of the spirit animating the flesh. Even though many were much less categorical than Bultmann in their abandoning of wonder, they shared his conviction, especially in the wake of the two world wars, that the spirit could never be understood apart from the requirements of the past, present, and future, nor in ignorance of the claims of science. But they developed forms of energetic healing that depended precisely on embracing modern medicine, and modern technologies more broadly, as conduits of the spirit to the flesh. They were attracted by the very mysteries that science opened up, as Belle Choné Oliver's mentor, Ernest Hocking put it: "No one who thinks twice can be in any danger of identifying the energy which is measurable in terms of mv^2 or fd with the 'energy' of his own will or its fluctuating 'tensions' of desire. Yet the ambiguity of these words is not accidental; no doubt the two phases of energy belong together; the one as substance and the other as shadow. But in this fact, there is nothing to indicate which is the shadow."[2]

Frederick Du Vernet's remarkable *Canadian Churchman* series on "spiritual radio," begun in 1922, was an anthropology that attempted to resolve the multivalence of energy, as he considered spiritual bodies to be simultaneously scientific, technological bodies, through which people could harness the healing current of God's love. Going beyond the mediation of healing via texts, Du Vernet argued for radio waves as channels for divine energy that would have therapeutic ends. Clearly, his commingling of electricity, radios, and God's healing power was at odds with the disenchanted, demythologizing views of Rudolf Bultmann. Du Vernet, however, was not alone among liberal Protestants in his robust technological supernaturalism; he was joined, in spirit if not in body, by many other sympathetic souls who utilized modern communication and medical technologies as pathways for the spirit. Along the way many of these technological experimentalists came to question how their missionary projects were embedded in racist Christian histories and mythologies that they no longer entirely embraced.

The time between the two world wars saw a flowering of a Protestant technological supernaturalism that would eventually contribute to both liberal anthropologies of spiritual equilibrium and charismatic anthropologies of spiritual intervention. I trace this technological supernaturalism through three related groups of people: missionaries in colonial contexts, Protestants engaged in psychic exploration, or as many liked to say, "psychic research," and those who began to engage with the tools and techniques of psychology. I group these Protestants together as "experimentalists," borrowing the category of their contemporary, Episcopalian biblical scholar Kirsopp Lake. Experimentalists were moderns who chose to put Christian texts and practices, including prayer, to the test of experience with the help of such ostensibly scientific methods as historical text criticism, psychic research, or psychoanalysis. They confidently evaluated (or confirmed) the union of Christian healing with new communication technologies, the new discipline of psychology, non-Christian techniques such as yoga, and psychic gifts such as telepathy, by turning to what they considered to be tools of science: impartial measures of an empirical reality that included the divine.[3] Although texts remained central to how they communicated their ideas, experimentalists sought out new sensational forms drawn from modern technologies, whether electricity, radio, or x-rays as both metaphorical and physical channels for healing.

The energetic healing of Protestant experimentalists fit within a theological and therapeutic tradition especially indebted to John Wesley, in which "electricity [was] an elemental form of power, derived from God."[4] Protestant experimentalists drew explanatory power from wider currents of harmonial religion—what historian Sydney Ahlstrom described as "forms of piety and belief in which spiritual composure, physical health, and even economic well-being are understood to flow from a person's rapport with the cosmos."[5] Their strong critiques of the injustices of capitalism distinguished them from prophets of prosperity, however, and their cosmic rapport came from a technologically mediated Christianity that was neither exactly metaphorical nor miraculous. They are perhaps better categorized as a Christian subset within Catherine Albanese's definition of metaphysical religion, in which the power of mind, including telepathic communication, new technologies, and theories of healing energy are predominant.[6]

This technological supernaturalism existed in the midst of a growing "secular" critique of communication technologies as themselves a kind of pathology of modernity. For example both Walter Benjamin and R. G. Collingwood argued, in different ways, that mechanized reproductions of artistic production were paltry substitutes for the direct experience of the human voice or the humanly crafted image.[7] Counter to this "audiovisual litany" that has lamented the incursion of media technologies into face-to-face human interaction, many liberal Protestants saw new communication technologies as ripe with possibility. Spiritual radio and even telepathic communication were part of what historian Jonathan Sterne has called a new age of "'Ensoniment,' a modern organization of sound [that] promotes a conception of nature (and human nature) as malleable, as something to be shaped and transformed."[8]

Turning to new technologies as vehicles for epiphanies and revelation, as well as sources of bodily healing, experimentalists used the tools of a supposedly disenchanted, mechanized age for spiritual ends. Bernard Faure, a scholar of Buddhism, has suggested that disenchantment is in part the refusal "to believe that our 'self' can be situated anywhere but in our body."[9] This contention is certainly borne out in the suspicion and ridicule that many Christians and scientists heaped on experimentalists as they sought to establish "evidences" for combinative pieties such as Christian spiritualism or radio mind—pieties that suggested the self could be in two places at once or even that the dead could speak to the living.[10] Yet throughout the twentieth century technologies of communication made it ever more possible for parts of the self—voices, images, words—to travel and stay put, to be here and there. The magic and amazement of these technologically travelling selves provided not only metaphors but also experiences that allowed experimentalists to cultivate an anthropology of the spiritual body that saw God acting on the body through the newly discovered laws of science. Blending scientific and romantic discourses of experience, as well as what they had learned of alternate practices of embodiment in the missionary encounter, Protestant experimentalists proclaimed the salvific and therapeutic benefits of technological and medical progress as tools for staying alert to the workings of the spirit.

EXPERIMENTALISTS AND A NEW HEALING MISSION

Experimentalists were an eclectic, educated, and often institutionally well-placed collection of people. At a less-physical level than Du Vernet's radio mind, Robert Edis Fairbairn, a minister of the newly formed United Church of Canada, also attempted radio theology. He argued that the same "polarity" underlying electricity and radio was also "a divine principle of the universe" that could turn disputes and contradictions among Christians—such as those quarreling over church union in the 1920s—into productive and complementary "contraries."[11] And even before the advent of radio broadcasting, when American Sherwood Eddy addressed an audience of women while on a 1913 missionary tour of China, the international Young Men's Christian Association (YMCA) evangelist shared not only the gospel, but also a demonstration of the possibilities of wireless telegraphy.[12] By 1922, when the first radio stations were on the air, Eddy compared prayer to a "vast electric railway system" and a "wireless apparatus," asking: "If man can thus increasingly utilize natural laws and forces, why cannot God also, if it is his world?"[13] Similarly to Emmanuel Movement founder Elwood Worcester, Sherwood Eddy later went on to declare his belief in the efficacy of psychic healing.[14]

Influenced by philosophers such as William James, Henri Bergson, and Ernest Hocking, who all wrote approvingly of the vitality of energy, experimentalists' versions of spiritual healing remained rather vague in terms of what illnesses could be cured through these means.[15] For some, experimentalism was a practice of wondering about possibilities and less a conviction of what was therapeutically attainable. For example when reading Bergson's discussion in *Mind Energy* of "healing by suggestion, or, more generally, by the influence of mind on mind," United Church minister and librarian F. Louis Barber mused in the margins of his copy: "Is this what Jesus did?"[16] Others more directly engaged in healing, such as Belle Choné Oliver, boldly claimed that the scientific method of learning from failure was proving the importance of prayer within a medical model: ". . . even modern medicine has had its many failures and these failures are helping men to realize that man is not merely a body, but mind and spirit as well, and that mind and spirit have their influence on the body for the worse and also for the better in functional and nervous diseases and also in organic disease."[17] Taking the power of prayer in another direction, Anglican Percy Dearmer argued that prayer was really just telepathy by another name and that both were techniques of spiritual communication that depended on "a power which we Christians have always believed in and have universally used."[18]

For experimentalists, God's power was not always directed to answering the prayers of supplicants. They considered the petitionary prayer of divine healing—that is, asking or demanding God for healing based on one's faith—to verge on "magic" that was spiritually immature, or, in the historically layered terminology shared with anthropology, "fetishistic."[19] According to the liberal critique, turning the body itself into a fetish, that is, "mistaking" the health or illness of the body as the material grounds in which God's power must be proved, left insufficient space both for theological notions of free will and unbidden grace and for scientific epistemólogies of human physiology. At the same time that experimentalists chastised Pentecostal healers for their magical demands of God, they often had charitable words for the openness to healing energy in non-Christian traditions, suggesting that these people were better able to live by "natural" laws because of their simpler life-styles. Ironically, given their love of technology, experimentalists also drew from the growing disciplines of anthropology and comparative religion to argue that non-Christians living outside the mechanistic, rushing pace of modernity held a precious aspect of human-divine connection in trust for the rest of humanity.[20]

Like many anthropologists of the time, Protestant experimentalists often came to their anthropological conclusions through contact with colonized peoples in North America, India, and Africa. Although many still called for the "Christianizing of the social order," by the 1920s liberal Protestants were suffering a crisis of missionary confidence as result of their recent experience of a bloody war among "Christian" nations, transformative encounters with non-Christians and anticolonial movements in the mission field, and persistent questions about what could be known about faith in a world not Christianized, but "scientized."[21] Their growing sense that missionary work was compromised by its consanguinity with colonialism led an increasing number of liberal Christians, including Hocking and Oliver, to question the goals and strategies of missions, in public and private.[22]

These liberal Protestant critiques were increasingly at odds with those of conservatives, whose confidence in the power of God continued to be rooted in a commitment to the supremacy of Christianity.[23] For example in 1924 the conservative, interdenominational Medical Missionary Association of London decided to transform its monthly periodical *Medical Missions at Home and Abroad* into a quarterly magazine with a more boldly imperialistic title, *Conquest by Healing*, with this explanation: "He who conquers heals, because he conquers the heart, the fount of love."[24] Reminiscent of Anglican Mabel Cartwright's 1907 appeal to Christian privilege and responsibility, Webb Anderson, the General Secretary of the Medical Missionary Association, asserted that medical missions were more than a duty, they were a privilege: "Privilege puts warmth into duty, lifts the burden of responsibility. Opportunity is golden in our grasp, because whether in medicine or the Church, alike under the Red Cross or the Cross of Calvary, we are out to help God to save His world for which He gave His son."[25]

For Anderson, the notion of privilege carried with it none of the burden of responsibility for exploitation and injustice that critics of colonialism, Christianity, or whiteness would later attribute to it. Instead privilege was meant to authorize and energize a practice of medical missions rooted both in the growing "humanitarianism" of networks such as the Red Cross and Christian efforts to proselytize the sick. A pamphlet published by the American Board, an ecumenical Protestant missionary organization more liberal than Anderson's group, also referred to dual allegiances to humanitarianism and Christianity but hinted at a growing tension in these paired loyalties: "It is an open secret about mission hospital units, that while they are followers of the Red Cross they are loyal to the White Cross. In one hand they carry healing for suffering bodies; in the other healing for weary souls."[26] For other Christian missionaries, however, the open secret of a conquest by healing was becoming something less worthy of boasting and more worthy of criticism and renunciation. Alongside a rise in journalistic accounts of the successes and failures of foreign missions grew the critiques of missionaries themselves, who no longer agreed that medical missions were the most effective path to convert non-Christians, or even that missions—medical or otherwise—were about conversion at all.[27] For those medical missionaries who eventually grew critical of the project of aggressive evangelization, such as Belle Oliver and her counterpart in China, Robert McClure, medicine became a Christian vocation not measured by souls saved but by numbers of local doctors trained and surgeries performed.

As Grant Wacker has argued in the context of Chinese missions, the 1920s were an especially intense time of self-critique among Protestant missionaries, who were experiencing the "waning of the missionary impulse." These progressive critics "had not solved all of the problems of cultural imperialism, but they were working on it," commented Wacker, as he traced Pearl S. Buck's path from missionary to Nobel-prize-winning critic of Christian imperialism.[28] The waning of the (medical) missionary impulse was simultaneous with a waxing of interest in an ever-widening sphere of experimental healing modalities—from Anglican Archbishop Frederick Du Vernet's notion of "radio mind" to Anglican missionary Jack C. Winslow's advocacy of a hybrid practice of "Christian Yoga."[29] A growing sense of a "universal spirituality" also enabled this ritual cosmopolitanism, just as the liberal sense of the "religious" individual was partly responsible for making such hybrid experimentation possible; with the universal notion of "religion" to hand, being a Christian did not prevent a person from employing the rituals and tech-

FIGURE 7. Belle Choné Oliver (far right) with Christian women physicians at a conference in India. Courtesy of United Church of Canada Archives, Toronto, Glenna Jamieson Fonds, 1988.029P96.

niques of another tradition. Christian experimentalism, often initiated by missionaries or former missionaries, could be read as a new form of Christian imperialism that sought to Christianize the world by absorption rather than wholesale destruction. Whereas experimentalism was considerably more porous and self-questioning than the conquest by healing, its attachments to science and even to the spirit meant that the work of translation between "religious" traditions could easily privilege a medicalized Christianity. Whether orientalist, hegemonic, progressive, or all three, experimentalism brought Protestants to rethink their relations to non-Christians and to reconsider the relative positions of Christian and scientific epistemologies.

THE SPIRITUAL FRONTIERS OF FREDERICK DU VERNET

Frederick Du Vernet (1860–1924) existed at the frontiers of the British Empire, Christianity, and science both literally and figuratively. Profoundly shaped by his encounters with First Nations peoples as he travelled by foot and canoe through the mountainous forests that the

Anglican Church had called the Diocese of Caledonia since 1879, Du Vernet sought to bring Caledonia, the last Canadian Diocese to owe its allegiance to Canterbury, into greater communion with Canadian Anglicanism. Known for his "wise leadership" of a diocese that had a long history of inner conflict and that had "no talent for cooperation," Du Vernet succeeded in his goals of union when Caledonia joined the newly formed Anglican Province of British Columbia in 1914, with Du Vernet as its first Archbishop.[30] At the same time that he cultivated new institutions of Anglicanism in a land largely peopled by First Nations, he imagined himself as a scientist breaking new ground with his experiments in telepathic communication. Committed to the transformative possibilities of telepathy (or what he called radio mind) for human communication and divine healing, Du Vernet fearlessly testified to his theo-scientific findings not only in the pages of the Anglican *Canadian Churchman* but also in secular news media including the *Montreal Daily Star* and *Maclean's Magazine*. He was a Protestant experimentalist with a mission and an audience.

Du Vernet graduated in the first class of the newly formed Wycliffe College, an Evangelical Anglican institution in Toronto. He began his career as a frontier missionary with rather typical goals of evangelization. On an 1898 missionary tour to northwestern Ontario, escorted by a part-Cree missionary, Jeremiah Johnston, Du Vernet kept a diary in which he detailed his encounters with several Ojibwe communities along the Rainy River. Coming into contact with Cree and Ojibwe traditions of healing, Du Vernet voiced an ambivalent condemnation of their "medicine tents," at times feeling compelled to respect their power: "It was most interesting but very sad, this propitiation offered in ignorance to a higher power. Even tho it was all such a fraud—the 3 medicine men getting the spoils—I stood with uncovered head with a feeling of reverence."[31] Not convinced intellectually—or theologically—by the healing practices before him, Du Vernet was nevertheless emotionally compelled to adopt a physical gesture that would show his respect. Similar unbidden "feelings of reverence"—whether in the presence of yogis or medicine men—led many missionaries to question, if gradually, the uniqueness of Christian claims to spiritual power.

The editor of the Toronto-based *Church Missionary Gleaner* until just prior to his appointment as missionary Bishop to the Diocese of Caledonia in 1904, Du Vernet would most likely have read the article in the July 1902 *Gleaner* written by his predecessor, the first Bishop of

Caledonia from 1879 to 1904, William Ridley. The Bishop offered this hesitating critique of imperial claims to Indian land, also expressed in the language of unbidden feeling.

> Missions made this [claim] easy and leave a twinge of uneasiness in the conscience. As a Nation we owe a debt of reparation to the red man. Civilization triumphs where the Gospel conquered for Christ the owners of a vast dominion that will more and more become the granary for feeding our Motherland. If this be among the providences of God, His love must surely bind us to deal beneficently with the original possessors of the rich domain.[32]

In his time as Bishop of Caledonia, Du Vernet also showed signs of this twinge of uneasiness, as he combined missionary work with support for maintaining aspects of Tsimshian culture, including its healing rituals. With parishioners such as Odille Morison, a Tsimshian/French Canadian Anglican, who was a gifted translator and correspondent of Franz Boas, and whose Tsimshian Anglican mother Mary was a renowned healer, Du Vernet was surrounded by Tsimshian Christians who combined Christian and Tsimshian traditions without necessarily giving up one for the other.[33] His earlier "feelings of reverence" for native healing ceremonies shaped Du Vernet's respect for First Nations cultures. He distinguished himself as an opponent of residential schooling: when lobbying both church and government for local day schools, he quoted the mother of a native child in residential school as saying, "My child might as well be dead."[34] Although he worked to convert First Nations people to Christianity, Du Vernet also struggled throughout his career to limit government and church disruption of their families and communities.[35]

By the end of his life Du Vernet had come up with his own healing techniques that demonstrated a considerably less dogmatic commitment to Christian orthodoxy. With more than a superficial similarity to Northwest Coast Native practices of healing, themselves dependent on convictions of traveling spiritual energies, Du Vernet argued for a Christian adaptation of psychological manifestations of energy, including telepathy and the power of suggestion.[36] Contending that "real religion" was exemplified in the "lonely prospector among the mountains, thrilled with the consciousness that he is one in spirit with God and one in spirit with his fellow-men," Du Vernet argued for a universal spirituality that could be experienced through new technologies as much as through scripture. He insisted that for the church to survive it must adapt to modern realities of psychology and communication technologies.[37] To explicate radio mind, Du Vernet posited that four types of interrelated energy allowed for telepathic communication between human minds, as well as between God and humans. Arguing that "conventional religion," with its focus on doctrinal orthodoxy, ignored Jesus's emphasis on "spiritual energy," Du Vernet insisted that all healing was "divine" in that it worked through the God-created "chain of life" in which mind energy worked on vital energy, which influenced nerve energy, which regulated muscular energy. The first link in the chain was the subconscious mind, "the storage battery of latent energy" where the "finite and the infinite meet and mingle."[38] For Du Vernet, the subconscious mind was a spiritual entity through which God could heal the body, but it was also a deep reserve that could be shaped by human actors, whether through oral or visual suggestion, auto-suggestion, or "collective telepathic suggestion," also known as "radio mind."[39]

Du Vernet considered himself a psychologist engaged in scientifically rigorous experiments that drew on "telepathic testimonies," including those of other Protestant clergy.[40] The "law of vibration" that under-wrote telepathy was particularly applicable in cases of illness or death within families: thus "a sleeping mother three thousand miles away can easily be awakened by a rhythmic wave of thought and feeling from her suffering son."[41] Du Vernet attempted to demonstrate this scientifically through conducting experiments with his daughter as the "passive" re-cipient, using a homemade Chevreul's Pendulum designed to register telepathic communication, in which a pencil attached to a wire and held by his daughter would point to particular letters that he sent her via "mental radiation."[42] In another family connection Du Vernet vouched for the efficacy of absent treatment, a healing technique of long-distance prayer usually associated with Christian Science, by describing the role of his prayers in bringing his adult son back from the brink of death from an unspecified illness: "As I prayed I knew with scientific certainty that, regardless of distance, my mind energy was penetrating his subcon-scious mind as he lay in the hospital very weak and susceptible to men-tal influence. . . . there suddenly flashed into his mind this thought, 'I must live for the sake of my wife and children.' This auto-suggestion, stimulated from afar, dropped into his subconscious mind, and there revived the latent energy of his soul."[43] Reflecting on the power of fam-ily ties or friendship to facilitate radio mind, Du Vernet described the "thrilling experience" of knowing that science and religion were in pro-found communion: "The law of psychic harmony pervades our whole religion. The vibrating Energy of God reaches its climax in the harmony of active Love."[44] Advocating a therapy of "resting in the Lord" akin to "meditation" that allowed the subconscious mind to rest, Du Vernet considered his eclectic mix of theory and practice to be scientific, Christian, and indispensable: thus "only by combining the help of both psychology and religion can we hope to offset the killing pace of this rushing age."[45]

Du Vernet was an experimentalist who pushed the bounds of orthodoxy—and pushed at the notion of orthodoxy itself—while remaining an Anglican of high office who was committed to Christianity and science. Even when addressing the contentious issue of the union of the Anglican and United Churches (a cause he supported), he turned to the history of electricity and the discovery that currents and waves could run through air as well as wire to argue for an expanded understanding of apostolic succession that would not be limited to traditional notions of lineage: "Loyalty to our Church traditions forces us to hold fast to the historic episcopate; but loyalty to the spirit of Christ will not allow us to erect this piece of ecclesiastical machinery as a barrier in the way of Christian fellowship."[46] He also supported the other controversial kind of postwar union, arguing for fairer labor practices and constraints on the untrammeled growth of capitalism. Du Vernet's theories were developed in a context remote from urban life but where he nevertheless witnessed the transformative powers of energy and developing technology in a vivid way as the railway steadily extended through the British Columbia interior, bringing increasing white settlement in its wake.

It is not entirely surprising that church historians have remembered Du Vernet more as an Evangelical who sought to bring together various factions both within and without the Anglican Church, and less as an experimentalist who cultivated a technological supernatural liberalism.[47] Despite being championed by the well-known (in his day) Episcopalian Gaynor Banks, Du Vernet's practice of radio mind did not become a runaway success. It may well have resonated with the work of more renowned authors, such as the American socialist and critic of organized religion, Upton Sinclair, who like Du Vernet, combined a harsh criticism of the corrosive effects of capitalism with a later-in-life fascination for psychic phenomenon: in 1906 he wrote his most famous book, the hard hitting novel *The Jungle*, which exposed the oppressive labor conditions in Chicago's meatpacking industry, and by 1930 he wrote *Mental Radio*, an account of psychic experiments he conducted with his wife as a medium. (He was also fascinated by Aimee Semple McPherson's blend of radio and healing.) Despite the quirky individuality of most Christian experimentalists, they did share some qualities: many were socialist-leaning, progressive thinkers who argued publicly for social and political transformation in several areas, including labor laws and racial discrimination.[48] They tied their interest in psychic communication between humans and the divine with the need to heal a war-ravaged world, and they spoke of love as a substance that could travel via currents, transforming all whom it touched.

THINKING DIFFERENTLY: BELLE OLIVER'S SUPERNATURAL LIBERALISM

Liberal Protestant missionaries concerned with questions of healing—which did not necessarily always mean medical missionaries, as Du Vernet demonstrates—came to their post–World War I critiques of the Christian triumphalism of missions from a variety of angles. Professionalization transformed some medical missionaries, as they were gradually enculturated into their identities as doctors and nurses in such a way that medical concerns took much greater precedence over those of evangelization.[49] Methodist missionary William Smith's predilection for selling tracts over curing cataracts was a quirk of a bygone era compared to many of the professionalized medical men and women of the postwar United Church, such as Robert McClure, who served as medical missionary in China, Gaza, and India, among other places, in addition to serving as the first lay moderator of the United Church of Canada.[50] For others a dawning appreciation of the virtues of non-Christian religions caused them to rethink the purpose of Christian mission altogether, understanding it as a powerful transformation (and re-embodiment) of Christianity in conversation with other rich religious traditions, as exemplified by Christian yoga. New ideas about the universality of the human psyche drawn from both psychology and psychic research led many to new hopes for a universal spirituality.

Although not fully in tune with the project of a universal spirituality, as the enthusiastically evangelical tenor of her book *Tales from the Inns of Healing* demonstrated, Belle Oliver was a woman poised between her youthful enthusiasm for evangelization and her mature questioning of the methods and goals of Christian missions. Her experiences as a doctor tending to suffering bodies and as a church worker who traveled the world were important pathways to the critical stance that led her to embrace a less evangelical and more ecumenical Christianity. Oliver was marked by ecumenism in both personal and public ways: her middle name came from that of a Roman Catholic priest who had saved her father from drowning; her sister, Agnes Galer, was a New Thought healer who established a Divine Science Church in Seattle; and Oliver herself chose to accompany those Presbyterians who decided to join the new United Church of Canada in 1925, later writing that "not only have we learned to ignore denominational lines but we have learned to deplore them. And we have taken action whenever possible to wipe them out."[51] Concerned to buy a nondescript Bible that she could read in public without attracting notice, Oliver was a committed Christian who wrote and spoke publicly about her faith but who chose to set limits on how and when she did so.[52] Reflecting on her contributions to Ernest Hocking's controversial report, *Rethinking Missions*, Oliver described the report as a compromise between "conservatives and liberals" that was an example of "good Christianity" as an "expression [of faith] that will not exclude others who think differently."[53]

Her own approach to mission, however, grew increasingly liberal with her insistence that medical mission should be an end in itself without harboring evangelism as a covert or declared goal. According to her diary Oliver was first introduced to the idea of "faith cures" at a prayer meeting while at home in Ontario during furlough in 1908.[54] She was clearly opposed to what she considered to be deliverance made easy, quoting in her notebook a passage from novelist George MacDonald's *Robert Falconer*: "Healing without faith in its source would have done them harm instead of good—would have been to them a windfall, not a Godsend; at best the gift of magic, even sometimes the power of Satan casting out Satan."[55] She maintained a space for the importance of well-directed faith, however: ". . . the view that is more and more winning its way is that God cares for the whole of a man—body, soul and spirit, and that through ministries directed in any of these channels His message may be transmitted." Turning to Jesus for her evidence, Oliver continued, "Christ never healed in order to gather a crowd or to advertise His teaching. His healing was an expression of His compassion and a releasing of people from what was hindering them in life. 'Ministry to the secular needs of men in the spirit of Christ, moreover, *is* evangelism, in the right sense of the word.' These acts of succor must be pure acts of disinterested service."[56] For Oliver, medical missions required a purity of intent that understood physical suffering as a call to care and not a chance for conversion. While commending the importance of the "spirit-filled, praying church" for the support of missionaries, Oliver also called for the "recognition of spiritual values in peoples of other faiths." She endorsed what would soon be called a holistic approach to "body, mind, and spirit" while she simultaneously accepted distinctions of secular, medical, and spiritual in carving out the terrain of her working life as a medical missionary.

Even Oliver's medically centered ecumenical approach was flavored with experimentalism, as shown by her discussion of healing via prayer in her book on medical missions in India. Careful to assert that medical means must be fully explored before turning to spiritual techniques, Oliver offered several anecdotes of successful healing via ritual practices uncommon among her United Church compatriots in Canada, including anointing with oil, laying on of hands, and petitionary prayer. Her first example, from the Nilgiri Hills in South India, told the story of a medical missionary who encountered an Indian woman with a rectal fissure, whose husband would not allow the doctor to operate. Counseled by the medical missionary to adopt the next best method and pray to "Yesu Swami," the woman followed the advice and later recounted her ensuing vision of Yesu Swami, who achieved the healing that her husband forbade.

> He said, "Do you believe that I can heal you?" I said, "Yes, oh, yes, I believe, I know that You can heal me. Have I not prayed as they have told me?" Then He said, "You will have no more pain, you are healed." Oh, it was so wonderful, and His face, it was so beautiful, I shall never forget. I am healed, quite healed." She then invited the doctor to examine her and the doctor was able to confirm her witness that complete healing had indeed taken place.[57]

In another anecdote included by Oliver, a doctor speaks of gaining insight into proper medical technique through a kind of mental receptivity very similar to that described by Du Vernet's spiritual radio. After a middle-of-the-night insight that two incompatible medicines were interfering with a patient's recovery, the doctor credited God: "It always seemed to me that God had flashed the thought into my mind when the mind was free to receive it."[58] Intriguingly, Oliver chose classic experimentalist sources to begin and end this chapter on prayer, commencing with an approving quotation from the controversial spiritualist Oliver Lodge and concluding with a quotation from the poet—and mesmeric healer—Tennyson: "More things are wrought by prayer than this world dreams of." Even for a resolutely biomedical Christian healer such as Oliver, a multiplicity of spiritual forces were at work in the mending of the body.

CHRISTIAN YOGA: A LOVE THAT THRILLS AND BURNS

India was a crucible for the interreligious encounters that served as important channels for the rethinking and re-embodying of Christian healing.[59] In her role as secretary of the Christian Medical Association of India, Burma, and Ceylon, Oliver would have been familiar with the work of Dewan Bahadur A. S. Appasamy, the first President of the Indian Mission Society, a group founded by Indian Christians who had worked with the YMCA. Appasamy went beyond the indigenization of Jesus as "Yesu Swami" to argue for yoga as a "mental discipline" and "technique" that was neither Christian nor Hindu. Arguing for yoga's many therapeutic benefits, including the calming of nerves through relaxation and an increase in vitality resulting from the control of the breath, Appasamy echoed William James's earlier endorsement of yoga for a Western audience.[60] In *The Use of Yoga in Prayer*, Appasamy cited both Hindu mystics and the latest scientific research on the "healing properties" of ultraviolet light to suggest that practicing yoga in the open air also accrued photovoltaic benefits: "My face turned toward the blue sky, I have often felt a new energy entering into my system."[61]

Appasamy's most passionate vindication of the Christian use of yoga lay in his description of his own experience: "Every day I catch glimpses, gloriously and utterly real, of these divine realities. I am firmly persuaded that I shall some day reach the divine land whose beauty I see far off now, and hold intercourse with the Father, the Son, and the Holy Ghost, on whom also I daily gaze to my indescribable joy."[62] Yoga gave Appasamy the certainty that other experimentalists craved: not only did it heal the body, it also confirmed the reality of the spiritual world and the immortality of the soul "in fellowship with the Divine Soul."[63] Not surprisingly, as an Indian Christian, Appasamy took care to establish the orthodoxy of the Christian practice of yoga, backing up his visionary ecstasy with scriptural warrants from Psalms and Revelation, among others. He extolled yoga as a "spiritual exercise" akin to vocal prayer and Holy Communion which "reduce[d] to its minimum the element of petition in prayer."[64] Arguing that his technique was neither occult depravity nor magical pleading, Appasamy differentiated his yogic mysticism both from the spiritualism that passed between England and

India via channels of theosophy and psychic research and from the "prim-itive" magic of non-Christian petitionary prayer.[65]

Appasamy's Christian yoga was not the only approach to such a therapeutic blending of traditions. Anglican missionary to India Jack Winslow (1882–1974), known as "Father Jack," founded the Christa Seva Sangha in 1922 as a Christian Ashram that drew from Indian tra-ditions of communal life and their contemporary Gandhian versions. Hoping that the ashram would serve as an "act of reparation for the racial arrogance of missionaries," Winslow also had great hopes for po-litical, therapeutic, and spiritual effects of the ashram's healing ministry that blended yoga with Christian liturgical traditions.[66] (Belle Oliver wrote in her 1929 diary of attending a "meeting for prayer for the sick" with Winslow and ashram members). According to a short 1923 book based on addresses he gave to the Society for the Propagation of the Gospel House in Westminster, England, Christian yoga was an attempt to merge the threefold path of yoga with Christian strains of mysticism. "Indian speech," he wrote, "describes this union with the Supreme Spirit as Yoga, literally 'yoking,' and tells us of three ways by which it may be achieved—bhakti-marga, or the way of loving devotion; dnyana-marga, or the way of knowledge; and karma-marga, or the way of works."[67] Emphasizing the superiority of Hindu approaches to devotional life when compared to what he considered to be Christian obsessions with law, will, and duty, Winslow declared that yoga would have "the whole life of the passions and emotions, as well as the will and the intellect, redeemed."

Drawing examples from Western movements in mental healing, psy-chology, and revivalist spiritual healing, Winslow suggested that yoga could accomplish all that these movements sought to do, but with a greater mystical exuberance: "It is the message of an absorbed, an al-most ecstatic, devotion to the Incarnate and Crucified Lord—a love that thrills and burns with an intense emotion to which we of the West are for the most part strangers, of which, if we tried to practise it, we should be secretly half-ashamed."[68] As with Du Vernet's lonely prospec-tor, "thrilled" by union with the divine in the mountains of British Co-lumbia, Winslow's "Christian Yogi" was to develop a passionate mysti-cism characterized by emotional intensity. Both clerics simultaneously emphasized the need for quietness of the soul to make healing—via spiritual attunement—possible. For Winslow this was to come in the form of a contemplative "stillness of body" through yogic techniques:

"its rules even in regard to such things as bodily posture worked out with a minute precision which often seems to us almost grotesque. Yet we cannot afford to ignore even our bodies."[69]

Winslow's spiritual liberality extended to James Moore Hickson, the Anglican lay healer traveling the British Empire in the early 1920s. Winslow celebrated "those wonderful days" of Hickson's traveling mission to India as a return to the "very atmosphere of the New Testament." Hickson did not stop anywhere long enough to imbibe the spiritual atmospheres of other traditions, offering instead a rather conventional (but still controversial) Anglican liturgical approach to healing. Winslow, however, thought that Indian traditions were the very path to an authentic New Testament spirituality: "There is, perhaps, no part of the Christian Gospel which we have more need to re-learn to-day, and which India may help us to re-learn, than the truth that Christians, being made one with Christ, the conqueror of sin, disease, and death, are *redeemed into a supernatural life.*" Winslow considered this supernatural life to include not only the possibility of miraculous healing but also the prospect that physical suffering that went unhealed could be a viable path to communion with God: "All exercise of supernatural powers for physical healing must be guided by such intuition of the divine Will as is gained more and more through prayer and quiet waiting upon God."[70]

An admirer and acquaintance of Gandhi, Winslow became supportive of Indian independence and what he called Gandhi's "aggressive pacifism."[71] He returned to England in 1934 and became active in another collective approach to Christian therapeutics, the Oxford Group movement, for which he wrote devotional pamphlets. Winslow's deep conviction that Christianity was to be transformed by its encounter with yogic traditions would not have been entirely unfamiliar to a 1920s London audience with increasing awareness of Indian religious and political sensibilities.[72] His message of an energized Christianity, shorn of what he considered to be doctrinal baggage that hampered true union with the "Supreme Spirit," fed a desire for religious universalism that could be found in the writings of both Gandhi and Du Vernet.

Belle Oliver, by contrast, was not the eclectic experimentalist represented by Du Vernet or Winslow—confident in her medical expertise, committed to the empirically based critique of whether medical missions actually worked in South Asia, and at the end of her career, primarily dedicated to the development of an ecumenical coeducational Christian medical college, Oliver was not spending her time developing techniques of Christian yoga or radio mind. But, like Du Vernet, Appasamy, and Winslow, she was committed to the sense that healing the body required receptivity to the spirit of God—a spirit that came from outside the body and from outside the forces of nature. A capacious category, the spirit was also a tricky entity—verified in experience and sensation, and often by the confirming "witness" of the doctor or scientist, the therapeutic power of the spirit was inherently unstable and open to interpretation.

PSYCHIC SUPERNATURALISM

As Leigh Schmidt has shown for an earlier era, the relations among Protestantism, science, and technology are not simply questions of belief that separate the science-friendly modernists from the antievolution fundamentalists; Protestant fascination with new technologies has also nurtured forms of "technological sacramentalism".[73] For post–World War I experimentalists this took the form of an eclectic combination of bodily healing and techniques for communicating with the spirits of the dead. Although many Protestants were deeply uncomfortable with psychic research (and its close but removed cousin, spiritualism) for its theological and scientific claims, there were also many mid-twentieth-century Protestants deeply engaged in reconciling psychic phenomena, new media, and Christian theology into a psychic supernaturalism with healing aims.[74] Christians joined the Society for Psychical Research (SPR), an organization with British, U.S., and Canadian branches that had its detractors but that also boasted scientists, including William James and Sigmund Freud, medical doctors, and science-friendly Christians willing to consider its claims to scientific legitimacy.[75]

As middle-class Christians with the intellectual and social capital to consider themselves valid commentators and researchers into the relationship of mind, body, and soul, psychic experimentalists brought their message to as wide an audience as possible via a range of genres including fiction, newspaper editorials, sermons, advice literature, and investigative prose that verged on the scholarly. Oxford-trained Anglican priest Percy Dearmer (1867–1936) and his Canadian friend and fellow Anglican, Lily Dougall (1858–1923), both set to this all-encompassing task. Dearmer, author of *Body and Soul: An Enquiry into the Effect of Religion upon Health, with a Description of Christian Works of Healing from the New Testament to the Present Day*, came to his views while living in the center of Anglicanism (and spiritualism), with brief forays into past and present British colonies, including India and the United States. Lily Dougall was a wealthy Canadian Anglican who moved to England for health reasons and opened her Oxford home to a network of Anglican experimentalists. Dearmer and Dougall were both deeply influenced by Ruskin and the Arts and Crafts Movement and shared a conviction that modernity called for new forms of Christian community and embodiment.

Dearmer's exploration of Christian healing began in the early 1900s and became increasingly experimental by the 1920s. Rooted both in sacramentalism and in his commitment to Christian socialism as a program to improve the living conditions of those exploited under capitalism, Dearmer's goal was to stimulate Christian study of the relationship of body and soul in matters of health while he also hoped to cultivate personal and societal health through reviving older traditions of Christian healing alongside medical means.[76] Dearmer's revival of older Anglican rituals of healing such as unction and laying on of hands was in conversation with the latest in medicine, psychology, and new religious movements. In 1912, for example, Annie Besant credited him with inviting a Theosophist to speak to his congregation at Primrose Hill about the possibilities of Eastern-influenced meditation in the Anglican Church.[77] He was not without his Anglican and medical critics, however, as condemnation of his excessive credulity demonstrated.[78]

Dearmer was also a member of the Society for Psychical Research and turned to spiritualist practices on several occasions. Mourning his son, a soldier killed in World War I, and his first wife Mabel, who died of enteric fever while serving together with him at a Serbian field hospital during the war, Dearmer consulted spiritualist mediums in an attempt to contact the spirits of his dead. In 1920 Dearmer returned home after a two-year absence during which he taught at an Anglican college in India—where he met Gandhi but was seemingly not impressed—and at several U.S. Episcopalian colleges.[79] That same year, he edited *The Fellowship of the Picture*, a book for which his second wife, Nancy, was the "automatist" or scribe for a dead World War I soldier. The phenomenon of automatic writing was in resurgence at the time—just three years earlier George Yeats, newlywed wife of the poet W. B. Yeats, had discovered the gift of being able to channel written messages from a variety of spirits of the dead.[80] Whereas George's automatic writing channeled the voices of many spirits, and at times focused on the sexual life and reproductive goals of the couple, Nancy Dearmer's automatic writing was the voice of one spirit and was much more prosaic, pious, and optimistic, focusing on ways that the reader could learn how to play his or her appropriate role in the fellowship of God's picture—God's larger divine plan. As the spirit put it, "When he [God] arranges life, it becomes enormously interesting and really very comfy, you know."[81]

The Dearmers's experience was in keeping with broader trends in spiritualism and automatic writing in which women were considered the more appropriately passive recipients of spirit messages. Nancy's spirit friend frankly commended her natural passivity and insisted that it was a necessary condition for both the automatic-writing process and the doing of God's will: "Passive folk are needed badly, and you know how to be passive: that is why I can use you for my book. God can use you for many things, if you are passive."[82] Percy's roles as witness to the moments of inscription and as editor of the text placed him in an appropriately active and masculine role; his introduction to the text ensured the reader that he consulted the SPR as soon as the automatic script began so that they could vouch for the authenticity of the spirit message within the terms of science. Showing the text to the secretary of the SPR, however, did not guarantee a good review in the *Journal of the Society of Psychical Research (JSPR)*: "I am told by those who know Mrs. Dearmer that there is ample reason for believing her subliminal to be quite capable of all that we have here. There is not a scrap of positive evidence for spirit intervention." [83] Ironically, given the suggestion in this review that Nancy, or at least her subliminal, actually wrote the book, Nancy displays little subjectivity in the published work—although the spirit friend addressed her directly when expounding his mediation of God's will, the editor, Percy, decided to edit out all but a few personal messages that were also part of the text. Nancy excised her own subjectivity further, by not mentioning the automatic script in her 1941 biography of her husband, an occlusion repeated by Dearmer's most recent biographer.[84]

In 1920 Dearmer also wrote a letter to *JSPR* warning his fellow researchers that public credibility would be elusive unless "we get rid of bogey-words and adopt scientific terminology."[85] Regardless of how scientific he claimed them to be, it seems that Dearmer did pay some price for his psychic interests. Already accused of dilettantism for his diverse interests, and disparaged for his penchant for fine garments and his passion for transforming the aesthetic elements of church decoration, Dearmer was judged by some within the Anglican hierarchy to be "a difficult square peg for which they only had conventional round holes."[86] His interests in psychic research and healing, combined with his support for women's ordination and Christian socialism, must have contributed to such judgments. Much to his frustration, he was repeatedly passed over for church appointments in the twenties.

Although a radical in terms of his socialist politics, his support of women's ordination, and his exploration of psychic phenomena, in his book *Body and Soul* Dearmer saw himself as a mediator between supporters of medical and spiritual healing and informed his reader that "our job is, through observation and with fair minds and friendly hearts, to enlarge the area of agreement [between doctors and faith healers] and to seek after the truth."[87] Even with an openness to the mixture of medicine, psychology, and religion similar to Elwood Worcester, (like Worcester, Dearmer supported the use of suggestion to "cure disease and awaken moral nature"), Dearmer rooted his approach in a sacramentalism absent from Worcester's more clinical techniques.[88] Dearmer's sacramentalism and his established authority as a liturgical expert helped to keep him credible enough within Anglicanism that he did not entirely pass from experimentalism over into heterodox occultism, so that he could finally be appointed Canon of Westminster Cathedral a few years before his death.

Lily Dougall shared Dearmer's interests in the Guild of Health, as well as his interest in psychic phenomena, as evidenced by her prolific output of novels and theological tracts, including *The Christian Doctrine of Health* (1916), which built on Dearmer's earlier work. Born and raised in Montreal as an heir to the Redpath sugar fortune, Dougall had long struggled with ill health. Whereas the English traveled to Mediterranean climates for their rest cures, the Canadian Dougall moved to England where she lived for many years with her companion, Sophie Earp. Dougall endorsed "scientific methods of curing disease" such as the "physical means" of drugs and surgery along with the "mental means" of hypnosis, telepathy, and psychoanalysis while she also contended that the spirit of God was a real source of healing.[89] Not so differently from the nineteenth-century proponents of "acting faith" described by religion scholar Heather Curtis, Dougall urged Christians to abandon the traditional view of sickness as a punishment from God and to engage in faithful prayer and an active love of others, thus releasing themselves of anxiety born of anger and hatred and allowing themselves to be filled with God's healing energy.

Insisting that daily habits of prayer would make the Eucharist more meaningful, as well as "bring increasing health" to the Christian, Dougall, however, sought to differentiate her liturgical approach from the "occasional miracles of healing" claimed by divine healers.[90] Arguing for an integrated dualism of body and soul in which the material and spiritual were mutually inextricable, Dougall asserted that the tripartite view of soul, spirit, and body (a marker of Pentecostal anthropology), was contrary to both the thought of Jesus and to modern thought and stood in the way of a fully embodied faith. For Dougall, faith in the "divine and natural" law of God's healing was also to extend toward others, taking on political consequences: "We believe that if the world is to be saved we must all make our venture of faith in this Divine power to heal and reinforce our individual lives, soul and body, from within, to heal and reinforce the life of each wounded nation spiritually and materially, to heal and reinforce the torn and divided life of humanity."[91] This was a mark of the experimentalist: healing the embodied spirit would transform the political world. Not always able to garner positive reviews (one writer described *The Christian Doctrine of Health* as "a singularly dry discussion of spiritual healing, which may be useful to victims of hyperaesthesia"),[92] Dougall managed to craft a place for herself as a lay theologian who gathered a circle of Anglican modernists about her. Unlike the confident treatises of Dearmer and Du Vernet, however, her writing was often tempered by gestures of feminine modesty and self-criticism, and she made no claims to being a healer herself.[93]

By contrast to Dougall, Anglican Dorothy Kerin, founder of an Anglo-Catholic divine healing movement, turned to what she believed were her own divinely bestowed gifts of healing to establish her authority. Concerned less with transforming the political and economic world around her and more with healing individual Christians of their ills, Kerin would go on to inspire a healing movement in the Canadian Anglican church that was poised between a charismatic and a liberal supernaturalism. According to her own testimony, and the numerous testimonies of doctors, family members, friends, priests, and journalists included in her first autobiography, *The Living Touch*, Kerin was bedridden for years with chronic and life-threatening illnesses, living in London under modest circumstances with her mother and siblings. In 1912, at the age of twenty-two, Kerin professed she experienced divine healing, when commanded by the voice of an angel to rise and walk. Commissioned by a "beautiful woman" in a dream vision to heal the sick despite the critics she would encounter, Kerin was further emboldened by visions of Jesus, who, she recounted, physically appeared to bestow healing on her with his "living touch."[94]

When a friend worried that Kerin "was in danger of being spoilt through speaking at too many spiritualist and theosophical meetings," she was taken in by a High Church Anglican priest, Richard Langford-James and his wife with whom she lived for fourteen years.[95] Under vows of obedience, poverty, and chastity made to Langford-James as her spiritual director, Kerin became a full-blown Anglican mystic, devoting her days and nights to prayer, exhibiting the stigmata, and engaging in wrenching bouts of self-negation in her prayers to various saints. With her friend and biographer, as well as several Bishops and clergy, describing her as a saint "who lived in complete obedience to her spiritual director" and who thus became "an instrument, tried and perfected to His purposes . . . forged by God," the accounts of Kerin's life as a young woman read like the narratives of medieval women mystics, who, in their bodily suffering and tortured obedience find sweet glimpses of the peace of faith.[96] Breaking from Langford-James in the wake of a spurned marriage proposal from an American cleric, Kerin experimented with various approaches to both her spirituality and her livelihood when she happened on the perfect combination of the two by opening the first of what would be several "Homes of Healing." Each one, financed by donations, was outfitted with a chapel and fine interior decoration in accord with her belief in the "healing agency of beauty" sanctioned by God, which led her to "give Him all the best and most beautiful things I can."[97] The last of these homes, opened in 1948, became Burrswood Christian Hospital, established on a country estate in Kent, just south of London.

A self-declared channel for God's healing power, Kerin was a controversial woman, in the lineage of Christian healers such as Mary Baker Eddy and Aimee Semple McPherson. She blended a testimony of personal healing with mysticism, charismatic authority, and shrewd real estate investments, always with an eye to gathering further testimonies and sanction for her healing gifts from clerics, Bishops, Archbishops, and even princesses. Whereas some were skeptical of what they saw as a healing mission focused on the wealthy and influential, others became her devoted disciples, writing numerous hagiographical accounts of her healing gifts.[98] Not sharing the political convictions of Dougall and Dearmer, Kerin was nevertheless a product of the same climate of Anglican healing experimentalism, whose version of the "privileged work" of healing would later resonate in Canada.[99]

Taking less liturgical paths, psychic supernaturalists were also scattered among the United Church and related ecumenical organizations such as the YMCA. In a pamphlet countering the Pentecostal approach to faith healing, United Church minister Robert Fairbairn used language strikingly similar to Du Vernet's to describe the "natural" role of Christianity in the process of healing: "the interaction of immanent divine energy with latent human capacity through the liberating influence of a mighty sympathetic personality."[100] The same year, he proclaimed in the *Christian Guardian* that the SPR was a "brave and brilliant" pathway to a scientific "rationale for prayer."[101] Just after the formation of the United Church, Fairbairn developed his own version of radio theology, arguing that the same "polarity" underlying electricity and radio was also "a divine principle of the universe" that could turn disputes and contradictions among Christians—such as those quarreling over church union in the 1920s—into productive and complementary "contraries."[102] United Church minister E.G.D. Freeman was more privately intrigued by the possibility of communication with the spirits of the dead via mediums and revealed in unpublished autobiographical reflections that in the 1930s he and several members of his congregation participated in regular sittings with a medium (who was also a United Church member). Noting that he had been on the way to being convinced of the healing power of spirit communication, Freeman maintained that he had reservations about the practice and that he gave it up in the 1940s.[103] By 1941, Freeman was a professor at United College in Winnipeg who communicated across distance in a more conventional style, giving war-time radio addresses from a Winnipeg church, in which he called on Christians to strive for social justice and to struggle against totalitarianism and praised the contribution of the Christian missionary in the spread of "scientific medical service."[104]

Fairbairn and Freeman did not go as far in their experimentalism as did some of their Methodist and United Church colleagues, whose commitment to the scientific and Christian legitimacy of psychic healing led to their eventual exclusion from the church. Although the 1899 heresy trial of Methodist minister-turned-spiritualist Benjamin Austin was an early example, there was a spate of spiritualist-leaning clergy who left the fold (or were kicked out) in the late 1920s and early 1930s.[105] Frederick Maines, a minister working as a YMCA secretary in southern Ontario, was suspended in 1931 from the United Church ministry after founding the spiritualist Church of the Divine Revelation in St. Catharines, together with his wife Minnie and his sister-in-law, Jenny Pincock. Convinced that spiritualism was a step in the evolution of true Christianity and that the survival of spirits after death helped to validate such points of orthodoxy as Jesus's resurrection, Maines continued to see himself as a committed yet inclusivist Christian: "Ancient Judaism and Christianity had no monopoly on divine revelation. God was in Confucius, Gautama, in Mohammed, in St. Francis of Assisi, in poets, authors, and artists."[106]

Heirs to the "cosmic consciousness" of the Walt Whitman devotee and medical doctor Maurice Bucke, another southernwestern Ontario mystic (the region that also produced Aimee Semple McPherson and Belle Oliver), Maines and Pincock eventually founded the Radiant Healing Centre.[107] Here, they practiced their own version of light therapy and distance healing that drew on spiritual Angelic Helpers as well as prayers such as the following: "I am a Light that radiates health. Through this RADIANT HEALING CENTRE I radiate health throughout the world. And unto those who need this power shall this radiation do wonders."[108] Disillusioned with the "intolerance" she met within the United Church, Jenny Pincock described her embrace of spiritualism and radiant healing rituals as a reluctant departure from her church home: "We continued attending our churches, loath to accept the situation. But we found ourselves gradually 'outgrowing our dwelling places.'"[109] It was only after establishing a new church outside the bounds of the United Church, however, that Maines was suspended from ministry.

While the Christian Spiritualism of Maines and Pincock attracted the private attention of a number of United Church members, including the well-known poet E. J. Pratt, the public reaction of the Church was vociferously negative as local clergy alternated among charging them with heresy for disbelieving the divinity of Christ, dismissing their writings as "twaddle," and anxiously warning that spiritualism was a regressive force for both Christianity and modernity, which would, presaging Bultmann, bring "an end to all our modern science and mechanics."[110] By moving their interests in psychic healing from the realm of the apologetic text to the public establishment of a new and competing institution with innovative ritual forms, Christians such as Pincock and Maines had crossed the line from Christian experimentalism to competitive heresy.

More prominent in his day than either Fairbairn or Du Vernet, and less polarizing than Maines and Pincock, American Sherwood Eddy (1871–1963) was an experimentalist who managed to walk the fine line between heresy and innovation as a robust example of supernatural liberalism. An ecumenical Protestant missionary who traveled the world for the YMCA, and who was frequently cited in the United Church newspaper, Eddy saw himself both as a champion of the dispossessed and an interlocutor of the powerful. Eddy was a wealthy man with the ability to finance his own travels and endeavors; his second wife, Louise Gates Eddy, past director of the Canadian YWCA, brought him into regular contact with Toronto audiences. Whether writing to Stalin from his Manhattan apartment with recommendations for how to improve the shoddy state of tourist facilities in the U.S.S.R., observing Hitler's speeches (and condemning him afterwards), or enjoying a personal audience with Gandhi, Eddy saw himself as a Christian man of the world whose mission was "not only to win or change individuals, all-important as that was, but to build a new social order and to Christianize the whole of life and all its relations, industrial, social, racial, and international."[111] A friend and benefactor to Union Theological Seminary professor Reinhold Niebuhr—both a defender and critic of liberalism—Eddy moved in circles that were at the heart of liberal Protestant thought and social action. In the 1920s and 1930s at the same time that he worked to organize African-American sharecroppers in the southern United States and engendered controversy for his socialist and pacifist leanings, Eddy found himself increasingly engaged with seeking scientific proof of personal immortality and psychic healing through experiments with psychic mediums. In 1925 encouraged by his brother and a Quaker friend, Eddy participated in a sitting with the renowned (or notorious) medium Marjorie Crandon and reported witnessing five pounds of ectoplasm moving in front of him for two hours.[112] (Ectoplasm was held to be an emanation from the spirit world that came from the medium's ears, nose, throat, or other orifices that looked like cheesecloth, or as a suspicious United Church *New Outlook* editorial suggested, *was* cheesecloth.)[113] From the 1930s to the 1950s Eddy had regular sittings with mediums, including E. A. Macbeth, whose spirit guide was a dead Irish priest and Arthur Ford, a former Disciples of Christ minister who became something of a spiritualist celebrity.

Similarly to Du Vernet and to Maines, Eddy's fascination for the possibilities of psychic and spiritual communication arose in the context of an active life as a missionary and YMCA secretary. Beginning his career as a YMCA missionary to India and treasuring his Christianity to the end, Eddy eventually came to the conclusion that all religions offer "the great mystic experience of the divine."[114] His universality was shaped by experience—after spending ten days with Gandhi in 1929 Eddy was seemingly more impressed than Dearmer had been and declared Gandhi the most spiritual man he had ever met.[115] Eddy's universalism and his

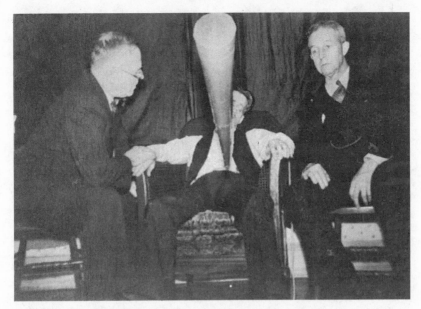

FIGURE 8. Sherwood Eddy (left) with medium Leonard Stott and Quaker friend Edward C. Wood, ca. mid-1940s, probably 1946, from a photograph pasted into a copy of *You Will Survive Death*. Courtesy of Special Collections, Yale Divinity School Library, Record Group 32, Eddy (George Sherwood) Papers.

exploration into psychic phenomena were both rooted in his earlier grappling with the role of doubt in the life of a Christian. With a liberal experimentalist's dedication to truths based on experience, Eddy contended that doubt was a necessary stage in achieving a strong personal faith, since it "marks a natural transition from a secondhand tradition to a firsthand faith, from a borrowed creed to a personal conviction, from the realm of authority to the reality of experience."[116] His experimentalism was not without its tensions however. By the time he wrote his second autobiography, Eddy had come to privilege scientific paths to "reality" and to cast his psychic interests as a quest "to find out if there actually is sufficient scientific evidence to support belief in survival, or personal immortality, or whether such belief is purely a question of blind religious faith."[117]

Eddy's writing about psychic phenomena was riven by anxiety, as he worried about fraudulent mediums, bemoaned the incredulity of both scientists and "orthodox Christians," and returned frequently to his own *almost* implacable doubt. He gained the confidence to write publicly about his psychic experiments only once he received his long-sought proof of the reality of spirits: the "apport" of an ash tray from his house to the home of the medium, via a form of lightning-quick spiritual transportation. In addition to this psychic materialization, Eddy's anxiety was somewhat appeased through the proofs that he drew from Christian scriptures and "personalities," including Jesus and Paul, the "great psychic Apostle."[118] Arguing in a vein similar to other Christian spiritualists, Eddy contended that "under different names the New Testament records the occurrence of trance, mediumship, telepathy, clairvoyance, clairaudience, precognition, and other psychic phenomena," which, taken together with Jesus's healing of the sick, provide scriptural evidence of psychic healing.[119] According to Eddy, the resurrection of Jesus demonstrated that "it was in the founding of the Christian religion . . . that there appeared the greatest manifestation of psychic experience and phenomena ever known in history."[120]

Although an Anglican modernist denounced the "strange *farrago* of psychic phenomena" in *You Will Survive Death* as "all very strange—and most of it very distasteful," in 1962 the *United Church Observer* saw fit to reprint an article written by a U.S. woman who cited Eddy's Christian spiritualism as her inspiration for employing psychic mediums to contact her son who died at nineteen years old.[121] Eddy—who himself had suffered the death of his teenage son—expected the critic and would have been happily surprised by his admirer.

> When I recall the bitter opposition that almost every new science has had to meet at its first appearance, I am not surprised at the reception that psychic investigation and evidence of survival meet on the part of the prejudiced majority . . . probably the majority of the orthodox, conventional Christians view the whole psychic field with deep antipathy or traditional prejudice.[122]

In addition to finding spiritual materializations such as ectoplasm "distasteful," modernist critics of Christian spiritualism (including those who criticized the Dearmer's automatic script) found the messages from the spirit world "pitiable" and platitudinous. Where spiritualists focused on the very "fact" of the spirit communication as proof of immortality, their critics pointed out that the mundane messages the spirits conveyed rarely went beyond "vague appeals to peace and goodwill," and failed to engage the moral values of an "enlightened Christian."[123]

A pragmatic Christian who was an early proponent of sexual education—and even of women's sexual pleasure within marriage—as a path to "healthy" morality, Eddy's forays into the epistemologies and experiments of psychic research reflected both his love and his fear of embodied existence. Arguing that psychic techniques such as telepathy were a tool of healing the physical body as well as authenticating the soul, Eddy sought to establish these techniques as both scientific and Christian. He did so as a man who had spent his life traveling the world, encountering and often embracing difference, while remaining tied to Christianity. Although eminent colleagues such as John Mott defended his economic and political radicalism (Mott also came to Belle Oliver's defense on occasion), Eddy's psychic experimentalism has not been so celebrated.[124] In trying to come to grips with Eddy's psychic turn, missionary historian Brian Stanley suggested that Eddy's interests in psychic healing were merely "bolted onto his existing theological framework." However superficial he considered it, Stanley also argued that Eddy's "supernaturalism" was reason enough to remove Eddy from the category of a liberal Protestant. The suggestion that "supernaturalism" was at odds with liberalism, however, is clearly at odds with the evidence. Even Reinhold Niebuhr, Eddy's lifelong friend and the paradigmatic North American realist theologian with harsh words for what he saw as optimistic excesses of liberalism, could laud liberal Protestants with psychic interests for their "real spirituality."[125] Clerics such as Du Vernet and ecumenical travelers such as Eddy experimented with psychic supernaturalism by bringing scientific language into conversation with scripture and spiritualism, while they also pursued more "typically" liberal concerns, such as questioning imperialism and working toward ecumenical and interfaith unions as modes of "healing."[126]

FRONTIERS OF THE UNCONSCIOUS

Narratives of the frontiers of mind, spirit, and empire—whether the Anglican remapping of First Nations lands as the "Diocese of Caledonia" or the Freudian remapping of the "soul" as the id, ego, and superego—occurred at the intersection of spiritual imaginations and sensing, suffering, bodies.[127] With new ways of conceptualizing the relation of mind, body, and soul thanks to such notions as the subconscious, liberal Christians experimented with techniques of healing that attempted to harmonize insights from Freudian psychoanalysis, psychic research, and continuing currents of electrically inspired therapies. They did so as Christians confronting not only a remapping of the soul at the hands of psychology, but also remapping of the world in a postwar and an imminently postcolonial world.

James Ward (1885–1958), an Alberta-raised, Oxford-educated priest of the parish of St. Stephen-in-the-Fields in Toronto, took an experimental direction less modeled on the laboratory and more focused on the liturgical. Ward, author of both novels and religious essays, drew on telepathy both as a handy plot device in his fiction and as a source of spiritual healing, but his greatest confidence lay in the possibilities for a "Christian conversion" of psychoanalysis. Largely based on his books, *The Commonwealth of the Soul* and *The Window of Life* (an eight-week series of bible studies and New Thought-style affirmations and meditations), Ward wrote a series on the "psychological aspects of religion" in the *Canadian Churchman*.[128] In this series he popularized Freudian theory without mentioning Freud (but he did give a nod to Jung). Arguing for the cultivation of "mental dietetics" that would recognize the power of the subconscious, especially when it was unwisely repressed, Ward thought that the "law" of suggestion should be applied to liturgies, prayer, hymns, and the visitation of the sick. By this he meant that clergy should "suggest" positive images to the minds of their parishioners gathered in their sanctuary, thus cultivating the will to believe and channeling human instincts to the benefit of both spirit and body. "In healing, in music, in art, in education, in religion, the aim is to get past a stress upon technique to the great joy of an ability to perform without effort," he wrote.[129] Such effortlessness required discipline, which Ward, directly citing Du Vernet, suggested could come through meditative prayer in which one "woo[ed] the mind into the Great Mystery of the larger self," or what he also called the Christ-self. He also recommended psychoanalysis over confession, since instead of tabulating sins, psychoanalysis allowed "free play for expression to suppressed energy."[130] Psychoanalysis, however, had to have a higher, Christian goal—a "modern and scientific" kind of conversion that allowed an "opening of the soul to health," in which "the mental clots within the soul must be cleared and self-converted."[131]

Noted in a *Canadian Churchman* report as a man with "considerable experience" in spiritual healing, Ward shared the ritual basis of his sacramentalist psychology with Dearmer. He was less interested in psychic phenomena, however, and more interested in the psyche. Reminding his readers that "the psychic is just the Greek for soul," Ward sought to popularize psychoanalysis as a ritual tool of healing in both liturgical and private settings.[132] Although on one hand he warned that psychoanalysis was the task of an expert, he also encouraged his readers to will themselves to "educate" their emotions through suggestion by retreating

FIGURE 9. Sanctuary of
St. Stephen-in-the-Fields
Anglican Church, Toronto,
photograph, interior, 1895.
James Ward became the
Priest of this parish in 1926.
Courtesy of Toronto Public
Library, (TRL): E 4-33c.

to a quite place and repeating slowly, "I am within the Infinite."[133] Echoing Christian Science and the Emmanuel Movement in their focus on idealism and suggestion, Ward's psychological sacramentalism differed from these movements in his explicit embrace of psychoanalysis—he espoused the virtues of a science of the mind and soul that intended to challenge both "prudish social convention" and "prejudicial religious convictions."[134]

Ward walked his talk by sharing a remarkably intimate and elaborate symbolic reading of one of his own complexes within the pages of the *Canadian Churchman*. According to Ward, this complex manifested itself in an obsessive dislike for the color red and an inability to write sufficiently appreciative reviews of the work of his mentor, the English Bishop Charles Gore (also a mentor to Dearmer). Ward traced these two issues to twin subconscious aversions to blood and the word "gore," which were prompted by a trip to a slaughterhouse as a young boy: "I was reacting to the impression (still active in my soul) of the slimy blood of the slaughterhouse floor and the fear that the maddened bullock would break loose and gore me." A few paragraphs later, after mentioning an "unpleasant experience" at Goring-on-Thames, Ward continued his self-analysis.

In the fear of the bullock, we were back at the instinct of self-preservation. The cow and the calf line of association would probably have borne on to the sex instinct. The Goring[-on-Thames] incident had such a connotation. Even the good Bishop in an association running back through another line of analysis was connected with the sex instinct . . . that is, sex used as Jung used the term, not necessarily with any sordid accompaniment of thought, but as the general urge by which life finds expression and even its very being.

Citing Jung as a means to legitimate his connection of the sex instinct to Bishop Gore, Ward—a lifelong bachelor—implied a heterosexual frame in the next paragraph by revealing that he had read his article aloud to a blonde- (and not red-) haired friend who "with something of a twinkle in her eye" asked, "Are you any more comfortable on a red cushion now?"[135]

Ward ventured beyond flirtation in his unpublished sonnets, short stories, and one novel, as he repeatedly hinged his narratives on what in his day would have been trangressive (heterosexual) love—sometimes communicated telepathically. His literary imaginings of the ways that subconscious drives and telepathic communion could transform human relationships took Du Vernet's family-based, Christian-rooted telepathic intimacy into much more unstable and erotic territory. One short story described an encounter between two strangers in a café—already a risqué beginning, especially for a clergyman. Don, the man whose point of view the reader shares, inadvertently thinks out loud and associates red strawberries with red lips, to which the woman, Peggy, responds, "'I think you are a psychologist sir,' she ventured in smiling banter. . . . 'A specialist in complexes, and trains of thought, and suggestions, and perhaps telepathy . . . who knows.'" Moments later, Don lays out his palm and Peggy grasps it. "'Quick,' he said, 'You spoke of telepathy . . . can you tell me what I am thinking of?' She laughed at his ruse, but there was nothing unmanly in the pressure of his hands."[136] Despite his toying with the feminized trope of mind-reading, Don ends up being invited back to Peggy's "dingy attic." After a complicated revelation of identities, the story ends not by Don reading Peggy's mind, but by the more conventional approach of him asking her to reveal what she was thinking: "I was thinking again how many beautiful things there are in life which are frowned on by society, yet which society longs to do. . . . and I was thinking of a rather dingy attic."

The notion of telepathy in the service of challenging society's conventions takes a very different shape in Ward's unpublished novel, *Pilgrim Haven*. Set in the early twentieth-century foothills of Alberta where Ward grew up, the novel is also filled with coincidental meetings and revelations of mistaken identity, this time against the backdrop of the frontier clash of Europeans and First Nations peoples. At one point in the novel, Dudley, a white woman rancher, earlier likened to a "guiding priestess of the soul," watches from a hill as women, men, and children of the Blood Nation mow the fields to prepare them for white farmers coming to the region: "She saw in vision the great westward march of empire, the inevitable, inexorable grip of the binding of the free lands to a harder husbandry, the passing of that class to which she herself belonged. And, as the vision came to her, there stood silently beside her one whom, in all his saturnine gravity, she had learned to revere." At her side she found her friend Hawkeye, of the Peigan First Nation, who tells her that he refuses to fence in the land and thus to contribute to white expansion. Dudley then thinks to herself, "This thing called western civilization—was it less barbarous, less crude, more Christian than that life which it had supplanted. Did the great Spirit All Father take such great cognizance of colour? Would her race not have to answer for their heritage? Could they answer in any equitable way?"[137] Somehow, "by some telepathic force," the narrator tells us, Hawkeye reads Dudley's mind, and replies by telling her that he plans to leave for the hills to maintain his freedom. The telepathic connection between Hawkeye and Dudley allows them to share their disgust for the advancing frontiers of empire, while adding to Dudley's developing characterization as priestess of the soul.[138] Whether using the active metaphor of mindreading or the passive one of telepathic thought transference, Ward's characters tapped into telepathy to challenge prudery or to question imperial expansion.

Unlike Du Vernet whose encounter with First Nations peoples led him to protest residential schools, Ward's "twinges" of uneasiness about imperial expansion were not translated into action. Ward wrote these unpublished stories, his articles on psychology, and his books on spiritual healing before assuming his position as the priest of St. Stephen-in-the-Fields in 1926 and before his eventual appointment as a Canon of St. Paul's Cathedral in Toronto. As with Dearmer, his career trajectory was not simple and was disrupted by World War I. In the words of the lawyer who interviewed him on behalf of the Bishop of Toronto in preparation for his St. Stephen's appointment, "The case is a peculiar one owing to the number of fields in which he appears to have worked and the temporary and non-parochial character of his engagements."[139] Credited with being a homesteader in Alberta, an Oxford student, a military chaplain in World War I, a dramatist, and a poet—all before being a parish priest—Ward translated this diversity of experience into published and unpublished prose that went a certain distance toward unsettling Christian mores and colonial assumptions.[140]

Once in a more formal role in the church hierarchy, however, Ward seems to have toned down his outspoken challenges to social convention. Despite having rooted his challenges in a Christology that tapped into the subconscious to cultivate the Christian who would be "a Christ-man with a Christ-mind." Ward's critique of empire and prudery seems not to have survived his change of ecclesiastical status.[141] He turned his energies to writing and producing church plays in collaboration with professional actors such as Dora Mavor Moore and Earle Grey as well as to utilizing the new technology of radio not for telepathic healing but for broadcasts of his sermons and plays. Seemingly leaving behind his critique of imperial expansion, but maintaining an interest in social and political criticism, Ward also turned his pen to writing odes to England and, eventually, to the new Queen on her coronation.[142] He joined the Society of St. George, a club entirely dedicated to glorifying England and her empire, and as his casket was carried out of St. Stephen's in 1958, one of his honorary pallbearers was the Society's president.

THE LONGED-FOR WORLD RELIGION

Experimentalists were found not only among seminary-educated Protestants contending with the rise of newly authoritative scientific discourses, but also among laywomen and new converts. As Protestants with an awareness of cultural difference and growing sensibilities of how their own cultures were differently implicated in the global politics of imperial expansion experimentalists proffered hopeful visions of a universalism that would bring peace and harmony through what was often a vague spirituality of connection. The technological supernatural liberalism of experimentalists repeatedly returned to the body as a specific site not only of divine-human encounter, but also of knowledge that articulated itself via scientific, biblical, and spiritual proofs. This experimentalist "knowing" was profoundly influenced by engagements with difference in missionary contexts. Ironically, perhaps, experimentalism led away from the indefatigably outward movement of medical missions and brought its practitioners toward more intimate and inwardly focused settings—whether the small group gathered around the séance table or the yogic practitioner at one in the sun with God.

In his 1927 book *Are Missions a Failure?*, U.S. journalist Charles Selden told his readers, "This book is by a disinterested correspondent who went to Asia thinking that the missionary enterprise was futile." Based on articles commissioned by the *Ladies' Home Journal* focused on the current state of Gandhi's home rule movement and the Nationalist movement in China, Selden's book concluded with an optimistic reversal. Although there were definitely "bad" missionaries out there, "of the kind who still call all Asiatics 'heathen,' " and who "know nothing about the ancient religions of the East or brush them aside as so much rubbish," Selden contended that most Christian missionaries were marked by their "interreligious courtesy" and their willingness to learn from and be transformed by other religions. For Selden this would have global significance: "It is by the rapidly increasing friendly relations between such men [devout adherents of an Eastern religion] and the intelligent Christian missionaries that an approach is being made possible which, centuries hence, may lead to the longed-for world religion."[143]

Their yearning for a universal peaceful religion that would bring healing from the ravages of bodily illness and from what Winslow called the "virus of our own [the West's] materialism,"[144] has clearly not come to pass. Having transcended neither medical materialism nor capitalist consumerism, the optimistic combination of Protestant experimentalism was deeply shaped by the ironies of colonial mimicry. Caught in a "double bind" similar to that described by Dipesh Chakrabarty in his account of Indian historiography, liberal Protestantism must be understood as both the "subject and object of modernity."[145] From a twenty-first century perspective, Du Vernet's and Winslow's engagements with Tsimshian and South Asian religions contained within them a mimicry (and appropriation) not only of other religions but also of discourses of science. Neither scientists nor yogis, their universalism was embedded in a progressive faith rooted in Christianity—a religion considered increasingly irrelevant by science and increasingly parasitical by non-Christian Indians, whether of the South Asian or North American sort. Mimicry or not, however, the experimentalist approaches of Du Vernet, Eddy, Winslow, and Appasamy were the forebears of much of the combinative spiritualities of our current age.

Radio mind and other versions of telepathy were sensational forms for divine communication that drew on the innovations of communication technologies as both metaphor and explanation. The idea of telepathy brought these Christians to think across frontiers of difference based on gender, racialization, religion, science, and empire, and, as Ward's novel demonstrated, to begin to realize the way their own traditions were built on the injustices perpetrated at frontiers. Linking prayer to telepathy, however, also made commonality out of difference in a way that was unsettling to both theological and biomedical orthodoxies. Christian experimentalists who sought justification for spiritual and psychic healing in the paradigm of the scientific experiment or the newly scientific discourse of psychology, as well as in the authority of biblical texts, were ultimately caught between two different kinds of skepticism. Both scientific and biblical epistemologies have skepticism, if not condemnation, of "energies" and "spirits" not within their realm, whether energy theories such as radio mind or channels for the spirits of the dead via automatic writing. Gendered subtexts, occult "heresies," and the religious practices of colonized others combined to shape experimentalists' anthropologies of the spiritual body as a space where difference could heal. Merging the physicality of healing with nascent communication technologies and theories of psychology, liberal Protestants brought the experiment into the arena of cultural and religious encounter seeking, in their view, to love and change the world and to be loved and changed themselves in turn.

CHAPTER 4

Evil Spirits and the Queer Psyche in an Age of Anxiety

With demons did this wide world swarm,
All eager to devour us,
We need not fear their threatened harm,
They shall not overpower us.

—"Our God's a Fortress," by Martin Luther, translated by Jay
Macpherson, in *The Hymn Book of the Anglican Church of Canada
and the United Church of Canada*, 1971

On September 29, 1967, the front-page headline in the morning edition of the *Toronto Star* proclaimed, "We Take Witchcraft Seriously but Don't Practise It: Priest." Later that day, the afternoon paper countered with: "Girl Spanked before Death to Cast out Devil—Ex-cultist." By October 3, the *Star* announced with restrained incredulity: "Witness Believes Evil Spirits Can 'Inhabit' Human Body." For four days that autumn, the local papers became the site for a fierce dispute over the anthropology of the spiritual body, as journalists covered the coroner's inquest into the death in June 1967 of a young woman, Katherine Globe, at the rectory of an Anglican church in downtown Toronto. Globe, eighteen years old, died of a brain abscess caused by meningitis. No doctors attended her during the last nine days of her life, as she lay moaning in her bed in the manse of St. Matthias Anglican Church, under the care of her guardians, the Anglican priest Canon G. Moore Smith and his wife.

In her last hours, the inquest revealed, Globe received repeated "spankings" from four men: Father Smith; his son David, who was also Globe's fiancé; the Assistant Priest, Douglas Tisdall; and her older brother Alexander, a Wycliffe College student (Du Vernet's alma mater). All the men were members of a tight-knit prayer group—which some called a cult—housed in the small red brick church of St. Matthias. The spankings were intended, according to various witnesses at the inquest, to "push the devil out of her," to chastise Globe for "vying for attention," or to demonstrate her fiancé's "disapproval of her childishness by treating her as a child."[1] After Globe's death, Father Smith, wearing purple vestments, went to the morgue along with Tisdall and Alexander Globe to anoint her dead body in an unusual liturgy of "last rites" that included beseeching God to raise Katherine from the dead, since, according to Smith, "healing doesn't stop with death."[2]

The mingled liturgy and violence that these four men, all intimately related to Katherine, directed at her in the hours before and after her death were in keeping with the wider approach of the group to "the cultivation and disciplining" of the spirit. In tune with its times, the prayer group used the jargon of 1960s slang—being spiritually "off" or "potting out," for example, were causes for discipline—although it distinguished itself both from hippie culture and from Pentecostal practices of speaking in tongues. The group's anthropology, however, was markedly focused on spiritual intervention, whether by Satan or God. As Tisdall put it, "the root of all illness is spiritual" and "God can heal disease directly—disease of body, mind, and spirit."[3]

Since 1948 G. Moore Smith had been the priest of St. Matthias Anglican Church, a pretty Anglo-Catholic parish founded in downtown Toronto in 1873. "Born again" in 1952, Smith became increasingly charismatic, joining forces with a young literature and theology student, Douglas Tisdall, and a female benefactor, Marjorie Rogers, who was dubbed the "leader of the cult" in the press coverage.[4] Both Smith and Tisdall came from prominent Toronto medical families; Rogers, the wife of a University of Toronto French professor, eventually left her husband for Tisdall. What began as a charismatic-influenced ministry of healing eventually became a hierarchical, tightly controlled community demanding complete obedience from its members and ensuring it through practices of shunning, exorcism, corporal punishment, and sexual abuse.[5]

Even the death of Katherine Globe, however, was not enough for the Anglican Diocese to call a stop to the prayer group. Even though high-ranking Anglican clergy had known of the increasingly coercive practices at St. Matthias, it was only after the coroner's inquest found Smith and his wife negligent in their care for Globe that Smith was forced to resign.[6] At the same time, the inquest into Katherine Globe's death was a remarkable example of the easy commensurability between the state and the Anglican Church. Although Coroner H. B. Cotnam acknowledged during the inquest that he was not an Anglican, he also declared that he knew from reading the *Anglican Book of Common Prayer* that the group's practices were beyond the bounds of Anglican doctrine. Willing to grant the power of God, Cotnam shifted between outrage and irony in his approach to the St. Matthias group. As *The Toronto Star* put it, "He said the group's 'stock reply seemed to be that "God can do anything" and that I will agree with.' But, Cotnam said, he thought it unusual to ask God to raise Miss Globe from the dead since God hasn't brought anyone back to life 'in almost 2,000 years' ".[7]

In the end Cotnam and the inquest's jury charged the Anglican Church to undertake a full probe of "faith healing" in the Toronto diocese, but no criminal charges were ever laid, as the circumstances of the death were deemed an affair of the church. As the Attorney-General Arthur Wishart mused, it was not "up to the attorney general to go prying into the faith (of people) in this field."[8] This respect for the church did not mollify Tisdall, however, who wrote his own outraged letter of resignation, in which he declared that the issue was really a theological dispute within the Anglican Church between the forces of disbelief and those faithful to spiritual reality. Indeed, he argued, the very fact of the inquest was a sign of the Church's capitulation to the secular: "I protest the fact that the bishop allowed an ecclesiastical matter to come before a secular court—a court completely unequipped to assess evidence on spiritual matters."[9] Even though many Anglican clergy defended some version of the "ministry of healing" in the course of the debate, both Tisdall and Smith contended that allowing medical doctors, psychiatrists, coroners, and lawyers to adjudicate the spirit was a telltale sign of declining faith.[10]

Although a United Church witness at the inquest made clear her condemnation of Smith's approach to healing, others within the United Church—and the *Toronto Star*—were somewhat more supportive of spiritual intervention, at least before the violent events at St. Matthias. In March of 1967, a few months before Globe's death, a *Toronto Star* article had enthusiastically profiled the healing mission of the Reverend Alex Holmes, under the headline "Quietness Replaces Emotionalism: Faith-Healing the United Way."[11] Holmes, a native of Scotland who had in the past spent nine years as minister of All Peoples' United Church in the northern Ontario city of Sault Ste. Marie, had returned to Canada from his new charge in Michigan in order to bring his healing service to Parkdale United Church in Toronto—a few miles down Queen Street from St. Matthias. Reminiscent of the media descriptions of James Hickson's

FIGURE 10. Newspaper image of Canon Moore Smith at court. Courtesy of the *Toronto Star*, October 4, 1967. From Norm James/GetStock.com.

"unemotional" liturgical style, the *Star's* coverage of Holmes turned to doctors, ministers, and the eyewitness testimony of the journalist to document the "amazing things" wrought by Holmes's prayers for the sick. In front of a crowd of about 500 people, Holmes quietly explained his approach:

> "Thought is powerful," he said, "and there is such a thing as the law of the materialization of belief: What you deeply believe tends to materialize in your experience. This law works negatively as well as positively—to make you sick as well as to heal. Tonight I want you to put this law to work positively. I want you to lift it up into your prayer life. Believe that what you deeply need, you will receive."

Listing the case of a middle-aged man in a "business suit" cured of a slipped disc and a shortened leg, of an elderly woman cured of gnarled arthritic fingers, and of a boy cured of his stammer, the article also recounted examples where Holmes's prayer had no visible effect. But the overall tone of the article—along with its picture of Holmes in action—was one of marveling approval.

With the visit of Holmes, Parkdale United Church continued its tradition of playing host to unusual testimonies to spiritual intervention; at the same church in 1899 Methodist minister Benjamin Austin gave

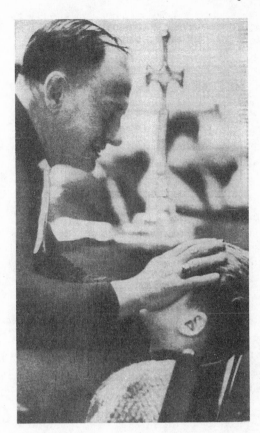

FIGURE 11. Newspaper image of Reverend Alex Holmes praying for sick child at a Healing Service in Toronto. Courtesy of the *Toronto Star*, March 11, 1967. From Frank Lennon/GetStock.com.

what the Methodist Church later declared to be a "heretical" sermon espousing the scientific veracity and healing effects of Christian spiritualism. Like Austin, Holmes also turned to the verification of "scientific" testing when in 1958 he allowed a Radio Corporation of America (RCA) engineer to photograph the "energy" emitted by his hands while healing.[12] Julius Weinberger, the director of research in RCA's New York laboratory, had taken another path to "radio mind," growing increasingly fascinated by parapsychology as proof for the existence of "disincarnate spirits" in his professional life as a telecommunications engineer.[13] Attaching photographic plates to Holmes's hands before the minister placed them on a young woman to heal her of "spastic curvature" of the spine, Weinberger found that the plates from Holmes, as well as those that he took of the hands of Episcopalian healer Agnes Sanford, revealed an unexpected "gray haze." In the newspaper account of the experiment, Holmes coyly avoided commenting on just what kind of proof this spirit photography offered, while clearly appreciating Weinberger's efforts at veridiction.

When compared to the intense "family" relationships cultivated at weeknight gatherings of the St. Matthias group, Holmes's performance of faith healing in a public liturgical setting was more akin to the ritual styles of earlier faith healers such as Hickson. His technological metaphors and "scientific testing," and his invocation of the "law of the materialization of belief," however, set him within a tradition of technological supernaturalism more in keeping with Du Vernet, with debts to the New Thought tradition. His cultivation of a language of energies and laws made for a scientistic mode of spiritual intervention that imagined power more mechanistically that the Satan-filled language of the charismatic St. Matthias group. Holmes's later career in the United States saw him affiliated with a diversity of healers, including the charismatic laywoman Kathryn Kuhlman and the medical mystic, psychologist Lawrence LeShan.[14] Although in the promotional material for his Parkdale visit Holmes situated himself among such luminaries as Karl Barth, Adlai Stevenson, and Henry Luce (all three spoke in the same Princeton Theological Seminary lecture series as Holmes), he inspired neither great admiration nor harsh rebuke from his United Church colleagues, who largely adopted a tone of curious surprise to find such a man in their midst.[15]

Not many liberal Protestants endorsed the varieties of spiritual intervention represented by Smith and Holmes, preferring instead the balance of spiritual equilibrium. Smith's satanic etiology, however, was more openly condemned than Holmes's spiritual technologies. In Anglican and United Church communities in the 1960s and 1970s, anthropologies of the spiritual body could go a number of ways: a pastoral counselor, committed to psychology as a tool of the Church, might criticize the "immature emotionalism" of a mass healing revival channeling interventions of the Holy Spirit but might cautiously appreciate the "shamanic" traditions of First Nations Christians. A charismatic might condemn the sexualized interpretations of overly "Freudian" Christians, or bemoan the excessive permissiveness of an "*I'm OK—You're OK*" self-help psychotheology, while praising the spiritual currency of a visiting faith healer.[16] The interdependent anthropologies of spiritual intervention and equilibrium carried different theologies of suffering, guilt, and responsibility within the holistic trinity of "body, mind, and spirit"—differences that remained at the core of later Protestant debates over sexuality, healing, and the spirit. Whereas advocates of spiritual equilibrium often set their analyses within wider contexts of what they saw as immoral capitalist economic systems, the pathological effects of imperialism, and distortedly inhibited views of sexuality, spiritual interventionists focused largely on the recesses of sin and distress that inhered in the individual body and memory that could be healed not by better social programs but, rather, by personal repentance and the forgiveness of God.

SPIRITUAL INTERVENTION: CHARISMATIC RENEWAL IN LIBERAL PROTESTANTISM

Liberal Protestants are not generally known for their spiritual charisms. When compared to charismatic Christians, however, they do hold equally strong convictions about the spirit. The pneumatic theologies of liberals and charismatics are in fact mutually—if often oppositionally—constituted. This mutuality has sometimes taken the form of recognizing similarities, as when, in a memorial to theologian Paul Tillich after his death in 1965, Rollo May, a well-known psychologist who studied with Tillich at Union Theological Seminary, chose to describe Tillich's wide popularity via glossolalia: "Let us take the distinguishing mark of Pentecost, 'speaking in tongues,' as Tillich's capacity to speak the language of the many diverse groups in our society." [17] More commonly, however, liberal and charismatic anthropologies of the spiritual body have been in tension, if not conflict. Whether bound by affinity or conflict, diverse approaches to healing and the spirit were inextricably linked—the spiritual intervention of the St. Matthias prayer group and that of Alex Holmes both grew within liberal Protestant enclaves that had long nurtured traditions of experimentalism in spiritual healing.

What is commonly known as the charismatic renewal in mainstream Protestantism is often credited with beginning in the 1960s, largely within Anglican/Episcopalian and Roman Catholic churches.[18] As with many "myths of origin" attached to spiritual eruptions—whether the controversial rappings of the Fox sisters in nineteenth-century spiritualism or the bible school glossolalia and Azusa Street excitement of the early Pentecostal movement—many narratives of the charismatic renewal do the simultaneous work of simplifying and mythologizing complex influences, contributing a sense of inevitability, or even divine intervention to these phenomena.[19] As a social movement, charismatic renewal emerged from many streams of influence and points of contact, including with (and within) liberal Protestantism. The U.S. Episcopalian priest Morton Kelsey epitomized the liberal charismatic: equally committed to a reinvigorated healing ministry that could include glossolalia, Jungian dream interpretation, and the depathologizing of homosexuality, Kelsey insisted that even "social-action oriented ministers" needed the spirit. In his words, "We can be continuously healing to others in soul, mind, and body, in their social oppression and poverty, only as we remain in touch with divine Love and let it move in and through us to others."[20]

Drawing its name from the "charisms" or gifts of God's grace narrated in Acts and described by Paul in 1 Corinthians—glossolalia, divine healing, and exorcism—charismatic renewal has brought Pentecostal practices and beliefs into more established churches, especially Anglican and Roman Catholic. Scriptural warrants such as 1 Corinthians 12:8–12 made space for a range of spiritual gifts within a unity of spirit. The claim of reaching directly back to New Testament times to "renew" spiritual gifts of healing is, as we have seen, not a particularly novel assertion. Joining in the persistent refrain of innovation that has accompanied experimentation with healing practices among North American Protestants, post–World War II charismatic Christians sought a new form of accommodation among mainstream Protestantism, charismatic practices, and biomedical care. But they had a range of forerunners beyond those conventionally found in the Pentecostal pantheon of healers.[21]

Beginning with the example of Frederick Du Vernet (other examples could be found among spiritualist Christians), we can trace a different genealogy of charismatic influence. Du Vernet's technique of spiritual radio was picked up and posthumously published in 1926 by Gaynor Banks, who in 1932, together with his wife Ethel Tulloch Banks, founded a U.S. Episcopalian spiritual-healing movement that became the International Order of St. Luke the Physician. Still functioning today within parish-based healing groups throughout Canada and the United States, primarily in Anglican churches but also in other denominations including a few United Churches, the Order of St. Luke has combined sacramental healing with charismatic influences. The parent organization offers regular "healing events" at local churches and at regional conferences, while it is always careful to note its complementarity with Anglican sacramentalism as well as biomedical techniques of healing. The members of individual branches of the Order of St. Luke , however, can sometimes be more charismatically focused than their local priest may advise —

enjoining not only healing prayer but also glossolalia and exorcism. As anthropologist Gail Grant found in her study of an Order of St. Luke group at an Anglican church in southwestern Ontario during the 1980s, women members—who made up an overwhelming majority of the group—experienced themselves as channels for God's healing spirit in ways not always sanctioned by their local priest. They were, however, encouraged by the deliverance ministries of Jesuit priests and Pentecostal evangelists they encountered at Order of St. Luke conferences.[22]

The Order of St. Luke's blend of sacramentalist and charismatic healing emerged at a time when several Anglican movements sought to achieve a medically legitimate High Church–Holy Spirit healing combination. Streams of what could be called Anglican charismatic healing, in the sense that it was based on channeling the healing power of Holy Spirit into the human body, have flowed in multiple international directions throughout the twentieth century. The Canadian branch of the Guild of Health, for example, moved from Percy Dearmer's moderate experimentalism on its founding in the 1920s to espousing a demonic etiology of disease in the 1980s.[23]

The strongest currents of post–World War II charismatic healing within the Anglican Church of Canada flowed from the United States and England, by the twin paths of books written by renowned healers, both clergy and lay, and by visits to Canadian churches by these healing celebrities. One frustrated *Canadian Churchman* writer lamented the slow pace of the spiritual healing movement in Canada in the 1950s but declared that two books would speed things up and "convince every Christian reader that Christ heals today"; one was written by American Episcopalian laywoman Agnes Sanford and the other by British minister R. A. Richard Spread. Although the *Churchman* writer found British Anglicans to be leading the way with James Moore Hickson as their model, the fact that "spiritual healing was in the air" was more likely attributable to U.S. healing celebrities, such as Sanford, whose books received particular attention in the *Churchman* and who established the "Agnes Sanford School of Pastoral Care" in 1958 as an axis for spiritual healing in Canada and the United States.[24] Offering traveling prayer clinics and workshops on spiritual healing to the Order of St. Luke, the Sanford School had many connections to the Anglican Church of Canada. The school was eventually led by a Canadian president, a retired Anglican priest, Charles Boole, of Ottawa, who also served as a consultant and practitioner on Deliverance and Exorcism to the Diocese of Ottawa.[25]

Sanford, daughter of Presbyterian missionaries to China and married to an Episcopalian priest, drew authority from narratives of her own experiences of divine healing both as a mother and an ill woman. Appreciatively called a combination of the "metaphysical and the sacramental" by another renowned Protestant healer, Glenn Clark, Sanford also made allusions to science and technology.[26] Undergirded by frequent biblical references, Sanford's approach to "healing light" was a theology of energy and experiment that was remarkably similar to that of Du Vernet. According to Sanford the scientific "discovery" that "the body is made up of specks of energy which attract and repel each other with tiny explosions of light" was the "literal manifestation" of Paul's claim in Ephesus that Christians must "walk as children of light." Sanford also turned to metaphors of electricity to explain that spiritual healing was all about the flow of divine energy: "We are the electric light bulbs through whom the light of God reaches the world."[27]

In order to become a vehicle of the "love-vibrations and the faith-vibrations of God," Sanford explained, one must cultivate both "thought-habits" and an "experimental" approach. The body, suggested Sanford, is a "laboratory exquisitely adapted to the working out of the power of God."[28] A habitual fourfold process would prepare a Christian to receive God's healing: (1) daily relaxation; (2) reminding oneself of "life outside yourself"; (3) asking "that life to come in and increase life in your body"; and (4) visualizing your body, or for the more advanced, forgetting the body and "concentrating the spiritual energies on God."[29] Just as Du Vernet considered the subconscious mind as the site where the "finite and the infinite meet and mingle" and Tillich understood it as the site of the demonic in the face of the ultimate, so too did Sanford understand the subconscious mind as the hub of divine-human interaction and healing. Sanford, however, held a more hierarchical view of the subconscious as a control center under orders from God: "For the forces of spirit, mind, and body are synchronized and ordered by the same inner control center, and that which affects one affects the other."[30] This synchronization could only be achieved by "re-education" of the subconscious through a "re-education in love" of God and of others: "God's life is a flow—it is a living water—it is active electricity—it is love vibrating at a definite wave length and intensity."[31] If this presumably metaphoric experiment in synchronizing living water with active electricity failed, Sanford argued that the fault was not that of God but of the human instrument.[32]

Careful to declare her appreciation of medical doctors as "God's servants," Sanford was not shy to testify to her convictions about instantaneous healings from wounds, cysts, and cancer. As long as the Christian "makes of his whole being, spirit, mind, and body, a receiving and transmitting center for the power of God," such miracles were possible.[33] Throughout her writings, Sanford carefully navigated the limits of her religious authority. Very conscious of the lack of sacramental authority she held because of her lay (and female) status, Sanford was nevertheless unwilling to let what Du Vernet called the "ecclesiastical machinery" stand in her way.[34]

Where Du Vernet's experiments with vibrational healing took the guise of a scientist directing his assistants, Sanford called for experimentation "combining the sacramental with the meditative" that would be both an individual and a group experience. Forming a prayer group, which she said would evolve naturally into a healing group, Christians would then be able to harness the vibrations of divine love via visualization, rote and spontaneous prayer, and meditation, thus achieving their own healing, the healing of others at a distance, and ultimately, the "healing of a sick world."[35] Meeting with both skeptical critics and valiant defenders in the pages of the *Canadian Churchman*, Sanford's vibrational theology had a lasting influence on Canadian Anglican healing practices from her writings, her "training school" visits to Canada as early as 1956, and her establishment of the School of Pastoral Care, which featured several Canadian Anglicans from across the country among its teachers.[36] She also had a long-lasting influence on Anglican clerics such as Canon G. Moore Smith and Morton Kelsey, who was bringing the message of the healing ministry to Canada into the 1980s.[37]

With both texts and travelers spreading the message, the charismatic version of an anthropology of body, mind, and spirit found its way into the pages of the *Canadian Churchman*, the pages of the *Anglican Prayer Book*, and into the parishes of the Anglican Church.[38] A series of articles "promoting Divine Healing" written by British Columbia–based Canon H. E. Taylor ran for almost two years in 1959–60, under the headline "Heal the Sick." Taylor was unremitting in his message that when Jesus spoke of abundant life, he meant that it should be "defined holistically, in body, mind, and spirit." Appearing just after the publication in 1958 of the Report of the Archbishops of Canterbury and York's Commission on "the Church's Ministry of Healing," Taylor's articles argued for a ministry of healing rooted in multiple sources: Jesus's example; the "sacramental principle" as found in the laying on of hands, Holy Unction, and Holy Communion; the prayers of the people, properly guided by the Church; and the divinely sanctioned gifts of medical professionals. Tempering his defense of divine healing with the caution that the Church must adjudicate the proper inflowing of the spirit, Taylor insisted every month that health was borne of balance and wholeness, closing his series with the prayer that "the love and healing power of our Blessed Lord will rest upon you, granting you peace, and strength of body, mind, and spirit."[39]

EVALUATING THE SPIRIT: MIDCENTURY COMMISSIONS ON HEALING

Even before the furor erupted over Katherine Globe's death, the Anglican hierarchy knew that it needed to think again about what constituted the "ministry of healing" in the post–World War II Church. Following the lead of the Archbishop of Canterbury, the Anglican Bishop of Toronto convened a committee in 1959 to determine how the Anglican Church should deal with the question of healing, calling together a group of clergy, psychiatrists, theologians, and former medical missionaries. Canon G. Moore Smith, of St. Matthias, sat on the committee, as did Dr. Florence Nichols, who, like Belle Oliver, had been a medical missionary to India. A psychiatrist, Nichols was noted in the *Canadian Churchman* for what many would now consider to be the problematic legacy of introducing electric shock treatments to her South Indian mission hospital.[40] Daniel Cappon, another Anglican psychiatrist and committee member, was a professor in the University of Toronto's Department of Psychiatry, with research interests in psychoanalysis, exemplified by his study of the dreams of the dying.[41]

In his contribution to the Committee's report, Cappon cast the problem of the ministry of healing this way:

> Once upon a time, the three were one: the body, the mind and the soul. They dwelt peacefully if temporarily together. Hence health, healing, wholeness, wholesomeness, and holiness have a common origin. Hence also the priest, the Shaman, the Indian Vedic and the witch doctor all practiced Medicine, Psychiatry and Religion. . . . With the advent of modern Medicine, the spirit was sheered off from the mind and body; and with the recent advances of Psychiatry, it seems as if a new kingdom has been created for specialist practice, a new mental realm. Thus today, guardians of the three: the body, the mind and the spirit, stand poised, eyeing each other, sometimes suspiciously, sometimes with friendly overtures to each other.[42]

If Cappon's nostalgic tale of the three guardians of the kingdoms of the self had a moral, it was this: priests and shamans should keep to the kingdom of the spirit. Cappon insisted that Christian clergy in particular must stop "meddling" with parishioners struggling with mental illness and must send them immediately to the realm of the trained psychiatrist. Poised between the kingdom of spirit and the kingdom of the mind as both an Anglican "churchman" and a professor of psychiatry, however, Cappon complicated these boundaries by cautiously endorsing the "wholeness" of what he called the "trinity of thought" of body, mind, and spirit. Although his psychoanalytic colleagues were not entirely convinced by Cappon's approach to delineating psychiatry and religion (one critiqued him for his "cloying piety"), his partitioning of the self into a holistic trinity of body, mind, and spirit was an attempted compromise between spiritual and psychoanalytic views of the self.[43] With a growing charismatic healing movement, however, the compromise was to become severely tested.

By the time the Bishop of Toronto's committee published its *Handbook on the Healing Ministry of the Church* in 1964, the psychologists on the committee seem to have won out over the charismatic Father Smith, which perhaps informed his breathless denunciation of experiment and dialogue in his statement to the press during the 1967 inquest.

> Not simply by theological nor liturgical renewal or the reaction to them, not by apologetically trying to look like the rest of the world nor by experimentation, dialogue, conference, committee meeting, financial campaign, or indeed the reaction to them, not by changing old truths to fit modern conditions, not by making God in our own image or by getting rid of Him altogether, not by denial of the supernatural, thereby forcing man to turn his instincts for these things in other directions, not by distrusting man's every motive nor by accepting him completely as he is will the visible church make a relevant contribution in our day or in any other, but by something so simple as to be seemingly unworthy of notice—the mission Christ announced for Himself and left for His Church: "The Spirit of the Lord is upon me because He has anointed me: He has sent me to announce good news to the poor, to proclaim release for prisoners and recovery of sight for the blind, to let the broken victims go free, to proclaim the year of the Lord's favor." Luke 4:18-19 (NEB)

Contrary to Smith's version of supernaturalism, the *Handbook's* rhetoric sounded more like Paul Tillich than either Smith or Agnes Sanford in stressing that Jesus's main goal was to bring people to "right relationship with ultimate things" and not to cast out their demons or to relieve their physical ailments: "Jesus' ministry must be seen as a whole, carried to the whole man and the primary part of it was not the healing of a man's body." Warning against the potential "quackery" of mass services of "charismatic" healing, the Committee delicately dismissed the terms "faith healing," "Divine Healing," and "spiritual healing," choosing instead the Anglican Prayer Book phrase, the "Church's ministry to the sick."[44] Clearly, their view of wholeness was not premised on either Smith's spiritual anointing or Agnes Sanford's "vibrationally charged, light-filled body."

THE MYSTIC CULT OF ST. MATTHIAS

After almost ten years of committees on healing, the St. Matthias scandal and publicity of the coroner's inquest sparked a new sense of crisis. The November 1967 *Canadian Churchman* was dominated by articles about the inquest and accounts of the practices at St. Matthias. An editorial sharply condemned the Diocese for not taking action based on its prior knowledge of what the editors' called Smith's "eccentric and mediaeval customs generally abhorred by most of Christendom." The editors insisted that the "reticence" of Anglican clergy to confront Smith was a grave problem: "The Church must air its mistakes and incompetence and heresies so that all may know it seeks to preserve the truth." Although several letter writers congratulated the newspaper for its frank coverage of the issue, another writer urged the church press to go further by discussing controversial movements and issues long before they became problems. In stark contrast, John B. Thompson, an Anglican priest, chastised the *Churchman* for its imitation of the sensationalism of the "daily press" and condemned the "morbidity and sadism of whoever is responsible for the production of *Canadian Churchman*." According to Thompson, the goal of the church press should be to elevate and inspire, not titillate, its readers, and it should not invade the privacy of clergy.[45]

Urged from within and without the church to confront directly the significance of the St. Matthias community, the Bishop of Toronto established yet another "Commission on the Ministry of Healing" made up of Anglican clergy, a United Church psychiatrist, a doctor, a lawyer, and Gordon Watson, the first Chair of the Department of Religious Studies at the University of Toronto, who was also active in the Toronto Institute for Pastoral Training. The Commission looked especially at the St. Matthias group, as well as at wider contexts of healing practices in the church, striking a largely conciliatory stance. After suggesting that medical doctors had not adequately monitored Globe's health, the Commission found the St. Matthias clergy to be characterized by "real love and devotion to the cause of the Church, and a concern for needy humanity." Somewhat reluctantly, the Commission Report concluded: "what began as a bold experiment in Christian outreach gradually degenerated into a mystic cult."[46] Calling Smith a "mere straw man" and a "victim of circumstances," the Commission laid most of the blame on Marjorie Rogers, "the all-wise matriarch," whom they considered to be the "key authoritative figure" with the real power.[47] Smith's mistake, the Commission decided, was that "he surrendered his lawful and rightful leadership into the hands of the inexperienced and untaught."[48] In addition to blaming the unlawfully powerful woman, the Report suggested that charismatic innovations, such as mass healing services and healing by proxy, made their way into the Diocese via "visitors" to the diocese "whose 'words and customs' have been received or followed uncritically by the unprepared."[49] This definition of visitor would have fit Agnes Sanford, along with a number of other charismatic healers.

In its larger conclusions the Commission advocated a pragmatic theology of the "wholeness" of body, mind, and spirit that accepted that the perfection of wholeness could never be fully achieved, and that a "healthy" self was always in a state of "becoming" but never "finished." The Report declared that healing should never be imposed, but only offered, and that all future exorcisms required the written permission of the Bishop. Suggesting that prayer for the Anointing of the Sick in the *Anglican Prayer Book* might contribute to inappropriate expectations for bodily healing, the Commission urged a revision: "If the word 'bodily' could be removed, it would permit 'health' in this prayer to be taken in its fullest sense—the whole person, including body, mind and spirit."[50] In shifting even more conclusively to a psychiatrically monitored spirituality, the Report also recommended the establishment of a Centre for Pastoral Services, the expansion of Clinical Pastoral Education, and the provision that chaplains must meet the accreditation standards of the Canadian Council of Churches. As for Smith and Tisdall, they were required to undergo psychiatric assessments, and Smith was to be supervised for two years before being placed in full charge of a parish again. Tisdall was to finish his doctorate in English literature and take another year of theological training before being allowed to have a probationary year in a parish.[51] The July–August 1968 *Canadian Churchman* included a long and detailed account of the findings of the Bishop's Commission on the Ministry of Healing with little editorial comment.[52]

Whereas Marjorie Rogers refused to meet with the Commission, her estranged husband William Rogers continued to play an active role in Anglican ecclesiastical life—a role marked by his unwilling encounter with satanic interventions. When serving on the committee that was producing a joint Anglican–United Church hymnal in preparation for a long-anticipated (but ultimately aborted) union of the two churches, Rogers was determined to expunge as much "devil" language from the hymns as possible. Rogers urged his United Church counterpart Jay Macpherson to retranslate Thomas Carlyle's version of Martin Luther's beloved hymn "A Mighty Fortress is our God," rendering the devil more subtly.[53]

Reading the Report's conclusions in the light of the recollections of Ann Smith, Canon Smith's daughter, provides a different perspective. Ann Smith spent four years in what she called the St. Matthias "cult" as a young adult and first spoke publicly about her experiences in a 1995 sermon, once she was herself an Anglican priest. Commanded to obey her father and other leaders while part of the prayer group, her sexuality was particularly policed. Assigned a boyfriend, she was also forced to participate in abusive rituals that included receiving the Eucharist and anointing with oil from her father when both were naked. Ann Smith finally resolved to leave the group after the death of Globe, who was her roommate, and after she had received an order to marry the boyfriend who had been chosen for her (and who was "struggling" with homosexuality). Coming to a conclusion very different from the Bishop's Commission when it considered the "matriarch" Marjorie Rogers to shoulder most of the blame for Globe's death, Ann Smith declared in a *Toronto Star* interview almost thirty years after Globe's death: "The power structures in the church have to change so that these abuses of power can no longer happen."[54] Although the Bishop's report favored a psychiatrically inflected spiritual equilibrium as an antidote to the abuses justified by spiritual intervention at St. Matthias, the report left unexamined, and even perpetuated, the liturgically and episcopally sanctioned patriarchal power that helped lead to Katherine Globe's death.

Despite the Commission's warnings and the regular appearance of articles critical of charismatic healing in the pages of the *Canadian Churchman*, spiritual healing did not disappear within the Diocese of Toronto. One of the Commission's members, Lewis Garnsworthy, became Bishop in 1972 and went on to set up his own committee on healing. Soon after, he commissioned a laywoman, Miriam Dobell, in her own ministry of healing. A disciple of Dorothy Kerin who had lived for six years at Burrswood, Dobell proceeded to speak at churches across the city and country. She described her "quiet, orderly service" of the laying-on-of-hands in her book *Healing Happens*, noting the time when an angry and "ardent Pentecostal" was surprised that her sedate services could be "so power-filled and so meaningful." Arguing that "spiritual malnutrition" afflicted the "children of the Western World" just as physical malnutrition plagued the "children of the Third World," Dobell insisted that "a person is a trinity, made up of spirit, mind, and body. In many families, the minds and bodies of our children are developed, but there is a complete neglect of the spiritual side. Many families are learning at a great price that their young are growing up imbalanced, seeking strange cults and strange teachings in connection with the spirit world."[55]

Offering abundant scriptural citations showing that "Jesus started it," and turning to many testimonies of physical healing including everything from cancer to blindness to emotional distress, Dobell stressed that healing happened not only because an individual had faith but because he or she was surrounded by a community of faith. Healing required openness to God's power and the patience to wait for the spirit, in Dobell's view, both qualities that she considered to be in short supply in Western countries: "People in the mission fields find that many receive instant healing, a far greater proportion than in the so-called Christian lands. They have no preconceived ideas and prejudices to be eradicated."[56] With an assumption of "primitive innocence" much like that of earlier Christian missionaries, Dobell contended that the non-Western, non-Christian inhabited a body, mind, and spirit ready for instantaneous healing, but the skeptical liberal Christian had failed to prime the spiritual pump by allowing the intellect to dominate over the body and spirit.

In 1973 Edward Aubert, the warden and resident physician of Burrswood (what was then known as the "Dorothy Kerin Home of Healing"), traveled to the Toronto area to address a conference organized by the Bishop's "Ministry of Healing." Aubert straddled the line between spiritual equilibrium and spiritual intervention. He insisted on the one hand that "psychological counselling" was mistaken in its refusal to demand that Christians admit guilt, personal responsibility, and repentance for their sins while he also endorsed the Archbishop of Canterbury's warning that the "semi-trained category of clergy with a smattering of scientific knowledge" needed to be replaced by clergy with real psychiatric training. Opposed to Freudian views of the self, Aubert emphasized the importance of good habits, positive emotions, and intercessory (but not insistent) prayer for the achievement of both physical and spiritual health. Aubert distinguished spiritual counseling from its psychological counterparts for its willingness to personally engage with patients on a spiritual plane, unlike the professional detachment called for by the psychiatric concept of transference. Psychiatry's unwillingness to undertake moral, biblically based persuasion of the patient doomed it to failure, according to Aubert: "Health or wholeness is basically a matter of right belief put into action by right living." The church had a responsibility, Aubert urged, to use medicine, prayer, and counseling to bring people out of illness and "spiritual pollution" and into health and "the wholeness of body, mind, and soul intended by God for man from the beginning."[57]

BROKEN SPIRITS

Charismatic renewal was never as profound an influence within the United Church as it was and continues to be among Anglicans. Alex Holmes lasted less than ten years in Canada before moving to the larger market of spirit-filled Protestants in the United States. Although the occasional *Observer* article mentioned an instance of "faith healing," these were rare occurrences and not institutionalized to anywhere near the same extent as in Anglican "ministries of healing." The post–World War II United Church preferred its healing in forms that were less squarely placed in Christian ritual forms—whether embracing psychology via pastoral counseling, or cautiously exploring psychic research.[58] For example, in the wake of World War II, the United Church lamented both the psychological distress of Canadians and their "feverish materialism" in their 1947 Annual Report "A Time of Healing." The report began with two epigraphs, one a biblical passage (Jeremiah 14:18–21) that served as a basis for the Stuttgart Declaration of Guilt in which prominent German Protestants acknowledged their guilt for the murderous Nazi regime.[59] The second quotation came from a U.S. Presbyterian publication lamenting the "racial tensions, economic maladjustment . . . moral license, and cynicism" of postwar society. Declaring that "a spiritual sickness demands a spiritual cure," the text focused not on assertions of wholeness but instead on diagnoses of "brokenness" at both societal and individual levels, insisting that "without a social gospel, evangelism heads toward superstition, but without evangelism, the social gospel is a sowing of the sand."[60]

Encompassing the disparate U.S. and German Protestant appeals to a metaphor of healing, the United Church sought a theology of "cosmic guilt" that would differentiate its particular approach from the personal guilt addressed by healing revivalists and could position the church as a Christian body with much to contribute to national and world affairs. However, in the celebratory year of Canada's centennial in 1967, the *Observer's* editor recalled to his readers that guilt was not the hallmark of a Protestant confessing church: "We have been on the guilt-complex, blame-assessing kick too long. After a while the ashes get into our nostrils and the sackcloth wears thin. It's time for a little joy. It is time to remember that the church is a great fellowship of confessing (and forgiven) sinners, that the God we try to serve is a great God with abundant resources for us."[61] A forerunner of this optimistic theology of abundance was biblical scholar Ernest Scott, who taught for twelve years at Queen's Theological College in Kingston, Ontario, before taking a position in 1919 at Union Theological Seminary in New York. At the end of his distinguished career as a biblical critic, Scott wrote the definitively entitled and posthumously published *I Believe in the Holy Spirit*, (1958), in which he argued that to allow the spirit to be relevant and necessary in a materialistic world deadened by conventionality and multiple threats to human freedom, "unity through difference" was the only path for Christians.[62]

Neither fully endorsing those revivals that "collect people together and stir them up into a mass excitement" nor accepting the "endless political discussion [that] all turns on what will be best for our material interests," Scott argued that the spirit was only truly manifest if its recipient lived as Jesus did, in word and deed. Not necessarily a dramatic, or even outwardly noticeable encounter, the indwelling of the Spirit came when "in our inmost nature we feel the truth of the Christian message. The Spirit bears witness with our spirits. In other words, the message comes to us, and we find it is in harmony with everything that is best in ourselves."[63] This was remarkably different in tone from Scott's earlier scholarly writing on the "supernatural" in ancient Christianity, where he cagily asked: "If the Christian beliefs and practices were in such wonderful harmony with the age, was it not possible that in some measure they were produced by it?"[64] Scott, facing the end of his life, had decided that the "spirit" was not to be analyzed but to be embraced as an experience open not only to ecstatic Christians, but also to quiet ones.[65] As the work of his colleague Paul Tillich demonstrated, the ecstasy of the spirit was something that could be expressed even through the new language of psychology.

PSYCHOLOGY AND THE SPIRIT

Psychology has long furnished a fertile language and symbolism for what E. Brooks Holifield has called the hallmark of Protestant liberalism, "the appeal to experience" that attempts to nurture both spiritual "receptivity" and ethical action in conversation with biblical texts.[66] Trying to be modern and traditional all at once, midcentury Protestants developed a psychiatrically based spiritual equilibrium that had its precursors in experimentalist therapies such as the Christian phrenology described by Christopher White, Elwood Worcester's Emmanuel Movement, Frederick Du Vernet's radio mind, and James Ward's psychoanalytic confessional. Hovering at the edges (or the far outer reaches) of psychology and also peripheral to the institutional centers of liberal Protantism, this earlier experimentalism was picked up—with much of its spiritual electricity switched off—in the encounter between psychoanalytic theories and Christian theology. Whether this meant theologian Paul Tillich's notion of the demonic or what pastoral counseling pioneer Seward Hiltner called the "modern sense of healing," mid-twentieth-century liberal Protestants used biblically rooted anthropologies of body, mind, and spirit to embrace and to contend with psychology, all the while casting suspicious glances at the "rising interest in all kinds of transcendent and supernatural phenomena like speaking in tongues, miraculous healings, and even demonology and exorcisms."[67] These were phenomena that, as we have seen, were very close to home.

In the midst of the new spiritualities of the 1960s and 1970s, liberal Protestants embraced psychology with a whole new enthusiasm as they encountered self-help movements, developed pastoral counseling clinics, and read the crossover bestsellers of theologians and ministers—books such as Thomas Harris' *I'm O.K., You're O.K.* and Paul Tillich's *The Courage to Be*. This embrace of psychology came at a time when Protestant approaches to healing were transforming along many axes. Not only was a charismatic movement making its way into sanctuaries, but medical missions were also facing declining ranks of missionaries and increasing questions about their ethical ramifications in a postcolonial and post-Holocaust world. Many church-founded hospitals in North America and internationally either closed or grew into bigger institutions sponsored by government agencies and were run by medical professionals who were not themselves clergy, or even necessarily Christian. Health-related political issues, such as lobbying the federal government to open access to birth control and legal abortion, and the launching of boycotts against multinational Nestlé for its promotion of baby formula in third-world countries were prominent topics in both the United Church and Anglican papers. And perhaps most importantly for competing anthropologies of the spiritual body, sexuality was becoming a topic newly open to discussion and critique thanks both to a dawning feminist movement and the popularization of psychology.[68]

After World War II, the language of psychology provided an increasingly important register for liberal Protestants to stake their claims as healers in a manner more "realistic" than the cheery advice of chaplains such as Grover Livingstone and Russell Dicks and more "scientific" than the satanic etiologies of Canon Moore Smith. While Seward Hiltner, a prolific contributor to the blending of psychology and Protestantism, praised *The Art of Ministering to the Sick* of Cabot and Dicks for its "unprecedented influence," he also critiqued what he considered to be its idiosyncratic Emersonian stress on self-reliance and its simplistic understanding of the clinical encounter.[69] Hiltner, a U.S. Presbyterian minister, professor at University of Chicago Divinity School and Princeton Theological Seminary, protégé of Tillich, and somewhat bombastic leader in the new field of pastoral counseling and clinical pastoral education, urged a more rigorous cross-fertilization between psychoanalysis and Protestant theology that had ripples north of the border as well.[70]

In 1943 Hiltner published a survey of Christianity and healing under the U.S. auspices of the Commission on Religion and Health of the Federal Council of Churches in which he argued at length for the symbiotic relationship between medicine and the church.[71] To back up his claim that Protestantism and medicine together repaired the brokenness of body, mind, and spirit, Hiltner turned to anthropologies of the self with Greek pedigrees: "'Psychic' may seem a queer word suggesting séances and table-tilting in the dark. But it is derived directly from the Greek word 'psyche,' which referred to the personality as mind, soul or spirit."[72] Sharing James Ward's earlier anxiety over the strangeness of the word "psyche," Hiltner nevertheless vouched for its use in a Christian context by pointing to authority derived both from its Greek etymology and its contemporary psychiatric usage. Referring repeatedly to the many medical doctors who understood the deep connection between body and "mind-spirit," Hiltner went on to argue that Jesus shared their understanding of the "whole person." Here too he turned to the evidence of etymology in a manner similar to many other Protestant writers: "The

Greek and Aramaic words for 'healing,' 'health,' 'being whole,' and 'salvation' are the same or very similar. To say that health is salvation would be wrong. But to indicate that there was in Jesus' mind a close connection between all these things would be almost self-evident."[73] The self-evident character of Jesus's mind aside, Hiltner argued for the complementarity of Jesus's holistic approach to healing with that of modern medicine and psychology, further signaling his difference from charismatic healers by reiterating the distinction between healing and salvation: "Theologians would say that health, even considered in the modern sense as relating to body, mind, and spirit, is not the same as salvation because health is 'temporal' or in time, and salvation is 'eternal' and beyond time."[74] Although the "whole body" was the focus of both medicine and Christian healing, Hiltner, and many other liberal Protestants, stressed that it was not to be mistaken for the whole truth.

Enthusiastic holistic synergies between psychology and Protestant theology were clearly evident in a 1957 collection, *Healing: Human and Divine, Man's Search for Health and Wholeness through Science, Faith, and Prayer*, published by the National Board of the YMCA.[75] Hiltner's contribution to the volume, published when he was a visiting professor at the Menninger Foundation, defended psychoanalysis (and Freud) against charges of being anti-religious. Hiltner argued that in addition to revealing how "actual life can be understood only in terms of its dynamic or driving forces," psychoanalysis helps to root out the "idolatrous" distortions of "pathological" religion: "People may and often do believe in a god who is a projection of father images, in a Christ or Mary who is a magic helper, in a holy spirit reputed to relieve one of personal responsibility. The psychic processes by which such distortions occur need to be known."[76] In this view, psychoanalysis would help Christians become healthy, honest, and accountable for their actions while it acknowledged the all-too-human drives within them that were neither inherently sinful, nor beyond adjustment.

Hiltner's most lasting effect was his cultivation of the field of pastoral psychology and its clinical affiliate, pastoral counseling. In this task he counted heavily on Paul Tillich's ability to bring both psychoanalytic and theological credibility to the project. Hiltner, along with many others engaged in psychiatric spirituality, drew his understanding of pathological religion writ large and the "cosmic" dimensions of health (and much else) from Tillich, his colleague in the 1940s "New York Psychology Group."

Tillich's blend of Christianity and psychology garnered a wide reception in theological, psychoanalytic, and medical circles while it also reached a popular reading audience channeled by both small-scale newsletters such as *Canada and Christendom* and glossy magazines such as *Life*.[77] His ability to communicate his version of spiritual equilibrium to such a broad audience meant that, as Brooks Holifield put it, it was "no accident that the Tillichian harvest coincided with the flowering of pastoral counseling in mainline Christian churches."[78] In 1973 a *United Church Observer* editorial heralded Tillich's writings as the blend of theology and psychology that would "help the wounded in spirit, and point to the source of Grace by which broken hearts are healed," thus serving as the liberal antidote to the rise of "conservative evangelical" churches that the editors worried were doing a better job of comforting those afflicted by the age of anxiety.[79] Taking a more mystical approach to the transformative power of Tillich, one woman wrote in a letter to the editor: "[T]o understand him calls for total immersion by people who have really lived."[80]

The totality and "wholeness" called for by Tillich's theology of ultimate concern provided a language of self-realization both traditional and modern that liberal Protestants could translate into psychological terms while maintaining a commitment to "communal wisdom that transcends the self."[81] Not all readers of the *Observer*, however, supported the marriage of theology and psychiatry. Arguing against what she saw as the claim of "new theology" that psychiatry has proven that "man" does not need God, Mrs. D. Trotter wrote to the editor: "Psychiatry has proven no such thing; in fact, as one who has been through the psychiatric 'mill' I know that here is the very place where this science reaches its limits. Christians, from Jesus himself through Peter, Paul, Martin Luther, John Wesley, and hundreds of thousands of others know from experience that only God (Holy Spirit if you will) can give man salvation and goodness. If the New Theologians deny this, they are humanists pure and simple."[82] What Trotter considered a denunciation, others might interpret as a benediction: many liberal Protestants would have happily accepted humanism as part of their inheritance and trajectory without thinking that it kept them from making room for the spirit.

In its day Tillich's singular sense of the ultimate enjoyed much more prominence among liberal Protestants than the plethora of parapsychological or satanic spirits that inhabited the corners of their churches.[83] Tillich's Marxist-inflected, psychoanalytic version of the demonic was heralded as a "modern" solution for the "burden of anxiety" that was said to plague mid-twentieth-century North American Christians. Tillich's solution was not the first attempt to solve the problem of the spirit by replacing unruly spirits with a singular, holistic divine principle or to turn to psychology in aid of the "ultimate." As Ann Taves has shown, William James did much the same thing in the *Varieties of Religious Experience*, some fifty years earlier, when he sought to divest "mysticism" of the taint of the occult by replacing a diversity of "spirits" with the singularity of an "unseen presence."[84] Although Tillich was unabashedly a theologian in a way that James was not, both were men who sought to carve out legitimacy for the spirit in psychological discourses by speaking across academic disciplines and to a wider public.

THE RISE OF PASTORAL COUNSELING

With roots in both Europe and the United States, pastoral counseling and clinical pastoral education first emerged in the 1920s led by a combination of clergy, theologians, medical doctors, and psychologists, as well as former psychiatric patients. With its blend of Christian views of the self and morality and the clinical techniques and theories of psychology, pastoral counseling gained momentum in the United States and Canada in the 1950s. Seminaries, in collaboration with university psychiatric departments and hospitals, introduced training institutes that could equip clergy with new techniques for counseling their troubled parishioners—techniques that were drawn not from the cure of souls, but from the latest academic theories of human psychology. Graduates applied their skills in congregational ministries, newly established church-run counseling centers, or hospital chaplaincies.[85]

Two Canadian programs, basing themselves on models from Boston and New York, were founded in 1958: the Toronto Institute for Pastoral Training was a collaboration among the University of Toronto's Faculty of Medicine (including the Department of Psychiatry) and the United Church and Anglican colleges, among others, while in Nova Scotia the Institute of Pastoral Training—with a motto of "wholeness and health"—was a similarly interdenominational program incorporated by the provincial legislature in the same year.[86] Whereas the Toronto Institute for Pastoral Training took some inspiration from British Methodist Leslie Weatherhead, the interdenominational Maritimes-based Institute of Pastoral Training traced its roots back to U.S. Protestants such as Seward Hiltner.[87] The co-founder of the Toronto Institute, Charles Feilding, was a professor and Dean at the Anglican Trinity College, who had earlier founded a short-lived newsletter, *Canada and Christen-*

dom.[88] Advancing a self-consciously "Canadian" Anglican voice that supported labor unions, condemned Japanese wartime internment, and advocated sex education, *Canada and Christendom* hoped to provide a Christian socialist corrective to what Feilding and his readers considered the "Super-Imperialist" flavor of more official publications such as the *Canadian Churchman*.[89] Citing the counseling work of Leslie Weatherhead, Feilding also hoped that his newsletter could explore the growing field of pastoral psychology. He finally achieved this goal in his work with the Toronto Institute for Pastoral Training, which offered a summer course based out of the Toronto General Hospital that was "designed to provide ministers of religion with an opportunity to deepen their understanding of pastoral care, and to develop greater skill and sensitivity in ministering to the needs of people."[90]

The United Church was particularly active in the establishment of pastoral counseling, setting up "clinics" in several urban congregations. For example in 1962 Edgar Mullen, a United Church minister, became the Director of the newly incorporated Pastoral Institute, housed in the basement of Calgary Centre United Church. Eventually outgrowing both the basement and the United Church identification, the Institute became the Calgary Counselling Centre in 1996 and now is a nonprofit organization with a multifaith (or no-faith) approach.[91] The concern to avoid a singularly Christian approach to pastoral counseling is evident even in early "manuals," such as the one written in 1958 by Samuel Laycock, a former Dean of Education at the University of Saskatchewan and published by the United Church's Ryerson Press under the auspices of the Canadian Mental Health Association. The preponderance of texts categorized as "Protestant" in the manual's suggested reading list demonstrated, however, that this multifaith approach was deeply shaped by a discourse of "religion" constituted largely by Protestant theological materials.[92] In 1968 the Canadian Mental Health Association continued its "interfaith" collaboration in Winnipeg running what was billed as the first Canadian conference to enable clergy to better help "people with emotional and mental health problems." Co-hosted by the Canadian Council for Supervised Pastoral Education, the conference gathered "delegates from the Mennonite, Baptist, Catholic, Anglican, Lutheran, Unitarian, United Church, Presbyterian, Jewish, and Salvation Army denominations."[93]

The ecumenical and interfaith energy behind these Canadian-born hybrids of psychiatry and theology drew much of their impetus from the United States and England. Many of the earliest Canadians to embark on counseling vocations traveled to the United States to study at institutions such as Princeton Theological Seminary, as did Wilena G. Brown, a graduate of the United Church's Emmanuel College, who began her studies as one of few women students of pastoral counseling at Princeton in 1962.[94] United Church ministers Mervyn Dickinson and Kenneth Allan, the founding directors of two pastoral counseling clinics that eventually merged into the Toronto Institute for Human Relations in 1967, both completed PhD programs in Psychology and Pastoral Counseling at the Methodist-based Boston University School of Theology. Although with less formal training, the Anglican nuns of the Sisters of St. John the Divine also took up counseling from their base at the St. John's Rehabilitation Hospital. A 1968 *Churchman* article described how the Sisters' traditional work of teaching and nursing had been increasingly "taken over by agencies" and that they had moved into "personal counselling" as a result. To the interviewer's question of whether "a nun [can] really do this type of counselling successfully," the Sisters defended their abilities by referring both to the courses they had taken and their receptive and loving listening skills and went on to argue for a greater role for laywomen in the church.[95]

Another place where liberal Protestants from across North America made space for the spirit in psychology was through the establishment of a scholarly clerical journal, *Pastoral Psychology* (a journal later edited by Hiltner). The journal brought together psychiatrists, ministers, pastoral counselors, and even anthropologists—Margaret Mead made several appearances in the 1960s with Tillich commenting on her work. Psychiatrist John Millet's 1950 contribution to the first volume had a title with a familiar ring to it: "Body, Mind, and Spirit." Millet argued, "From my own standpoint, [spirit] seems applicable to that feeling of urgency in man to struggle toward an integration of his mental and physical self in the direction of some ideal, an ideal whose pursuit will result in a decreasing burden of anxiety, a more effective social role, and a deep respect for the eternal mysteries which the finite and limited nature of man can never be expected to penetrate."[96] Arguing that cooperation between science and religion was crucial in the "atomic age," Millet advocated both the insights of "social science" and a science-friendly Christianity as paths to reducing individual anxiety and social conflict.

SEX AND THE SPIRIT

One of the most important yet little explored effects of the rise of psychiatric-inflected spirituality was the manner in which psychological discourses, mediated via the anthropology of body, mind, and spirit, provided a way station for liberal Christians to reevaluate sexuality in conversation with feminist- and gay- and lesbian-liberation movements of the 1960s and 1970s. Susan Myers-Shirk has shown that pastoral counseling and the larger movement of what she calls "Protestant psychotherapeutic culture" provided a context for Protestant men to begin to challenge patriarchal gender norms—something that women in their churches and homes were increasingly demanding.[97] In her work on Alfred Kinsey's "religious encounters" in the wake of his wildly popular reports on male and female sexual practices, Marie Griffith has shown that Kinsey's reports, although inspiring vitriolic attacks from conservative Catholics and Protestants, were well received by many liberal Protestants, including Seward Hiltner. Adeptly woven into the goal of pastoral counseling as a church-supported conversation in which Christians could frankly address their concerns about sexuality, Kinsey's revealing portrait of the sexual histories of "average" Americans emboldened liberal Protestants who were already on their way to questioning predominant sexual mores.[98]

Pastoral counseling institutes became places for couples and youth to learn about "healthy" sexuality and even became centers from which to lobby provincial education systems to introduce sex education into schools. In Alberta the United Church-based Pastoral Institute was at the heart of the struggle to introduce sexual education into the schools in 1969. A fiery public meeting drew 750 people to a Calgary high school, where fourteen-year-old girls demanded that their schools and parents address the topic of sexuality frankly, and Anglican and United Church clergy echoed their plea. Clergy went a step further to host discussion groups for youth groups, on such topics as "The Beauty of Sex" (led by a doctor) and "Youth's Social Responsibility."[99] Ironically, forty years later in 2009, conservative Christians successfully lobbied the Alberta government to place restrictions on the teaching of sexual education in schools.

The plea among proponents of pastoral counseling for a Christian acceptance of sexuality as a positive inflowing of the spirit, worthy of "reverence" in the earlier words of Belle Oliver, led liberal Protestants to become pioneers in challenging the pathologizing of homosexuality as itself an ideological distortion of Christian theology. Elwood Worcester was an early, cautious proponent of this view, whereas, by contrast, Anglican psychiatrist Daniel Cappon argued in his 1965 book *Toward an Understanding of Homosexuality* that homosexuality could (and should) be "cured." United Church author Samuel Laycock, however, argued in his 1958 advice manual on pastoral counseling that although clergy may help homosexuals "adjust" to their society, this was "not necessarily the same thing as a cure."[100]

Once liberal Protestants started thinking about sexuality as a question not only of the body but of mind and spirit as well, several clergy, consigned to their sphere in the kingdom of spirit, took even more radical stands. In the wake of a small group of Anglican clergy organizing the Council on Religion and the Homosexual, Anglican priest William Nicholls, who had just founded the Department of Religious Studies at the University of British Columbia in 1964, wrote a letter to the Vancouver Sun arguing that laws prohibiting homosexual sex were "barbaric" and that repealing them could have the effect of *improving* moral standards.[101] A few months later Mervyn Dickinson, United Church minister and then Director of the Pastoral Counselling Service of Toronto, who also led workshops on "spiritual healing," published an article in the *Observer* condemning the church's support for the "highly repressive sexual ethic of western culture." Based on his conversations with gay men at a downtown Toronto bar, Dickinson's article suggested, with reference to psychiatric theories, that homosexuality "may not be as totally 'unnatural' or pathological as we like to think." Going further, Dickinson urged that the church openly welcome homosexuals and bless committed homosexual relationships, while also pressuring the government to revoke "prejudicial legislation."[102]

Of the four letters in response to Dickinson printed by the *Observer*, only one was critical. The three others praised the *Observer* for its courage, "truth and compassion" and lauded Dickinson for his "deep understanding." One anonymous letter, from a homosexual and recovering alcoholic with bitter memories of his priest's hostile response when he came out, challenged those who labeled homosexuality a perversion: "Those who are so strong in their condemnation and prejudice have a lot to answer for, not only spiritually by making outcasts of those God loves, but by wrecking physical and mental health on a large scale." Five years before the legendary Stonewall riots in New York City, Canadian ministers writing in national church newspapers were calling for the depathologizing of homosexuality, along with its legal and liturgical

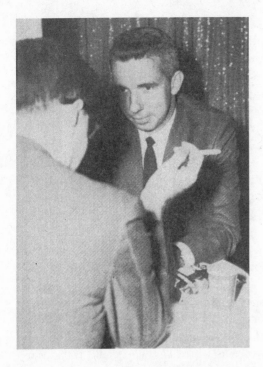

FIGURE 12. Photo of Reverend Mervyn Dickinson interviewing men at a Toronto gay bar, November 15, 1965. Courtesy of the *United Church Observer*.

recognition. This suggests that the charismatic renewal is not the only cultural movement that has an untold liberal Protestant lineage.[103]

Almost ten years later in the *Christian Century*, Seward Hiltner took another approach to the assertion that homosexuality was not an "illness" by calling for attention to the "neglected phenomenon of female homosexuality." Imagining a "pansexualist utopia" in which women "had the psychic inclination to realize their full orgasmic potentialities," Hiltner concluded—or rather lamented—that given such a utopia women would engage in sex with other women much more often than with other men, and would thus profoundly disrupt the domestic order as well as the male ego.[104] Nonetheless, he joined the call for openness to sexual diversity voiced a decade earlier by Canadian Protestants.

Since the holistic *unity* of body, mind, and spirit simultaneously preserved the *difference* of these three sites of the self, it thus made space for reevaluating—and revaluing—bodiliness in particular, giving a sense of sacredness to the body by virtue of its equilibrium with mind and spirit. Arguing for sexual education for young women and men, as well as for married couples, liberal Christians started tackling questions of women's sexual satisfaction and patriarchal dominance in marriage.

With scientific justification via medical discourses that argued for the naturalness of homosexual desire, liberal Christians came to reject the metaphor of healing as adequate to homosexuality, arguing that it inappropriately pathologized sexual orientations that were neither illnesses nor sinful whims. Adopting a language of justice, compassion, and self-realization, liberal Protestants, both gay and straight, argued for the spiritual authenticity of a diversity of sexualities.[105]

DISCERNING THE SPIRIT

Spiritual equilibrium and spiritual intervention both arose as aspects of a "modern sense of healing" that insisted on a holism of the material, the psychic, and the spiritual. Their overlapping holism, however, contained serious cleavages; the clearest difference between the two lay in the emphases they placed on the three pivots in the balance of body, mind, and spirit. Supporters of spiritual equilibrium, in concert with their psychological affinities, were more likely to argue that healing came from honestly accounting for mental anxieties and fears, including those that were culturally induced, acknowledging the limits of the body, and acting with spiritual confidence as Christians who could transform a materialistic world in cooperation with tools of modern social organization. In the words of United Church writer, E. Gilmour Smith, God "wants us to live and organize the life of the individual, family, nation, and world, that diseases shall be eliminated or reduced to the minimum. When sickness does come, God also will come near to uphold, strengthen and sustain. . . . Surrounded by super-abundance there is need to develop self-discipline lest there be gluttony."[106] It was this kind of view that fueled the many liberal Protestants who worked, together with allies of various sorts, to secure the passing of the Medical Care Act in the Canadian Parliament in 1966, granting universal, publicly funded access to the care of physicians.[107] Health care, in their view, was not to be primarily oriented by capitalist models of economic and social organization, and healing need not be limited to explicitly Christian energies. Spiritual interventionists, on the other hand, gave an explicitly Christian shape and power to spiritual energies, alternately mediated by Jesus, by divine vibrational energies, and in more perilous forms, by Satan. At the forceful insistence of such spirits, they thought, mind and body were permeable and open to change, whether through "instantaneous healings" or psychic realignment. There was nothing in the body that could not be cured by the spirit—whether cancer or sexual desire—if the Christian were receptive and truly patient.

The significance of guilt was another fault line. For the supporters of spiritual equilibrium, whose influence was most pervasive among clergy and church officials, psychology provided a new language for thinking about and acting on guilt, as well as a way of distancing oneself from it and accepting it simultaneously. Cosmic guilt was largely understood as a collective emotion that came in response to structural and historical injustice. As journalist Will Oursler reflected on guilt and sin in *Religion: Out or Way Out*, his account of Christianity in 1960s North America, "The church does not abandon a metaphysical position in healing; rather, in modern terms, it orients that role to the broad concept that much of our sickness—physical, mental, and emotional—is brought upon us by our own hatreds and prejudices, our need for vengeance, our need to hurt others."[108] For the smaller, but persistent stream of spiritual interventionists, guilt was a personal emotion, a first step toward recognizing one's sinfulness and becoming open to the abundant healing of the spirit. Different perspectives on guilt would become especially important in the 1970s and onward, as the United Church and the Anglican Church came to grapple head on with the three structural, historical issues that provoked the greatest conflict within their churches: women's changing roles in the church, the active participation of openly gay and lesbian Christians, and the Church's responsibility for the practice and legacies of native residential schools.

As the embrace of sexual diversity as an issue of community justice shows, spiritual equilibrium, while tied to self-realization, was also rooted in commitments to broader notions of social justice. Near the end of his life, Seward Hiltner considered the United States particularly vulnerable to an idolatrous "imperialism of health" in which the biblical view of health as a "cosmic phenomenon" was lost to a focus on the individual: "In countries like our own there is a great danger not of undervaluing health but of treating it too highly or idolatrously. Health is regarded as so desirable that we are supposed automatically to be in favor of anything that promotes health. Even our religion and our ethics are often judged simply by their being healthy or otherwise."[109] Regretting the depoliticizing effects of a psychologically inflected Christianity, Hiltner argued for the importance of the "queer" notion of the psyche while he also called for a theological critique of the assumption that "health" was to be pursued at all costs.

However tricky it may be to disentangle proponents of spiritual equilibrium from those of spiritual intervention, and however vague and capacious the notion of the holistic trinity might appear, Protestants are clear that anthropology can be contentious terrain.[110] Wholeness has operated as a metaphor that could contain markedly divergent ideologies: social responsibility versus personal guilt as the etiology of illness; individual self-knowing mediated by biomedicine versus divine intervention by the "finger of God" as paths to healing. The idea that wholeness necessarily makes for unity has been most seriously challenged—and contradicted—at times when disciplines of the body have come to the fore: when a young woman died as a result of being exorcised and slapped instead being given antibiotics, and in a very different context, when a seed of transformation was planted by the revolutionary suggestion that the church stop trying to heal gays and lesbians and welcome them as healthy and whole in their embodied selves. The Bishop's Commission on the Ministry of Healing hoped that excising the word "bodily" from the prayer for the Anointing of the Sick would allow Anglicans to take "'health' . . . in its fullest sense" and would help to restore the appropriate weighting of body, mind, and spirit. The very demarcations of body, mind, and spirit in the holistic trinity, however, ended up not so much establishing the equilibrium of the healthy Christian self, as revealing the precariousness of its balance.

CHAPTER 5

Ritual Proximity and the Healing of History

I also know that I am in need of healing, and my own people are in need of healing, and our church is in need of healing. Without that healing, we will continue the same attitudes that have done such damage in the past. I know that healing takes a long time, both for people and for communities. I also know that it is God who heals, and that God can begin to heal when we open ourselves, our wounds, our failure and our shame, to God. I want to take one step along that path here and now.

—Primate of the Anglican Church of Canada, Archbishop Michael Peers, apologizing to the National Native Convocation, Minaki, Ontario, 1993[1]

There will be no health in the Western world until, in a new hearing of faith, the quality of life among the "least of these" is understood, valued and appropriated and, until we get off the backs of those we profess to be serving.

—Ian M. Fraser, quoted by United Church missionary Katharine B. Hockin, "My Pilgrimage in Mission," 1988

In the last few decades of the twentieth century and on into the twenty-first, the meanings and modes of Christian healing within Anglican and United Churches had proliferated in a dizzying array of directions. Transcendental meditation, yoga, traditional First Nations rituals, medieval-based labyrinth walks, energy healing such as Reiki and therapeutic touch, and healing services with anointing and laying on of hands could all be found in sanctuaries and parish halls across North America, not to mention in the health expos and bookstores of ecumenically "New Age" networks.[2] As well, parish nursing, a hybrid of biomedical expertise and pastoral care, introduced a new, less evangelical version of the medical missionary. This proliferation of healing brought with it an intensified supernatural liberalism that celebrated ritual and spiritual innovation, while it also prompted charges of heresy and appropriation. A prayer quoted by a United Church minister on her church's website ironically named such "heresies":

> We are confused—
> By New Age spirituality and crystals,
> By goddess-talk and Christa,
> By borrowings of Native American traditions
> And Zen Buddhism,
> By charismatics, faith healers,
> And snake-handlers,
> By Tai-chi and yoga,
> By 12-step spirituality and spiritual direction, by contemplatives
>   and revivalists, by Christian Scientists and Mormons, by
>   Jehovah's Witness and the Jesus Seminar.
> We can have respectable dialogues with at least six clearly defined
>   world religions, but not with these upstart heresies.
> But your holy spirit doesn't care about orthodoxy. The Spirit's gift
>   is poured out on those who don't come to churches, who don't
>   sing our hymns, who don't need committees.[3]

Bolstered by an unorthodox sense of the Holy Spirit, yet also counting on the authority of Christian tradition, these proliferating techniques of healing connected with familiar Christian rituals while they also borrowed from other traditions. They accorded with earlier vibrational theologies of Frederick Du Vernet and Agnes Sanford, and they were grounded in the conviction that human life was sustained by a universal spirit, recognized by different names. Spiritual intervention, as it turns out, may have won the day after all but with a plenitude of spirits that could not be easily fit within either the demonic or the holy.

This capacious universality was in plentiful evidence at St. Luke's, a Toronto Anglican church that I first decided to visit when I read the notices for Saturday yoga classes and weeknight Meditation/Bible Studies on its outdoor sign. Adele, for example, a longtime Caribbean-Canadian parishioner who did not attend the yoga classes, had developed her own version of experimentalism, drawing both from traditional Anglican liturgies and a conviction of the power of spiritual intervention. Speaking with Adele in her suburban apartment, I learned that she had begun training as a lay anointer in the Anglican Church, at the suggestion of the priest, Father Patrick. This training would enable her to anoint her fellow Christians with consecrated oil at the church's healing services. Although tied by their commitment to Anglican healing liturgies, Adele and Patrick did not share entirely commensurable anthropologies of the spiritual body. Adele, who also attended Pentecostal services on Sunday evenings, was moved by a view of spiritual intervention that pitted the Holy Spirit against demons, whereas Patrick, a self-described "child of the Enlightenment," was more attuned to the kinesthetic disciplines of yoga and meditation as paths to spiritual healing.

A grandmother who since the 1970s had regularly traveled the long distance by subway to come to St. Luke's, Adele told me of her strategy for getting around Patrick's skepticism of thaumaturgy. Knowing that Patrick was not partial to exorcism or to practices of blessing inanimate objects, Adele would come to St. Luke's healing services with her biomedically-prescribed medication for various ailments hidden in her purse. When it was her turn to step forward for anointing, she carried her purse under her arm, and thus considered her medications to have also received a blessing. With Pentecostal healing services bringing an even greater mix to her spiritual pharmacy, Adele drew widely from various traditions, finding great inspiration in the devotional writings of the Scottish evangelist Oswald Chambers. With her daily reading of Chamber's best-selling devotional text, *My Utmost for His Highest*, Adele imbibed a message of the triumph of the supernatural over the natural life.[4]

Though Patrick turned more to yoga than to charismatic spirits, his encouragement of Adele as a lay anointer testified to the breadth of what could fit within his conception of healing, rooted as it was in a widely shared liberal Protestant conviction about the universality of spirituality. Haunting this optimistic universalism, however, has been the specter of history: for many Euro-American liberal Protestants, these newly blended and borrowed traditions came along with an uncomfortable awareness of the past, in which liberal Protestants came to understand the history of Christian imperialism as itself a pathology of modernity in need of healing. This has been nowhere more apparent than in the ways the metaphor of healing has set the very terms for Anglican and United Church reparations to aboriginal peoples in the wake of the churches' responsibility for administering the residential schools that so severely damaged First Nations communities in Canada. When Anglican Archbishop Michael Peers used the rubric of healing in his 1993 apology to First Nations' peoples, and the United Church moderator, Robert Smith, did the same in his earlier 1986 apology, they drew in part from a discourse of healing common to First Nations communities. Both churches invested healing with a significance that went well beyond techniques for the restoration of an individual's body, mind, and spirit, making it an uncertain path to attempt to address and atone for legacies of injustice.

Both the Anglican Church of Canada and the United Church of Canada established Healing Funds in the 1990s as their First Nations members called them to face their historic role in the establishment and running of state-funded residential schools that had sought to turn aboriginal children into English-speaking, fully "assimilated" Canadians. Adding this atonement to the earlier, psychologically inflected reconceptualization of human sexuality, healing became a concept and a process called on to bear—and transform—the burdens of colonialism, racism, sexism, homophobia, and Christian triumphalism. Whether the idea of healing was up to this daunting task is not something that I can hope to settle. Instead, in this last chapter, I turn to my fieldwork within Anglican and United Church settings in Toronto, along with textual sources, to consider the ways that liberal Protestants envisioned this expanded—or impossibly stretched—sense of healing as a technique for confronting and reconciling Christian legacies of triumphalism and violence. Grounded in biblical reasons and interreligious exchanges, this approach to healing history sought not to resurrect the past but to exorcise it in the present.[5]

EXPERIMENTALISM ANEW

Turning to a broadly eclectic range of therapies drawn from a diversity of religious and cultural traditions did not mean that liberal Protestants relinquished biomedical practices. After the Medical Care Act was made law in 1966, ecumenical Christian networks continued to draw on biomedical and human rights discourses to press for improvements to health care systems in Canada and around the world. Insisting that health was a universal right for everyone (and not just Christians), the Canadian Council of Churches' 2002 "Health Care Covenant for all People in Canada" based itself on the United Nations Declaration of Human Rights, as well as the World Health Organization's definition of health.[6]

Another space of biomedical encounter was the new academic field of bioethics that emerged in the 1960s within Protestant and Catholic seminaries, as well as within religious studies departments. Deliberating on the ethics of modern biomedical innovations, and the hubris of doctors "playing God," bioethicists from many religious traditions have spoken to issues such as reproductive technologies, euthanasia, organ donation, and cloning.[7]

Alongside articles on bioethics and advocacy for greater access to biomedical health care, church newspapers also ran articles and letters that weighed the merits and validity of an increasingly wide range of alternative therapeutic approaches, entertaining the idea that biomedicine was just one epistemology of healing among others. In time this inquiry into alternative healing techniques ascribed virtue to the very fact of religious difference itself: perfecting yoga asanas would heal not only the body but also the dogmatic and insufficiently embodied aspects of Christianity itself. Quite in contrast to the warnings against syncretism that, as we shall see, began to emanate at the turn of the millennium from the historically liberal ecumenical organization the World Council of Churches, many liberal Protestants forged therapeutic and religious combinations that they saw as the solution to Christian exceptionalism. As early as 1954, the Ontario Ladies' College, a United Church-related girls' high school with a traditional arts and science curriculum, was also home to a Christian ashram, in which the organizers "adapted the Indian Ashram idea for Christian use as a Conference Retreat."[8] In another example, Paul Tillich developed an interest in Zen Buddhist practices of meditation near the end of his life while he simultaneously made important contributions to the growing field of biomedical ethics. Taking experimentalism even further, the British-born Alan Watts left the Episcopal Church in 1950 after a brief stint as a chaplain, and went on to become one of the most well-known of authors to popularize Buddhism for a Western audience, while also "experimenting" with drugs, sexuality, and the spiritual community of Esalen.[9] Religious borrowing, for some, became an antidote for the toxic legacies of missionary imperialism and Christian triumphalism in which religious difference had been read solely in terms of pathological heathenisms to be overcome rather than as currents of spiritual energy to be celebrated and tapped.

The elasticity of liberal Protestant healing was made possible by its embodiment in practice rather than its articulation in doctrine. Remaining largely skeptical of demonic spiritual intervention and preferring an equilibrium of body, mind, and spirit, late-twentieth-century Anglicans and United Church members shifted toward a new emphasis on bodily practices, without entirely shunning psychological discourses, as the starting point for healthy Christian selves. Marjorie, the minister at Confederation Street United Church where I attended services, noted the difference between her church's new healing services and the rituals of her Presbyterian forebears: "healing services are tactile—you're actually touched." More akin to the energy-based faith healing of Alex Holmes than the talk therapies of pastoral counseling, this tactility constructed bodies-in-relation as themselves sensational forms conveying experience of the spirit.

No longer entranced by the power of new communication technologies as tools of bodily healing, liberal Protestants nevertheless used innovations in transportation and communication to develop an awareness and encounter with non-Christian traditions, whether by flying to India or reading websites. Seeking a spirituality that acknowledged and worked through the body, liberal Protestants came to poise different religious practices in "ritual proximity," whereby diverse rituals, symbols, and epistemologies—including those of biomedicine and spiritual intervention—coalesced within particular bodies situated in particular places. Whereas Marjorie largely kept her healing experimentalism within Christian and psychological bounds, Father Patrick of St. Luke's started with seeking out non-Christian religious teachers found within his urban North American communities. Not alone in being transformed by the missionary practices of Buddhist, Hindu, and Reiki teachers in North America, Patrick represents a controversial yet persistent undercurrent of contemporary Christianity that welcomes this interreligious transformation as an authentic, faithful path.[10]

As anthropologist Arjun Appadurai has shown, assertions of religious authenticity in the present build on a "debatable" past, mediated by cultural norms including the authority of textual evidence, assertions of interdependence with other pasts, claims to continuity with a larger historical narrative, and appeals to antiquity.[11] The debatable past of Christianity has been newly configured by ritual proximity, in which liberal Protestants value the bodily practices of non-Christian traditions as sources of spiritual insight and even healing. Inescapably, however, this ritual proximity has been saturated with the tensions, confusions, and parallels implied by the historically laden opposition of "East" and "West," Christian and non-Christian.

HISTORY, HISTORICITY, AND RITUAL INNOVATION

Given the force of postcolonial critiques of "Orientalism" and its "epistemic violence," any analysis of popular Western Christian syncretisms of Asian traditions must be aware of how colonialism, Christian missionaries, and Orientalist scholars prepared the way for such borrowings.[12] Syncretic religiosity (which arguably means all religiosity) implies historicity: interaction with the pastness of particular objects, places, people, and traditions. Despite popular assertions of the spontaneity of "true" spirituality, invoking deities, rituals, myths, and symbols within and across traditions entails a relationship—whether of responsibility, ignorance, or influence—with the pastness of religions. Christianity, in all its varieties, exudes robust historicity through textual, ritual, dogmatic, visual, and storied forms that all draw on the power of the past to assert authenticity. Religious alterity is a persistent, although often sublimated, current in these constructions of "historic Christianity"; the otherness of Jews, Muslims, First Nations peoples, and the mystic East have all shaped Christian self-definitions and practices and continue to do so. Anglo-Canadian Christians integrating Asian and First Nations traditions via ritual carry this past while fostering something new. They historicize with the agency to remember, forget, and revive their pasts (or those of others) in particular ways, while they are at the same time more passively shaped by the weight—or support—of tradition.

Understanding the uses of the past for liberal Protestants as they have reinvented their approaches to healing requires a brief clarification of historicity and history. Historicity is not identical to the discipline of history, a point Dipesh Chakrabarty illuminates by particular reference to the dilemma of historical accounts of religious consciousness. Chakrabarty describes the rationalist historian who cannot fit claims of divine agency, in which historical actors consider divine intervention more powerful than human action, into what Chakrabarty names as the two premises of rationalist history: "Can the story be told/crafted? And does it allow for a rationally-defensible point of view or position from which to tell the story?"[13] Rationalist history looks to anthropology for epistemological assistance here, as the supernatural is first "anthropologised (i.e., converted into somebody's belief or made into an object of anthropological analysis) before it finds a place in the historian's narrative."[14] For Chakrabarty, anthropology has none of the ambiguous ontological baggage of its theological origins—instead it is a filter that seeks to winnow out the supernatural from the really real by the very gestures of its inter-pretive task.

Chakrabarty insists, however, that the historian's or the anthropolo-gist's discipline is not the only way to remember or even reconstruct other times, places, and peoples. Prominent among these alternative approaches to historicization—what Chakrabarty terms "subaltern pasts, pasts that cannot enter history ever as belonging to the historian's own position"—are religious narratives and practices in which divine agency is a foremost reality.[15] The distinction between these subaltern pasts and historical narrative is real, but not impassible, since historical narratives are only possible when the historian recognizes some aspect of what she narrates: "[subaltern pasts] remind us that a relation of contemporaneity between the nonmodern and the modern, a shared 'now', which expresses itself on the historical plane but the character of which is ontological, is what allows historical time to unfold."[16] Twenty-first-century liberal, North American Protestants fully immersed in modernity but also fully engaged with the supernatural are a challenging case for considering the contemporaneity of which Chakrabarty writes, in which "a plurality of times [exist] together."[17] Although their Enlightenment heritage often obliges these Christians to undergo a certain ironic distancing from their own religious practices, they resolutely pursue a mingling of rituals, reli-gions, spirits, and energies in their twenty-first-century versions of a heal-ing mission.[18] They revalue those traditions once considered heathen—subaltern—not only through revising (or forgetting) their own western Christian history, but also through renovating their own ritual with the help of the very traditions—such as yoga—rendered subaltern by Christian-influenced Western colonialism. Making this plurality even more intense is the fact that the subaltern other may often also herself be Christian, whether Caribbean-Canadian Adele, who brought together Anglican sacramentalism and Pentecostalism, or a First Nations Christian who participates in both the sweat lodge and communion, thus embodying layers of historical conflict and cooperation.

THE VARIETIES OF ANGLICAN SYNCRETISM

One spring day in 2005 I gathered together with several older British women in the dining hall of Burrswood Christian Hospital, Dorothy Kerin's legacy, to share a sedate dinner of baby shrimp and rice, along with a view of the colorful flowers and greenery of the Burrswood gar-dens just outside the window. As the women told me of their regular

& architecture &
measure

FIGURE 13. The grounds of Burrswood Christian Hospital, founded by Dorothy Kerin in 1948, Tunbridge Wells, England. Photo by John Marshall, 2005.

extended visits to Burrswood, one woman declared with subdued enthusiasm, "There's nothing quite like Burrswood." During my short visit there, the clientele of Burrswood's hotel-style wing were largely older women, coming from around England in search of some rest and relaxation, a dip in the hot baths, a stroll in the garden, and quiet prayers in the chapel or church. These were not the more seriously ill patients in another wing of the hospital, who were mostly there for recuperation from surgery or as psychiatric inpatients. Rooted in a blend of Anglican liturgical tradition, biomedical practice, and Dorothy Kerin's particular charisma, Burrswood had been recently renovated in the 1990s by an Evangelical Anglican influence. I had come to visit it after learning that a group of Canadian Anglicans was taking Burrswood as their model for a Toronto-based healing center.

Once the site of more experimentalist practices, Burrswood had undergone an Evangelical transformation in the 1990s. Working on at least three fronts, the Burrswood leadership divested itself of "questionable" practices of earlier leaders that were thought to be New Age, pared down much of the rococo, High-Church "excess" of Kerin's

Church of Christ the Healer, and employed a modified Anglican version of exorcism to relieve some of its patients of their psychological demons. Healing at Burrswood was now at once appropriately biomedical and firmly Evangelical Anglican. Neither radically combinative in the fashion of the socialist-spiritualist, Anglo-Catholic Percy Dearmer, nor experimental in the frequency of radio mind, most of Burrswood's clients sought a form of healing more akin to a Christian rest cure than an encounter with radical difference on a spiritual or earthly plane.[19]

In the wake of the healing ministry of Miriam Dobell, Dorothy Kerin's Canadian disciple, a group of clergy, doctors, nurses, and laypeople sought to establish the Miriam Dobell Healing Centre on the grounds of the convent of the Sisters of St. John the Divine north of Toronto.[20] The Sisters offered a likely home for a Kerin-inspired healing center, having established one of the first Christian hospitals in the city as a blend of Anglo-Catholic sacramental healing and biomedicine. Opened in 2002 as a pilot project, the Centre's first director, Ronald Van Auken, described it as "a place where an individual can step back from the ordinary ongoing pressures and demands of life and seek healing whether of body, mind or spirit."[21] Van Auken's version of the holistic trinity set specific limits, as he expressed reservations about "the offering of other modalities, body work, and such, [or] exercise whether it be yoga or Tai Chi. You know those two, simply I think largely because of their names and their origin raises some flags for some people." The devotional techniques of the Centre would focus on explicitly Christian modalities: "In terms of the Christian component, [we're] looking at some obvious things such as prayer, anointing, laying on of hands, worship services, meditation, spiritual direction, journaling, pastoral counseling, spiritual guidance, a variety of those things that would easily be understood to be Christian practices or spiritual disciplines." The Centre did not become fully functioning, due in part to the financial hardship of the Anglican Church in an era both of declining membership and payments to redress its historical injustices to First Nations. With grand visions and professionally rendered architectural drawings, along with the support of several church leaders, the Miriam Dobell Centre did not have a healer at its core with the charismatic gifts or fundraising savvy of Dorothy Kerin.

By contrast to the Christian pedigree of healing practices at the ill-fated Miriam Dobell Healing Centre, St. Luke's Church was a linguistically, economically, and ethnically diverse downtown Toronto church combining Christian liturgical traditions of sung prayer, incense, and anointing with oil with non-Christian traditions of yoga and medita-tion. Once a church with a strong British heritage, both in its architec-ture and its congregation, by the early twenty-first century St. Luke's declared its embrace of yoga without apology, providing related "spiri-tual links" on its website. Sharing in a wider tradition of Christian yoga stimulated partly by twentieth-century yoga evangelism on the part of South Asian Hindus, St. Luke's was broadly concerned with healing body, mind, and spirit through social engagement and personal contem-plation.[22] Meditation/Bible- study groups, yoga classes, and Taizé prayer and healing services—based on the sung chants of the Taizé ecumenical monastic community in France—were all further manifestations of energy sacramentalism at St. Luke's.[23]

Nadia, a certified yoga instructor and the wife of Patrick, St. Luke's priest, taught yoga classes in the church hall on Saturdays. A woman who spoke with the confidence of someone who has thought through her philosophy of life, Nadia moved with the suppleness of a long-time yoga practitioner. She viewed her classes as a form of community out-reach; without the marketing or paraphernalia of for-profit yoga schools, Nadia's classes attracted about ten to fifteen participants, including be-ginners and those more advanced. On one Saturday that I was there, a disabled woman in a wheelchair joined the class, with the help of her companions. Speaking with Nadia one afternoon in the parish hall, she told me of her ambivalent negotiation of Christian tradition with East-ern practices: "Yoga sparks me more than the Christian things." Never-theless, Nadia was quite active in St. Luke's. Growing up in a nominally Lutheran home but unmoved by church, Nadia began her own solitary, teenage yoga practice in her bedroom, with the help of a mail-order yoga booklet from *Seventeen* magazine: "And I remember one day walking down the school hall, and kind of feeling that the world was different somehow, that I was in this altered space. . . . And I knew it had to do with the yoga." Nadia eventually began practicing liturgical dance in Christian settings, returning to yoga in the past decade.

Attracted to Christian practices of meditation and chanted prayer because "they're a little bit more eastern and I've always, I guess just had that kind of predisposition," Nadia wished that she had learned earlier about Christian contemplative practices. She considered her im-pulse toward kinesthetic contemplation to be somehow innate, or, in the half-joking words of a friend, evidence of a "past life" as a yoga practitioner. Instead of understanding her attraction to yoga and to contemplative Christianity as a matter of mere preference, Nadia historicized it, both by nodding to a past life, and by rooting it in her predispositions. Without a ritual tradition embraced from her childhood, she crafted a contemplative legacy that was at once organic and lodged in an artistic and spiritual tradition bigger than her own inclinations.[24]

Similarly to Dorothy Kerin, who in her day could not have been ordained an Anglican priest even had she wanted, Nadia has developed her healing practice without ecclesiastical authority. Frustrated by what she described as Christianity's patriarchal structures and its indifference to "the inner life" of bodily movement, Nadia felt called to bring her yoga discipline into the context of her Christian community, although not in a formal liturgical manner. Nadia began to teach yoga classes each Saturday in the parish hall and sometimes in the church sanctuary, inviting all interested church and local community members. Mixing Hindu practice in Christian space, these yoga classes were an intervention into the implied "Western-ness" of the neo-Gothic space of the church. The goal of St. Luke's original nineteenth-century architect was to remind parishioners of their English heritage, transporting them to feelings of medieval awe, preferably without the memories of Roman Catholicism. Later architects of neo-Gothic Anglican churches had the additional goal that architecture would serve, in the words of Ralph Adams Cram, "as a language and as a mighty missionary influence, winning back the world from heathenism."[25] Nadia's innovative reorganization of the space inverted this missionary thrust, as twenty-first century participants lay on yoga mats gazing up at the afternoon light streaming through stained-glass windows—the same windows that once shed light on early twentieth-century Anglicans dedicated to converting "the Hindu" in other British colonies.

In order to set the tone for the yoga classes in the parish hall, Nadia brought a Black Madonna icon from its usual position of honor in the sanctuary and placed it on an ersatz altar, with candles and other icons, including one of the seventeenth-century Iroquoian Christian Kateri Tekakwitha. Bordered by a poster of martyred El Salvadorean Roman Catholic Archbishop Oscar Romero on the wall behind, the altar evoked Native Christianity, women's spirituality, and liberation theology. Nadia sought to "combine the images, because [the Black Madonna] is a Christian icon, and the idea of icon is, it's a window through which to see God." The careful setting for the class—the darkened room, the altar, the warm blankets Nadia placed on participants during the time of relaxation at the end of the class—shaped the physical kinetics of yoga into a spiritual practice that was at once Christian and not. Linking the meditative quality of her teaching to iconic and historical exemplars of Christianity, Nadia's yoga class engaged Christian space and history while also transforming it.

Conflating historical spaces, times, and bodies, Nadia's yoga classes, especially when held in the main church sanctuary, used ritual proximity to challenge the Christian past of missionary triumphalism. Working with an ontology of contemporaneity akin to Chakrabarty's, Nadia described the church as housing years of sedimented memory and energy: "Like any kind of consecrated space, there's a layering of energy, because this [space] has been used for years and years and years. I mean, it's like when you have an altar at home or a prayer room, vibrations build up." This layering contained conjunctions of past and present, as twenty-first-century bodies practiced *ujjayi* breathing in a nineteenth-century building.[26]

Whether working with therapeutic touch or leading a yoga class, Nadia sought to create sacred space and channel divine healing energy without imparting religious labels: "That was part of my discipline, if you want to call it . . . to be available and open to whoever came, to try to create a nice space and to also try to find ways of including spirituality but without naming it in a particular way."[27] Nadia freely moved between the Sanskrit terminology of yoga and the scientific language of physiology to describe what she called the "spiritual release" that came from yogic gestures and breathing. Nadia sought to authenticate her combination of yoga and Christianity via a personal lineage of experience and authoritative textual and pedagogical sources, including Hindu teachers. Housing her religious fusion within a particularly Christian past (or future) was not crucial to her, but she did share the desire to transform Christianity—and the Christian body—by bringing together disparate histories of East and West through ritual proximity.

Nadia's husband, Patrick, supported this fusion of Christianity and yoga in both his liturgical and personal practice. Sitting in his small office adjacent to the sanctuary, Patrick, a quietly focused man in midlife, described the way he has sought to combine his embrace of Hindu traditions with a revival of what he considered to be the forgotten wisdom traditions of Christianity. That his experimentalism has also corresponded with the burgeoning popularization of yoga was a benefit, in his view: "You can go to yoga classes on Sunday morning that are much better attended than many church services, so what is it? Part of it is probably fad and a kind of fitness faddism . . . but there's also, you know, people are always looking for a sense of feeling connected, and yoga is a means of union." Suggesting that yoga may function as a spiritual practice, Patrick said he would "be delighted if some of them, former Christians, actually discovered that Christianity also knows something about conscious, intentional spiritual practices, and yoga is an excellent vehicle that you can pull some of those things together from your own tradition, as well as learning something from other people." Patrick had recently spent a four-month sabbatical in India, living at a Syrian Orthodox seminary and practicing yoga at a variety of places. Occasionally, he taught the yoga classes at St. Luke's when Nadia was unavailable.

Patrick rooted his ritual innovation in a long history of Christian practices of contemplation and healing. He has drawn most centrally from Eastern Orthodox traditions of prayer, which were also of great interest to his forefathers in the nineteenth-century Oxford Movement within the Anglican Church in England. A nineteenth-century Anglo-Catholic movement dedicated to retrieving liturgical traditions from the Catholic past that their fellow Anglicans had sometimes violently cast aside, the Oxford Movement was highly sacramental, provoking controversy among more Evangelical Anglicans. What his Oxford Movement ancestors might not have foreseen, however, is how Patrick would elaborate their Anglo-Catholic liturgical sensibilities through recourse to even more Eastern religious traditions, namely Hinduism and Buddhism. In positioning his ritual focus on healing as Anglo-Catholic with Asian influences, Patrick also differentiated his approach from charismatic styles of faith healing. Although not entirely hostile to charismatic streams within the Anglican Church—which he knew were also flowing in St. Luke's among parishioners such as Adele—Patrick, with his self-proclaimed Enlightenment heritage, held them at a skeptical but respectful distance.

In shaping an embodied spirituality, Patrick turned to yoga partly from Nadia's influence and partly because of its synergy of empirical observation and wisdom traditions (neglected in modern Christianity, according to Patrick). In good experimentalist fashion, Patrick argued: "Yoga is a huge, complex tradition, but it involves—it's not just a kind of revelation or something like that, but 'let's try this out and see how it works for people.'" Similarly to Nadia, Patrick turned to the concept of "energy" to dissolve the historical oppositions between Eastern religious traditions and Christianity, finding in energy, "qi," "ch'i," and

Reiki (a Japanese-based energy therapy) a transhistorical principle of "tapping into universal life force." As with yoga, Patrick argued that this universal energy could also be found Christianity: "That kind of language is also in the Christian tradition, especially in the Orthodox. The energies of God, especially related to the spirit, prana, and we're back founding connections again: people noticing certain common human experiences that they understand as also being charged with divinity."[28] Although "there are Christians who regard it with fear and loathing," Patrick considers such hostile reactions to interreligious energies to be founded on inadequate and xenophobic historicizing: "I just think they don't know their own tradition that well and are unduly suspicious of wisdom coming from other places." For Patrick, bodily disciplines offered diverse sensational forms for accessing universal wisdom recognized by different names.

When Patrick held healing services during Sunday liturgies, they were simple rituals of anointing with holy oil, in which parishioners lined up in the small sanctuary, stepping forward to let Patrick touch their foreheads with oil that had been blessed by the Bishop of the diocese. He also held an alternate service occasionally on weeknights, which attracted small groups of parishioners to the darkened, candlelit sanctuary to join in quiet Taizé chanting, meditative silence, and prayer, and closing with a circle for the sacrament of anointing. Patrick's weekly Tuesday-night meditation sessions in the church sanctuary were also a place of religious fusion, combining Buddhist- and Eastern Orthodox–influenced meditative prayer, Bible reading, and frank discussion of the biblical text, all under the watchful gaze of the same Black Madonna icon that Nadia had incorporated into her yoga practice.[29] Praying the Jesus Prayer by inhaling on "Lord Jesus Christ" and exhaling on "Have Mercy on Me," the six to ten participants would sit for twenty minutes with their right hands cradled in their left palms, with thumbs touching. Following a contemplative reading aloud of the biblical text, the group began a more conventional style of Bible study, grappling with biblical texts whose puzzling antiquity often challenged their own twenty-first-century cultural contexts. Closing with a prayer for all who suffered, the meditation sessions were carefully structured rituals in which participants could sit with a range of emotions and express them in prayer and conversation if they so desired. The healing that Patrick sought to cultivate in these gatherings was not so much physical, bodily repair as the restoration of the spirit through bodily, intellectual, and emotional work.[30]

As Patrick was quite aware, not all participants in his healing liturgies understood them in quite the same way. Where Adele's Pentecostal anthropology was one example, the meditation/Bible-study group brought forward even more challenging discrepancies in viewpoints. One evening, a woman who was not a regular to the group shared at length her anxious visions of the Eucharistic "blood of the Lamb" with an intensity and fervor that was uncommonly vivid for the group. After listening for a time, Patrick gently suggested that she return to speak with him about her concerns at a later time, and carried on with the Bible study. The hospitality of churches—their invitation to one and all to come for an evening of stretching the body or the mind—makes them particularly combinative places in and of themselves, in which unexpected encounters are always a possibility.

For those who sought a more direct kind of bodily therapy than yoga or meditation, two Reiki practitioners not affiliated with the church occasionally rented the parish hall to hold free or low-cost Reiki workshops, which Patrick often attended. On the evening that I came for a treatment, four rectangular tables of the sort often found in older churches—plywood tops with brown metal legs—were covered in sleeping bags, and arranged in the dimly lit parish hall. The five female "clients" sat on chairs in a circle as the four Reiki channels (one man and three women) began the treatment with breathing exercises and a short primer on Reiki as a "non-religious" technique for "accessing the universal energy" which required only the openness to receive it. Once the clients lay on their tables, the channels quietly circulated around the room, their hands hovering over and alighting on the bodies of their clients. As my channel settled in beside my table and placed her hands on my belly, she asked why I wanted to receive Reiki. Replying that I sought to "relax and be calm," the channel then intoned, "May the universe grant your wish," and added in a whisper, "Reiki can work right away, or sometimes it can take years." Since my curious young daughter had accompanied me to the session, unwilling to let me leave her yet again for another evening of "going to church," my worries that she might disrupt the atmosphere as she rustled through the darkened hall left my wish unfulfilled, at least for that moment.

ENERGY SACRAMENTALISM

At the urging of Patrick, I travelled to Cambridge, Massachusetts to visit the Society of St. John the Evangelist (SSJE), a male monastic community first founded in England in 1866 under the influence of the Oxford Movement. From 1927–1983, several SSJE brothers lived in a monastery in Bracebridge, Ontario a town up the road from Grover Livingstone's Muskoka Sanitarium, but they eventually folded into the Cambridge community.[31] Advised by Patrick that I should speak in particular with Brother John, I set out to visit the neo-Gothic monastery on the banks of the Charles River, where the energy of Reiki was also circulating. Designed in the 1920s by Ralph Adams Cram, the architect with triumphalistic hopes of winning the world back from heathenism, the monastery now sits in the shadow of the Harvard School of Government. Similarly to St. Luke's, the SSJE took an approach to blending traditions in line with what anthropologist Roger Bastide called "religious accumulation."[32] Unlike Nadia's accumulation, Brother John's version was resolutely historical. Like Dorothy Kerin and other self-consciously Christian healers, Brother John considered healing to be an historic legacy of Jesus and the earliest Christians. To carry this healing "energy" across two thousand years, however, Brother John did not feel limited to Christian lineages. He borrowed what he viewed as complementary sources of healing energy: Buddhist meditation and Reiki.[33]

A white-bearded grandfather in his eighties, John met with me in the sunny sitting room of the monastery, where we shared a pot of tea as he told me of his path to becoming an SSJE brother. John was initially drawn to the Anglican monastic community after returning "in bad shape" from service as a marine in the South Pacific during World War II. Feeling too young to commit to a vocation of poverty, celibacy, and obedience, he left the monastery after three years to finish his history degree and then to teach and to raise his daughter as a single parent. Once his daughter left home, he sought out Buddhist teachers who taught the Ch'an and Theravada traditions in America. On the verge of ordination as a Theravada Buddhist monk, John was informed by his teacher that he would never attain enlightenment because he "was born and baptized in Jesus Christ and that's for life." Learning that his teacher considered him to be irrevocably Christian because of his long distant ritual of initiation caused John to rethink his spiritual path. In the late 1980s he returned for good to the Cambridge monastery that is the North American home of the Society of Saint John the Evangelist.[34]

The SSJE's Cambridge chapel is a quietly impressive space of carved stone, stained glass, marble floors, and rows of wooden chairs. At a monthly healing service, John performed the Anglican rite of laying on of hands and anointing with oil, but as a monk and not an ordained priest, he would not consecrate the Eucharist. The Society had tried but ultimately failed to establish a monastery in India in the first half of the twentieth century, but thanks in part to the ministrations of John, aspects of South Asian religions, namely Buddhism and Hinduism, have succeeded in creating a niche for themselves in the American community.[35] Parallel to the ritual innovation in which the Oxford Movement revived the spurned liturgies of Anglicanism's Catholic past, John became part of a similar wave of ritual innovation in which some Anglicans (many influenced by the Oxford Movement) began absorbing the rituals of formerly "heathen" religions. John insisted that human beings need to "find a universal path, a planetary path" and that "Christianity that gets itself bogged into a corner" is not such a path. Although John's hybrid liberalism would be unrecognizable to the Oxford Movement's founders, John cast his embrace of Asian religious traditions of healing entirely in continuity with the Oxford Movement's sacramentalist inheritance.[36]

John was studying to become a Reiki master, inspired by a fellow monk's positive experience of Reiki treatment for a congenital heart ailment. Searching for the right words to describe his healing practices, he contended that "we need an expanded theological ability to speak about these things." Appropriating scientific and Chinese vocabularies, he described channeling the energy of Reiki when laying hands on Christian worshippers seeking healing through the Holy Spirit.[37] John acknowledged that speaking of energy could alarm more conservative Christians, but when that happens, he advised, "You just call it the spirit." Although some who attend the intimate services at the monastery chapel have questioned his willingness to "mix it up"—blending Reiki, the Holy Spirit, and Buddhist practices of meditation—he has followed his planetary path with the full blessing and support of his religious community.[38]

John justified his hybrid approach to spiritual healing or "in modern terms, getting in tune with energy" by turning to a source of legitimacy that bundled together the authoritative norms of textual evidence and antiquity—namely, the historical Jesus. Asserting that "Jesus wouldn't have turned aside Reiki," John contended that the healing energy of Reiki was also preserved in such biblical texts as the Books of Wisdom, and the Acts of the Apostles. In a familiar refrain, John argued that healing "was the promise, but the church lost it, except for a few people." For John, this promised healing was not necessarily curing, but instead a coming to terms with bodily suffering that may or may not eliminate

the suffering.[39] John told a particularly Anglo-Catholic version of the rec-
lamation of Jesus' first-century healing gifts: "For us, it's the Oxford
Movement revival when people began to examine what was lost and to
reinstate it and to reuse it. [Healing] is available as an energy. The energy
hasn't gone away; it's peoples' awareness of it [that has]." John's theology
of energy, similar to that of Du Vernet, argued that not only was energy
universally accessible, it was also transhistorical, whether or not people
were aware of it in different historical eras.

John's strongest claim of lineage, however, lay in his assertion of continuity with the Christian past through ritual, or more particularly,
sacramentalism—an approach that distinguishes him from Du Vernet's
technological enthusiasm. According to John, traditional sacramentalism rooted in the ritual and liturgy of the Anglican Church—not in a
charismatic mode—distinguishes his appeal to healing energy. In his
view, sacramentalism allowed him to draw not on the historical Jesus
who was there, in first-century Palestine, but on the Jesus who is here in
ritual proximity in the twenty-first century, inhabiting John every time
he participated in the sacrament of the Eucharist: "We believe in the real
presence. It's more than a memorial. We are stained by the presence
through the body and the blood." For John, the corporate ritual of the
Eucharist allowed him to eat and drink his way into his Christian faith
via a historicizing ritual that was more than a memorial gesture. For
Anglican sacramentalists, the Communion services of other Protestants
seem watered-down gestures of memory, rather than embodied rituals
in which time, place, and spirit merge.[40] Layering the orthodoxy of his
sacramentalism onto his public (and private) identity as a monk, John
embodies traditions of Christian liturgy that claim lineages stretching
back almost two millennia.

Secure in the authenticity evoked by ritual, architectural, and vo-
cational embodiments of historical Christianity, John embraced Asian-
inflected energy sacramentalism within an ontology of contemporaneity.
Layering continuity with antiquity, his participation in Eucharistic ritual
serves as a backdrop of Christian legitimacy when John "mixes it up" in
other ritual contexts, such as when channeling an "interfaith" healing
energy or when he and his fellow monks welcomed unexpected Buddhist
visitors—also monks—to share in the Eucharist despite their unbap-
tized status. For John, taking the practices and concepts of other religions and enacting a "translation into Christian terms" is neither appropriation nor heresy. Instead, it is an embrace of an evolving future-focused

planetary path that, for him, depends on the Christian past in narrative and ritual forms to tell new stories and enact new rituals of healing and hybridity.

Early in the twentieth century, Anglican commentators on the "hybrid religion" of Christianity and "Eastern systems" had prophesied that "there would come a trying phase of contamination, and then a great enrichment by which our too Western, too exclusively ethical and practical, conceptions would be balanced by Oriental conceptions, predominantly mystical."[41] The "great enrichment" had already commenced with the gestures toward Christian yoga of both British and South Asian Anglicans in the 1920s, but by the end of the century, liberal Anglicans, and other liberal Protestants, had overtly rejected assumptions that Christianity could be "contaminated" by contact with the practices and conceptions of other religions. Instead, liberal Protestants argued that ritual innovation would both create something new and allow Christians to "rediscover" their own pasts. As postcolonial, North American Christians, they historicized in three directions at once: they connected their devotional practices to Christian pedigrees; they delved inward to root their syncretic practices in personal histories of long connection with Asian and other non-Christian religions; and they also cast outward to call forth a tradition of common human religiousness in what Brother John called a "planetary path."

TACTILITY AND MEMORY IN THE UNITED CHURCH

Although without the same historical resources of sacramentalism and liturgical renewal as in the Anglican Church, United Church members have evinced the same energetic practices of ritual combination in the service of healing. True to their union past in which "blending traditions" of Presbyterian, Methodist, and Congregationalist "manifestations of the Spirit" was the heart of their very founding, United Churches have gone far beyond those early visions of what needed unification.[42] Maintaining their long tradition of working from Christian notions of justice and love to urge the Canadian government to provide biomedical health care for all, United Church clergy and members also began turning to new forms of experimentalism in the 1970s. Similar to more renowned spiritual retreats such as Esalen, where anthropologists such as Gregory Bateson and (former) liberal Protestants such as Alan Watts undertook experimentation of many kinds, liberal Protestants throughout North America and Britain developed their own spaces outside of traditional sanctuaries in which ritual experimentation was encouraged. For example, the United Church's Five Oaks Education and Retreat Centre in southern Ontario sought to foster ecumenical encounter and "personal growth," offering weekend seminars in topics such as human sexuality, sacred music with the Roman Catholic Medical Mission Sister Miriam Therese Winter, and more recently, "Labyrinth Solstice Walk: The Sacred Circle."[43]

If Burrswood became the model for Evangelical Anglican healing communities in Canada, the Iona Community in Scotland provided a similar template for liberal Protestants gathered at places such as Five Oaks. Founded in 1938 as an ecumenical community working for "social justice" based in a refurbished medieval abbey on the island of Iona, the Iona Community included healing liturgies from its earliest days. At the same time, many of its adherents worked for the National Health Service and still do.[44] In 1963 the United Church historian John Webster Grant argued that Iona should be an inspiration for "radical renewal" in a United Church too insular in its sense of what counted as Christian tradition: "In such experiments as the Iona Community and the French monastic brotherhood at Taizé they are seeking to make the timeless contemporary and to relate the present world to the eternal order."[45] Such an ontology of contemporaneity would give radically expanded horizons to the project of "union."

Steeped in metaphors of healing as wholeness, Iona community members understood their "ministry of healing" as directed both toward individual suffering and the "wounds of the body politic." According to a former Warden of the community, Peter Millar, the very plurality of religious traditions encountered in the "modern" world has led both modern and postmodern Christians to a "quest for healing": ". . . we are discovering (or rather rediscovering) the *power* of prayer in healing. This is partly because the modern mind, in my opinion, wants a *direct experience* of the divine rather than some mediated experience. Within post modernism there is this search for the transcendent; we cannot live in a world denuded of transcendence."[46]

Orienting this supernaturalism toward social and political concerns, Ian M. Fraser, another member of the Iona Community, considered healing liturgies to be one means for the "purification of memory" that could transform insidious forces such as racism. Drawing from the Jubilee Year repentance of Pope John Paul II, "The Church and the Mistakes of the Past," Fraser argued that "purified memory can draw that past into the present so that it becomes a vivid force." For Fraser, ritualized remembrance of the past, in conjunction with biblical texts, could overcome the fear provoked by difference: "We are not to take our cue for living from the emotions and fears which may well up within us when we encounter people of different ethnic groups, histories, cultures, whom we may consider to be strange or threatening. We are to take our cue from God, who is not respecter of persons and who 'loves the foreigner' (Deuteronomy 10:19)." Ritual proximity, in this view, could bring together the God of the Hebrew Bible, the violence of past Christian triumphalism, and the millennial embrace of the stranger to effect the purification of the "sinful past."[47]

Earlier Protestant languages of contamination in which they fired vitriol at the infectious danger of Christian Science make imagining *redemptive* practices of purification a potentially treacherous thought experiment. As Bruno Latour and others have shown, "purification," whether as an explicit ideal or an implicit social process, can very often be a path to exclusionary violence, or at least to the reification of cultural and religious differences.[48] Liberal Protestants, however, have clearly considered their faith to be tested and refined, if not always purified, through their embrace of difference and their acknowledgment of past injustice. Endorsing Ian Fraser's call to "value and appropriate" the ways of life of "those we profess to be serving," Katharine Hockin, a highly respected United Church missionary, reflected on her own "pilgrimage in mission," in which she shifted from a desire to convert the other to a desire to affiliate with her.[49] Appropriation, in this case, meant the recognition on the part of biomedical and Christian practitioners that non-Western communities have their own understanding and practices of what makes for a good and healthy life, and that Western Christians would remain "sick" without this awareness.

Taking their cue from the healing ministries of places like Iona, and with faint resonances to the rituals of faith healers who had earlier practiced in the United Church, the monthly healing services that I attended at Confederation Street United Church in downtown Toronto were small, quiet, and deliberate gatherings. A large church building with an illustrious past, Confederation Street now has a smaller congregation but still has many people moving through its doors, since its many rooms are rented out for dance and yoga classes, psychotherapy clinics, and talks by prominent left-wing political activists, among other purposes. Marjorie, the minister, led the midweek evening healing services, explaining clearly that one's level of participation was entirely voluntary: one could choose whether to move to the steps leading to the chancel to join the group as they laid hands on a fellow worshipper or one could remain seated in the semicircle of chairs placed close to the foot of the steps.

The first healing service that I went to occurred shortly after the events of September 11, 2001. While a man quietly played Taizé chants on a grand piano, the group of about eight people, mostly older women, both Euro-Canadian and Asian-Canadian, gathered in the circle of chairs. Marjorie, a tall woman with short grey hair, arranged small candles and a bowl of sand on an altar positioned in the middle of the chairs, and had earlier placed large photographs, including one of the twin towers of the World Trade Center, on the steps. The candles, it turned out, were for us to light and place in the sand, after offering a prayer for healing, either aloud or silently. Several people prayed for friends or family they knew who were ill, while others prayed for the healing of the world in the wake of the destruction in New York City. Anyone who wanted the group to pray for her was then invited to come forward to the steps, where she knelt down and the rest of the group laid hands on her as Marjorie gave a brief prayer for her health. The prayed-for person then stood to join the group, and another took her place. Discussing these healing services with me later in her office, Marjorie noted how the services were a remarkable shift from the counseling psychology approach to healing that had dominated her seminary training, and she was quite sure that "our Presbyterian ancestors would flip over in their graves" were they to witness the "Papist" candles and "touchy-feely" laying on of hands of the service. She recalled that she overcame her own fear and discomfort with the aesthetics and tactility of these healing services and with their focus inward rather than "outward to social justice," once she became convinced that they met an important need.

Anglican and United Churches are porous institutions—housing communities of people long familiar with each other, they also, ostensibly, welcome all newcomers. For the most part, the same people attended the Confederation Street healing services each time, although at one service, an aboriginal man who was not a regular, and who was grappling with alcoholism, joined the group. As he talked of his own pain and of the painful weight of his people's history, the rest of the group sat quietly, if awkwardly, listening, opening itself to this man's testimony in a manner similar to the response to the woman who vividly described her visions of the blood of the Lamb to Patrick's meditation and Bible-study group.

The poignant awkwardness of these encounters, as regular group members looked to their leaders to gauge their reactions of hospitality and puzzlement, points to the challenge that urban liberal Protestants face as they try to live out a disposition of welcome: although their hospitality has not always translated into the vibrantly diverse communities that they desire, their imposing buildings are both reminders of their past prominence and the sites for their present attempts to enliven their churches through embracing ritual innovation. Situated on downtown streets that are home to psychiatric survivors, homeless people, and people with various addictions, these churches have opened themselves up as homeless shelters and street health clinics. Every so often, through ritual, they also become sites for encounter between strangers not as clients or beneficiaries, but as people sharing the desire for healing from an increasingly vast panoply of modern pathologies.

PARISH NURSING AND THE SPIRITUALITY GAP

In addition to bringing healing services to Confederation Street, Marjorie has also been a strong supporter of parish nursing, a particularly fertile space of ritual proximity. A blend of biomedical, theological, and ritual expert, parish nurses are registered nurses—virtually all women—who work as part of the ministerial team of a church, dispensing health care advice but not prescription medicines. Parish nursing has become a pliable rubric over the past thirty years—appealing to everyone from evangelical Jesus People to Catholic nuns—in large part because of its conscious approach to historicizing itself within a Christian lineage. As with most genealogies of Christian healing, when advocates of present-day parish nursing account for its rise, they almost invariably place parish nurses at the forefront of a long line of Christian healers, which, depending on the writer, can stretch back to include the Lutheran deaconesses of nineteenth-century Germany, John Wesley's visits to the sick in eighteenth-century England, Jesus's healing ministry in first-century Galilee, or even Shifrah and Puah, the Hebrew midwives who refused Pharaoh's orders to kill male babies born to Hebrew women, as told in Exodus 1:15.[50] Most of these narratives depict Christianity as a tradition that has always nurtured a holistic approach to healing that knits together body, mind, and spirit, whether in Jesus's healing miracles or in parish nursing's effort to "bridge the gap that has separated religion and spirituality from healing and wholeness."[51] Heralded as the "reincarnation of the Deaconess movement," parish nursing has its roots in the intersection of Christianity and nursing that formed the very beginnings of modern nursing practice.[52] Unlike the Deaconess, however, the parish nurse who emerged in the 1980s was no longer located in a household of women dedicated to the poor and the newly immigrated. Instead, she operated from within specific congregations as a registered nurse who was part of the ministerial team, and usually focused more on the needs of Christian congregants than on those of the non-Christian stranger. Parish nursing's appeal to a tradition of early Christian healing must be set in the particular contexts of its growth in the United States in the mid-1980s, a time when women's ordination was a controversial topic in many denominations and when charismatic forms of spiritual healing grew increasingly popular.

Although not necessarily in conscious response to debates in theological anthropology, parish nursing has adopted a tripartite anthropology of the self with unwavering clarity. The frequent incantation of "body, mind, and spirit" by those trying to explain the goals of parish nursing, and by Christians engaged in the cultivation of "spiritual wellness" more broadly, functions as a rhetorical reminder that parish nursing roots itself in plural epistemologies of physical suffering, including biomedical, psychological, and theological views. Although acknowledging the authority of biomedicine in their licensing requirements and many of their practices, parish nurses are medical personnel who have chosen to step outside of ostensibly secular medical workplaces (forgoing higher levels of pay as well) and into religious roles where they are free to directly invoke spiritual resources in their therapeutic work. Found among Lutherans, Anglicans, Roman Catholics, the United Church, and Pentecostals, parish nurses understand their vocation in radically different ways with some focused on biomedical referrals and diagnostics, such as blood pressure checks, others adopting a charismatic approach in cooperation with the Order of St. Luke, and still others widening their scope to include energy healing.

Most narratives of the development of parish nursing credit its founding to Granger Westberg (1911–1999), a seminary professor, hospital chaplain, and minister within the Evangelical Lutheran Church in America, who worked throughout his life to carve out organizational spaces where Christianity and biomedicine could meet.[53] Although Westberg was not the first to use the phrase, he popularized it, arguing that parish nurses could serve as ". . . catalysts in getting representatives of medicine and theology to talk with each other. Nurses seemed to have one foot in the humanities and one foot in the sciences and thereby were able to bridge the unnecessary gap between these two very old and esteemed positions."[54] Starting up in Canada in the early 1990s, with its teaching arm based in the United Church's Emmanuel College, parish nursing organizers soon turned their attention to professional accreditation. In 1998 the American Nurses Association recognized parish nursing as a specialty nursing practice, and in 2007 the Canadian Association of Parish Nursing Ministry was admitted as an associate member of the Canadian Nurses Association. By 2006 approximately 10,000 parish nurses worked primarily in the United States and Canada but could also be found in Great Britain, Korea, Australia, New Zealand, Swaziland, Zimbabwe, and South Africa.[55]

Where Nadia, John, and Patrick found a lack within Christianity that bodily disciplines such as yoga could address, parish nurses widely consider the materialism of biomedicine to suffer from a spirituality gap. Retaining a connection to their biomedical authority, while being freer to critique aspects of biomedical care systems, has been an important premise for many parish nurses. For example Sue, a parish nurse at a thriving 300-member United Church in a southeastern Ontario town, learned about parish nursing from reading articles in the *Toronto Star* and the *United Church Observer*. I spoke with Sue, a grandmother who had been recently widowed, in the basement of her church after I attended her workshop on child development for young mothers. She described how after more than thirty years as a registered nurse, she felt the lack of "depth" in the medical model of treatment and was attracted to the possibility of bringing a "spiritual connection" to her work. Although in her first volunteer position she found it difficult to explain just what a parish nurse did—a common concern among parish nurses— through training from the Interchurch Health Ministries and her own trial and error, she came to blend a range of modalities into her part-time paid position as a parish nurse to a largely rural and generationally diverse congregation.

As the first parish nurse in her congregation, Sue quickly recognized that she needed to educate the congregation about her role and that she needed to establish her credibility. In addition to making hospital and home visits to church members with health problems and leading workshops on health-related issues, she organized mothers' groups, a "Health Matters" group, and a group for widows and widowers. With the support of the church's minister and a congregational "health cabinet" that met with her regularly to discuss her work, Sue also introduced a wide diversity of "healing" activities: yoga classes, kite-making workshops for families, labyrinth walks, Lenten prayer beads, and healing services. Her healing services featured candles and laying on of hands and were the most liturgically traditional and "intimate" of her ritual innovations. However, compared to the popular yoga classes, for which Sue hired a certified yoga instructor, the healing services were not well attended. Recognizing that the reception of these innovations depended on "the credibility of the people involved" and that "some people are not interested at all," Sue said she was careful not to "force these things." Trained in therapeutic touch, Sue offered it to some people who have come to her with health problems and who seemed open to the possibility.

In the midst of all this ritual innovation, United Church parish nurses were adamant that their work was not meant to compete with the state-funded health care system. At Marjorie's church, where I attended meetings of the parish nurse health cabinet, whereas some members worried that the parish nurse would render obsolete lay traditions such as visiting the congregation's sick, others raised the concern that parish nursing should not fill the cracks in a public health care system threatened by neoconservative privatization. Sue, however, clearly saw "medical issues" as the base of her work, distinguishing her approach from the "social visits" of pastoral care. Guiding people through the complexities of a health care system, which in rural areas suffers from a shortage of doctors and walk-in clinics, Sue understood the biomedical aspects of her ministry to be very important. But she also saw the blood pressure checks and health care advice she proffered as ultimately "spiritually based because they [her clients] see the support they can obtain from the church environment, without anything being asked back. That's a big thing."

While cautious to avoid stepping in to bail out an underfunded health care system, parish nurses sought to offer their biomedical expertise as religious practitioners. Like their medical missionary precursors, they have understood how potent the combination of biomedicine and spirituality could be, as Sue described her attempts at "going a little deeper and introducing the concept of prayer, the importance of prayer, interaction of prayer, making people and congregations just more comfortable in the prayer environment. Because it seems that when people reach their deepest pain, it is prayer that is left to them. And to have somebody to just work with that, or pray for them, it seems to be important." Not endorsing an unwavering confidence in spiritual intervention that understands prayer to bring about bodily healing, Sue nevertheless was convinced of the necessity of prayer and the need to cultivate habits and dispositions of prayer in her congregation. Working in a church marked by a membership with more historical continuity and cultural similarity than in many urban contexts—"people . . . have their whole history of their family in this church building"—Sue did this work of cultivation via both traditional and innovative rituals.

Sue learned much about ritual innovation from her colleague, Debra, from whom she borrowed the labyrinth ritual. Debra, an energetic, middle-aged woman who was also a parish nurse in a small-town United Church within commuting distance from Toronto, was widely described to me as a leader in therapeutic ritual innovation by her parish nursing colleagues. She described her work as "bodyprayer": the integration of therapeutic touch, Reiki, labyrinth walks, and healing services with the laying on of hands that would ideally bring a new awareness and appreciation of bodiliness as a realm of spirituality. Instead of opening up the church to Reiki practitioners, Debra started her own therapeutic touch "clinic" with a Christian orientation, a trend that continues in many liberal Protestant churches. True to the philosophy of parish nursing, in which the parish nurse encourages members of the congregation to take responsibility for their health, Debra taught willing members of her congregation how to practice therapeutic touch and then opened a clinic that now attracts members of other congregations and "those who do not attend any church." Similarly to the Christian framing of the yoga classes and meditation services at St. Luke's, Debra described each clinic session as beginning with "a Christian guided meditation, followed by therapeutic touch treatments and a closing intercessory prayer circle. In this way we practiced therapeutic touch in a Christian context."[56] Debra also described her practice of giving individual therapeutic touch treatments to members of her congregation, in many circumstances: "pre and post operative, during the course of chemotherapy, depression, injury, throughout the dieting process, etc. I have always thought of it as a bodyprayer. Most people were open to it and if they weren't that was okay too. The minister would never have a treatment himself, but he frequently referred people to me for treatments."

Where therapeutic touch and Reiki evoked skepticism that was not easily met with a historicizing counterargument, Debra authenticated

FIGURE 14. Labyrinth on the grounds of Vancouver School of Theology, Vancouver, BC, 2007. Photo by author.

walking the labyrinth in a Christian pedigree that cast it as an indigenous European ritual. The labyrinth is a "vague" ritual practice that speaks at once to a generic "spirituality" while it also claims a Christian lineage via medieval labyrinths plotted in the stone floors of European monasteries and Cathedrals, such as Chartres.[57] Explanations of the labyrinth often start with three key points: (1) labyrinths are "centuries old" and deliberatively walking through their channels was a part of medieval Christian devotional practice; (2) walking the labyrinth slows the pace of life allowing for encountering emotions, new insight, and healing; and (3) labyrinths are not mazes—"if you follow the path you cannot get lost." The proliferation of labyrinths across North America has traversed Christian, biomedical, and public space: medieval-style labyrinths have been added to churches, seminaries, and public parks (including the Lewis Memorial United Church in rural Alberta, the Anglican Church of the Holy Trinity in downtown Toronto, the Vancouver School of Theology, and the Waterford Hospital in Newfoundland).[58] The recent rise of the labyrinth as a devotional and therapeutic tool in the gardens of public hospitals is evidence that Christian rituals still "fit" in some biomedical contexts.

Parish nurses such as Debra and Sue draw from a broad range of techniques as they seek to make "spiritual connections" with others, establishing their credibility on the basis of their medical training and their ability to design and lead a good ritual. Their stories of healing were at once more clinical and more intimate that those told by Patrick or Brother John—they focused less on healing via universal, transhistorical energy, and more on helping others to come to their own understandings of healing as wholeness, informed by the liberal Protestant view that one cannot expect miraculous cures. For example when asked how she would describe her view of a healthy body, Debra explained:

> I think that it is achieving the best that we can with the limitations that we have. So, you know, I have had a couple of experiences with people who are going through the journey of terminal illness. And I can think of one woman in particular who was really well. Now that doesn't mean that her body was cured or perfect, but she was truly whole and well, and lived her life within the limitations that she had. And so she was, she saw herself as whole and well and sort of lived into her dying instead of dying every day. So it has to be a balance of being well in body, mind, and spirit. A healthy body, you know there are people with healthy bodies and they are not well. And that's only a piece of it. And I guess a healthy body to me would be one that's in relationship, in right relationship, so that it would mean you weren't abusing it in various ways, and caring for it in the way that it would need to be cared for.

Right relationship, as a balancing act within the self and between self and others, expects spiritual equilibrium to bring not miraculous cure but imperfect wellness.

That Granger Westberg found nurses to be his perfect point of contact between theology and medicine is in keeping with medical historian Charles Rosenberg's insight that holistic care of the "whole patient" (as opposed to medical curing of a particular ailment) has always been central to nursing: "In some ways the nursing profession's acceptance of holistic thinking is that profession's central ideological tradition."[59] In the context of parish nursing, the ideological work of holistic healing is partly to carve out a space of authority for nurses that draws from both biomedical and spiritual therapies, thus claiming a holism of perspective and practice that is at once ceaselessly flexible and open to a variety of very different interpretations. By virtue of its position as a medically and ecclesiastically sanctioned movement, liberal versions of parish nursing have also opened a route for feminist and alternative forms of ritual practice to find their way into more traditional church communities.

MEDICINE AND RELIGIOUS DIFFERENCE IN
GLOBALIZED CHRISTIANITY

The ritual flexibility of parish nursing has its detractors—one parish nurse from New York told me of her congregation's increasing suspicion of the non-Christian origins of the variety of practices in her "wellness center" to the point that the church authorities scaled back her resources significantly. Parish nursing has embodied the expansiveness of holistic healing by evoking a syncretism of biomedical authority, ritual experimentation, and Christian tradition in which nurses literally work on and with bodies in a way that ministers do not. Touching the skin, laying on hands, reading blood pressure, leading the way in the labyrinth, parish nurses inhabit their own bodies and the bodies of those they serve as sensational forms by which divinity, in a diversity of registers, is mediated. But what is mediation for one is heresy for another.

A revealing lens for this adjudication of innovation versus heresy is the World Council of Churches (WCC), especially in the work of its Christian Medical Commission, which has long encouraged Christians to understand healing in a more globalized and pointedly political manner in the wake of independence movements among colonized countries, as well as with the rise of liberation and feminist theologies. Both the Anglican Church and the United Church have long participated actively in the WCC—the United Church's first woman moderator, Lois Wilson, became a WCC President in 1983. In the words of a WCC report, "Our body/mind/spirit can be broken by social injustice, misuse of power, unhealthy relationships and life style, lack of care for and abuse of creation, individualism, materialism, and false spirituality."[60] In the context of WCC forums on health care, renewed awareness of the colonialism and paternalism of medical missions prompted many Euro-American liberal Protestants to develop appreciation for indigenous, traditional healing practices, as well as for the indigenous Christians who kept these practices alive. At the same time, disenchantment with the limits of biomedical explanations and treatments have prompted calls for biomedicine to make room for new kinds "spiritual" collaboration with Christianity and have set some liberal Protestants on a path toward "complementary" and/or non-Christian healing modalities, such as therapeutic touch, yoga, or acupuncture.

In other parts of the WCC, when the appreciation of nonbiomedical and non-Christian healing came into full flower, it provoked great controversy. Oft condemned by conservative Protestants for its political,

economic, and theological liberalism (or radicalism), two WCC events
in the 1990s—their Seventh Worldwide Assembly in Canberra, Australia in 1991 and a WCC-sponsored "Re-Imagining" conference on feminist theology in Minneapolis in 1993—sparked furious debate for their
openness to interreligious blending and their unabashed celebration of
feminist theology. Healing became a site for fusing these two themes, as,
for example, in the ritual experimentation of one woman at the center
of both events, Korean theologian Chung Hyun-Kyung. In Canberra
Chung presided over a plenary ritual in which she invited the spirits of
Korean shamanism to partake in the assembly theme of "Come Holy
Spirit, renew the whole creation." In Minneapolis she led conference-
goers in rituals of "pranic healing" (prana being a Sanskrit word for
breath or spirit) and encouraged them to draw on a variety of spiritual
energies from trees, rocks, and the natural world. Declaring herself an
unapologetic "syncretist" in contrast to the covert syncretism that has
characterized much of Christian missionary encounter, Chung's experimentation prompted a strong backlash from both mainline and Evangelical Christians.[61]

In the wake of these highly publicized moments of syncretic, feminist, rituals of healing, the WCC seems to have taken a step back from
its embrace of the "complementary." The Christian Medical Commission's earlier attempts to reconcile a holistically biomedical spirituality
with traditional, non-Christian practices appeared largely absent from
a 2002 WCC Commission on World Mission and Evangelism "Consultation on Faith, Healing, and Mission" held in Accra, Ghana. In a move
away from the WCC's liberal Protestant base, the majority of participants at the consultation were from Pentecostal or Charismatic churches
that were not members of the WCC. Not surprisingly, the discussion
did not focus on how to learn from non-Christian versions of holistic
healing but, instead, debated the benefits of the exorcism of evil spirits
and the relative importance of "the world of spirits or of social structures, on people's suffering."[62] The social structure versus spirits debate
took a decidedly spiritual turn in a follow-up WCC paper, "The Healing Mission of the Church," prepared by an ecumenical group for the
2005 meeting of the Commission on World Mission and Evangelism
held in Athens. The authors seemingly realized that the discourse of
spiritual intervention was on the rise, and focused on how best to
moderate the tensions between the healing anthropologies of those
churches shaped by "post Enlightenment scientific rationality" and

those churches shaped by charismatic traditions of demonology and the "power encounter" between God and other (diabolical) spiritual entities.[63]

Whereas earlier reports from the Christian Medical Commission could embrace (if vaguely) the benefits of traditional, non-Christian healing practices, the 2005 paper made specific mention of Reiki and Yoga as disputed practices, favored largely by "Christians in the West." Although all healing comes from God, the paper argued, in the case of non-Christian practices "caution or even explicit rejection are recommended wherever religious dependency is created on the healer or Guru, absolute spiritual, social, or economic obedience is demanded, humans beings are kept in a spirit of threat, anxiety or bondage due to healing practices, the success of a healing is made dependent on fundamental changes in the religious worldview of Christians."[64] Earlier critics of materialist, capitalist models of biomedical care might have replaced "guru" with "biomedical system," but these WCC authors were clearly not implicating modern medicine in their argument—their focus was "Western" Christians such as (ironically) Chung Hyun-Kyung, who had by then moved to the famously liberal Union Theological Seminary in New York City. Recommending a much more conservative version of experimentalism than that espoused by Chung, the 2005 paper suggested that the Bible invites Christians to "test everything" (1 Thessalonians 5:21–22), but cautioned, "When encountering practices of healing and energetic therapeutic work rooted in other religions, Christians should always first of all feel encouraged to rediscover the rich diversity and ancient spiritual traditions of healing within the Christian church itself." Contrary to the WCC embrace of the traditional practices of Asians and Africans in the 1980s, by the new millennium, WCC documents asserted that indigenous practices were only assimilable if they could be woven into a Christian pedigree. The "Healing Mission of the Church," the WCC authors concluded, would best be served by turning to Anglican, Orthodox, and Roman Catholic liturgies of healing and by exploring an ecumenical, i.e. intra-Christian, movement for the "rehabilitating of the office of the exorcist as Christian ministry in those church traditions where it does not exist."[65]

The earlier health-as-justice approach of the Christian Medical Commission was not entirely forgotten however, as the contribution by Aram I, the WCC's then-moderator, demonstrated. The Armenian Orthodox leader argued that healing is an ontological basis of Christianity—a holistic, ecumenical, ground upon which Christians should work for community-oriented justice, challenge abuses of power, strive for the healing of the ecological system, work for reconciliation and forgiveness while honoring memories of injustice, and reflect upon the anthropology of Christian healing. He too, however, worried about healing becoming a financial transaction and cautioned that although "indigenous cultural forms and approaches in a healing ministry [are] sign[s] of strength and richness, [they] may easily lead to syncretism when cultural forms are considered as norms and are not checked by the Gospel."[66] Offering an account of healing much more in line with the justice and right-relations language of liberal Protestants, Aram I still described an ontology of healing that was suspicious of extra-biblical norms.

Though its wholeness was always with cracks, by the new millennium holistic Christianity could not encompass all anthropologies of healing. In a world where Charismatic and Pentecostal Christianities were growing rapidly in both North America and the global south, healing and wholeness became a rubric under which the WCC invoked Christian liturgical traditions, welcomed charismatic notions of spiritual intervention, and exorcised non-Christian spirits in one fell swoop. The tension between affirming the "indigenous" and "exorcising" it took on new meanings in postcolonial, global Christianity. On the one hand, movements of "enculturation" and overt syncretism celebrated the combination of Christianity with the "traditional." On the other hand, African, Asian, North American, and European Christian critics of non-Christian healing practices allied across varying theological persuasions in defiant opposition to a range of practices, whether Reiki, Yoga, or New Age therapies.

In contrast, liberal "Christians in the West" (including some Catholics) have increasingly embraced a blending of Christian and non-Christian healing practices and theologies, heedless of the kinds of cautions issued by the World Council of Churches. The heirs of a post-Enlightenment skepticism, they looked to other Enlightenment notions, such as cosmopolitanism, to open up the boundaries of their theological anthropologies and the disciplines of their bodies. Speaking a language of affiliation rather than exorcism, liberal Protestants built new versions of "affective communities" in which they sought to learn from religious others rather than convert them.[67] When the Protestants in question were themselves indigenous peoples who were once the target of medical and other missions, crafting healing as a site for affiliative spirituality made for a particularly charged space of contestation and combination.[68]

THE MEETING GROUND OF HEALING

The expectation that healing encompass justice has been put to its greatest test in the encounter between First Nations and Christian practices of healing. Combinations of Christian and Native practices have grown increasingly important for liberal Protestants since the time that Du Vernet practiced a kind of ritual proximity with Tsimshian spirits in his notion of spiritual radio.[69] A more recent example is that of Andrew Ahenakew, a Plains Cree Anglican priest from Saskatchewan whose story was recounted in the *Canadian Churchman* by Ernie Willie, also a First Nations Anglican. After a long career as what he described as a "brainwashed Anglican clergyman," Ahenakew received a vision that bestowed upon him the gift of healing. While traveling in Manitoba and worried about his brother ill with cancer, Ahenakew experienced a vision of a "beautiful creature, a creature of God, sent by God" that instructed him to make a special bear medicine and take on the gift of healing. Encouraged and aided by his wife Alice, Ahenakew made the medicine and started attending whoever requested a healing. Too frightened to tell his bishop of the vision and the medicine, he kept them secret for a year. When he did reveal his story, the bishop gave Ahenakew his blessing, acknowledging that "the gift of spiritual healing was indeed part of the church's work." Ahenakew then openly practiced his gift, anointing with medicine and praying for all who visited his healing tepee.[70]

Similar stories of Native clergy discovering their healing gifts, often with trepidation and reluctance, are also found in the *United Church Observer*. Although not herself becoming a healer in the manner of Ahenakew, Jessie Saulteaux, an Assiniboine woman from Saskatchewan, drew on her stories of her grandmother, a Plains medicine woman, to ground her own approach to Christianity.[71] At the Jessie Saulteaux Resource Centre, a United Church theological college oriented toward First Nations students, the blending of Native and Christian rituals has taken many forms, including four-day seasonal ceremonies open to all, which feature a sweat lodge and potluck feast as a way to "renew and refresh your body, mind, and spirit."[72] In discussing this ritual blending, Stan McKay, the co-director of the Centre and the first Native (Cree) moderator of the United Church, has cautioned that bringing together Christian and First Nations traditions requires changes in the ritual pace of Anglo-Protestant liturgies that might be hard to achieve.[73] Despite these challenges, McKay freely brings rituals such as smudging into broad-based

United Church gatherings, as a mode of both personal "cleansing" and preparation for community participation.[74] McKay roots his blend of Christian and First Nations traditions in an ontology of wholeness stemming from a very different spiritual resource than that of Pentecostal or liberal healers, but nevertheless one shaped by the larger holistic discourse: "The value that comes from the spirituality of my people is one of wholeness. It certainly is related to a view of life which does not separate or compartmentalize. The relationship of health with ourselves, our community and with all creation is a spiritual relationship."[75] This Native ontology of wholeness circulates within the wider Protestant communities with both friction and fluidity.

In 1986, seven years before Anglican Archbishop Michael Peers' apology at a convocation of First Nations Anglicans, the United Church moderator Robert Smith apologized for his church's historic subjugation of First Nations peoples and spiritual traditions, via a statement that Stan McKay had helped to draft:

> We imposed our civilization as a condition for accepting the gospel. We tried to make you be like us and in so doing we helped to destroy the vision that made you what you were. As a result you, and we, are poorer and the image of the Creator in us is twisted, blurred, and we are not what we are meant by God to be. We ask you to forgive us and to walk together with us in the Spirit of Christ so that our peoples may be blessed and God's creation healed.[76]

In both Anglican and United Church apologies, the metaphor of healing itself sought to create a kind of ritual proximity, as it gestured to First Nations traditions of healing, embodied in the lives of First Nations Christians such as Andrew and Alice Ahenakew and Jessie Salteaux, at the same time that it drew from a long tradition in which healing was a fundamental task of Christian witness. Whether the history of medical missions and First Nations traditions can share such space is a question in process. Indisputably, however, healing has been an important metaphor and practice through which some non-Native Anglican and United Church members and congregations have become more receptive to Native spirituality as practiced by the First Nations Christians among them. The metaphor has persisted in both churches' establishment of "healing funds" as granting agencies that fund Native-run projects of language retrieval, healing workshops, and community health clinics as ways to "repair the damage" that residential schools wrought on First Nations communities.[77] It also persists in the language of the

FIGURE 15. Derelict St. Michael's Anglican Residential School in Alert Bay, BC, 2007. The school began in 1882, and this building opened in 1929 and was under Anglican control until 1968. It is now owned by the 'Namgis First Nation community in Alert Bay. Photo by author.

Truth and Reconciliation Committee. Exercises in imperfection by definition, these attempts at healing history have brought the debatable past into the present.

APPROPRIATING THE PAST

Liberal Protestant embrace of Asian and First Nations' traditions of embodied ritual has come as a result of personal experiences as well as wider historical trajectories of Christianity, colonialism, orientalism, Hindu and Buddhist proselytizing in North America, and the rise of communities of First Nations Christians. Charting lineages of religious transmission both Christian and non-Christian, liberal Protestants have embedded their syncretic embrace of yoga, meditation, and Reiki within webs of Christian ritual. As they stretch their bodies in the sun salutation in a church sanctuary, meditate with the help of a biblical verse, or channel universal healing energy through an anointing service, liberal Christians inhabit spaces and rituals with long histories of both exclusion and experimentation. Making proximate what was once the "other"—adopting "Gurus" or becoming Reiki Masters—liberal Christians have drawn criticism for their syncretism, a highly controversial but useful term.[78] Some fellow Christians charge them with heresy, while other critics (including some scholars) consider their syncretism a consumerist fad, or worse, an orientalist "exotic fantasy" appropriating religious traditions that colonialist Christians once condemned.[79]

At their most extreme, heresy and appropriation are categories that depend on the assumption that traditions can and should be pure and that hybridity or syncretism is contamination.[80] The hybridizing discourse of liberal Protestants avoids claiming purity or uniqueness, without abandoning claims of authenticity.[81] Maneuvering around charges of faddism, appropriation, and heresy, ritually innovative liberal Protestants deploy the past to articulate a Christian embrace (but not conversion) of non-Christian healing traditions, demonstrating that historicizing is not only about claiming one's own history through lineages of cultural or religious purity; it can also include selective embrace of another's tradition with all the complicated relationships such retroactive kinship entails. Judging this cross-cultural experiment solely as unrecognized "imperialist projection" is not sufficient.[82] These lives cannot be cast as beyond the legacies of orientalism or colonialism, but nor should they be confined to a reductionist narrative that leaves exotic fantasy as the only trope with which to describe popular Western, South Asian, or First Nations' efforts of cross-religious relation.

The "ancestral history" of liberal Protestants contrasts with a common theme discussed by many anthropologists of Christianity, namely the tension experienced by many non-Western Christians between "traditional" ritual obligations to ancestors and newer Christian models of the autonomous self standing in relation to God or a congregation, but free from the encumbrances of kinship with the dead. Birgit Meyer points to how, in Ghana, African-led Pentecostalism was able to accept Ewe ancestral spirits as real spiritual forces in a way that German Lutheran mission churches could not, even if Pentecostals turned ancestors into "diabolical" spirits in the process. Webb Keane shows how Dutch Calvinist missions among the Sumbanese in Indonesia led to a Sumbanese Calvinism for which the past was a "threat" standing in the way of cultivating "modern" Christian subjects who were not burdened by ancestral relations, and thereby were open to the progress promised by Protestant and secular liberal narratives.[83]

Though the question of their ancestors' effects as spirits per se has not been one that perturbs most Anglicans or United Church members (save for the spiritualists among them), the ongoing spiritual and political effects of their ancestors has been of great concern. Marjorie's comment that her "Presbyterian ancestors would flip over in their graves" were they to know of her healing services demonstrates an ironic awareness of the disjunction between past and present. The 1998 apology to former students of Indian Residential Schools offered by the United Church Moderator Bill Phipps acknowledged a more tragic ancestral weight: "We know that many within our church will still not understand why each of us must bear the scar, the blame for this horrendous period in Canadian history. But the truth is, we are the bearers of many blessings from our ancestors, and therefore, we must also bear their burdens."[84]

Acknowledging their ancestral history and bearing the scar precisely because they had come to reevaluate what it means to be a Christian in a world of religious difference, liberal Protestants have at once chosen *and* been forced—by legal processes, the Canadian government, and First Nations people, including Anglicans and United Church members—to carry the burden of the past. There are limits to what carrying this burden has meant, as liberal Protestants, and most Canadians, do not consider it realistic to entirely abandon the blessings of land and sovereignty that their ancestors gave them through creating Canada in part via the forcible containment of First Nations people. For Anglicans and United Church members in particular, however, if they seek to maintain a continuity with their historic churches—and to avoid "zooming around" in the words of Courtney Bender's account of the "spiritual imperialisms" of some contemporary American mystical traditions—they cannot escape their ancestors.[85] They also cannot give up on the possibility of "progress," even if it is a chastened sensibility that they can learn from their mistakes.

Living within Christian community, and sometimes with deep attention to Christian history, liberal Protestants have turned not to doctrine but to ritual to evoke and articulate their religious blending. They have claimed an authenticity for their ritual adaptations based in a simultaneous valorization of innovation and tradition that invokes intimate stories of their own pasts together with grand narratives of energy flows in the past and future.[86] As Wade Clark Roof has argued, the question of "how to appropriate the past into a meaningful present" is one of the most pressing of issues for North Americans negotiating the relationship between historical tradition and individual choices in a world of shifting religious (and other) borders.[87] That these Christians seeking to heal history do so with a multiplicity of spirits, ancestors, and traditions at play within their own families and their own churches means that ritual proximity can neither escape responsibility for the past, nor stop experimenting in the present.

Conclusion

Critical Condition

The idea of the crisis of modernity is born with modernity;
it is the ingredient modernity can never do without.
—Claude Lefort, *Writing, the Political Test,* 2000

Invoking healing as the way to achieve their goals both political and
spiritual, liberal Protestants championed a metaphor hard to counter.
Who could disagree with healing as a goal with wide, if not universal,
resonance? Liberal Protestant anthropologies of the spiritual body drew
from a wide array of sources—biomedicine, yoga, Reiki, Jesus's healing
miracles—to craft an ideal of healing as wholeness that would make
space for a diversity of spirits. Arguing not that everyone could have a
right to be physically healed, but that everyone should have a right to
the process of healing, liberal Protestants sought to embrace the weakness and finitude of the body, without giving up the Holy Ghost. Over
the course of the twentieth century, healing shifted from being the grounds
for solidarity with science and vitriolic condemnation of heresies and
heathens to becoming a process of autocritique through which Euro-
American liberals in the Anglican and United Churches apologized for
their history as settler-colonialists while they held out hope for reconciliation with First Nations peoples. All the while, healing incorporated
both the supernatural and the scientific, as a realm in which liberal Protestants could calibrate their experiences of and "tune" their reactions to
a range of modern technologies of the self, whether biomedicine, radio
mind, or psychoanalysis. Being "liberal Protestants" gave many middle-
class, and largely white, Canadians a space in which to imagine and to
work toward a cosmopolitan world that would be founded on peace
with justice. But being a member of the Anglican Church or the United

Church placed them in a denomination, and a nation, with burdens from the past both moral and monetary.

After years of interrogating their own complicity with the pathologies of modernity, and in the wake of the growing power of conservative Protestants, many North American liberal Protestants have recently sought to recuperate their critical temperament as a tradition with its own virtues. Instead of writing with their cultured despisers in mind, however, they now orient their arguments to their "Christian detractors," as did U.S. novelist Marilynne Robinson in her 2006 essay, "Onward, Christian Liberals." Tracing the contours of Christian liberalism via biblical and theological texts, American religious history, and scientific method, Robinson argued for an "ethic of liberality" in which "doubt and self-doubt are allied with truth—teaching as they do that truth as we know it remains forever partial and provisional." In response to those Christians who disdain liberals as "not really religious" dilettantes, Robinson defended the liberal habit of self-critique as a doctrine of "inescapable fallibility":

> This doctrine is very liberal in its consequences, an excellent basis for the harmony in diversity that is an essential liberal value now under attack as relativism or as an unprincipled concession to what is now called secularism. This secularism, which is supposed to alarm us, in fact may be nothing more alien to religion than the common space our many flourishing religious traditions have long been accustomed to share. In any case, it is worth remembering that such a common, nonjudgmental space is fully consistent with faithful doubt, as it were, which has not only the very humane consequence of allowing us to live together in peace and mutual respect, but also a strong theological and Scriptural grounding. It is first of all the responsibility of liberal or mainline Protestants to remember this, because insofar as it is an aspect of their tradition, they should understand it and be able to speak for it.[1]

Finally, in making the case that liberal Protestants are not the same as libertines, Robinson hazarded an epidemiological argument: "In present terms, no statistics indicate that any of the vices or pathologies of modern life are more prevalent among liberal Protestants than among any other group."[2]

Robinson's clarion call to reclaim liberal Protestantism as a *tradition* comes on the heels of both popular and scholarly depictions of liberalism as an unrooted, relativizing *attitude*, that has demanded little of its advocates. As church historian George Marsden declared of early twentieth-century Protestantism in the United States, "Liberal religion was essentially culture-affirming and hence would appeal to more cosmopolitan individuals as a form of Christianity that would not unduly disrupt their established forms of life."[3] Similarly, sociologist Donald Luidens and his colleagues contended that "lay liberalism, with its highly individualized faith and its wide-open acceptance of cultural variety, has been a pragmatic response to the challenges of modernity." Arguing that lay liberals turn outward in their acknowledgment that truth may inhere in other religious traditions beside Christianity, they predicted that its "personalized" style would be its demise: "[W]hile lay liberalism may be a creative response to modern pluralism, our findings are not an unqualified affirmation of this perspective. Lay liberalism is very shifting sand on which to build a religious community. It has no inherent loyalty factor upon which institutions can depend for sustained support."[4] In the terrain of Protestant liberalism, novelists are often its most eloquent advocates, whereas many scholars diagnose its very "modernity" as a terminal condition.[5]

But what happens when we work to understand liberal Protestantism as a community of interpretation—however imagined, virtual, or face-to-face—that cannot be fully understood by the standards or desires of an evangelical Protestant orthodoxy or by the numerical marker of bodies in the pews? Much of the recent analysis of liberal Protestantism in Canada and the United States comes from conservative evangelicals such as Marsden, who end up implicitly using their version of theological orthodoxy as the point of departure for telling a story of the "decline" of liberal denominations. Sometimes, they even display *Schadenfreude* as they recount how liberal Protestants' flagrant embrace of worldly secularism has led to their dispersal and demise. Holding this numerical eschatology at bay, what might be other ways to understand liberal Protestant sensibilities of critique and dispositions of cosmopolitanism? And how have these critical dispositions been formed through debates and practices of healing?

Liberal Protestants have dwelt within—while also articulating—the crisis of modernity through habits of critique—habits that moved many of them from liberalism to liberationism. In the 1960s, for example, the Anglican Church of Canada, largely at the behest of its liberal-leaning leaders and membership, commissioned not one but two external critiques of their church. First, in 1965 Pierre Berton, a prominent Canadian journalist who had embraced "liberal humanism" over and against his childhood Anglicanism, wrote the surprisingly best-selling *The Comfortable Pew*, a controversial and brash critique that admonished Canadian Protestantism for failing to engage with the social and political

crises of the day. Turning the screws further, a group of Canadian Anglicans edited another book in response, in which an international group of
authors largely embraced Berton's diagnosis of a church at risk of dying
by conventionality, as all around it people grappled with the prospect of
nuclear war, changing sexual mores, and the continuing effects of racism
and colonialism.

One British contributor, Anglican writer and journalist Monica Furlong, (and eventual biographer of Alan Watts), argued that a renewed
understanding of "spiritual health" was required, one not rooted solely
in traditional liturgies: "[T]oo many who faithfully practise these things
do not seem liberated people. In many cases, the faith which should
have led to enlightenment and self-knowledge has become a means of
evading reality, of retiring into a fantasy world which is safe and nicer
than the real one."[6] Contending that, in concert with the medical breakthroughs of the century, the church needed to cultivate a "new understanding of love" that would realize that "as there is a hygiene of the
body which properly carried out, strengthens its resistance to disease,
so there is a hygiene of the mind and of the spirit." Furlong argued that
this hygiene of body, mind, and spirit would be based in a love that
made Christians vulnerable and nonjudgmental, in ways that might
very well mean their demise: "As for our fear that . . . Christian beliefs
and practices as we know them, are in imminent danger of being swept
away on the tide of secularism; I believe that we must learn to face with
equanimity, even with enthusiasm, the prospect that it might happen,
working out for ourselves in the process the kind of faith which could
survive and make sense to us, even in the most hostile conditions."[7] An
early supporter of rights for homosexuals in the Church, Furlong, who
held an abiding interest in mysticism, went on to be a leader in the fight
to ordain women in the Church of England.

Furlong's enthusiastic embrace of an ethic of liberation that might
hasten the church's demise had its echoes in the second church-
commissioned critique of the 1960s, the "Hendry Report" on the Anglican Church's work with First Nations. In 1968, the Anglican Church
asked Charles Hendry, professor of social work at the University of Toronto, graduate of Union Theological Seminary in New York City, and
United Church member, to candidly assess the Church's work with Native
peoples. At a time when Native Anglicans were themselves organizing in
newly ecumenical and North American networks to advance a concerted
program of political and ecclesiastical change, the 1969 Hendry report
helped to provoke new kinds of solidarity between Anglican Church lead-

ers and activist groups such as the National Indian Brotherhood. As a result, the Anglican Church voted to support First Nations struggles for treaty rights and land claims at a crucial time in Canadian politics.[8]

The autocritique of the Hendry Report also heralded the inception of a new openness among Anglicans to First Nations' spiritual traditions, including the healing ministry of Anglican Priest Andrew Ahenakew. Marking the beginning of an official process in which the Anglican and United Churches confronted their own complicity and "burden of guilt" for residential schools, the Hendry Report played a part in leading these Canadian churches to literally pay for what some called their "original sin."[9] By the 1990s the General Synod of the Anglican Church of Canada was facing the possibility of bankruptcy, as legal cases brought against the Church by First Nations peoples grew into millions of dollars. After a great deal of negotiating among churches, the Canadian government, and First Nations groups, the Indian Residential Schools Settlement Agreement was finalized in 2005, in which the Anglican Church was assigned a fixed sum for reparations of $15.6 million (the United Church, with fewer schools, was assigned almost $7 million). The money was directed to a range of purposes, including settlements to First Nations individuals, the Native-run Aboriginal Healing Fund, and the newly established Truth and Reconciliation Commission.[10] Although the settlement averted bankruptcy of the General Synod, several churches, and even dioceses, have closed in Western Canada. Not an entirely voluntary kind of decline (and not the only reason for the closure of Anglican churches in Canada), some Anglicans saw these closures as a chance to enact a "living apology" in which they both atoned for and reconsidered their history and their future.[11] In the words of Mark MacDonald, appointed in 2005 as the National Indigenous Bishop within the Anglican Church of Canada, such reconsideration called for non-Native Anglicans to admit "that they carried the seeds of that horrific evil."[12] Trying to not live in "fear of small numbers," some liberal Protestants have come to accept that their own numerical decline is both their due and their potential, as they embrace what Arjun Appadurai has called new transnational "utopian cellularities," based not on universal mandates but locally sensitive solidarities.[13]

The full story of the process of dealing with the legacy of residential schools has not yet been told, and it will not likely be a story in which the churches acted only with virtue and never with self-justification or duplicity; nevertheless liberal Protestant sensibilities of critique are partly responsible for their confrontation with the past. At their most critical, liberal Protestants have worked from the understanding that they expose the pathologies of modernity at the same time that they inhabit them. Urged on by what Paul Tillich called the "Protestant principle" or what Robinson called inescapable fallibility, they abide by the conviction that since God's sovereignty means that human beings can never know the whole truth, critique of self and society is a necessary and ongoing responsibility.

Steeped in their own tradition of "critical inquiry," Canadian liberal Protestants have sought to enact an ideal very similar to that described by Michel Foucault, echoing Kant: "critique's primordial responsibility [is] to know knowledge."[14] At the same time, however, their "disciplined intelligence" entailed more than habits of mind—critique was also what Foucault would call a "technique of the self" in a long tradition of Christian subjectivation, by which confession and self-examination were the routes for Christians to recognize themselves as subjects. For Foucault, techniques of the self "allow individuals to perform a certain number of operations on their bodies, their souls, their thoughts, their conduct in such a way as to produce in themselves transformations or modifications, and attain certain states of perfection, happiness, purity, or supernatural power."[15] Whereas Ruth Marshall has adeptly translated Foucault's words to apply to Nigerian Pentecostals, in another register, Canadian liberal Protestants were similarly engaged in what Marshall, following Foucault, calls "political spiritualities": the ongoing "will to found anew" the link between modes of governing the self and distinguishing between the true and the false. Whereas Nigerian Pentecostals elaborate new modes of government and politics of truth through work on the self, liberal Protestants have been preoccupied by work on the "social," implicating the diseased and healthy body in a politics of the spirit on both national and international scales. Articulating and experiencing the "wholeness" of healing through the trinity of body, mind, spirit, liberal Protestants bound the transformation of healing with the spirit of critique in a cosmopolitan optimism undergirded by both the "tragic consciousness" and the "melancholic freedom" of their narratives of modernity.[16]

Justification by critique, however, is a "game of truth" that can never be won but only played over and over again. With the possibility of self-justification always lingering in any act of self-critique, this is not a path to purity or innocence—it is a necessarily perpetual process.[17] As a remedy to the perpetuity and partial truth of critique, however, liberal

Protestants have long put their faith in love as an unending obligation that cannot be fully fathomed or otherwise measured. Whether animated by the colonial project of conversion, or a feminist desire to revalue incarnation, or a supernatural liberalism, liberal Protestants have lived by the hope that love made tangible could change—or even heal—the world.

By the turn of the second millennium, most liberal Protestants had abandoned a quest for the "long hoped for world religion." (There are still many Christians, however, including many medical missionaries, who aspire to make Christianity into the religion of the world.)[18] Moving from an evangelical ecumenism that sought to Christianize the whole inhabited world to a postcolonial cosmopolitanism that sought to engage others without erasing religious difference, liberal Protestants—contrary to the diagnosis of Marsden—knowingly disrupted their established lives. Following the changing shape of healing demonstrates how engaging with cultural movements—medical missions, psychotherapy, anticolonialism, the spread of yoga, feminism, gay and lesbian liberation, and First Nations self-determination—brought liberal Protestants to repeatedly question their taken-for-granted assumptions and practices about what made for ethical, and healthy, human subjects.[19] Not motivated by the kind of perfectionism that shaped nineteenth-century versions of Christian healing, the late twentieth-century quest for "health as liberation" rooted itself in political theories of praxis that deferred any hope for instant healing or moral perfection.[20]

Whether liberal Protestantism can revive itself as a Christian tradition in the way that Marilynne Robinson advocates is yet to be seen, especially since the category itself is only loosely applied and not regularly policed from within. A chorus of voices from outside is already calling (or calling for) its demise. The deep fissures within the Anglican Communion over homosexuality have led to new kinds of "postcolonial" global alliances between conservative North American and African Anglicans that have ritually severed relations within the North American communion, on the grounds that liberal Anglicans are apostate. Similarly, some conservative commentators have written off the United Church of Canada as so radical that it is no longer even fit to be ecumenical—that is, it cannot claim enough common doctrine with other Christian groups to be in union with them.[21]

Even scholars more sympathetic to liberal Protestantism lament its "decline" by way of a logic that refuses to recognize the cosmopolitanism of a growing number of liberals as an authentic form of Christianity. Catherine Gidney, for example, in *A Long Eclipse*, argued that for historical reasons beyond their control, liberal Protestants lost their prominence within Canadian universities in the 1950s and 1960s: "[T]he postwar era witnessed a 'second disestablishment': no longer would a single religious perspective comprise the authoritative religious voice of the university community."[22] Not alone in naming this disestablishment a demise, by doing so Gidney misrecognized the ways in which many liberal Protestants were actively seeking *not* to be the single authoritative voice in Canadian society. Shaped by postwar theology strongly critical of the anti-Semitism within Christian history both ancient and modern, many liberal Protestants came to realize that they did not live in a "Christian Canada", but inhabited a world of Jews, atheists, and an increasingly broad range of religious diversity.[23] Beginning to realize their own historic injustices toward varieties of religious difference, some liberal Protestants no longer wanted to speak for everyone.

Liberal Protestants have another set of critics beyond those lamenting—or documenting—the decline of Christian power. By virtue of their enduring connection to wider traditions of liberalism in which cosmopolitan optimism and self-critique form the grounds for human relationships and the transformation of political structures, liberal Protestants are subsumed within critiques of liberalism as well. In the past few years anthropologists of religion have crafted powerful arguments demonstrating that optimistic, liberal democratic expectations of progress have undergirded and distorted anthropological analysis of agency and cultural combination. Saba Mahmood's insightful critique of the intersections of feminist theory with the anthropological fixation on agency as empowerment showed how liberal (and feminist) understandings of autonomy could not be the standard for interpreting the practices of devotion of the Egyptian Muslim women of her study. Instead of a "naturalization of freedom as a social ideal," these women strove for a habitual practice of fitting themselves to a tradition of prayer, Quranic reading and pious comportment.[24] Anthropologist Aisha Khan, in her reflections on religious combination in Trinidad, argued that the scholarly concept of creolization was itself an admixture of "agency and teleological optimism" in the service of ideological ends, including those of liberalism.[25] Questioning both the romanticism and the assumptions about free will implicit in the teleological optimism of creolization, Khan urged anthropologists to attend self-critically to how their categories are shaped by their own politics and desires. For Mahmood and Khan, however, liberalism largely remained an ideology and not a practice.

Similarly, Webb Keane's work on "Christian moderns" narrates a very different story of Protestantism and modernity when compared to my own. Keane's analysis of Sumbanese Calvinists in Indonesia concludes that conversion to Protestantism in colonial and postcolonial contexts has often been a path to modernity via transcendence over the material world: "Protestantism and modernity (and, one might add, capitalism) *alike*, and even *conjointly*, seek to abstract the subject from its material and social entanglements in the name of freedom and authenticity."[26] Writing of Protestants in the Canadian colonial context, however, one could just as correctly say that in the twentieth century, observations and experiences of capitalism and colonialism brought many liberal Protestants to insist that material and social entanglements were precisely the grounds for critical immanence, via a supernaturalism that took the health of bodies both near and far as test of both faith and political will.

The important critiques of Mahmood and Khan, among others, make clear the need for a sustained analysis of the ways scholars have used the category of liberalism itself as they do the work of "anthropology of religion." Offering one foray into such analysis, I have explored the cosmopolitan optimism of liberal Protestants by endeavoring to think in a way that Sheldon Pollock and his co-editors described as "archivally cosmopolitan." I have considered, over time, a specific instantiation of "how people have thought and acted beyond the local."[27] The cosmopolitan optimism undergirding liberal Protestants' growing openness to transform their healing practices—and their very understanding of healing itself—by way of non-Christian epistemologies and rituals is a hopefulness that cannot escape its history. Not all liberal Protestants are equally aware or equally articulate about the ways a tragic past and a tragic consciousness inhabit their present projects of healing; nevertheless the historicity of colonialism haunts the present and future of their churches.

By neglecting to look at liberalism archivally or ethnographically, anthropologists of religion and the Christian detractors of liberal Protestantism develop a peculiar commonality. Both views consign liberalism, whether by intention, disinterest, or trope, to a polyglot assembly of individualistic experimentalists cast adrift on the shifting sands of provisional truths, or alternatively, a band of romantics bound by their devotion to freedom of thought and perpetual resistance to an oppressor that is indeed themselves. This is partly due to disciplinary habits, in which political theorists and philosophers have the most to say about "liberalism" as a normative political tradition, whereas theologians and church historians have given the most attention to liberal Protestantism largely as a theological movement. I do not speak for liberal Protestants—I am not an Anglican, a Methodist, or a member of the United Church—but I do think that it is worth speaking about them. In the present moment, an account of twenty-first century liberal Christianity cannot be written without an historical perspective—the vestiges of its past "righteous empire" necessarily intrude into the narratives of its present, whether they be stories of its decline in the face of Pentecostal Christianities, or accounts of its unrelinquished and illegimate hegemony, or narratives of a common space of multireligious flourishing.[28]

The changing assumptions and historicity underlying our concepts— whether healing, modernity, holism, the spirit, or even anthropology— demand perpetual recognition, critical acts of perception done both by scholars and the people we study. Recognizing that a robust supernaturalism accompanied the liberal Protestant embrace of medicalization challenges the assumption that liberal versions of healing quarantined the spirit. Instead, the plethora of spirits that have inhabited liberal Protestant bodies and debates over the past century demonstrate habits of experimentalism that cultivated critique itself as a practice of healing. Transforming their anthropologies of the spiritual body through their encounters with the healing practices and histories of others both global and local, liberal Protestants have enacted a commitment to knowing that resembles, if not infuses, the work of critical scholarship itself.

Notes

PREFACE

1. Eugene R. Fairweather, "Christianity and the Supernatural I. The Meaning of the Supernatural" *Canadian Journal of Theology* 9, no. 1 (1963), 15; Eugene R. Fairweather, "Christianity and the Supernatural II. Historical Notes on Christian Supernaturalism" *Canadian Journal of Theology* 9, no. 1 (1963), 102. Fairweather was referring to Paul Tillich in this last quote, and is described as liberal Anglo-Catholic (or High Church) Anglican in Alan Hayes, *Anglicans in Canada: Controversies and Identity in Historical Perspective* (Urbana: University of Illinois Press, 2004), 149.

2. Peter van der Veer, *Conversion to Modernities: The Globalization of Christianity* (New York: Routledge, 1996).

3. Matthew Engelke, ed., *The Objects of Evidence: Anthropological Approaches to the Production of Knowledge* (Oxford: Wiley-Blackwell, 2009), 12. See also Louis Dumont's analysis of the Christian roots of what he considers to be anthropology's misrecognized individualism. Louis Dumont, *Essays on Individualism: Modern Ideology in Anthropological Perspective* (Chicago: University of Chicago Press, 1986).

4. United Church Health Services Web page, http://www.unitedchurchhealth.ca/uchs_experience.php (accessed June 25, 2010); Bob Burrows, *Healing in the Wilderness: A History of the United Church Mission Hospitals* (Madeira Park, BC: Harbour Publishing, 2004), 230.

5. "Plan of Anglican Work in Support of a New Partnership between Indigenous and Non-Indigenous Anglicans: A New Agape," Report 003, General Synod 2001, http://www.anglican.ca/gs2001/rr/reports/report891b.html?rep=003A (accessed June 25, 2010).

6. See Bruno Latour, *We Have Never Been Modern* (Cambridge, MA: Harvard University Press, 1993); Dilip Parameshwar Gaonkar, *Alternative Modernities* (Durham: Duke University Press, 2001); Peter Osborne, "Modernity Is a

Qualitative, Not a Chronological, Category," *New Left Review* I, no. 92 (March–April 1992), 65–84; and Roger O'Toole, "Canadian Religion: Heritage and Project," in *Rethinking Church, State, and Modernity*, ed. David Lyon and Marguerite Van Die (Toronto: University of Toronto Press, 2000), 34–51.

7. Dipesh Chakrabarty, *Habitations of Modernity: Essays in the Wake of Subaltern Studies* (Chicago: University of Chicago Press, 2002), xx.

8. I am grateful to Webb Keane for the phrase "pathologies of modernity," which he used in a different context during a discussion at the "Ordinary Ethics Workshop" at the University of Toronto, October 2008. See also, Dipesh Chakrabarty, *Habitations of Modernity*, xxi.

9. Paul Farmer, *Pathologies of Power* (Berkeley: University of California Press, 2004). See also, Deborah Gordon, "Tenacious Assumptions in Western Medicine," in *Biomedicine Examined*, ed. M. Lock and D. Gordon (Dordrecht: Kluwer Academic, 1988), 19–56; Margaret Lock, "Cultivating the Body: Anthropologies and Epistemologies of Bodily Practice and Knowledge," *Annual Review of Anthropology* 22 (1993): 133–155; Charles Rosenberg, "Framing Disease: Illness, Society, and History," in *Framing Disease: Studies in Cultural History*, ed. Charles E. Rosenberg and Janet Golden (New Brunswick, NJ: Rutgers University Press, 1992), xiii–xxvi.

10. Michel Foucault, *The Birth of the Clinic: An Archaeology of Medical Perception* (New York: Vintage Books, 1975); *History of Sexuality* (New York: Vintage Books, 1980); and "The Crisis of Medicine or Antimedicine?" *Foucault Studies* 1 (December 2004): 5–19.

11. Ivan Illich, *Medical Nemesis* (Edinburgh: Edinburgh University Press, 1974). See also Susan Sontag, *Illness as Metaphor and AIDS and Its Metaphors* (New York: Farrar, Strauss and Giroux, 1989), who argues persuasively for the overreaching effects of healing and illness used metaphorically.

12. Mary-Ellen Kelm, *Colonizing Bodies: Aboriginal Health and Healing in British Columbia, 1900–1950* (Vancouver: UBC Press, 1998); Megan Vaughn, *Curing their Ills: Colonial Power and African Illness* (Stanford: Stanford University Press, 1991); Warwick Anderson, *Colonial Pathologies: American Tropical Medicine, Race, and Hygiene in the Philippines* (Durham: Duke University Press, 2006); Warwick Anderson, "Where is the Postcolonial History of Medicine?" *Bulletin of the History of Medicine* 72, no. 3 (1998): 522–530; Maureen K. Lux, *Medicine That Walks: Disease, Medicine, and Canadian Plains Native People, 1880–1940* (Toronto: University of Toronto Press, 2001).

13. E. Brooks Holifield, *A History of Pastoral Care in America: From Salvation to Self-Realization* (Nashville, TN: Abingdon Press, 1983), 201.

14. Philip Rieff, *The Triumph of the Therapeutic: Uses of Faith after Freud* (New York: Harper & Row, 1966), 24–25. For a different but related perspective, see T. J. Jackson Lears, *No Place of Grace: Antimodernism and the Transformation of American Culture, 1880–1920* (New York: Pantheon Books, 1981).

15. Rieff, *The Triumph*, 3, 18.

16. Keith Meador, "'My Own Salvation': The Christian Century and Psychology's Secularizing of American Protestantism," in *The Secular Revolution*, ed. Christian Smith (Berkeley: University of California Press, 2003), 271. But

see the work of other scholars that challenges this argument from inherency, including Christopher White, *Unsettled Minds: Psychology and the American Search for Spiritual Assurance, 1830–1940*, Berkeley: University of Californtia Press, 2009. For a counterargument to Rieff that demonstrates a strong antipathy between U.S. liberal Protestants and Freudian psychoanalysis, see Jon H. Roberts, "Psychoanalysis and American Christianity, 1900–1945," in *When Science and Christianity Meet*, ed. David C. Lindberg and Ronald Numbers (Chicago: University of Chicago Press, 2003), 225–244; for a Canadian example, see Alison Falby, "The Modern Confessional: Anglo-American Religious Groups and the Emergence of Lay Psychotherapy," *Journal of History of the Behavioral Sciences* 39, no. 3 (2003), 251–267.

17. Rieff's view has also been echoed in many Protestant theological critiques, such as, Keith G. Meador and Shaun C. Henson, "Growing Old in Therapeutic Culture," in *Growing Old in Christ*, ed. Stanley Hauerwas, Carole Bailey Stoneking, and Keith G. Meador (Grand Rapids, MI: Eerdmans, 2003), 90–111; Stanley Hauerwas, "Salvation and Health: Why Medicine Needs the Church," in *The Hauerwas Reader* (Durham: Duke University Press, 2001), 539–555; and Joel J. Shuman and Keith G. Meador, *Heal Thyself: Spirituality, Medicine, and the Distortion of Christianity* (Oxford: Oxford University Press, 2003).

18. For example, Talal Asad, *Formations of the Secular: Christianity, Islam, Modernity* (Stanford: Stanford University Press, 2003) and Charles Taylor, *A Secular Age* (Cambridge: Harvard University Press, 2007).

19. Wendy Brown, *Regulating Aversion: Tolerance in the Age of Identity and Empire* (Princeton, N.J.: Princeton University Press, 2006), 7.

20. Jeffrey Stout, *Democracy and Tradition* (Princeton, N.J.: Princeton University Press, 2005), 130–131.

21. Randall Balmer, *Grant Us Courage: Travels Along the Mainline of American Protestantism* (Oxford: Oxford University Press, 1996), 5; Brown, *Regulating Aversion*. See also John Milbank, "Liberality versus Liberalism," in Michael Hoelzl and Graham Ward, eds., *Religion and Political Thought* (New York: Continuum, 2006), 225–236.

22. Michael Warner, "Is Liberalism a Religion?" in Hent de Vries, ed. *Religion: Beyond a Concept: The Future of the Religious Past* (New York: Fordham University Press, 2008), 612.

23. See Chris Hann, "The Anthropology of Christianity *per se*" *Archives Européennes de Sociologie* 48, no. 3 (2007), 391–418. Matthew Engelke thinks creatively and anthropologically about liberal Protestants but limits himself to eighteenth- and nineteenth-century theologians. Matthew Engelke, *A Problem of Presence: Beyond Scripture in an African Church* (Berkeley: University of California Press, 2007).

24. Laurie F. Maffly-Kipp, Leigh E. Schmidt, and Mark Valeri, eds. *Practicing Protestants: Histories of Christian Life in America, 1630–1965* (Baltimore: The Johns Hopkins University Press, 2006), 199–221.

25. Joel Robbins, "Continuity Thinking and the Problem of Christian Culture: Belief, Time, and the Anthropology of Christianity," *Current Anthropology* 48, no. 1 (2007): 1. Webb Keane gestures to this "liberal tradition" in his

article "Sincerity, 'Modernity', and the Protestants" *Cultural Anthropology* 17, no. 1 (2002), 65–92.

26. Edward Sapir, "The Meaning of Religion" *Selected Writings in Language, Culture, and Personality*, ed. David G. Mandelbaum. (Berkeley: University of California Press, 1949), 346–356. Sapir was the first anthropologist employed by the government of Canada, working for the Royal Geographic Survey, with its own Christian genealogies: see Ian Dyck, "Founding of the Anthropology Division at the National Museum of Canada: An Intertwining of Science, Religion, and Politics," in *Revelations: Bi-Millennial Papers from the Canadian Museum of Civilization* (Hull, QC: Canadian Museum of Civilization, 2001), 3–34.

27. For related arguments, see Robert Orsi, "Snakes Alive: Religious Studies between Heaven and Earth" *Between Heaven and Earth* (Princeton, N.J.: Princeton University Press, 2006), 177–204, Robert Bellah, *Beyond Belief: Essays on Religion in a Post-Traditional World* (New York: Harper & Row, 1970); Stanley Tambiah, *Magic, Science, Religion and the Scope of Rationality* (Cambridge: Cambidge University Press, 1990); Talal Asad, *Formations of the Secular*; Talal Asad, *Genealogies of Religion: Discipline and Reasons of Power in Christianity and Islam* (Baltimore: The Johns Hopkins University Press, 1993); and Tomoko Masuzawa, *The Invention of World Religions* (Chicago: University of Chicago Press, 2005).

28. Mark Lewis Taylor, "At the Crossroads of Religion and Medical Anthropology," Conference of the Nordic Society of Medical Anthropologists, University of Helsinki, Mekrijarvie, Finland, March 2002, medanthro.kaapeli.fi/nordic2002/papers/plenary/taylor.pdf (accessed June 25, 2010).

29. Joel Robbins, "Anthropology and Theology: An Awkward Relationship?" *Anthropological Quarterly* 79, no. 2 (Spring 2006): 288. See also, Fenella Cannell, "The Anthropology of Christianity" in Fenella Cannell, ed. *The Anthropology of Christianity* (Durham: Duke University Press, 2006), 1–50.

30. John Milbank, *Theology and Social Theory: Beyond Secular Reason*, 2nd ed. (Malden and Oxford: Blackwell, 2006); John Milbank, "Liberality versus Liberalism."

31. Leigh Schmidt, *Restless Souls*; Joseph Kip Kosek. *Acts of Conscience: Christian Nonviolence and Modern American Democracy* (New York: Columbia University Press, 2009); Courtney Jung, "The Burden of Culture and the Limits of Liberal Responsibility," *Constellations* 8, no. 2 (June 2001): 219–235. Other recent research drawing more complicated accounts of the intersection of secularity, religion, and liberal subjects in North America include Tracy Fessenden, *Culture and Redemption: Religion, the Secular and American Literature* (Princeton, N.J.: Princeton University Press, 2007); Andrea Most, "The Birth of Theatrical Liberalism," in *After Pluralism*, ed. Courtney Bender and Pamela Klassen (New York: Columbia University Press, 2010), 127–155. For an account of liberal Protestantism from within, see Diana Butler-Bass, *Christianity for the Rest of Us* (San Francisco: HarperSanFrancisco, 2006).

32. Judith Butler, "The Sensibility of Critique: Response to Asad and Mahmood," in *Is Critique Secular? Blasphemy, Injury, and Free Speech*, ed. Talal Asad, Judith Butler, Saba Mahmood, and Wendy Brown (Berkeley: The

Townsend Center for the Humanities, University of California, Berkeley, 2009),
101–136.

INTRODUCTION: HEALING CHRISTIANS

1. Belle Choné Oliver, *Anandi's Question: For Parents of Little Children*
(Madras, Allahabad, Rangoon, Colombo: Christian Literature Society for In-
dia, 1930), 22. Nancy Christie argues that a later sacralization of sex in the
United Church was largely to restrict women to the home, an argument that
applies less well to Oliver's case. Nancy Christie, "Sacred Sex: The United Church
and the Privatization of the Family in Postwar Canada," in *Households of Faith:
Family, Gender and Community in Canada, 1760–1969*, ed. Nancy Christie
(Montreal and Kingston: McGill-Queen's University Press, 2002), 348–376. On
Christian progressives in the social hygiene movement more generally, see John
D'Emilio and Estelle B. Freedman, *Intimate Matters: A History of Sexuality in
America*, 2nd ed. (Chicago: University of Chicago Press, 1997).

2. Belle Choné Oliver, *Tales from the Inns of Healing of Christian Medical
Service in India, Burma, and Ceylon*, Canadian ed. (Toronto: The Committee
on Missionary Education, The United Church of Canada, 1944[1942]), 123.

3. William Ernest Hocking, *Human Nature and its Remaking* (New Haven:
Yale University Press, 1918), 7.

4. Frederick Du Vernet, *Spiritual Radio*. (Mountain Lakes, NJ: The Society
of the Nazarene, 1925), 28.

5. Du Vernet's supernaturalism has received no attention from scholars.
Ruth Compton Brouwer notes that "if Oliver's religious discourse sometimes
seemed fervent, even by the standards of Indian and mission Christianity . . .
there was another, more "modern" and secular side to her personality." Ruth
Compton Brouwer, *Modern Women Modernizing Men: The Changing Missions
of Three Professional Women in Asian and Africa, 1902–69* (Vancouver: UBC
Press, 2002), 64.

6. Important exceptions include Christopher White's *Unsettled Minds: Psychology and the American Search for Spiritual Assurance, 1830–1940* (Berkeley: University of California Press, 2009) and Leigh Schmidt's *Restless Souls:
The Making of American Spirituality* (San Francisco: HarperSanFrancisco,
2005).

7. Max Weber, "Science as a Vocation," in *From Max Weber* (London: Routledge, 1991), 139, and Max Weber, *The Protestant Ethic and the Spirit of Capitalism* (New York: W. W. Norton & Co., 2009), 182. Weber was quoting Nietz-
sche without attribution; see Claude Lefort, *Writing, The Political Test*, trans.
David Ames Curtis (Durham: Duke University Press, 2000), 183.

8. Robert Orsi, *Thank You St. Jude: Women's Devotion to the Patron Saint
of Hopeless Causes* (New Haven: Yale University Press, 1996); Karen McCarthy Brown, *Mama Lola: A Vodou Priestess in Brooklyn*, updated and expanded
edition, (Berkeley: University of California Press, 2001).

9. Benedict Anderson, *Imagined Communities: Reflections on the Origin
and Spread of Nationalism* (London: Verso, 2006 [1983]).

10. A list of archives consulted is found at the end of this book.

11. Homi Bhabha, *The Location of Culture* (London: Routledge, 1994).

12. Gary Dorrien, "American Liberal Theology: Crisis, Irony, Decline, Renewal, Ambiguity," *Cross Currents* (Winter 2006): 55. Dorrien's three-volume account of the development of liberal Protestant theology is the most thorough and up-to-date intellectual history of Protestant liberalism, and this article is a very much abridged version of volume 3: *The Making of American Liberal Theology: Crisis, Irony, and Postmodernity, 1950–2005* (Louisville, KY: Westminster John Knox, 2006).

13. William R. Hutchison, *The Modernist Impulse in American Protestantism* (Durham: Duke University Press, 1992). See also Robert Wuthnow, *The Restructuring of American Religion: Society and Faith since World War II* (Princeton, N.J.: Princeton University Press, 1988), and Nancy Christie and Michael Gauvreau, *A Full-Orbed Christianity: The Protestant Churches and Social Welfare in Canada, 1900–1940* (Montreal and Kingston: McGill-Queen's University Press, 1996).

14. Cartwright was referencing the biblical passage from Nehemiah 2:20 (KJV): "Then answered I them, and said unto them, The God of heaven, he will prosper us; therefore we his servants will arise and build: but ye have no portion, nor right, nor memorial, in Jerusalem." For more on Cartwright, see Johanna Selles-Roney, "A Canadian Girl at Cheltenham: The Diary as an Historical Source," *Historical Studies in Education/Revue d'histoire de l'éducation* 3, no. 1 (1991): 93–103.

15. The quotations are from a discussion of the meeting in the *Canadian Churchman* (May 23, 1907), 347, and may be paraphrases of Cartwright's address.

16. Hannah Riddell, *Canadian Churchman* (November 14, 1907).

17. Julia Boyd, *Hannah Riddell: An Englishwoman in Japan* (London: Tuttle, 1996).

18. See the home page of the Hanna Riddell Memorial Society: http://www.riddell-wright.com/E/index.htm (accessed July 9, 2006). See http://www.cmai.org/about/history.htm (accessed June 26, 2009). For a parallel example, see Janet Beaton and Marion McKay, "Profile of a Leader: Caroline Wellwood," in *Canadian Journal of Nursing Leadership* 12, no. 4 (1999): 30–33. For a related discussion, see William McKinney, "Mainline Protestantism 2000," in *Annals of the AAPSS* 558 (July 1998): 59.

19. Martin E. Marty, "Tradition and the Traditions in Health/Medicine and Religion," in *Health/Medicine and the Faith Traditions: An Inquiry into Religion and Medicine*, ed. Martin E. Marty and Kenneth L. Vaux (Philadelphia, Fortress, 1982), 18. For a range of perspectives on Christianity and medicine in North America, see James Opp, *The Lord for the Body: Religion, Medicine, and Protestant Faith Healing in Canada, 1880–1930* (Montreal: McGill-Queen's University Press, 2005); Heather D. Curtis, *Faith in the Great Physician: Suffering and Divine Healing in American Culture, 1860–1900* (Baltimore: Johns Hopkins University Press, 2007); Rennie B. Schoepflin, *Christian Science on Trial: Religious Healing in America* (Baltimore: Johns Hopkins University Press, 2003); Yvonne Chireau, *Black Magic: Religion and the African-American Conjuring*

Tradition (Berkeley: University of California Press, 2003); Richard Ostrander, *The Life of Prayer in a World of Science: Protestants, Prayer, and American Culture, 1870–1930* (Oxford: Oxford University Press, 2000); Robert Bruce Mullin, *Miracles and the Modern Religious Imagination* (New Haven: Yale University Press, 1996); and Robert K. Burkinshaw, *Pilgrims in Lotus Land: Conservative Protestantism in British Columbia, 1917–1981.* (Montreal: McGill-Queen's University Press, 1995). Many of these texts have built on the pioneering work of Raymond J. Cunningham, such as "From Holiness to Healing: The Faith Cure in America, 1872–1892," *Church History* 43, no. 4 (1974): 499–513. Negotiations between Christianity and biomedicine also profoundly shaped Catholicism; for example, see Robert Orsi, *Thank You St. Jude.* For a comparative approach, see Susan Sered and Linda Barnes, eds., *Religion and Healing in America* (Oxford: Oxford University Press, 2005).

20. Nikolas Rose, "Governing Advanced Liberal Democracies," in Peter Miller and Nikolas Rose, *Governing the Present: Administering Economic, Social, and Political Life* (Cambridge: Polity, 2008), 206, 211.

21. Courtney Jung, *The Moral Force of Indigenous Politics: Critical Liberalism and the Zapatistas* (New York: Cambridge University Press, 2008), 21.

22. See especially the work of Gary Dorrien and William Hutchison and the early work of Richard Wightman Fox, such as William Hutchison, "Liberal Protestantism and the End of Innocence," *American Quarterly* 15, no. 2, part 1 (1963): 126–139; and Richard Wightman Fox, "The Niebuhr Brothers and the Liberal Protestant Heritage," in *Religion and Twentieth-Century American Intellectual Life,* ed. Michael J. Lacey (Cambridge: Cambridge University Press, 1989), 94–115; Catherine L. Albanese, *A Republic of Mind and Spirit: A Cultural History of American Metaphysical Religion* (New Haven: Yale University Press, 2007); Schmidt, *Restless Souls.* For other recent scholarship that starts with practice, see Laurie F. Maffly-Kipp, Leigh E. Schmidt, and Mark Valeri, eds., *Practicing Protestants: Histories of Christian Life in America, 1630–1965* (Baltimore: Johns Hopkins University Press, 2006), and Catherine Gidney, *A Long Eclipse: The Liberal Protestant Establishment and the Canadian University* (Montreal and Kingston: McGill-Queen's University Press, 2004).

23. Richard Allen offers a full account of historiographical debates about the category of liberalism in studies of Canadian Anglo-Protestantism in particular. Richard Allen, *The View from the Murney Tower: Salem Bland, the late Victorian Controversies, and the Search for a New Christianity* (Toronto: University of Toronto Press, 2008). See also Richard Allen, *The Social Passion: Religion and Social Reform in Canada, 1914–28.* Toronto: University of Toronto Press, 1971. For more on how attention to Canadian Christianity can challenge and reframe perspectives on U.S. Christianity, see William Westfall, "Voices from the Attic: The Canadian Border and the Writing of American Religious History," in *Retelling U.S. Religious History,* ed. Thomas Tweed (Berkeley: University of California Press, 1997), 181–199; and Phyllis D. Airhart, "As Canadian as Possible Under the Circumstances: Reflections on the Study of Protestantism in North America," in *New Directions in American Religious History,* ed. Harry Stout and D. G. Hart (New York: Oxford University Press, 1997), 116–140.

24. Charles Long, "The Question of Denominational Histories in the United States: Dead End or Creative Beginning?" in *Reimagining Denominationalism: Interpretive Essays*, ed. Robert Bruce Mullin and Russell E. Richey (New York: Oxford University Press, 1994),104; see also, Peter Beyer, "Modern Forms of the Religious Life: Denomination, Church, and Invisible Religion in Canada, the United States and Europe" in *Rethinking Church, State, and Modernity: Canada between the United States and Europe*, ed. David Lyon and Marguerite Van Die (Toronto: University of Toronto Press, 2000), 189–210; Tweed, *Retelling U.S. Religious History*.

25. Talks for a "Plan of Union" bringing together the United Church of Canada with the Anglican Church and the Disciples of Christ were initiated in the 1940s, and the Plan was published and accepted in 1972, only to be rejected by the Anglicans in 1975. General Commission on Church Union, *Plan of Union and By-laws: The Anglican Church of Canada, Christian Church (Disciples of Christ) in Canada, the United Church of Canada* (Toronto: The Commission, 1972).

26. Jonathan Z. Smith, *Relating Religion: Essays in the Study of Religion* (Chicago: University of Chicago Press, 2004), 27.

27. R. Laurence Moore, *Religious Outsiders and the Making of Americans* (New York: Oxford University Press, 1986), ix. For a helpful discussion of "mainstream Protestantism" based both in historical and theological claims, see Milton J. Coalter, John M. Mulder, and Louis B. Weeks. *Vital Signs: The Promise of Mainstream Protestantism* (Grand Rapids, MI: W. B. Eerdmans, 1996). For other depictions of mainstream Protestantism, see William McKinney, "Mainline Protestantism 2000," *Annals of the AAPSS* 558 (July 1998); Robert Wuthnow, *The Quiet Hand of God: Faith-Based Activism and the Public Role of Mainline Protestantism* (Berkeley: University of California Press, 2002).

28. Moore, *Religious Outsiders*, xiii.

29. See John S. Baick, "Cracks in the Foundation: Frederick T. Gates, the Rockefeller Foundation, and the China Medical Board," *Journal of the Gilded Age and Progressive Era* (January 2004), http://www.historycooperative.org/cgi-bin/justtop.cgi?act=justtop&url=http://www.historycooperative.org/journals/jga/3.1/baick.html (accessed June 13, 2005).

30. Marty, "Tradition and the Traditions."

31. Ibid., 17.

32. Dorrien, "American Liberal Theology," 456.

33. Richard Wightman Fox, "The Culture of Liberal Protestant Progressivism, 1875–1925, *Journal of Interdisciplinary History* 23, no. 3 (3, Winter, 1993), 641.

34. My definition of "liberal Protestant" largely fits with the term's use in George Rawlyk, ed. *The Canadian Protestant Experience, 1760–1990*, 2nd ed. (Montreal and Kingston: McGill-Queen's University Press, 1993). See also the Canada-U.S. comparison of William Katerberg, *Modernity and the Dilemma of North American Anglican Identities, 1880–1950* (Montreal and Kingston: McGill-Queen's University Press, 2001). More recently, Kevin Flatt draws a

strong line between "evangelicals" and "liberals" in the United Church, using a largely theologically derived distinction. Kevin Flatt, "The Survival and Decline of the Evangelical Identity of the United Church of Canada, 1930–1971," PhD Dissertation, McMaster University, 2008. For an Anglican account that uses the language of "social concern" more than "liberal," see Edward Pulker, *We Stand on Their Shoulders: The Growth of Social Concern in Canadian Anglicanism* (Toronto: Anglican Book Centre, 1986).

35. On the rise of biomedicine see Paul Starr, *The Social Transformation of American Medicine*. (New York: Basic Books, 1982); John Harley Warner, "Grand Narrative and Its Discontent: Medical History in the Social Transformation of American Medicine," *Journal of Health Politics, Policy and Law*, 29 (2004): 757–780, 2004; Frank Huisman and John Harley, eds., *Locating Medical History: The Stories and their Meanings*. (Baltimore: Johns Hopkins University Press, 2004). For Canadian approaches to the historiography of biomedicine, see C. David Naylor, ed. *Canadian Health Care and the State*. (Montreal and Kingston: McGill-Queens University Press, 1992).

36. Medical anthropology, in particular, has developed the curing/healing distinction in which the first term is physiologically focused and the latter term considers the social and cultural contexts of embodied suffering. For example, Thomas Csordas argues that religious healing in particular employs a "rhetoric of transformation" that reinterprets bodily conditions as meaningful and transformative, without necessarily "curing" those conditions. Thomas J. Csordas, *Body/Meaning/Healing*. (New York: Palgrave Macmillan, 2002), 53. See also, Arthur Kleinman, *Writing at the Margin: Discourse between Anthropology and Medicine*. (Berkeley: University of California Press, 1995).

37. For narratives of the significance of healing within the development of Christianity, see Amanda Porterfield, *Healing in the History of Christianity*. (Oxford: Oxford University Press, 2005), and Ronald Numbers and Darrel W. Amundsen, eds. *Caring and Curing: Health and Medicine in the Western Religious Traditions*. (Baltimore, Johns Hopkins University Press, 1998[1986]). In the twentieth century, both the social gospeler Walter Rauschenbusch and the Emmanuel Movement leader Elwood Worcester made this kind of argument about Jesus's scientific prescience; see Fox, "The Culture of Liberal Protestant Progressivism, 1875–1925," 652, and Elwood Worcester, Samuel McComb, and Isador Coriat, *Religion and Medicine: The Moral Control of Nervous Disorders.*, (New York: Moffat, Yard, 1908).

38. Pamela Klassen, *Blessed Events: Religion and Home Birth in America* (Princeton, N.J.: Princeton University Press, 2001).

39. Neil Semple, *The Lord's Dominion: The History of Canadian Methodism* (Montreal: McGill-Queen's University Press, 1996); Marguerite Van Die, "Introduction," in *Religion and Public Life in Canada*, ed. Marguerite Van Die (Toronto: University of Toronto Press, 2001), 3–19; and William Westfall, *Two Worlds: The Protestant Culture of Nineteenth Century Ontario* (Montreal and Kingston: McGill-Queen's University Press, 1989).

40. Reinhold Niebuhr, *Leaves from the Notebook of a Tamed Cynic* (Louisville, KY: Westminster John Knox Press, 1990[1929]), 25.

41. Ramsey Cook, *The Regenerators: Social Criticism in Late Victorian English Canada* (Toronto: University of Toronto Press, 1985); David B. Marshall, "Canadian Historians, Secularization, and the Problem of the Nineteenth Century," *Historical Studies* 60 (1993–1994): 57–81.

42. Alison Falby, "The Modern Confessional: Anglo-American Religious Groups and the Emergence of Lay Psychotherapy," *Journal of the History of Behavioural Sciences* 39, no. 3 (2003): 251–67.

43. Nathan O. Hatch, "The Puzzle of American Methodism," *Church History* 63, no. 2 (2, 1994): 175–189; Marty, "Tradition and the Traditions," p. 18. See also, Martin E. Marty, "The Intertwining of Religion and Health/Medicine in Culture: A View through the Disciplines," in *Health/Medicine and the Faith Traditions: An Inquiry into Religion and Medicine,.* Eds. Martin E. Marty and Kenneth L. Vaux. (Philadelphia: Fortress Press, 1982), 48; Numbers and Amundsen, *Caring and Curing*; Brooks Holifield, *Health and Medicine in the Methodist Tradition: Journey Toward Wholeness.* (New York: Crossroad, 1986); Margaret Poloma, *Main Street Mystics: The Toronto Blessing and Reviving Pentecostalism.* (Walnut Creek, CA: Alta Mira, 2003). Less denominationally committed research includes Meredith McGuire, *Ritual Healing in Suburban America.* (New Brunswick, NJ: Rutgers University Press, 1998); Robert Orsi, *Thank You St. Jude*; and Thomas Csordas, *The Sacred Self: A Cultural Phenomenology of Charismatic Healing.* (Berkeley: University of California Press, 1994).

44. Hatch, "Puzzle," p. 177. See also Webb Keane's parallel comment about the "ordinariness" of Reformed Churches in Indonesia and "mainstream Protestants" in the United States. Webb Keane, *Christian Moderns: Freedom and Fetish in the Mission Encounter.* (Berkeley: University of California Press, 2007), 30.

45. Some historically focused studies have attended to the importance of healing for the wide array of new, Christian-inflected healing movements of the late nineteenth and early twentieth centuries but have not followed this healing "revival" very far into the more established denominations. For example, see Catherine Albanese, *Nature Religion in America.* (Chicago: University of Chicago Press, 1990); David Harrell, *All Things are Possible: The Healing and Charismatic Revivals in Modern America.* (Bloomington: Indiana University Press, 1975); Beryl Satter, *Each Mind a Kingdom: American Women, Sexual Purity, and the New Thought Movement, 1875–1920.* (Berkeley: University of California Press, 2001); James Opp, *The Lord for the Body*; Marie Griffith, *Born Again Bodies: Flesh and Spirit in American Christianity.* (Berkeley: University of California Press, 2004). Several essays of Raymond Cunningham give more attention to mainstream Protestantism at the turn of the twentieth century.

46. Joel J. Shuman and Keith G. Meador, *Heal Thyself: Spirituality, Medicine, and the Distortion of Christianity* (Oxford: Oxford University Press, 2003); Stanley Hauerwas, "Practicing Patience: How Christians Should be Sick," in *Beyond Mere Health: Theology and Health Care in a Secular Society*, ed. Hilary Regan, Rod Horsfield, and Gabrielle McMullen (Melbourne: Australia Theological Forum, 1996); McKinney, "Mainline Protestantism"; Wade Clark Roof,

Spiritual Marketplace: Baby Boomers and the Remaking of American Religion (Princeton, N.J.: Princeton University Press, 1999).

47. Kenneth Mills, *Idolatry and its Enemies: Colonial Andean Religion and Extirpation, 1640–1750* (Princeton, N.J.: Princeton University Press, 1997); Joel Robbins, *Becoming Sinners: Christianity and Moral Torment in a Papua New Guinea Society* (Berkeley: University of California Press, 2004).

48. For another approach to liberal Protestant cosmopolitanism, see Gary Miedema's discussion of the Christian Pavilion at Montreal's Expo 1967, in *For Canada's Sake: Public Religion, Centennial Celebrations, and the Re-making of Canada in the 1960s* (Montreal: McGill-Queen's University Press, 2005).

49. On visions of cosmopolitanism, see Anthony Appiah, *Cosmopolitanism: Ethics in a World of Strangers* (New York: W. W. Norton, 2006); Leigh E. Schmidt, "Cosmopolitan Piety: Sympathy, Comparative Religions, and Nineteenth-Century Liberalism," in Maffly-Kipp, *Practicing Protestants*, 199–221; Leela Gandhi, *Affective Communities: Anticolonial Thought, Fin de Siecle Radicalism, and the Politics of Friendship* (Durham: Duke University Press, 2006).

50. Thomas Browne, *Religio Medici* (London: Dent, 1965[1643]); John Wesley, *Primitive Physick, or, an Easy and Natural Method of Curing Most Diseases* 14th ed. (Bristol: William Pine, 1770). See also Numbers and Amundsen, *Caring and Curing*; Holifield, *Health and Medicine in the Methodist Tradition*.

51. Brian Clarke, "English Speaking Canada from 1854," in *A Concise History of Christianity in Canada*, 261–360. Eds. Terrence Murphy and Roberto Perin. (Oxford: Oxford University Press, 1996), 262. Although some Anglo-Catholic Anglicans argued that they were not Protestant, having never forsaken Catholic episcopal lineage, for my purposes (and for those of many Anglicans), Anglicans are Protestants. See Alan L. Hayes, *Anglicans in Canada: Controversies and Identity in Historical Perspective.* (Urbana and Chicago: University of Illinois Press, 2004), 115.

52. For an accessible account of the demographics of religious identity in Canada, see Kurt Bowen, *Christians in a Secular World: The Canadian Experience.* (Montreal and Kingston, McGill-Queen's University Press, 2004), especially chapter 2.

53. Alan L. Hayes, *Anglicans in Canada*; J. R. Miller, *Shingwauk's Vision: A History of Native Residential Schools* (Toronto: University of Toronto Press, 1996).

54. See also Miranda Hassett, *Anglican Communion in Crisis: How Episcopal Dissidents and Their African Allies Are Reshaping Anglicanism* (Princeton, N.J.: Princeton University Press, 2007).

55. http://www.orderofstluke.org/index.htm (accessed June 14, 2005). See also Gail Paton Grant, "Miracle Lore and Metamorphoses," in *Undisciplined Women: Tradition and Culture in Canada* (Montreal: McGill-Queen's University Press, 1997), 203–212.

56. John Wesley, *Primitive Physick*; Holifield, *Health and Medicine*; Porterfield, *Healing in Christianity.*

57. Semple, *The Lord's Dominion*; Marilyn Fardig Whiteley, *Canadian Methodist Women, 1766–1925: Marys, Marthas, Mothers in Israel* (Waterloo, ON: Wilfrid Laurier University Press, 2005); John Wigger, *Taking Heaven by*

Storm: Methodism and the Rise of Popular Christianity in America (Oxford: Oxford University Press, 1998).

58. Catherine Brekus, *Strangers and Pilgrims: Female Preaching in America, 1740–1845* (Chapel Hill: University of North Carolina Press, 1998); Whiteley, *Canadian Methodist Women*.

59. James W. Opp, "Healing Hands, Healthy Bodies: Protestant Women and Faith Healing in Canada and the United States, 1880–1930," in *Women and Twentieth-Century Protestantism*, ed. Margaret Lamberts Bendroth and Virginia Lieson Brereton (Urbana: University of Illinois Board of Trustees, 2002), 236–256; Curtis, *Faith in the Great Physician*; and Cunningham, "From Holiness to Healing."

60. See William Westfall, "Constructing Public Religions at Private Sites," in *Religion and Public Life in Canada: Historical and Comparative Perspectives*, ed. Marguerite Van Die (Toronto: University of Toronto Press, 2001), 23–49; William H. Katerberg, "Redefining Evangelicalism in the Canadian Anglican Church, Wycliffe College and the Evangelical Party, 1867–1995," in *Aspects of the Canadian Evangelical Experience* ed. George Rawlyk (McGill-Queen's University Press, 1997), 176; and Terence Ranger, "Medical Science and Pentecost: The Dilemma of Anglicanism in Africa," in *The Church and Healing: Papers Read at the Twentieth Summer Meeting and the Twenty-first Winter Meeting of the Ecclesiastical History Society*, ed. W. Sheils (London: Basil Blackwell, 1982), 333–365.

61. Raymond J. Cunningham, "James Moore Hickson and Spiritual Healing in the American Episcopal Church," *Historical Magazine of the Protestant Episcopal Church* 39, no. 1 (1970): 2–16; Robert Bruce Mullin, *Miracles and the Modern Religious Imagination* (New Haven: Yale University Press, 1996), 237–42; Stuart Mews, "The Revival of Spiritual Healing in the Church of England, 1920–26," in *The Church and Healing*, 323.

62. Professor H. Mitchell, "The Christian Mission of Healing," *Canadian Churchman* (July 1, 1920).

63. Phyllis Airhart, *Serving the Present Age: Revivalism, Progressivism, and the Methodist Tradition in Canada* (Montreal and Kingston: McGill-Queens University Press, 1992).

64. In Canada, health care funding comes from the federal government but is implemented by provincial governments.

65. http://www.ucobserver.org/about/ (accessed January 14, 2009). For editorial histories of both papers, see T. R. Millman, "Canadian Anglican Journalism in the Nineteenth Century," *Canadian Church Historical Society* 3, no. 5 (1959): 9. See also Katerberg, "Redefining Evangelicalism," 176; Hayes, *Anglicans in Canada*, 125; Phyllis Airhart, *Serving the Present Age*, 78; Christie and Gauvreau, *A Full-Orbed Christianity*, 25. On Creighton's love of books, see Donald Creighton, "My Father and the United Church," in *The Passionate Observer: Selected Writings* (Toronto: McClelland and Stewart, 1980), 95–96. For reasons of time and because of the historic link among Methodist, Holiness, and Pentecostal currents of healing, I decided to focus on the main Methodist newspaper (there were many in early-twentieth-century Canada) and not on the

Presbyterian Record, which is still published by the wing of the Presbyterian Church that did not join the United Church.

66. I draw this phrase from Janice Boddy, "Spirit Possession Revisited: Beyond Instrumentality," *Annual Review of Anthropology* 23 (October 1994), 411.

67. For more on Christianity and print culture in North America, see David Hall, *Worlds of Wonder, Days of Judgment: Popular Religious Belief in Early New England* (New York: Alfred A. Knopf, 1989); Candy Gunther Brown, *The Word in the World: Evangelical Writing, Publishing, and Reading in America, 1789–1880* (Chapel Hill: University of North Carolina Press, 2004); David Paul Nord, *Faith in Reading: Religious Publishing and the Birth of Mass Media in America* (Oxford: Oxford University Press, 2004), 35–36.

68. Anderson, *Imagined Communities*, 35–36.

69. Ibid., 35.

70. Martin E. Marty, *The Religious Press in America* (New York: Holt, Rinehart, and Winston, 1963).

71. "Poisonous Books," *Canadian Churchman* (January 20, 1910).

72. I have given pseudonyms to those people whose quotes I gathered in the course of fieldwork, and to the two Toronto churches that I discuss.

1. ANTHROPOLOGIES OF THE SPIRITUAL BODY

1. The English translation of Mao Tse-Tung's text was completed in 1967 for publication by the Chinese government. The original Chinese text is in the *Selected Works of Mao Tse-Tung, vol. II*. See Mao Tse-Tung, *Serve the People; In Memory of Norman Bethune; The Foolish Old Man Who Removed the Mountains* (Peking: Foreign Languages Press, 1967).

2. Accounts of Bethune's life are numerous, the latest being Adrienne Clarkson, *Extraordinary Canadians: Norman Bethune* (Toronto: Penguin Canada, 2009).

3. Salem Goldworth Bland, *The New Christianity or the Religion of the New Age* (Toronto: McClelland and Stewart, 1920), 49.

4. Grover Livingstone, *Through Sickness to Life* (Toronto: The Ryerson Press, 1954), 42.

5. Richard C. Cabot and Russell L. Dicks, *The Art of Ministering to the Sick* (New York: McMillan, 1959 [1936]), quoted in Livingstone, *Through Sickness to Life*, 56, 64.

6. Matthew Engelke, *A Problem of Presence: Beyond Scripture in an African Church* (Berkeley: University of California Press, 2007). Engelke draws the concept of semiotic ideologies from Webb Keane. See, for example, Webb Keane, *Christian Moderns: Freedom and Fetish in the Mission Encounter* (Berkeley: University of California Press, 2007).

7. Birgit Meyer, *Religious Sensations: Why Media, Aesthetics, and Power Matter in the Study of Contemporary Religion* (Amsterdam: Faculteit der Sociale Wetenschappen, Vrije Universiteit, 2006), 9.

8. For example, see James N. Lapsley, *Salvation and Health: The Interlocking Processes of Life* (Philadelphia: Westminster Press, 1972), 71. Conservative

Protestant anthropologies are often sharply critical of using anything but biblical sources to formulate a theological anthropology. For further examples of theological anthropologies, see D. J. Louw, *A Mature Faith: Spiritual Direction and Anthropology in a Theology of Pastoral Care and Counseling* (Louvain: Peeters Publishers, 1999).

9. R. Marie Griffith, *Born Again Bodies: Flesh and Spirit in American Christianity* (Berkeley: University of California Press, 2004); Dale Martin, *The Corinthian Body* (New Haven: Yale University Press, 1995). See also, Robert S. Cox, *Body and Soul: A Sympathetic History of American Spiritualism* (Charlottesville: University of Virginia, 2003).

10. Michael Lambek, "Provincializing God? Provocations from an Anthropology of Religion," in *Religion: Beyond a Concept*, ed. H. de Vries (New York: Fordham University Press, 2008), 122.

11. Fenella Cannell, "The Christianity of Anthropology," *Journal of the Royal Anthropological Institute* 11, no. 2 (2005): 335–356; Joel Robbins, "Anthropology and Theology: An Awkward Relationship?" *Anthropological Quarterly* 79, no. 2 (2006): 285–294; and Talal Asad, *Formations of the Secular* (Stanford: Stanford University Press, 2003). See also Webb Keane, *Christian Moderns*, and Robert J. Priest, "Missionary Positions: Christian, Modernist, Postmodernist," *Current Anthropology* 42, no. 1 (2001): 29–68.

12. William Garriott and Kevin Lewis O'Neill, "Who Is a Christian? Toward a Dialogic Approach in the Anthropology of Christianity," *Anthropological Theory* 8 (2008): 381–398.

13. "Anthropology," in *Oxford English Dictionary*, 2nd ed. (Oxford: Oxford University Press, 1989).

14. Manfred Kuehn, "Introduction," in Immanuel Kant, *Anthropology from a Pragmatic Point of View*, trans. ed. Robert Louden (Cambridge: Cambridge University Press, 2006), xxviii. See also John Zammito, *Kant, Herder, and the Birth of Anthropology* (Chicago: University of Chicago Press, 2002); Michel Foucault, *Introduction to Kant's Anthropology* (Los Angeles: Semiotext[e], 2008); and Michel Foucault and Ludwig Binswanger, *Dream and Existence*, trans. Jacob Needleman (Atlantic Highlands, NJ: Humanities Press Int., 1986).

15. "Anthropology," in *Encyclopedia of Biblical, Theological, and Ecclesiastical Literature* (New York: Harper and Brothers, 1883).

16. Engelke, *The Problem of Presence*.

17. For related genealogies see Talal Asad, *Genealogies of Religion* (Baltimore: Johns Hopkins University Press, 1993); George W. Stocking Jr., *Victorian Anthropology* (New York: Free Press, 1987).

18. See Grant Wacker, "A Plural World: The Protestant Awakening to World Religions," in *Between the Times: The Travail of the Protestant Establishment in America, 1900–1960*, ed. William R. Hutchison (Cambridge: Cambridge University Press, 1989), 253–277; Tomoko Masuzawa, *The Invention of World Religions* (Chicago: University of Chicago Press, 2005).

19. Murray G. Murphey, "On the Scientific Study of Religion," in *Religion and Twentieth-Century American Intellectual Life*, Michael J. Lacey, ed. (Cambridge: Cambridge University Press, 1989), 168.

20. Anthony F. C. Wallace, "Rituals: Sacred and Profane" *Zygon* 1, no. 1 (1966): 60–81. This chapter is a shortened version of *Religion: An Anthropological View* (New York: Random House, 1966).

21. Donald Szantho Harrington, "Science and the Search for a Rational Religious Faith" *Zygon* 1, no. 1 (1966), 107.

22. James goes on to say: "'Self,' 'body,' in the substantial or metaphysical sense—no one escapes subjection to those forms of thought. In practice, the common-sense *denkmittel* are uniformly victorious." William James, *Pragmatism: A New Name for some Old Ways of Thinking* (New York: Longman Green and Co., 1907), 65, 69.

23. Although Barth was not a liberal, he was read by them. Fred Dallmyr, "Politics of the Kingdom: Pannenberg's Anthropology." *The Review of Politics* 49, no. 1 (1987), 88. The *Anchor Bible Dictionary* of 1992 has a sole entry dealing with anthropology labeled "Anthropology in the Old Testament" that only treats anthropology as an academic discipline bringing together archaeology with theorists such as Mary Douglas: "Anthropology in the Old Testament," in *Anchor Bible Dictionary*, David Noel Freedman, ed. (Toronto: Doubleday, 1992). On Barth's relationship to liberal Protestantism, see Hartmut Ruddies, "Karl Barth als liberaler Theologe. Eine Skizze zu den Anfängen seiner Theologie" *Protestantismus zwischen Aufklärung und Moderne: Festschrift für Ulrich Barth* Roderich Barth, Claus-Dieter Osthövener, and Arnulf von Scheliha, eds. (Frankfurt am Main: Peter Lang, 2005), 389–402.

24. Karl Barth, Church Dogmatics, vol. 3, *The Doctrine of Creation* (Edinburgh: T & T Clark, 1936), 346.

25. Barth, *Church Dogmatics,* 344.

26. Hannah Arendt, *The Human Condition* (Chicago: University of Chicago Press, 1958).

27. On reading Barth in Protestant seminaries, see, Don Browning, "Immanence and Transcendence in Pastoral Care and Preaching," in *The Treasure of Earthen Vessels: Essays in Theological Anthropology*, ed. Brian H. Childs and David W. Waanders (Louisville, KY: John Knox, 1994), 123.

28. See David Riches, "The Holistic Person," and Hilde Hein, "Liberating Philosophy: An End to the Dichotomy of Spirit and Matter," in *Women, Knowledge, and Reality: Explorations in Feminist Philosophy*, ed. Ann Garry and Marilyn Pearsall (London: Routledge, 1996), 437–453; and Grace M. Jantzen, "Healing Our Brokenness: the Spirit and Creation," *The Ecumenical Review* 42, no. 2 (1990). On overemphasis and reification of the role of "Cartesian dualism" in modern medicine, see Anne Harrington, *The Cure Within: A History of Mind-Body Medicine* (New York: W. W. Norton, 2008).

29. Arendt, *The Human Condition.*

30. Anne Harrington, *Reenchanted Science: Holism in German Culture from Wilhelm II to Hitler* (Princeton, N.J.: Princeton University Press, 1996), xxiii.

31. Belle Oliver, Banswara notebook, 1929–1935. United Church of Canada Archives, Glenna Jameison Fonds, no. 3330.

32. Christopher Hookway, *Truth, Rationality, and Pragmatism* (Oxford: Oxford University Press, 2003), 192. For another approach to the vagueness of

the holistic see Christoph Benn and Erlinda Senturias, "Health, Healing, and Wholeness in the Ecumenical Discussion," *International Review of Missions* 90, no. 356/357 (2001), 21.

33. William James, "Pragmatism and Common Sense," in *Pragmatism and Other Writings*, ed. Giles B. Gunn (New York: Penguin Classics, 2000), 81.

34. Paul Tillich, "Heal the Sick," in *The Eternal Now* (New York: Scribner, 1963); Agnes Sanford, *The Healing Light* (St. Paul, MN: Macalester Park Publishing, 1947).

35. Kenneth Rogers, "Mental Health and Hygiene," *Canadian Churchman*, October 4, 1951. See also Daniel Cappon, "Physical, Mental, and Spiritual Healing," in *Handbook on the Healing Ministry of the Church* (Toronto: Office of the Bishop of Toronto, 1964); Dr. R. F. Warren, "Common Ground of Cooperation between Doctors and Clergy and Areas of Conflict," in *Handbook on the Healing Ministry of the Church* (Toronto: Office of the Bishop of Toronto, 1964). For other examples in which the "holistic" has operated as an ideological tradition, mediating concepts of the body within specific cultural and political contexts, see Harrington, *Reenchanted Science*; David Riches, "The Holistic Person; Or, the Ideology of Egalitarianism." *Journal of the Royal Anthropological Institute N.S.* 6 (2000): 669–85; Michael Hau, "The Holistic Gaze in German Medicine, 1890–1930," *The Bulletin of the History of Medicine* 74 (2000): 495–524; Charles Rosenberg, *Our Present Complaint: American Medicine, Then and Now* (Baltimore: Johns Hopkins University Press, 2007).

36. Alison Stokes, *Ministry after Freud* (New York: Pilgrim Press, 1985). See also Dale Martin's discussion of models of equilibrium and "spiritual invasion" in Greco-Roman, Jewish, and early Christian approaches to illness in Martin, *The Corinthian Body*.

37. For a view that conflates mainline with charismatic and Pentecostal healing practices, see Margaret M. Poloma, "A Comparison of Christian Science and Mainline Christian Healing Ideologies and Practices," *Review of Religious Research* 32, no. 4 (June 1991), 337–350. For another perspective, see Meredith B. McGuire and Debra Kantor, *Ritual Healing in Suburban America* (New Brunswick, NJ: Rutgers University Press, 1988).

38. Webb Keane, "The Evidence of the Senses and the Materiality of Religion," *Journal of the Royal Anthropological Institute* 14, no. 1 (2008), 120.

39. On repetition and reshaping the self in a different context of liberal Protestant anxiety, see Christopher White, "Minds Intensely Unsettled: Phrenology, Experience, and the American Pursuit of Spiritual Assurance, 1830–1880," *Religion and American Culture* 16, no. 2 (2006), 227–261.

40. Robert J. Thornton, "Rhetoric of Ethnographic Holism," in *Rereading Cultural Anthropology*, ed. George E. Marcus (Durham: Duke University Press, 1992), 19.

41. Arjun Appadurai, "Putting Hierarchy in its Place" in *Rereading Cultural Anthropology*, ed. George E. Marcus (Durham: Duke University Press, 1992), 38.

42. On the persistence (and success) of this dualistic thinking, see Ian Hacking, "Our Neo-Cartesian Body in Parts," *Critical Inquiry* 34 (Autumn 2007), 78–105.

43. Mark Johnson, *The Meaning of the Body: Aesthetics of Human Understanding* (Chicago: University of Chicago Press, 2007). Johnson's account says little about the particularities of the visceral body—skin color, gender, disability—he theorizes about none of these aspects of embodiment in what becomes a universalizing discourse, making his version of the embodied mind peculiarly disembodied, and oddly disconnected from several important theoretical approaches to embodiment, including feminist and queer theory. See also the discussion of dualism, embodiment, and Bourdieuian oxymoron in Thomas Csordas, *The Sacred Self: A Cultural Phenomenology of Charismatic Healing* (Berkeley: University of California Press, 1994), pp. 278–280.

44. Thomas A. Harris, *I'm OK—You're OK: A Practical Guide to Transactional Analysis* (New York: Harper & Row, 1969).

45. James Opp, *The Lord for the Body: Religion, Medicine, and Protestant Faith Healing in Canada, 1880–1930* (Kingston and Montreal: McGill-Queen's University Press, 2005), 201–202.

46. Ian Hacking, *Rewriting the Soul: Multiple Personality and the Sciences of Memory* (Princeton, N.J.: Princeton University Press, 1995); See also, Ann Taves, *Fits, Trances, and Visions: Experiencing Religion and Explaining Experience from Wesley to James* (Princeton, N.J.: Princeton University Press, 1999).

47. Opp, *Lord for the Body,* 19.

48. Opp, *Lord for the Body,* 141.

49. Doctors, ministers, epidemiologists, and alternative health care practitioners have all argued for the importance of holistic perspectives that consider the ways health is shaped not only by physiology or brain synapses but also by psychological, spiritual, social, and economic influences. Harrington, *Reenchanted Science*; Christopher Lawrence and George Weisz, eds., *Greater Than the Parts: Holism in Biomedicine, 1920–1950* (New York: Oxford University Press, 1998); Mary Elizabeth O'Brien. *Spirituality in Nursing: Standing on Holy Ground* (Sudbury, MA: Jones and Bartlett, 2003), 9.

50. Jan C. Smuts, *Holism and Evolution* (London: Macmillan, 1926).

51. Ibid., 270.

52. Harrington, *Reenchanted Science,* xxii.

53. Louis Dumont, *Essays on Individualism: Modern Ideology in Anthropological Perspective* (Chicago: University of Chicago Press, 1986).

54. Percy Dearmer, *Body and Soul: An Enquiry into the Effects of Religion upon Health, with a Description of Christian Works of Healing from the New Testament to the Present Day* (London: Sir Isaac Pitman & Sons, Ltd., 1910); James Bissett Pratt, *Matter and Spirit: A Study of Mind and Body in Their Relation to the Spiritual Life* (New York: Macmillan, 1922).

55. Pentecostals based their dramatic miracles of faith healing on a tripartite anthropology of the self drawn in part from Paul's first letter to the Thessalonians: "May your spirit and soul and body be kept sound and blameless at the coming of our Lord Jesus Christ" (5:23). In this triad, Pentecostals have cast the spirit as that most sanctified part which directly experiences God, while the soul stands between the body and the spirit. Pentecostals also paid particular attention to Paul's distinction between the natural body and the spiritual body (1 Cor. 15).

56. Lily Dougall, *The Christian Doctrine of Health: A Handbook on the Relation of Bodily to Spiritual and Moral Health* (London: Macmillan, 1916), 92, 133–134.

57. "Missionary, Medico, and Musician." *Canadian Churchman*, September 4, 1952.

58. Elwood Worcester and Samuel McComb, *Body, Mind, and Spirit* (New York: Charles Scribner's Sons, 1932), xvii.

59. Ibid., 206. Worcester shifts between the terms "mind" and "soul."

60. Ibid., 73, 214.

61. Andrew Heinze, *Jews and the American Soul: Human Nature in the Twentieth Century* (Princeton, N.J.: Princeton University Press, 2004), 171–172.

62. See also Christopher G. White, *Unsettled Minds: Psychology and the American Search for Spiritual Assurance, 1830–1940* (Berkeley: University of California Press, 2009).

63. Ibid., 345.

64. Ibid., 94. Worcester also took credit for popularizing James's essay "The Energies of Men" by publishing it as a tract distributed by the Emmanuel Church, 239. See also Elwood Worcester, *Life's Adventure: The Story of a Varied Career* (New York: Charles Scribner's Sons, 1932).

65. Worcester, *Body, Mind and Spirit*, 32–38.

66. Ibid., 122.

67. Ibid., 22.

68. Ibid., 175.

69. Cabot and Dicks, *Ministering to the Sick*, 3.

70. Livingstone, *Through Sickness to Life*, 42.

71. Ibid., 66.

72. Ibid., 12

73. See "Religion and Psychiatry," *Canadian Churchman* November 6, 1952.

74. For an example of this argument, see the work of Canadian Anglican, Arthur N. Thompson, *Haelend: The Church's Ministry of Healing* (Burlington, ON: Welch Publishing, 1985), 10–11. For a discussion of whether such a tripartite view was heretical or not according to nineteenth-century Anglicans, see Karina Side, "Christopher Smart's Heresy," *Modern Language Notes* 69, no. 5 (May 1954), 316–319.

75. Leslie Weatherhead, *Life Begins at Death* (Nashville: Abingdon, 1969), 40–41. Abingdon Press was (and is) a well-known American Methodist publisher. For a glowing review of Weatherhead's *Religion, Psychology and Healing*, recommending it as a "gift book," see *Canadian Churchman*, December 4, 1952.

76. Leslie D. Weatherhead, *The Mastery of Sex through Psychology and Religion* (Toronto: McClelland and Stewart, 1936), 20. Weatherhead quotes Sherwood Eddy, *Sex and Youth* (New York: Doubleday, 1929), 43.

77. Weatherhead, *Life Begins at Death*.

78. Paul Tillich, "The Meaning of Health (1961)." *Main Works/Hauptwerke, vol. 2, Writings in the Philosophy of Culture* (Berlin: Walter de Gruyter, 1990), 344–353.

79. On Rogers's popularity among liberal Protestants, see Susan E. Myers-Shirk, "'To Be Fully Human': U. S. Protestant Psychotherapeutic Culture and the Subversion of the Domestic Ideal, 1945–1965." *Journal of Women's History* 12(1, 2000):112–136.

80. "Paul Tillich and Carl Rogers: A Dialogue," *Pastoral Psychology* 19, no. 2 (1968): 55–64.

81. "The Demonic" was translated into English and published for an American audience in 1936. Paul Tillich, "The Demonic: A Contribution to the Interpretation of History," in *The Interpretation of History* (New York: Scribners, 1936). See also Paul Tillich, *Systematic Theology* (Chicago: University of Chicago Press, 1973), 218.

82. Tillich, "The Demonic," 121.

83. Ibid., 120.

84. Ibid., 222.

85. Ibid., 224.

86. Lesslie Newbigin, "The Healing Ministry in the Mission of the Church," in *The Healing Church: The Tübingen Consultation* (Geneva: World Council of Churches, 1965), 10, 13. Newbigin was part of a wider current of liberal Christian engagement with the secular as epitomized by Harvey Cox, *The Secular City: Secularization and Urbanization in Theological Perspective* (New York: Macmillan, 1965).

87. Janet R. Jakobsen and Ann Pellegrini, eds., *Secularisms* (Durham: Duke University Press, 2008); Asad, *Formations of the Secular*; Charles Taylor, *A Secular Age* (Cambridge, MA: Harvard University Press, 2007).

88. "Findings," *The Healing Church*, 35.

89. Erling Kayser, "Medicine and Modern Philosophy: An Introduction," in *The Healing Church*, 23.

90. Ibid., 21, 23.

91. Martin Scheel, "Some Comments on Pre-Scientific Forms of Healing," in *The Healing Church*, 28.

92. James C. McGilvray, "The Next Steps," in *The Healing Church*, 46.

93. On local Chinese doctors in Canadian medical missions, see the biography of United Church medical missionary Robert McClure, Munroe Scott, *McClure: A Biography* (Toronto: Penguin Books Canada, 1979).

94. Benn and Senturias, "Health, Healing, and Wholeness," 9; Socrates Litsios, "The Christian Medical Commission and the Development of the World Health Organization's Primary Health Care Approach," *American Journal of Public Health* 94, no. 11 (2004), 1884–1893. For more on the CMC, see Gillian Paterson, "The CMC Story, 1968–1998," *Contact* 161–162 (1998): 2–52.

95. The pages of the *Canadian Churchman* and the *United Church Observer* are filled with discussions of the Nestlé boycott and, later on, the responsibility for churches to respond to the global crisis of HIV/AIDS.

96. Christian Medical Commission (CMC), *Healing and Wholeness: The Churches' Role in Health* (Geneva: World Council of Churches, 1990). This definition drew on that of the World Health Organization.

97. Christian Medical Commission, *Healing and Wholeness*, 32.

98. Ibid., iv, 8, 30, 14.

99. Ibid., 13.

100. For the WHO definition, see http://www.who.int/suggestions/faq/en/ index.html (accessed December 18, 2008). Benn and Senturias, "Health, Healing, and Wholeness," 21. For the CNA definitions of health, see http://www.cna -aiic.ca/CNA/about/meetings/resolutions_2005/resolutions_08_e.aspx (accessed December 18, 2008). The Parish Nursing Interest Group reported that the response from the WHO was not encouraging and that "prayer, patience, and persistence" were required; see http://rnao-pnig.org/joomla/index.php?option= com_content&task=view&id=19&Itemid=32. For an account of the difficulties of including spirituality in the WHO definition of health, which ends with the perplexingly simplistic suggestion to use "the Bible as a universal standard" for "assessing spiritual health throughout the world in nations which practice the Christian faith," see James S. Larson, "The World Health Organization's Definition of Health: Social vs. Spiritual Health," *Social Indicators Research* 38 (1996), 181–192.

101. Winnifred Fallers Sullivan, "Religion Naturalized: The New Establishment," in *After Pluralism: Reimagining Models of Religious Engagement,* ed. Courtney Bender and Pamela Klassen (New York: Columbia University Press, 2010), 82–97.

102. By the new millennium, however, the WCC, because of lack of funds, had drastically cut back their health "team" to 1.8 people.

103. Ostrander drawing from Schleiermacher: Rick Ostrander, *The Life of Prayer in a World of Science: Protestants, Prayer, and American Culture, 1870–1930* (Oxford: Oxford University Press, 2000), 121.

104. Edward J. Larson, *Summer for the Gods: The Scopes Trial and America's Continuing Debate over Science and Religion* (New York: Basic Books, 1997).

105. On "sad Christians" see Opp, *Lord for the Body,* 141. R. Marie Griffith discusses how Women Aglow participants label mainstream Protestantism "spiritually dead," while scholar Donald Miller advances such a critique as his own. R. Marie Griffith, "A 'Network of Praying Women': Women's Aglow Fellowship and Mainline American Protestantism," in *Pentecostal Currents in American Protestantism,* ed. Edith L. Blumhofer, Russell P. Spittler, and Grant A. Wacker (Urbana and Chicago: University of Illinois Press, 1999), 134. Donald Miller, *Reinventing American Protestantism: Christianity in the New Millennium* (Berkeley: University of California Press, 1997), 8. For a critique of this view from within, see Dorothy Bass, *Christianity for the Rest of Us: How the Neighborhood Church Is Transforming the Faith* (San Francisco: Harper San Francisco, 2006).

106. Cabot and Dicks, *Ministering to the Sick,* quoted in Livingstone, *Through Sickness to Life,* 64.

2. THE GOSPEL OF HEALTH AND THE SCIENTIFIC SPIRIT

1. Anna Henry, *Life from the Dead* (Toronto: Women's Missionary Society of the Methodist Church, Canada, n.d.), 3.

2. Larry Hannant, *Rereading Bethune* (Toronto: University of Toronto Press, 1998), 15.

3. B. Choné Oliver, *Dr. Margaret MacKellar: The Story of her Early Years* (Toronto: Women's Missionary Society of the Presbyterian Church in Canada, 1920), 42. United Church Archives, PAM BX 9225 M25704.

4. Benedict Anderson, *Imagined Communities: Reflections on the Origin and Spread of Nationalism.* 2nd ed. (New York: Verso, 1991).

5. Mary Baker Eddy, *Science and Health with a Key to the Scriptures* (Boston: First Church of Christ, Scientist, 1994). See Paul Gutjahr, "Sacred Texts in the United States: The State of the Discipline," *Book History* 4 (2001); 335–370."

6. Janice Boddy, "Spirit Possession Revisited: Beyond Instrumentality," *Annual Review of Anthropology* 23 (October 1994), 411.

7. David Hall, *Worlds of Wonder, Days of Judgment: Popular Religious Belief in Early New England* (New York: Alfred Knopf, 1989); Candy Gunther Brown, *The Word in the World: Evangelical Writing, Publishing, and Reading in America, 1789–1880* (Chapel Hill: University of North Carolina Press, 2004); David Paul Nord, *Faith in Reading: Religious Publishing and the Birth of Mass Media in America* (Oxford: Oxford University Press, 2004); David Cressy, "Books as Totems in Seventeenth-Century England and New England." *Journal of Library History* 21, no. 1 (1986), 94. For a fuller argument, see Pamela E. Klassen "Textual Healing: Mainstream Protestants and the Therapeutic Text, 1900–1925," *Church History* 75, no. 4 (December, 2006), 809–848.

8. See Lisa Gitelman, *Scripts, Grooves, and Writing Machines: Representing Technology in the Edison Era* (Stanford, CA: Stanford University Press, 1999).

9. On distrust of biblical criticism, see Michael Gauvreau, *The Evangelical Century: College and Creed in English Canada from the Great Revival to the Great Depression* (Montreal and Kingston: McGill-Queen's University Press, 1991); and "Revival of Religion and Higher Criticism," *Christian Guardian* (January 3, 1906). On biblical texts as talismanic, see John L. Comaroff and Jean Comaroff, *Of Revelation and Revolution: The Dialectics of Modernity on a South African Frontier*, vol. 2 (Chicago: University of Chicago Press, 1997), 338–346.

10. See Derek Peterson, "The Rhetoric of the Word: Bible Translation and Mau Mau in Colonial Central Kenya," in *Missions, Nationalism, and the End of Empire*, ed. Brian Stanley (Grand Rapids, MI: Eerdmans, 2003), 166, and Jack Goody, ed. *Literacy in Traditional Societies* (Cambridge: Cambridge University Press, 1968).

11. Homi K. Bhabha, *The Location of Culture* (New York: Routledge, 1994), 105.

12. Leigh Schmidt, *Hearing Things: Religion, Illusion, and the American Enlightenment* (Cambridge, MA: Harvard University Press, 2000), 48. See also, Peter Thuesen, *In Discordance with the Scriptures: American Protestant Battles over Translating the Bible* (New York: Oxford University Press, 1999).

13. Mr. Black's Bible Class, "The Duty of Good Health," *Christian Guardian* (March 30, 1921).

14. "The Duty of Physical Fitness," *Christian Guardian* (March 15, 1911); "Preparing to Live Long," *Christian Guardian* (July 28, 1920); *Canadian Churchman* (May 4, 1911); "A Department of Health" *Christian Guardian* (November 29, 1911); "Pankhurst in Canada" *Canadian Churchman* (April 28, 1921); "Controlling the Nerves" *Christian Guardian* (March 8, 1922); *Christian Guardian* (November 22, 1916). For a discussion of the notion of "Christian citizenship", see Kevin O'Neill, *City of God: Christian Citizenship in Guatemala* (Berkeley: University of California Press, 2009).

15. Bernice A. Pescosolido and Jack K. Martin, "Cultural Authority and the Role of American Medicine: The Role of Networks, Class, and Community," *Journal of Health Politics, Policy and Law* 29, nos. 4–5 (2004): 736.

16. John Harley Warner, "Grand Narrative and Its Discontents: Medical History and the Social Transformation of American Medicine," *Journal of Health Politics, Policy, and Law* 29, nos. 4–5 (2004): 770; Rhodri Hayward, "Demonology, Neurology, and Medicine in Edwardian Britain," *Bulletin of the History of Medicine* 78, no. 1 (2004), 58. For Canadian contexts, see C. David Naylor, ed., *Canadian Health Care and the State: A Century of Evolution* (Montreal and Kingston: McGill-Queen's University Press, 1992).

17. See Michel Foucault "The Crisis of Medicine or Antimedicine?" *Foucault Studies* 1 (December 2004), 13. Turning to religious terms, Foucault laments: "What is diabolical about the present situation is that whenever we want to refer to a realm outside medicine we find that it has already been medicalized" (14). See also, Michel Foucault, *The Birth of the Clinic: An Archaeology of Medical Perception* (New York: Vintage Books, 1975), and *History of Sexuality* (New York: Vintage Books, 1980).

18. Deborah R. Gordon, "Tenacious Assumptions in Western Medicine," in *Biomedicine Examined*, ed. Margaret Lock and D. R. Gordon (Dordrecht: Kluwer, 1988), 19; Bryan Turner, *The Body and Society: Explorations in Social Theory* (London and Thousand Oaks, CA: Sage Publications, 1996).

19. Malcolm Bull, "Medicalization and Secularization," *British Journal of Sociology* 41, no. 2 (June 1990), 251.

20. Bull, "Medicalization and Secularization," 252, 253. See also, Jason Szabo, "Seeing is Believing? The Form and Substance of French Medical Debates over Lourdes," *Bulletin of the History of Medicine* 76 (2002), 199–230; Rennie B. Schoepflin, *Christian Science on Trial: Religious Healing in America* (Baltimore: Johns Hopkins University Press, 2003); James Opp, *The Lord for the Body: Religion, Medicine, and Protestant Faith Healing in Canada, 1880–1930* (Montreal: McGill-Queen's University Press, 2005).

21. See Ronald L. Numbers, *Science and Christianity in Pulpit and Pew* (Oxford: Oxford University Press, 2007).

22. See Barry A. Lazarus, "The Practice of Medicine and Prejudice in a New England Town: The Founding of Mount Sinai Hospital, Hartford, Connecticut," *Journal of American Ethnic History* 10, no. 3 (1991): 21–41, and Andrew Heinze, *Jews and the American Soul: Human Nature in the Twentieth Century* (Princeton, N.J.: Princeton University Press, 2004).

23. For example, *Christian Guardian* (January 31, 1900); *Christian Guardian* (January 15, 1915). See also, "Patent Medicines and Methodism," *Christian*

Guardian (February 1915). Lori Loeb, "Beating the Flu: Orthodox and Commercial Responses to Influenza in Britain, 1889–1919," *Social History of Medicine* 18, no. 2 (August 2005), 203–24; T. J. Jackson Lears, *No Place of Grace: Antimodernism and Transformation of American Culture, 1880–1920* (New York: Pantheon Books, 1981); Nancy Tomes, "Merchants of Health: Medicine and Consumer Culture in the United States," *Journal of American History* 88, no. 2 (September 2001) 519–547; Mariana Valverde, *The Age of Light, Soap and Water, 1885–1925* (Toronto: McClelland and Stewart, 1991).

24. See Richard Wightman Fox, "The Culture of Liberal Protestant Progressivism, 1875–1925," *Journal of Interdisciplinary History* 23, no. 3 (1993), 639–660.

25. See Laurie F. Maffly-Kipp, "Writing Our Way into History: Gender, Race, and the Creation of Black Denominational Life," in *Women and Twentieth-Century Protestantism*, ed. Margaret Lamberts Bendroth and Virginia Lieson Brereton (Urbana: University of Illinois Press, 2002), 164–183; R. Marie Griffith, "Female Suffering and Religious Devotion in American Pentecostalism," in *Women and Twentieth-Century Protestantism*, 184–208. Between the years 1908 and 1925, the *Christian Guardian* had a consistent subscriber base that ranged from 20,000 to 23,000, with a jump in 1920 to 32,126 (United Church of Canada/Victoria University Archives, United Church of Canada Board of Publication Collection fonds, financial operations: Methodist/Ryerson, fonds 513/2, 83.061C-box 30-file 21, "Methodist Book and Publishing House Financial Statements," 1915, 1919, 1920, 1924, 1925). Ministers were the main agents for the paper, but it was also peddled door to door (United Church of Canada/Victoria University Archives, United Church of Canada Board of Publication Collection fonds, Ryerson History, fonds 513/2/3, 83.061C-box 12-file 2, *Christian Guardian*, n.d., 7). Archival records and subscription rates for the *Canadian Churchman* from 1900 through 1925 are seemingly nonexistent. In the 1950s, a low point, its subscribers numbered approximately 5000 ("*Anglican Journal/Journal Anglican*: A Brief History" Anglican Journal—Historical Information, GS96-07, Anglican General Synod Archives).

26. *Christian Guardian* July 19, 1905 (United Church of Canada/Victoria University Archives, United Church of Canada Board of Publication Collection fonds, Ryerson History, fonds 513/2/3, 83.061C-box 12-file 2, "The Christian Guardian," n.d.). Both denominations were deeply influenced by their British and American counterparts. See Phyllis Airhart, *Serving the Present Age: Revivalism, Progressivism, and the Methodist Tradition in Canada* (Montreal and Kingston: McGill-Queen's University Press, 1992); William Westfall, *Two Worlds: The Protestant Culture of Nineteenth-Century Ontario* (Montreal and Kingston: McGill-Queen's University Press, 1989); Richard W. Vaudry, "Evangelical Anglicans and the Atlantic World: Politics, Ideology, and the British North American Connection," in *Aspects of the Canadian Evangelical Experience*, ed. G. A. Rawlyk (Kingston and Montreal: McGill-Queen's University Press, 1997), 154–170. Even among Pentecostals, for whom bookishness was highly suspect, newspapers abounded and were used not only for communicative purposes but also on occasion as objects with supernatural healing power. Grant Wacker, *Heaven Below: Early Pentecostals and American Culture* (Cam-

bridge, MA: Harvard University Press, 2001), 94; and Randall J. Stephens, "'There is Magic in Print': The Holiness-Pentecostal Press and the Origins of Southern Pentecostalism," Part 1 and Part 2. *Journal of Southern Religion* (December 2002), http://jsr.fsu.edu/2002/Stephens.htm, accessed January 20, 2009.

27. *Christian Guardian* September 21, 1904. On the centrality of texts within Canadian Methodism, see Lorne Pierce, *On Publishers & Publishing* (Toronto: The Ryerson Press, 1951), in United Church of Canada/Victoria University Archives, United Church of Canada Board of Publication Collection fonds, Ryerson History, fonds 513/2/3, 83.061C-box 12-file 2, "*The Christian Guardian*," n.d. See also, United Church of Canada/Victoria University Archives, United Church of Canada Board of Publication Collection fonds, Ryerson History, fonds 513/2, 83.061C-box 12-file 2, *The United Church Publishing House: A Brief Look at its Origin, Development, and Present Structure*, n.d.

28. *Christian Guardian* (January 17, 1914); *Christian Guardian* (January 31, 1900); *Christian Guardian* (May 5, 1914); *Canadian Churchman* (October 8, 1914); *Canadian Churchman* (February 3, 1910).

29. For different perspectives on this confidence, see Gauvreau, *An Evangelical Century*, 220; Neil Semple, *The Lord's Dominion: The History of Canadian Methodism* (Montreal and Kingston: McGill-Queen's University Press, 1996).

30. R. R. Hare, "V.D. and the School," *Christian Guardian* (March 2, 1921). Hare endorsed a pamphlet called "A Pure Citizenship" by Arthur Beall, a sex educator employed by the Ontario Education Department. Michael Bliss, "How We Used to Learn about Sex," *Maclean's Magazine* (March 1974). See also *Canadian Churchman* (February 8, 1917), and *Canadian Churchman* (March 1, 1900).

31. *Canadian Churchman* (March 1, 1900).

32. Gail Edwards, "'The Picturesqueness of His Accent and Speech': Methodist Missionary Narratives and William Henry Pierce's Autobiography," in *Canadian Missionaries, Indigenous Peoples: Representing Religion at Home and Abroad*, ed. Alvyn Austin and Jamie S. Scott (Toronto: University of Toronto Press, 2005), 67–86; Andrew F. Walls, "'The Heavy Artillery of the Missionary Army:' The Domestic Importance of the Nineteenth-Century Medical Missionary," in *The Church and Healing*, ed. W. J. Sheils (London: Basil Blackwell, 1982), 287–297; C. Peter Williams, "Healing and Evangelism: The Place of Medicine in Later Victorian Protestant Missionary Thinking," in Sheils, *The Church and Healing*, 271–285.

33. *Canadian Churchman* (November 21, 1901).

34. *Canadian Churchman* (February 15, 1900).

35. A. R. MacDuff, *Canadian Churchman* (January 8, 1903). See C. B. Kelly, "Healing the Sick in Chung-Chow, China," *Christian Guardian* (December 30, 1914).

36. *Canadian Churchman* (February 22, 1900). In 1904 the Methodist Women's Missionary Society read Arthur Henderson Smith, *Rex Christus: An Outline Study of China* (New York: Macmillan, 1903); *Christian Guardian* (November 9, 1904). In 1905 they read "Japan: Woman in Japan," a chapter from William Elliot Griffis, *Dux Christus: An Outline Study of Japan* (New York: Macmillan, 1904); *Christian Guardian* August 9, 1905.

37. For example, Walter R. Lambuth, *Medical Missions: The Twofold Task* (New York: Student Volunteer Movement for Foreign Missions, 1920); R. Fletcher Moorshead, *The Way of the Doctor: A Study in Medical Missions* (London: The Carey Press, 1926); and Tatchell, *Medical Missions in China*.

38. Henry, *Life from the Dead*, 6.

39. Ibid., 7.

40. Anna Henry, quoted in "Medical Work," *Christian Guardian* (June 28, 1916). See also Rosemary R. Gagan, *A Sensitive Independence: Canadian Methodist Women Missionaries in Canada and the Orient, 1881–1925* (Montreal and Kingston: McGill-Queen's University Press, 1992); Lambuth, *Medical Missions*, 125; and on Bible women, see R. S. Sugirtharajah. *Postcolonial Criticism and Biblical Interpretation* (London: Oxford University Press, 2002).

41. On the "desperate situation" of women, see "The Needs and Possibilities of Medical Work for Women in China," *Christian Guardian* (April 21, 1909). Also see Anglican Caroline Macklem's comment: "It is the women of India, who, by their gross superstition, are retarding the growth of Christianity," *Canadian Churchman* (May 23, 1901). See also *Canadian Churchman* (February 22, 1900).

42. *Canadian Churchman* (March 1, 1900).

43. Mary-Ellen Kelm, *Colonizing Bodies: Aboriginal Health and Healing in British Columbia, 1900–1950* (Vancouver: University of British Columbia Press, 1998), Maureen K. Lux, *Medicine That Walks: Disease, Medicine, and Canadian Plains Native People, 1880–1940* (Toronto: University of Toronto Press, 2001). For a similar discussion of opium addiction, see Ruth Rogaski, *Hygienic Modernity: Meanings of Health and Disease in Treaty-Port China* (Berkeley: University of California Press, 2004). For a discussion of the health benefits of dried seaweed and fish eggs, see the comments on the back of a photo taken by Dr. R. W. Large and labeled "3 Kiusquit women; Coming to Bella Bella for medical treatment," (United Church of Canada Archives, From Mission to Partnership Collection, 93.049 p/31, R. W. Large, 1909).

44. *Christian Guardian* (November 18, 1914). On Darby, see Bob Burrows, *Healing in the Wilderness: A History of the United Church Mission Hospitals* (Madeira Park, BC: Harbour Publishing, 2004), 58.

45. Bhabha, *The Location of Culture*, 118.

46. Lambuth, *Medical Missions*, 116–17.

47. Diary 1903, Box 2, no. 10, William Edward Smith Papers, Mission Research Library Archives: 2, in the archives of the Burke Library at Union Theological Seminary, New York. On Canadian missionaries to China more generally, see Alvyn Austin, *Saving China: Canadian Missionaries in the Middle Kingdom, 1888–1959* (Toronto: University of Toronto Press, 1986).

48. Diary 1897, Box 1, no. 76 William Edward Smith Papers, Mission Research Library Archives: 2, in the archives of the Burke Library at Union Theological Seminary, New York. See also W. W. Peter, *Broadcasting Health in China: The Field and Methods of Public Health Work in the Missionary Enterprise* (Shanghai: Council on Health Education, 1926).

49. Jean Comaroff, *Body of Power, Spirit of Resistance: The Culture and History of a South African People* (Chicago: University of Chicago Press, 1985), 143.

50. "The Heathen Way," *Christian Guardian* (March 24, 1909). See the caution about attributing undue influence to literacy in terms of social and cultural difference in Leah Price, "Reading: The State of the Discipline," *Book History* 7 (2004): 316.

51. See also Comaroff, *Body of Power, Spirit of Resistance,* 143.

52. *Christian Guardian* (June 5, 1901).

53. James W. Opp, "Healing Hands, Healthy Bodies: Protestant Women and Faith Healing in Canada and the United States, 1880–1930," in *Women and Twentieth-Century Protestantism,* ed. Margaret Lamberts Bendroth and Virginia Lieson Brereton (Urbana and Chicago: University of Illinois Press, 2002), 236–252, 237.

54. Healthy-minded religion is characterized by a faith that makes one happy, through "the deliberate adoption of an optimistic turn of mind." William James, *The Varieties of Religious Experience: A Study in Human Nature* (Cambridge, MA: Harvard University Press, 1985), 87.

55. *Christian Guardian* (June 27, 1906). On the left wall: "He shall give you another comforter, that he may abide with you for ever; Even the spirit of truth whom the world cannot receive, because it seeth him not. But ye know him for he dwelleth in you. Christ Jesus." This is a slight alteration of John 14:16–17 as found in the Authorized Version translation. On the right: "If sin makes sinners Truth and Love can unmake them. If a sense of disease produces suffering and a sense of ease antidotes it, disease is mental. Hence the fact of Christian Science that the human mind alone suffers and the divine mind alone heals it. Mary Baker Eddy." This is an earlier version of the passage in the current edition of *Science and Health* 270:22. Also on the right: "Preach the word; be instant in season, out of season; reprove, rebuke, exhort with all wrong suffering and doctrine. Paul" (2 Timothy 4:2, AV).

56. *Christian Guardian* (August 7, 1901). On Protestant reactions to Christian Science see Stephen Gottschalk, *Rolling Away the Stone. Mary Baker Eddy's Challenge to Materialism* (Bloomington: Indiana University Press, 2006); Rennie B. Schoepflin, *Christian Science on Trial*; Raymond J. Cunningham, "The Impact of Christian Science on the American Churches, 1880–1910," *The American Historical Review* 72, no. 3 (April 1967): 885–905; Patricia Jasen, "Mind, Medicine, and the Christian Science Controversy in Canada, 1888–1910," *Journal of Canadian Studies* 32, no. 4 (1998), 5–22; Stephen Gottschalk, *The Emergence of Christian Science in American Religious Life* (Berkeley: University of California Press, 1973).

57. S. D. Chown, *Christian Science Examined* (Toronto: J. Richardson, 1901). See also Gillian Gill, *Mary Baker Eddy* (Reading, MA: Perseus Books, 1998; Gottschalk, *Rolling Away the Stone,* 45, 86, 87, 258.

58. See, Rev. Canon R. C. Blagrave, "The Inadequacy of Christian Science Theology" *Canadian Churchman* (November 1, 1923); "Where Christian Science Broke in Two," *Christian Guardian* (August 14, 1907); "Relation of Christian Ministers to Christian Science," *Zion's Herald* (July 31, 1907); J. P. Sheraton, *Christian Science* (n.p. published by request,1891). Sheraton was principal of the Evangelical Anglican Wycliffe College in Toronto; Chown, *Christian Science Examined.*

59. "Follow the White Star of Truth," *The News*, Toronto, (September 18, 1907). CP241 Archives of the Mary Baker Eddy Library.

60. Chown, *Christian Science Examined*, 143.

61. W. G. Nicholson, "Christian Science," *Canadian Churchman* (April 6, 1916); H. Michell, "Visiting with the Sects" *Canadian Churchman* (April 5, 1923); P. Marion Simms, "Christian Science: Suggestive Therapeutics," *Christian Guardian* (October 16, 1907); "Death of Eddy," *Canadian Churchman* January 19, 1911); H. Michell "Five Modern Heresiarchs: Mother Ann," *Canadian Churchman* (May 8, 1924). See also Rodney Stark, "The Rise and Fall of Christian Science," *Journal of Contemporary Religion* 13, no. 2 (1998):189–214; and Rodney Stark, William Sims Bainbridge, and Lori Kent, "Cult Membership in the Roaring Twenties: Assessing Local Receptivity," *Sociological Analysis* 42, no. 2 (1981):137–162.

62. Sheraton, *Christian Science*, 1891, 16; Rev. R. S. MacArthur quoted in "Curse of Christian Science" *Weekly Scotsman* (March 11, 1907). CP 241, Archives of the Mary Baker Eddy Library.

63. D. F. Mackenzie, *Bromely Chronicle* (England) (November 21, 1907). CP241, Archives of the Mary Baker Eddy Library.

64. Sheraton, *Christian Science*, 1891, 43; Patterson Dubois, "Bahaism and Its Claim," *Philadelphia Book News Monthly* (December 1915). CP948, Archives of the Mary Baker Eddy Library.

65. "Mrs. Eddy and Eddyism," *Canadian Churchman* (January 19, 1911). See also "Mrs. Eddy Again" *Christian Guardian* (November 7, 1906); Sheraton, *Christian Science*, 1891, 42.

66. Editorial, "Jesus' Method of Healing," *Christian Guardian* (February 25, 1920).

67. *Erie* [PA] *Dispatch* (March 18, 1907), CP241, Archives of the Mary Baker Eddy Library. See also William B. Creighton, "Editorial," *Christian Guardian* (April 21, 1920).

68. N. C. Moller, *La Crosse Wisconsin* (October 14, 1907). CP241, Archives of the Mary Baker Eddy Library.

69. T. C. Martin, *Republican* [Springfield MA] (May 10, 1907). Archives of the Mary Baker Eddy Library.

70. *Canadian Churchman* 26 (October 26, 1922).

71. Letter from "An Anglican," *Canadian Churchman* (October 18, 1923). On Jews and Christian Science, see John J. Appel, "Christian Science and the Jews," *Jewish Social Studies* 31, no. 2 (1969): 100–121; and Ellen M. Umansky, *From Christian Science to Jewish Science: Spiritual Healing and American Jews* (New York: Oxford University Press, 2005).

72. William W. Washburn, "Pundita Ramabai and Christian Science," *Christian Guardian* (October 21, 1903), 11. See, Ramabai Sarasvati and Meera Kosambi, *Pandita Ramabai's American Encounter: The Peoples of the United States (1889)* (Bloomington: Indiana University Press, 2003).

73. Rev. H. R. Stevenson, "God, Philosophy, and Psychology: Kant and Hegel," *Canadian Churchman* (February 28, 1924); Stephen Gottschalk, *Rolling Away the Stone*, 86, 130.

74. *Canadian Churchman* (October 26, 1922); Byron H. Stauffer, "The Spell of St. Anne de Beaupre," *Christian Guardian* (October 4, 1916).

75. Jason Szabo, "Seeing is Believing."

76. J. N. Carpenter, "Christian Science," *Canadian Churchman* (February 14, 1918).

77. Pickles, "Relation of Christian Ministers," *Zion's Herald*. Archives of the Mary Baker Eddy Library. See also Rev. Edgar J. Helms in the same article.

78. *Canadian Churchman* (February 14, 1918); Rev. Canon R. C. Blagrave, "The Inadequacy of Christian Science Theology," *Canadian Churchman* (November 1, 1923); Foster, "Letter to the Editor," *Canadian Churchman* (September 6, 1923); C. E. Luce, "Letter to the Editor," *Canadian Churchman* (February 28, 1918).

79. On idealism and "medical materialism," see William James, *The Varieties of Religious Experience*.

80. Percy Dearmer, *Body and Soul: An Enquiry into the Effect of Religion upon Health, with a Description of Christian Works of Healing from the New Testament to the Present Day* (London: I. Pitman and Sons, 1910), 117–118.

81. Review of P. N. Wagget, *Religion and Science: Some Suggestions for the Study of the Relations between Them* (London: Longmans, Green, 1904). (1904); *Canadian Churchman* (April 7, 1904).

82. See for example, Frederick George Scott, "Unction of the Sick." A paper read before the Synod of the Diocese of Quebec, June 11, 1903. (Quebec: Chronicle Print Co., 1903).

83. Though in early publications Worcester described his Christian therapeutics as an answer to Christian Science, he later denied that it had any influence on his approach. See Gottschalk, *The Emergence of Christian Science*, 213. On Coriat, see Heinze, *Jews and the American Soul*.

84. Leslie D. Weatherhead, *Psychology, Religion and Healing* (London: Hodder and Stoughton, Limited, 1955), 225. See Raymond J. Cunningham, "The Emmanuel Movement: A Variety of American Religious Experience," *American Quarterly* 14, no. 1 (1962): 48–63; and Robert Bruce Mullin, *Miracles and the Modern Religious Imagination* (New Haven: Yale University Press, 2005).

85. See also "The Gospel of Health," *Christian Guardian* (July 29, 1908); "Divine Healing" *Canadian Churchman* (January 14, 1909).

86. "The Ministry of Healing," *Canadian Churchman* (September 29, 1910).

87. *Boston Record* (November 22, 1906). CP 189, Archives of the Mary Baker Eddy Library.

88. *Buffalo Times* (October 19, 1907); *Boston Magazine* (April 9, 1907), both CP 241, Archives of the Mary Baker Eddy Library. Elwood Worcester, Samuel McComb, and Isador Coriat, *Religion and Medicine: The Moral Control of Nervous Disorders* (New York: Moffat, Yard & Company, 1908); Nathan G. Hale Jr. *Freud and the Americans: The Beginnings of Psychoanalysis in the United States, 1876–1917* (New York: Oxford University Press, 1971), 231.

89. Carol V. R. George, *God's Salesman: Norman Vincent Peale and the Power of Positive Thinking* (Oxford: Oxford University Press, 1993), 11.

90. Worcester, *Religion and Medicine*, 339, 351, 380, 385, 386.

91. Samuel McComb, "Psychotherapy," in *The New Schaff-Herzog Encyclopedia of Religious Knowledge*, vol. 9 (New York: Funk and Wagnalls, 1911); Worcester, *Religion and Medicine*, 40, 69; Samuel McComb, *New York Evening Post* (March 30, 1907), CP241, Archives of the Mary Baker Eddy Library.

92. "Suggestions Help Reason: Mental Healing Class Begins Session," COP, *Boston Daily Globe* (December 6, 1906), Archives of the Mary Baker Eddy Library.

93. Worcester, *Religion and Medicine*, 45, 65–66, 67, 68, 138–39.

94. Worcester, *Religion and Medicine*, 2; McComb, "Psychotherapy," in Dearmer, *Body and Soul*, 103.

95. "Hundreds of Neurotics" COP, *Boston Record* (November 22, 1906); "Psychology in Church," *Boston Sunday Globe* (December 9, 1906), Archives of the Mary Baker Eddy Library.

96. William James, "The Energies of Men," *Science* N.S. 25, no. 635 (1907): 321–32.

97. See Clifford Putney, *Muscular Christianity: Manhood and Sports in Protestant America, 1880–1920* (Cambridge, MA: Harvard University Press, 2001).

98. "Psychology in Church," *Boston Sunday* Globe, (December 9, 1906), Archives of the Mary Baker Eddy Library.

99. Worcester, *Religion and Medicine*, 146.

100. On charity, see Tomes, "Merchants of Health."

101. Sanford Gifford, *The Emmanuel Movement (Boston, 1904–1929). The Origins of Group Treatment and the Assault on Lay Psychotherapy* (Cambridge, MA: Harvard University Press, 1996), 116; and Hale, *Freud and the Americans*.

102. *Canadian Churchman* (September 6, 1923); Rev. A. R. Taylor (Episcopalian), Warren, PA (December 4, 1915), CP948, Archives of the Mary Baker Eddy Library; Dean Lloyd, "Notes on Spiritual Healing," *Canadian Churchman* (July 14, 1921).

103. Gifford, *The Emmanuel Movement*, 116; Elwood Worcester, "Dr. Prince as a Psychic Researcher and as a Psychiatrist," in *Walter Franklin Prince: A Tribute to His Memory* (Boston: Boston Society for Psychic Research, 1935).

104. Rev. F. J. Moore, "The Body and the Soul," *Canadian Churchman* (September 6, 1923); "What is Spiritual Healing?" *Christian Guardian* (August 9, 1911); Daniel Sack, "Men Want Something Real: Frank Buchman and Anglo-American College Religion in the 1920s," *Journal of Religious History* 28, no. 3 (2004): 260–275; Alison Falby, "The Modern Confessional: Anglo-American Religious Groups and the Emergence of Lay Psychotherapy," *Journal of History of the Behavioral Sciences* 39, no. 3 (2003): 251–267. On Buchman and the Oxford Group in Canada, see Kevin Kee, *Revivalists: Marketing the Gospel in English Canada, 1884–1957* (Kingston and Montreal: McGill-Queen's University Press, 2006).

105. W. G. Nicholson, "Christian Science," *Canadian Churchman* (April 6, 1916); "The Gospel of Health" Christian Guardian (July 29, 1908).

106. Dean Lloyd, "Notes on Spiritual Healing," *Canadian Churchman* (July 14, 1921).

107. Heather D. Curtis, *Faith in the Great Physician: Suffering and Divine Healing in American Culture, 1860–1900* (Baltimore: Johns Hopkins University Press, 2007), 90, 114. See also, Wacker, *Heaven Below.*

108. This also happened within Catholicism, in the midst of the great medical debates about the legitimacy of the cures at Lourdes; see Szabo, "Seeing is Believing."

109. Boddy, "Spirit Possession Revisited," 421; Deborah Gordon and Margaret Lock, eds. *Biomedicine Examined* (Dordrecht and Boston: Kluwer Academic Publishers, 1988); Opp, *The Lord for the Body*; and Charles Rosenberg, *The Therapeutic Revolution.*

110. Timothy Lenoir, "Inscription Practices and Materialities of Communication," in *Inscribing Science: Scientific Texts and the Materiality of Communication,* ed. Timothy Lenoir (Stanford: Stanford University Press, 1998), 1–19. See also Gitelman, *Scripts, Grooves and Writing Machines,* and Opp's discussion of the use of x-rays to contest testimonial evidence for faith healing: Opp, *The Lord for the Body,* 184–191.

111. Michel de Certeau, "The Scriptural Economy," in *The Certeau Reader,* ed. Graham Ward (Oxford and Malden, MA: Blackwell Publishers, 2000), 167. See also Johns, "The Physiology of Reading," and Bhabha's discussion of writing as "recordation" in Bhabha, *The Location of Culture* (London: Routledge, 1994), 94–96. Also see Peter Harrison, *The Bible, Protestantism, and the Rise of Natural Science* (Cambridge: Cambridge University Press, 1998), and Lisa Jardine, *Ingenious Pursuits: Building the Scientific Revolution* (London: Little, Brown, 1999).

112. Gauvreau, *An Evangelical Century,* and Marguerite Van Die, *An Evangelical Mind: Nathaniel Burwash and the Methodist Tradition in Canada, 1839–1918* (Montreal and Kingston: McGill-Queen's University Press, 1989), 98.

113. For example, "The Christian Science Case," *Christian Guardian* (May 31, 1905), "Table Talk," *Christian Guardian* (November 1, 1905); J. M. Waggett, "An Editor and Christian Science," *Christian Guardian* (July 18, 1917); "Superstition and Spiritualism," *Canadian Churchman* (May 24, 1900); Rev. A. Haire Forster, "Christian Science," *Canadian Churchman* (June 26, 1919).

114. *Christian Guardian* (January 31, 1900).

115. Donald Gray, *Percy Dearmer: A Parson's Pilgrimage* (Norwich, Norfolk: Canterbury Press, 2000).

116. Dearmer, *Body and Soul,* 120–121.

117. Percy Dearmer, *Everyman's History of the Prayer Book* (London: Mowbray, 1912). In Acts 19:19 (NRSV), Paul's preaching and acts of healing in Ephesus are so convincing to the Ephesians that "a number of those who practiced magic collected their books and burned them publicly."

118. "Sic Transit," *Christian Guardian* (March 13, 1907); "Faith Healing," *Christian Guardian* (May 30, 1906). See also *Canadian Churchman* (October 29, 1903); "Dowie in the Depths," *Christian Guardian* (November 14, 1906); "Lourdes," *Christian Guardian* (December 7, 1910); "Shrine of St. Anne de Beaupre," *Canadian Churchman* (October 22, 1908). On Dowieism in Canada,

see Opp, *The Lord for the Body*. See also, Rev. Paul Sterling, *Canadian Church-man* (February 3, 1910). Some of these early accounts of healing were influenced by the Holiness messages of the Keswick Convention, an annual interdenominational Protestant gathering in England, with strong Anglican ties.

119. "Miracles" and "Spiritual Intercourse," *Canadian Churchman* (March 28, 1910). John Huntley Skrine, *Creed and the Creeds: Their Function in Religion* (London: Longmans, Green, 1911). Skrine went on to write *The Survival of Jesus: A Priest's Study in Divine Telepathy* (New York: George H. Doran Company, 1917). "Spiritualism Will Make Us a Nation of Neurotics," *Canadian Churchman* (April 22, 1920). For Methodist examples, see "Spiritualism," *Christian Guardian* (September 30, 1908); "Miracle Workers?" *Christian Guardian* (May 29, 1907); "A Disturbed Séance," *Christian Guardian* (October 23, 1907); "The Fallacy of Spiritualism," *Christian Guardian* (May 12, 1920).

120. The original editorial was "Miracle Workers?" *Christian Guardian* (May 29, 1907); the response was given the headline "'Divine' or 'Faith Healing,'" *Christian Guardian* (July 24, 1907).

121. "Legend," *Canadian Churchman* (January 24, 1924); "Illness of Elijah II" *Christian Guardian* (November 22, 1905).

122. See Opp, "Healing Hands, Healthy Bodies," and Mullin, *Miracles and the Modern Religious Imagination*.

123. *Christian Guardian* (January 31, 1900).

124. Ibid.; see also "The Limits of Faith Healing," *Christian Guardian* (May 27, 1914).

125. J. T. P. *Christian Guardian* (July 18, 1906).

126. Semple, *The Lord's Dominion*, 349; Nancy Christie and Michael Gauvreau, *A Full-Orbed Christianity: The Protestant Churches and Social Welfare in Canada, 1900–1940* (Montreal and Kingston: McGill-Queen's University Press, 2001); Airhart, *Serving the Present Age*, 50–51.

127. Semple, *The Lord's Dominion*, 224.

128. *Christian Guardian* (July 18, 1906).

129. Helen E. Bingham, *An Irish Saint: The Life Story of Ann Preston, Known Also as "Holy Ann,"* 27th ed. (Toronto: Evangelical Publishers, 1927),18. Digital publication: http://wesley.nnu.edu/wesleyctr/books/0001-0100/HDM0016.PDF

130. Bingham, *An Irish Saint*, 28.

131. "What is Spiritual Healing?" *Christian Guardian* (August 9, 1911); "Religion and Insanity," *Christian Guardian* (April 22, 1908); "Preparing to Live Long," *Christian Guardian* (July 28, 1920). See Wacker, *Heaven Below*; Grant Wacker, "The Holy Spirit and the Spirit of the Age in American Protestantism, 1880–1910," *Journal of American History* 72, no. 1 (June 1985): 45–62.

132. "The Healer of Men," *Christian Guardian* (June 23, 1915).

133. For example, see "From a Hospital Ward," *Canadian Churchman* (February 8, 1917).

134. "Shell Shock," *Canadian Churchman* (December 5, 1918); "Controlling the Nerves," *Christian Guardian* (March 8, 1922); Hale, *Freud and the Americans*, 169. See also Ruth Leys, "Traumatic Cures: Shell Shock, Janet, and the Question of Memory," *Critical Inquiry* 20, no. 4 (1994): 623–662.

135. See Curtis, *Faith in the Great Physician*; Cunningham, "From Holiness to Healing"; Opp, *The Lord for the Body*.

136. *Christian Guardian* (August 6, 1919); *Christian Guardian* (December 10, 1919).

137. "Mr. Hickson's Healing Mission," *Christian Guardian* (July 7, 1920); "Healing the Sick," *Christian Guardian* (May 8, 1921); *Christian Guardian* (December 12, 1923); *Christian Guardian* (February 13, 1924); "The Church and Healing," *Christian Guardian* (September 16, 1925); "The Church and Healing," *New Outlook* (September 16, 1925).

138. *Canadian Churchman* (July 1, 1920). For a more detailed account of Hickson's healing campaign, see Raymond J. Cunningham, "James Moore Hickson and Spiritual Healing in the American Episcopal Church," *Historical Magazine of the Protestant Episcopal Church* 39, no. 1 (1970): 2–16 and James Moore Hickson, *Heal the Sick* (London: Methuen, 1924).

139. "A Spiritual Healer" *Canadian Churchman* (January 8, 1920).

140. Jesmond Dene, "This Perfect Soundness," *Canadian Churchman* (August 13, 1925).

141. Ibid.

142. For this tone of appeasement see "Mr. James Moore Hickson and the Medical Profession," *Canadian Churchman* (June 17, 1920) and "Editorial," *Canadian Churchman* (July 1, 1920).

143. Hickson, *Heal the Sick*.

144. George M. Long, "Christian Healing," *Canadian Churchman* (August 23, 1923).

145. Anonymous, *The Ministry of Healing* (London: Society for the Propagation of Christian Knowledge, 1924).

146. See Anonymous, *A Time to Heal: A Report for the House of Bishops on the Healing Ministry* (London: Church House Publishing, 2000).

147. On Methodist reaction to Price, see Airhart, *Serving the Present Age*. For a detailed account of Price's revivals in Victoria and Vancouver, see Robert Burkinshaw, *Pilgrims in Lotus Land: Conservative Protestantism in British Columbia, 1917–1981* (Montreal and Kingston: McGill-Queens University Press, 1995), 100–120.

148. H. Michell, *Canadian Churchman* (July 1, 1920). This was in contrast to F. Oliver, an earlier (nonhealing) revivalist who exacerbated fundamentalist/liberal divisions within Vancouver's ministerial community. Burkinshaw emphasizes the media's attraction to Price's "personal eloquence, charm, and grace" in *Pilgrims in Lotus Land*, 101, 105.

149. H. R. Trumpour, "A Great Faith-Healing Clinic," *Canadian Churchman* (January 10, 1924).

150. Edward Trelawney, "Western Faith Healing Campaign," *Christian Guardian* (June 20, 1923).

151. John W. Saunby, *Christian Guardian* (July 11, 1923).

152. *Christian Guardian* (July 18, 1923).

153. *Christian Guardian* (February 13, 1924); "The Church and Healing," *Christian Guardian* (September 16, 1925); "The Church and Healing" *New Outlook* (September 16, 1925); *Canadian Churchman* (October 26, 1922); "Some

Prayer Problems," *Canadian Churchman* (March 1, 1923); "Churchman Bible Class," *Canadian Churchman* (February 26, 1925).

154. *Christian Guardian* (November 19, 1925); *New Outlook* (November 18, 1925).

155. The series, initially authored by Dr. T. C. Routley, the General Secretary of the Canadian Medical Association, ran in the *Canadian Churchman* from December 4, 1924 until November 26, 1925, in the *Christian Guardian* from December 3, 1924 until May 27, 1925, and in *New Outlook* from September 16, 1925 until November 25, 1925. For more on Routley, see C. David Naylor, *Private Practice, Public Payment: Canadian Medicine and the Politics of Health Insurance, 1911–1966* (Montreal and Kingston: McGill-Queen's University Press, 1986).

156. Mullin, *Miracles and the Modern Religious Imagination*, 46, 97.

157. *Christian Guardian* (May 19, 1909). See also Christopher White, *Unsettled Minds*.

158. Moorshead, *The Way of the Doctor*, 60–61.

159. Percy Dearmer, ed., *The Fellowship of the Picture: An Automatic Script Taken Down by Nancy Dearmer* (New York: E. P. Dutton, 1920). Mullin classifies Dearmer as a sacramentalist for his championing of anointing the sick—given his spiritualist interests, I would argue that he was equally "thaumaturgical," though not in a Pentecostal sense. See Mullin, *Miracles and the Modern Religious Imagination*, 199–202.

160. See John D. Root, "Science, Religion, and Psychical Research: The Monistic Thought of Sir Oliver Lodge," *Harvard Theological Review* 71 (July–October 1978): 245–263.

161. *Christian Guardian* (January 26, 1910).

162. *Christian Guardian* (February 9, 1910); *Christian Guardian* (March 2, 1910).

163. C. L. Bedson, "We Have Not Turned Spiritualist," *Christian Guardian* (January 26, 1910).

164. George A. Bainborough, "Sir Oliver Lodge's Creed," *Christian Guardian* (February 16, 1910).

165. C. E. Naylor, "Sir Oliver Lodge and Psychic Research," *Christian Guardian* (March 2, 1910). John Murphy, *Christian Guardian* (February 3, 1915).

166. *Christian Guardian* (March 2, 1910).

167. See Leigh Schmidt, *Hearing Things*.

168. Gail Bederman, "The Women Have Had Control of the Churchwork Long Enough: The Men and Religion Forward Movement of 1911–1912 and the Masculinization of Middle Class Protestantism," in *A Mighty Baptism: Race, Gender, and the Creation of American Protestantism*, ed. Susan Juster and Lisa MacFarlane (Ithaca, NY: Cornell University Press, 1996), 116, and Christie and Gauvreau, *A Full-Orbed Christianity*, 65. For a caution regarding the ubiquity of feminization, see Ann Taves, "Feminization Revisited: Protestantism and Gender at the Turn of the Century," in *Women and Twentieth-Century Protestantism*, 304–324. On bureaucratization, see Christie and Gauvreau, *A Full-Orbed Christianity*, 164. On feminization and healing, see Opp, "Healing Hands, Healthy Bodies"; Beryl Satter, *Each Mind a Kingdom: American Women,*

Sexual Purity, and the New Thought Movement, 1875–1920 (Berkeley: University of California Press, 1999); R. Marie Griffith, *Born Again Bodies: Flesh and Spirit in American Christianity* (Berkeley: University of California Press, 2004). *Christian Guardian* (March 14, 1900); Christie and Gauvreau, *A Full-Orbed Christianity*, 77; William Westfall, "Constructing Public Religions at Private Sites: The Anglican Church in the Shadow of Disestablishment," in *Religion and Public Life in Canada: Historical and Comparative Perspectives*, ed. Marguerite Van Die, (Toronto: University of Toronto Press, 2001), 23–49.

169. *Canadian Churchman* (January 14, 1909).

170. Ibid.

171. Christie and Gauveau, *A Full-Orbed Christianity*, 129.

172. Phyllis Airhart and Roger C. Hutchinson, "Christianizing the Social Order: A Founding Vision of the United Church of Canada," *Special Issue of Toronto Journal of Theology* 12, no. 2 (1996); Christie and Gauveau, *A Full-Orbed Christianity*, 77, 220; Paul T. Phillips, *A Kingdom on Earth: Anglo-American Social Christianity, 1880–1940* (University Park, PA: Pennsylvania State University Press, 1996), 83–116.

173. *Canadian Churchman* (March 16, 1922). On the history of deaconesses and Protestant sisterhoods, see D. S. Schaff, "Deaconess," in *The New Schaff-Herzog Encyclopedia of Religious Knowledge*, vol. 3 (London: Funk & Wagnalls, 1909), 371–84; Janet Grierson, *The Deaconess* (London: C10, 1981); Mary S. Donovan, *A Different Call: Women's Ministries in the Episcopal Church, 1850–1920* (Wilton, CT: Morehouse-Barlow, 1986); Susan Mumm, *Stolen Daughters, Virgin Mothers: Anglican Sisterhoods in Victorian Britain* (Leicester: Leicester University Press, 1999); Sioban Nelson, *Say Little, Do Much: Nurses, Nuns, and Hospitals in the Nineteenth Century* (Philadelphia: University of Pennsylvania Press, 2001); Alison Kemper, "Deaconess as Urban Missionary and Ideal Woman: Church of England Initiatives in Toronto, 1890–1895," in *Canadian Protestant and Catholic Missions, 1820s–1960s: Historical Essays in Honour of John Webster Grant*, ed. John S. Moir and C. T. McIntire (New York: P. Lang, 1988); and John D. Thomas, "Servants of the Church: Canadian Methodist Deaconess Work, 1890–1926," *Canadian Historical Review* 65 (September 1984): 371–395.

174. Grierson, *The Deaconess*, 3; Prelinger, *Episcopal Women*; on secularization of nursing, see Siobhan Nelson, "From Salvation to Civics: Service to the Sick in Nursing Discourse," *Social Science & Medicine* 53, no. 9 (2001): 1217–1225.

175. "What Christians Are For," *Christian Guardian* (September 21, 1904). See also "Deaconess World," *Christian Guardian* (April 27, 1904).

176. *Christian Guardian* (December 20, 1911); see also *Christian Guardian* (March 28, 1906); *Christian Guardian* (October 25, 1905); *Christian Guardian* (April 12, 1911).

177. *Christian Guardian* (December 7, 1910).

178. On fumigation, see "Not Exactly a Case of Luck," *Christian Guardian* (September 3, 1919).

179. *Christian Guardian* (March 28, 1906); *Canadian Churchman* (December 7, 1922); *Christian Guardian* (September 25, 1912). See also a laywoman's

support for this kind of program in *Christian Guardian* (May 29, 1916). See Eleanor J. Stebner, "More than Maternal Feminists and Good Samaritans: Women and the Social Gospel in Canada" in *Gender and the Social Gospel*, ed. Wendy J. Deichmann Edwards and Carolyn De Swarte Gifford (Champaign: University of Illinois Press, 2003), 53–70; Kathryn K. Sklar, "The Last Fifteen Years: Historians' Changing Views of American Women in Religion and Society," in *Women in New Worlds: Historical Perspectives on the Wesleyan Tradition*. ed. Rosemary Skinner Keller, Louise L. Queen, and Hilah F. Thomas (Nashville, TN: Abingdon Press, 1982), 48–65; Carolyn D. Gifford, "For God and Home and Native Land," in Thomas and Keller, *Women in New Worlds*, 310–327; and Mary E. Frederickson, "Shaping A New Society," in Thomas and Keller, *Women in New Worlds*, 345–361. On social gospel theology, see William McGuire King, "An Enthusiasm for Humanity: The Social Emphasis in Religion and its Accommodation in Protestant Theology," in *Religion and Twentieth-Century American Intellectual Life*, ed. Michael J. Lacey (Cambridge: Cambridge University Press, 1989), 49–77.

180. See J. M. Shaver, "Civic Problems and the Immigrant," *Christian Guardian* (October 4, 1916); Editorial, "The Undesirable Immigrant," *Christian Guardian* (April 25, 1906); *Christian Guardian* (January 4, 1911). *Canadian Churchman* (December 7, 1922).

181. *Christian Guardian* (December 7, 1910); Hilda Hellaby, *Canadian Churchman* (September 13, 1923). Hellaby later moved to the Yukon to serve as a Deaconess near Whitehorse. See Hilda Hellaby, *Hilda Hellaby's Story and Poems* (Whitehorse, Yukon: Anglican Churchwomen of Christ Church Cathedral Parish, 1983).

182. "Among the Eskimos," *Canadian Churchman* (July 25, 1918).

183. For example, see "Women's Medical Work," *Canadian Churchman* (July 11, 1912).

184. *Christian Guardian* (December 11, 1920).

185. Alice Chown, "Not Deaconesses, but Deaconess Training," *Christian Guardian* (December 6, 1911), reprinted in Diana Chown, "Alice Chown's Criticism of Deaconess Education in the Methodist Church," *Historical Studies in Education* 8, no. 1 (1996), 95, 98. Chown's reference to "cosmic consciousness" is likely based on the book by that name by the Canadian mystic Whitmanite and medical doctor R. Maurice Bucke, *Cosmic Consciousness: A Study in the Evolution of the Human Mind* (Philadelphia: Innes, 1901).

186. *New Outlook* (June 17, 1925).

187. *Christian Guardian* (November 22, 1916).

188. "A Nurse's Ministry," *Christian Guardian* (May 2, 1906); *Christian Guardian* (August 10, 1921). See also Valverde, *The Age of Light, Soap and Water: Moral Reform in English Canada, 1885–1925*; Cecilia Morgan, "Turning Strangers into Sisters? Missionaries and Colonization in Upper Canada," in *Sisters or Strangers? Immigrant, Ethnic, and Racialized Women in Canadian History*, ed. Franca Iacovetta (Toronto: University of Toronto Press, 2004), 23–48; and Franca Iacovetta and Valerie J. Korinek, "Jell-O Salads, One-Stop Shopping, and Maria the Homemaker: The Gender Politics of Food," in Iacovetta, *Sisters or Strangers?* 190–230.

189. *Christian Guardian* (March 29, 1916); Christie and Gauvreau, *A Full-Orbed Christianity*. On calls for government responsibility for health care, see *Christian Guardian* (September 27, 1916); *Christian Guardian* (August 9, 1916); F. N. Stapleford, "The Price of Illness," *Christian Guardian* (January 12, 1921).

190. *Canadian Guardian* (October 25, 1916); *Canadian Churchman* (September 15, 1910).

191. *Canadian Churchman* (January 23, 1913).

192. Mary Anne MacFarlane, "Faithful and Courageous Handmaidens: Deaconesses in the United Church of Canada, 1925–1945," in *Changing Roles of Women within the Christian Church in Canada*, ed. Elizabeth Gillian Muir and Marilyn Fardig Whiteley (Toronto: University of Toronto Press, 1995), 246.

193. "Good Reading Popular," *Christian Guardian* (October 5, 1910).

194. Harrison, *The Bible, Protestantism, and the Rise of Natural Science*.

195. See Opp, *The Lord for the Body*.

196. "TB Sunday," *Christian Guardian* (March 15, 1911); "A Good Health Gospel," *Christian Guardian* (April 27, 1910).

197. Robert Milliken, "Baptism of a Scientific Spirit," *Christian Guardian* (January 3, 1923).

198. Richard Golden, "Lyman Powell, William Osler, and Oliver Wendell Holmes," *Osler Library Newsletter* 72 (February 1993): 1; Lyman P. Powell, *Mary Baker Eddy: A Life-Size Portrait* (New York: Macmillan, 1930). For more on Osler and his Anglican identity, see Michael Bliss, *William Osler: A Life in Medicine* (Toronto: University of Toronto Press, 2002).

199. *Christian Guardian* (May 29, 1912). DD refers to Doctor of Divinity.

200. On dis-ease, see *Canadian Churchman* (December 22, 1910); "Romance of Science," *Christian Guardian* (August 24, 1924); "Scientists Ask for Prayer," Worldwide News of the Progress of Religion, *Christian Guardian* (November 4, 1925).

3. PROTESTANT EXPERIMENTALISTS AND THE ENERGY OF LOVE

1. Rudolf Bultmann, *History and Eschatology: The Presence of Eternity. Gifford Lectures* (Edinburgh: University Press, 1957). Italics added. The epigraph is from Rudolf Bultmann, "New Testament and Theology" in *The New Testament and Theology and Other Basic Writings*. Edited and translated by Schubert M. Ogden. (Philadelphia: Fortress Press, 1984), 4.

2. William Ernest Hocking, *Human Nature and its Remaking*, new rev. ed. (New Haven: Yale University Press, 1923 [1918]), 79.

3. Kirsopp Lake, *The Religion of Yesterday and To-morrow* (Boston: Houghton Mifflin, 1926), 64, 72; see also John Huntley Skrine, *The Survival of Jesus: A Priest's Study in Divine Telepathy* (New York: Hodder & Stoughton, 1917). Some Anglicans have rejected being categorized as Protestants, but those who were experimentalists were more ecumenical in their approach. Given their questioning of dogma and their embrace of experience, these clerics would have also fit within the more common category of "modernists" as defined by Angli-

can Henry Major, who wrote the introduction to Frederick Du Vernet's collected essays (H. D. A. Major, *English Modernism: Its Origins, Methods, Aims* (Oxford: Oxford University Press, 2002), 8; F. H. Du Vernet, *Out of a Scribe's Treasure* (Toronto: Ryerson Press, 1927). Lake was not the first to use the term—for example, some nineteenth-century liberal Protestants considered themselves experimentalists. See Christopher White, "Minds Intensely Unsettled: Phrenology, Experience, and the American Pursuit of Spiritual Assurance, 1830–1880," *Religion and American Culture* 16, no. 2 (2006): 227–261.

4. Amanda Porterfield, *Healing in the History of Christianity* (Oxford: Oxford University Press, 2005).

5. Sydney E. Ahlstrom, *A Religious History of the American People*, 2nd ed. (New Haven: Yale University Press, 2004), 1019.

6. Catherine Albanese, *A Republic of Mind and Spirit: A Cultural History of American Metaphysical Religion* (New Haven: Yale University Press, 2006).

7. Walter Benjamin, "Reflections on Radio," in *Walter Benjamin: Selected Writings*, vol. 2 *(1927–1934)* (Cambridge, MA: Harvard University Press, 1999), 543–544; and R. G. Collingwood, "Art and the Machine," in *The Philosophy of Enchantment: Studies in Folktale, Cultural Criticism, and Anthropology*, ed. David Boucher, Wendy James, and Philip Smallwood (Oxford: Clarendon Press, 2005), 291–304.

8. Jonathan Sterne, *The Audible Past: Cultural Origins of Sound Reproduction* (Durham: Duke University Press, 2003), 340.

9. Bernard Faure, *Double Exposure: Cutting Across Buddhist and Western Discourses*, trans. Janet Lloyd (Stanford: Stanford University Press, 2004), 115.

10. For examples of this critique that often verged on ridicule, see Horton Davies, *Christian Deviations* (London: SCM Press, 1954). See also Roger Luckhurst, *The Invention of Telepathy* (Oxford: Oxford University Press, 2002); and R. Laurence Moore, *In Search of White Crows: Spiritualism, Parapsychology, and American Culture* (New York: Oxford University Press, 1977).

11. R. Edis Fairbairn, "Polarity—A Divine Principle of the Universe," *New Outlook* (September 29, 1926): 4; see also, Edith Waldvogel Blumhofer, *Aimee Semple McPherson: Everybody's Sister* (Grand Rapids, MI: Eerdmans, 1993); and F. H. Du Vernet, *Spiritual Radio* (Mountain Lakes, NJ: The Society of the Nazarene, 1925).

12. Sherwood Eddy, *The New Era in Asia* (New York: Missionary Education Movement of the United States and Canada, 1913).

13. Sherwood Eddy, *Facing the Crisis: A Study in Present Day Social and Religious Problems* (New York: Association Press, 1922), 123–124. Radio was widely considered "miraculous" and pathbreaking in 1920s North America; see Mary Vipond, *Listening In: The First Decade of Canadian Broadcasting, 1922–1932* (Montreal and Kingston: McGill-Queen's University Press, 1992), 22; Tona Hangen, *Redeeming the Dial: Radio, Religion, and Popular Culture in America* (Chapel Hill: University of North Carolina Press, 2002). Radio broadcasting began in Canada and the United States in 1920 and became widely accessible (in terms of both numbers of radio stations and the affordability and availability of radio sets) by the late 1920s (Vipond, *Listening In*, 14–15, 37). See also, Michele Hilmes, "Rethinking Radio," in *Radio Reader: Essays in the Cultural*

History of Radio, ed. Michele Hilmes and Jason Loviglio (New York: Routledge, 2002), 1–20.

14. Sherwood Eddy, *You Will Survive Death* (Surrey: Omega Press, 1954).

15. William James, "The Energies of Men." *Science,* N.S. 25, no. 635 (1907): 321–332; Henri Bergson, *Mind-Energy* (New York: Henry Holt, 1920) (the original French title was, interestingly, *L'Energie Spirituelle*); William Ernest Hocking, *Human Nature and its Remaking* (New Haven: Yale University Press, 1918). See also David A. Hollinger, "'Damned for God's Glory': William James and the Scientific Vindication of Protestant Culture," in *William James and a Science of Religion: Reexperiencing the Varieties of Religious Experience,* ed. Wayne Proudfoot (New York: Columbia University Press, 2004), 9–30.

16. Henri Bergson, *Mind-Energy,* 99. Barber's copy is held in Pratt Library, Victoria College.

17. Belle Choné Oliver, ed. *Tales from the Inns of Healing of Christian Medical Service in India, Burma and Ceylon.* Prepared under the direction of the Executive Committee of the Christian Medical Association of India, Burma and Ceylon, Canadian edition (Toronto: Committee on Missionary Education, United Church of Canada, 1944 [1942]), 123.

18. Percy Dearmer, *Body and Soul: An Enquiry into the Effect of Religion upon Health, with a Description of Christian Works of Healing from the New Testament to the Present Day* (London: I. Pitman, 1909), 170.

19. See Oliver, *Tales,* 126; Emily Apter and William Pietz, *Fetishism as Cultural Discourse* (Ithaca, NY: Cornell University Press, 1993); Tomoko Masuzawa, "Troubles with Materiality: The Ghost of Fetishism in the Nineteenth Century," *Comparative Studies in Society and History* 42, no. 2 (2000), 242–267; Webb Keane, *Christian Moderns: Freedom and Fetish in the Mission Encounter* (Berkeley: University of California Press, 2007).

20. Tisa Wenger provides an Episcopalian example of a liturgical experimentalist in "The Practice of Dance for the Future of Christianity: 'Eurythmic Worship' in New York's Roaring Twenties," in *Practicing Protestants: Histories of Christian Life in America, 1630–1965,* ed. Laurie F. Maffly-Kipp, Leigh E. Schmidt, and Mark Valeri (Baltimore: Johns Hopkins University Press, 2006), 222–249.

21. Phyllis D. Airhart and Roger C. Hutchison, eds., *Christianizing the Social Order: The Founding Vision of the United Church of Canada* (Waterloo, ON: Wilfrid Laurier University Press, 1996).

22. The best account of this shift, dealing largely with U.S. liberal Protestants, is by William R. Hutchison, *Errand to the World: American Protestant Thought and Foreign Missions* (Chicago: University of Chicago Press, 1987).

23. See, for example, J. Wesley Robb, "Hendrik Kraemer versus William Ernest Hocking," *Journal of Bible and Religion* 29, no. 2 (1961): 93–101.

24. "Editorial," *Conquest by Healing* 1, no. 1 (March 1924): 5. In 1962 the title changed again to *Saving Health.*

25. Webb Anderson, "The Red Cross," *Conquest by Healing* 1, no. 1 (March 1924): 8.

26. The American Board, "After Red Cross Group Work Something More, Very Like It," Boston, MA, n.d. MRL 12: American Board of Commissioners

for Foreign Missions, The Burke Library Archives at Union Theological Seminary in the City of New York.

27. Charles Selden, *Are Missions a Failure?* (New York: Fleming H. Revell, 1927), and Hypatia Bradlaugh Bonner, *Christianizing the Heathen: First-Hand Evidence Concerning Overseas Missions* (London: Watts and Co., 1922).

28. Grant Wacker, "The Waning of the Missionary Impulse," in *The Foreign Missionary Enterprise at Home*, ed. Daniel H. Bays and Grant Wacker (Tuscaloosa: University of Alabama Press, 2003), 201. Other examples of recent exemplary collections on missionary research include Mary Taylor Huber and Nancy C. Lutkehaus, *Gendered Missions: Women and Men in Missionary Discourse and Practice* (Ann Arbor: University of Michigan Press, 1999); Alvyn Austin and Jamie Scott, *Canadian Missionaries, Indigenous Peoples: Representing Religion at Home and Abroad* (Toronto: University of Toronto Press, 2005); Jean Comaroff and John L. Comaroff, *Of Revelation and Revolution*, vol. 2 (Chicago: University of Chicago Press, 1991); Elizabeth Elbourne, *Blood Ground: Colonialism, Missions, and the Contest for Christianity in the Cape Colony and Britain, 1799–1853* (Montreal and Kingston: McGill-Queen's University Press, 2002).

29. On Winslow, see William W. Emilsen, "The Legacy of John Copley Winslow" *International Bulletin of Missionary Research* 21, no. 1 (1997), 26–28, 30. For an account of this process of colonial "knowledge transfer" on the part of German missionaries, and its significance for the study of religion and for notions of religious pluralism, see Rebekka Habermas, "Wissenstransfer und Mission: Sklavenhändler, Missionare und Religionswissenschaftler" *Geschichte und Gesellschaft* 36 (2010), pp. 257–284.

30. Philip Carrington, *The Anglican Church in Canada* (Toronto: Collins, 1963), 220, 231.

31. F. H. Du Vernet, "Diary of a Missionary Tour," Anglican Church of Canada Archives, 1898. Du Vernet also narrated encounters with "medicine men" and several older women, in which he described these men and women as people with reasonable arguments against Christianity and white settlement, and he described what he saw as their valiant but doomed attempts to stop Christian missionary advancement.

32. William Ridley, "His Majesty's Dominions: The Dominion of Canada," *The Canadian Church Missionary Gleaner* (July 1, 1902): 100.

33. Maureen Atkinson, "'Affection and Kindness' and 'Utterly Fearless': The Living Legacy of Odille Morison. http://www.livinglandscapes.bc.ca/northwest/odill/index.html. Website of the Royal B. C. Museum, accessed December 21, 2006.

34. J. R. Miller, *Shingwauk's Vision: A History of Native Residential Schools* (Toronto: University of Toronto Press, 1996), 345.

35. Alan L. Hayes, *Anglicans in Canada: Controversies and Identity in Historical Perspective* (Urbana: University of Illinois Press, 2004), 31. For a survey of encounters between First Nations peoples and Christian missionaries, see John Webster Grant, *Moon of Wintertime: Missionaries and the Indians of Canada in Encounter since 1534* (Toronto: University of Toronto Press, 1984). Du Vernet could also be fit within the parameters of what John Ralston Saul

recently described as the "Métis civilization" that is Canada. John Ralston Saul, *A Fair Country: Telling Truths about Canada* (Toronto: Penguin, 2008).

36. Du Vernet, *Spiritual Radio*; Sylvia DuVernet, ed., *Portrait of a Personality: Archbishop Frederick Herbert DuVernet* (Toronto: Sylvia DuVernet, 1987).

37. Du Vernet, *Out of a Scribe's Treasure*, 30.

38. F. H. Du Vernet, "Reality in Religion," *Canadian Churchman* (November 23, 1922); Du Vernet, *Out of a Scribe's Treasure*, 30.

39. F. H. Du Vernet, "Divine Healing," *Canadian Churchman* (September 13, 1923); F. H. Du Vernet, "Telepathic Testimonies" *Canadian Churchman* (November 1, 1923).

40. Du Vernet, "Telepathic Testimonies"; Du Vernet, *Spiritual Radio*, 26.

41. Du Vernet, *Spiritual Radio*, 45.

42. Ibid., 24–26.

43. Ibid., p. 50. Sylvia DuVernet describes the illness of Du Vernet's son, her father-in-law Horace, as pleurisy, a lung ailment. Sylvia DuVernet, *Portrait of a Personality*, 7.

44. Ibid., p. 53.

45. Du Vernet, "Divine Healing"; F.H. Du Vernet, "The Psychology of Resting" *Canadian Churchman* (August 21, 1924).

46. Du Vernet, *Out of a Scribe's Treasure*, 114.

47. Robert Connell in Du Vernet, *Out of a Scribe's Treasure*, v; Philip Carrington, *The Anglican Church*, 231.

48. On the "progressive" politics and scientific disposition of nineteenth-century spiritualism in Canada, see Ramsay Cook, "Spiritualism, Science of the Earthly Paradise," *Canadian Historical Review* 60, no. 1 (1984), 4–27.

49. For example, see R. M. Barton, "Hospital Evangelism," *The Journal of the Christian Medical Association of India, Burma, and Ceylon* (November 1941).

50. Munroe Scott, *McClure: A Biography* (Toronto: Penguin Books Canada, 1979).

51. Belle Choné Oliver, "Adventures in Denominationalism," United Church of Canada Archives, Belle Choné Oliver fonds, 88.029C-box 001-file 13.

52. Ibid.

53. B. Choné Oliver, "On 'Re-Thinking Missions.'" *The New Outlook* (January 18, 1933). See also, William Ernest Hocking and the Commission of Appraisal, *Re-Thinking Missions: A Lay-Man's Inquiry after One Hundred Years* (New York: Harper, 1932); Robert E. Speer, *"Re-Thinking Missions" Examined* (New York: Fleming H. Revell Co., 1933), 7–15.

54. Belle Choné Oliver, Diary (February 19, 1908). United Church of Canada Archives, Glenna Jamieson Fonds, no. 3330.

55. Oliver, Banswara Notebook, 1929–1935, United Church of Canada Archives, Glenna Jamieson Fonds, no. 3330.

56. Oliver, "On 'Re-Thinking Missions.'" Oliver quotes Hocking's report here, Hocking, *Re-Thinking Missions*, 326. See also Christian Medical Association of India, *The Ministry of Healing in India: Handbook of the Christian Medical Association of India* (Mysore: Wesleyan Mission Press, 1932), and Ruth Compton Brouwer, *Modern Women Modernizing Men: The Changing Missions*

of *Three Professional Women in Asia and Africa, 1902–69* (Vancouver: UBC Press, 2002), pp. 42–44.

57. Oliver, *Tales*, 130.

58. Ibid.

59. I cannot do justice in this context to the considerable literature on Christianity and colonialism in India, but I have the following works most helpful: Judith M. Brown, Robert Eric Frykenberg, Alaine M. Low, eds. *Christians, Cultural Interactions, and India's Religious Traditions* (Grand Rapids: Eerdmanns, 2002), Richard Fox Young, ed. *India and the Indianness of Christianity* ((Grand Rapids: Eerdmanns, 2009), Leela Gandhi, *Affective Communities: Anticolonial Thought, Fin de Siecle Radicalism, and the Politics of Friendship* (Durham, NC: Duke University Press, 2006); Richard King, *Orientalism and Religion: Postcolonialism and the "Mystic East"* (London: Routledge, 1999); Peter van der Veer, *Imperial Encounters: Religion and Modernity in India and Britain* (Princeton, N.J.: Princeton University Press, 2001); Gauri Viswanathan, *Outside the Fold: Conversion, Modernity, and Belief* (Princeton, N.J.: Princeton University Press, 1998); Dipesh Chakrabarty, *Provincializing Europe: Postcolonial Thought and Historical Difference* (Princeton: Princeton University Press, 2000).

60. William James, "The Energies of Men," 321–332.

61. Dewan Bahadur A. S. Appasamy, *The Use of Yoga in Prayer* (Madras: The Christian Literature Society for India, 1926), 22. See also Joseph Alter, *Yoga in Modern India: The Body between Science and Philosophy* (Princeton, N.J.: Princeton University Press, 2004); and Sarah Strauss, *Positioning Yoga: Balancing Acts across Cultures* (Oxford: Berg, 2005).

62. Bahadur, *The Use of Yoga in Prayer*, 25–26.

63. Ibid., 19.

64. Ibid., 29.

65. On the Indian-British currents of theosophy and Christianity, and their relation to Gandhi's thought, see Michael Bergunder, "Gandhi, Esoterik und das Christentum" *Esoterik und Christentum: Religionsgeschichtliche und theologische Perspektiven*. Michael Bergunder and Daniel Cyranka, eds.. (Leipzig: Evangelische Verlagsanstalt, 2005), 129–148.

66. Emilsen, "The Legacy of John Copley Winslow," 27.

67. J. C. Winslow, *Christian Yoga*. Printed by request for the SPG. (Croydon: Roffey and Clark, 1923), 10.

68. Ibid., 14. On mental and spiritual healing, see pp. 29, 41.

69. Ibid., 27.

70. Ibid., 41–42, 44, 46.

71. J. C. Winslow, "Mahatma Gandhi and Aggressive Pacifism," in *Mahatma Gandhi: Essays and Reflections on His Life and Work*, ed. S. Radhakrishnan (London: George Allan and Unwin, 1939).

72. Gauri Viswanathan, "The Ordinary Business of Occultism," *Critical Inquiry* 27, no. 1 (2000): 90–121; van der Veer, *Imperial Encounters*; Roger Luckhurst, *The Invention of Telepathy*.

73. Leigh Eric Schmidt, *Hearing Things: Religion, Illusion, and the American Enlightenment* (Cambridge, MA: Harvard University Press, 2000), 241.

74. Rene Kollar, *Searching for Raymond: Anglicanism, Spiritualism, and Bereavement between the Two World Wars* (Lanham, MD: Lexington Books, 2000); H. L. Puxley, "The Church and the Paranormal," in *The Psychic Force*, ed. Allan Angoff (New York: G. P. Putnam, 1970), 219–228; J. D. Pearce-Higgins and G. Stanley Whitby, eds., *Life, Death and Psychical Research: Studies on Behalf of the Churches' Fellowship for Psychical and Spiritual Studies* (London: Rider, 1973).

75. Two of the best accounts of Christian engagement with psychic research are Ann Taves, *Fits, Trances, and Visions* (Princeton, N.J.: Princeton University Press, 1999), and Roger Luckhurst, *The Invention of Telepathy*. For the wider culture of occultism, see Alex Owen, *The Place of Enchantment: British Occultism and the Culture of the Modern* (Chicago: University of Chicago Press, 2004). Also see Masuzawa, "The Trouble with Materiality."

76. Dearmer, *Body and Soul*, 90.

77. Annie Besant, "Meditation in the Anglican Church," *The Theosophist* (April–June 1912): 268.

78. T. Clifford Allbutt, ed. *Medicine and the Church: Being a Series of Studies on the Relationship between the Practice of Medicine and the Church's Ministry to the Sick* (London: K. Paul, Trench, & Trübner, 1910).

79. Nancy Dearmer, *The Life of Percy Dearmer* (London: Book Club, 1941), 212. Dearmer's writings, while decrying the injustices of capitalism, left colonialism uninvestigated. In one 1933 essay positing Christianity as the solution to a range of international "crises," he even argued that the British Commonwealth and its "free" Dominions, including Canada (but not India), were examples of the "ancient Christian principle" of "liberty combined with order." Percy Dearmer, ed., *Christianity and the Crisis* (London: Victor Gollancz, 1933), 11.

80. Margaret Mills Harper, "Nemo: George Yeats and her Automatic Script," *New Literary History* 33 (2002): 291–314, 2002.

81. Percy Dearmer, ed., *The Fellowship of the Picture: An Automatic Script Taken Down by Nancy Dearmer* (New York: E. P. Dutton, 1920), 5.

82. Ibid., 10.

83. M. A. Bayfield, "Review of *The Fellowship of the Picture*." *Journal of Society for Psychical Research* 20 (January 1921): 25. A more scathing review complained that "The unconscious of *so* many automatic writers seems to be singularly barren of content . . . modern automatic writing seems to produce nothing more worthy of notice than these exhortations in the style of the new theology" (Anonymous, "Review of *The Fellowship of the Picture*," *The New Age: A Socialist Review of Religion, Science, and Art* 28, no. 10 (1921): 119.

84. Donald Gray, *Percy Dearmer: A Parson's Pilgrimage* (Norwich: Canterbury Press, 2000).

85. Percy Dearmer, Letter, *Journal of the Society for Psychical Research* 19 (1920): 180.

86. Gray, *Percy Dearmer*, 196.

87. Dearmer, *Body and Soul*.

88. Robert Bruce Mullin, *Miracles and the Modern Religious Imagination* (New Haven: Yale University Press, 1996).

89. Lily Dougall, *The Christian Doctrine of Health* (London: Macmillan, 1916), 136.

90. Ibid., 144, 196.

91. Ibid., 196.

92. Charles Gardner, *In Defence of the Faith* (Oxford: Basil Blackwell, 1927), 60.

93. For an insightful analysis of Lily Dougall as a theological writer, see Joanna Dean, *Religious Experience and the New Woman: The Life of Lily Dougall* (Bloomington: Indiana University Press, 2006).

94. Dorothy Kerin. *The Living Touch* (Tunbridge Wells: KSC Printers, 2002 [1914]), 17–18.

95. Dorothy Arnold. *Dorothy Kerin: Called by Christ to Heal* (Tunbridge Wells: KSC Printers, 1965), 26.

96. See Carolyn Walker Bynum. *Holy Feast and Holy Fast: The Religious Significance of Food to Medieval Women* (Berkeley: University of California Press, 1987).

97. Ibid., 72–73.

98. Daphne Du Maurier and Oriel Malet, *Letters from Menabilly: Portrait of a Friendship*, (New York: M. Evans, 1994); Smiley Blanton, "Portrait of a Seer," *Pastoral Psychology* 11, no. 4 (1960), 56–57.

99. Another less institutionally successful Episcopalian example is that of a woman who claimed to have received spiritual dictation from Canadian doctor William Osler, as well as from William James. Jane Revere Burke, *Messages on Healing: Understood to Have Been Dictated by William James, Sir William Osler, Andrew Jackson Davis, and Others, and Received by Jane Revere Burke Sitting with Edward S. Martin* (New York: Scribner's, 1936), 7. Burke's earlier collection of automatic writings from 1922 was published by the same press, E. P. Dutton, that put out the Dearmers' contribution in 1920.

100. R. Edis Fairbairn, *Faith Healing* (Toronto: Ryerson Press 1923), 9.

101. R. Edis Fairbairn, "Science and Psychic Research," *Christian Guardian* (October 24, 1923).

102. R. Edis Fairbairn, "Polarity—A Divine Principle of the Universe," *New Outlook*, (September 29, 1926): 4.

103. I thank Lois Wilson for sharing her father's unpublished writings with me, and for allowing me to refer to them without quoting them.

104. E. G. D. Freeman, "The Church and Social Reconstruction," in *Four Addresses of the Church of the Air Series* (Toronto: United Church of Canada, 1941).

105. Ramsay Cook, *The Regenerators: Social Criticism in Late Victorian English Canada* (Toronto: University of Toronto Press, 1985); Stan McMullin, *Anatomy of a Séance* (Montreal and Kingston: McGill-Queen's University Press, 2004). Also see, however, McMullin's account of Albert Durrant Watson (1859–1926), a medical doctor, poet, and psychic researcher who retained strong ties to the Methodist Church.

106. F. J. T. Maines, "Do You Believe in the Resurrection?" GA 64 File 176 Maines/Pincock Family Fonds, University of Waterloo Library; "Spiritualist Church Begins Its Services." (October 13, 1930) (unnamed newspaper clipping). GA64 Accrual 1995, File 6, Maines/Pincock Family Fonds, University of

Waterloo Library. For more on The Church of Divine Revelation see McMullin, *Anatomy of a Séance.*

107. Maurice Bucke, *Cosmic Consciousness: A Study in the Evolution of the Human Mind* (Philadelphia: Innes, 1901). For more on Bucke, see Michael Robertson, *Worshipping Walt: The Whitman Disciples* (Princeton: Princeton University Press, 2008).

108. "Radiant Healing Centre: Form of Service and Private Instructions." GA64 File 160. Maines/Pincock Family Fonds, University of Waterloo Library.

109. Jenny O'Hara Pincock, "What Going to Church Meant to Us," n.d. GA64 Accrual 1995, File 26, Maines/Pincock Family Fonds, University of Waterloo Library.

110. Rev. J. A. Tuer quoted in Anonymous, "Challenge to Spiritualists," *St. Catharines Standard* (n.d.). University of Waterloo Library, Maines/Pincock Family Fonds, GA64 File 73; Rev. J. A. Pue-Gilchrist, *St. Catharines Standard* (January 1929). University of Waterloo Library, Maines/Pincock Family Fonds, GA 64 Accrual 1995, File 6.

111. Sherwood Eddy, *Eighty Adventurous Years: An Autobiography* (New York: Harper, 1955), 119. The letter to Stalin is found at the Yale University Divinity School Library, George Sherwood Eddy Papers, RG32. For more on Eddy's life see Rick Nutt, "G. Sherwood Eddy and the Attitudes of Protestants in the United States toward Global Missions. *Church History* 66, no. 3 (1997): 502–521; Rick L. Nutt, *The Whole Gospel for the Whole World: Sherwood Eddy and the American Protestant Mission* (Macon, GA: Mercer University Press, 1997); and Brian Stanley, "The Legacy of George Sherwood Eddy," *International Bulletin of Missionary Research* 24, no. 3 (2000): 128–131.

112. Eddy, *You Will Survive Death.*

113. "What is Ectoplasm?" *New Outlook,* n.d. GA 64 File 176 Maines/Pincock Family Fonds, University of Waterloo Library.

114. Sherwood Eddy Papers, notes and draft of "Why I Believe: A Modern Reason for Faith." File 10-171, George Sherwood Eddy Papers, Record Group No. 32, Special Collections, Yale Divinity School Library.

115. Sherwood Eddy, "Gandhi—An Interpretation," *The Christian Century* (April 19, 1923), 489–494. File 6-107, George Sherwood Eddy Papers, Record Group No. 32, Special Collections, Yale Divinity School Library.

116. Sherwood Eddy, *Doubt: Practical Suggestions for Those Having Intellectual Difficulties Regarding the Christian Faith* (New York: Association Press, 1920).

117. Eddy, *Eighty Adventurous Years,* 218.

118. Eddy, *You Will Survive Death,* 148, 156. 172.

119. Sherwood Eddy, unpublished manuscript, "How to Live" (ca. 1954–1956). File 10-167, George Sherwood Eddy Papers, Record Group No. 32, Special Collections, Yale Divinity School Library.

120. Sherwood Eddy, *You Will Survive Death,* 169.

121. D. L. Scott, "Spiritualism and Christian Faith," *Modern Churchman* 65, no. 1 (1955): 43; Frances Dunlap Heron, "My Experience with Spiritualism," *United Church Observer* (August 1962).

122. Sherwood Eddy, *You Will Survive Death,* p. 10.

123. D. L. Scott, "Spiritualism and Christian Faith," 45.

124. "Sherwood Eddy and Free Speech." File 6-114, George Sherwood Eddy Papers, Record Group No. 32, Special Collections, Yale Divinity School Library; Harry Emerson Fosdick, "Dr. Fosdick on the Eddy Attack," *Christian Century*. File 6-135; "Ministers Reject Rebuke to Nazis"; "Dr. Eddy Quit 'Y' to Join Socialists"; "McCarthy Fought by Church Group." George Sherwood Eddy Papers, Record Group No. 32, Special Collections, Yale Divinity School Library. See Brian Stanley, "The Legacy of George Sherwood Eddy." *International Bulletin of Missionary Research* 24, no. 3 (2000), 131. I discuss this historiographic erasure more fully in "Radio Mind: Christian Experimentalists on the Frontiers of Healing," *Journal of the American Academy of Religion* 75, no. 3 (2007): 651–683.

125. As a student in 1912, Niebuhr praised the spirituality of the Dean of Yale Divinity School, Charles Reynolds Brown, who also engaged in psychic research. Richard Wightman Fox, *Reinhold Niebuhr: A Biography*, 2nd ed. (Ithaca, NY: Cornell University Press, 1996).

126. For another example of an experimentalist, see Kerry Fast's discussion of United Church missionary Agnes Wintemute Coates. Kerry Fast, "But What a Strange Commixture Am I": Borders of Self and Religion in the Making of Women's Lives. PhD Dissertation, University of Toronto, 2008.

127. Viswanathan, "The Ordinary Business of Occultism"; Ian Hacking, *Rewriting the Soul: Multiple Personality and the Sciences of Memory* (Princeton, N.J.: Princeton University Press, 1995).

128. James E. Ward, *The Commonwealth of the Soul: A Study of the Reason Behind Spiritual Healing* (Toronto: Wm. Tyrrell, 1921); James E. Ward, *The Window of Life* (Toronto: Macmillan, 1925).

129. James E. Ward, "Psychological Aspects of Religion: 5: Psycho-Analysis" *Canadian Churchman* (September 10, 1925).

130. James E. Ward, "Conversion and Personal Responsibility," *Canadian Churchman* (October 1, 1925).

131. Ibid.

132. James E. Ward, "Psycho-Analysis"; F. H. Du Vernet, *Spiritual Radio*, 44.

133. James E. Ward, "Suggestion and Self-Realization," *Canadian Churchman* (August 27, 1925); Ward, "Conversion and Personal Responsibility"; Ward, *The Window of Life*, 13.

134. Ward, "Psycho-Analysis."

135. Ibid.

136. James E. Ward, "The Smile of Peggy Morland" (Unpublished manuscript, Diocesan Archives of the Diocese of Toronto, Anglican Church of Canada, n.d.).

137. James E. Ward, "Pilgrim Haven" (Unpublished manuscript, Diocesan Archives of the Diocese of Toronto, Anglican Church of Canada, n.d.).

138. For a detailed discussion of depictions of white and aboriginal women in western Canada, see Sarah Carter, *Capturing Women: The Manipulation of Cultural Imagery in Canada's Prairie West* (Montreal and Kingston: McGill-Queen's University Press, 1997).

139. J. A. Worrell, Letter to the Lord Bishop of Toronto (January 9, 1926). Diocesan Archives of the Diocese of Toronto, Anglican Church of Canada.

140. Anonymous, "Canon Had Varied Career," *Toronto Globe and Mail* (January 4, 1958): 4.

141. James E. Ward, "Prayer: Personal Religion" *Canadian Churchman* (August 20, 1925).

142. James E. Ward, *This England* (Toronto: Longmans, Green, and Co., 1948).

143. Selden, *Are Missions a Failure?* 25.

144. J. C. Winslow, *Christian Yoga*, 44.

145. Dipesh Chakrabarty, *Provincializing Europe*, 40.

4. EVIL SPIRITS AND THE QUEER PSYCHE IN AN AGE OF ANXIETY

1. Mrs. Dale Webb, quoted in Ron Lowman and Loren Chudy, "We Take Witchcraft Seriously, but Don't Practise It: Priest," *Toronto Star* (September 29, 1967), 4 star ed., 1, 8; David Moore Smith quoted in "Jury Asked: Did Spirit Cult Affect Girl's Death?" *Toronto Daily Star* (October 4, 1967), 1, 2; Alexander Globe, quoted in "Witness Believes Evil Spirits Can 'Inhabit' Human Body," *Toronto Daily Star* (October 3, 1967), 4 star ed., 1, 2.

2. G. Moore Smith, quoted in "Dead Girl's Dad Charges Blackmail by Minister," *Toronto Daily Star* (September 30, 1967), 4 star ed., 1–2.

3. Douglas Tisdall, quoted in Lowman and Chudy, "We Take Witchcraft Seriously," 8.

4. "Cult Split Couple, Inquest Told," *Toronto Daily Star* (October 3, 1967), 1–2.

5. Judy Steed, "Priest Tells of Cult Horror in Dad's Rectory," *Toronto Star* (February 12, 1995).

6. The Report of the Bishop of Toronto's Commission on the Church's Ministry of Healing, Diocese of Toronto, May 1968, 28.

7. "Jury Wants All Cults Probed," *Toronto Daily Star* (October 4 1967), 1, 2.

8. "Anglican Bishop Says He'll Stop Faith Healing Cult That 'Cast out Demons,'" *Toronto Daily Star* (October 5, 1967), 1, 3.

9. "Faith Healing Probe to Cover All Diocese," *Toronto Daily Star* (October 6, 1967), 1, 2.

10. See Smith's press release at the beginning of the inquest, for his clear distinction between the faithful, supernatural church and the faithless, hopelessly modernizing church. "Not 'Possessed,' Dead Girl Was 'Holy', says Anglican minister," *Toronto Daily Star* (September 27, 1967).

11. "Quietness Replaces Emotionalism: Faith-Healing the United Way," *Toronto Daily Star* (March 11, 1967). Alex Holmes Bio file, United Church of Canada Archives.

12. Cuth Mann, "Faith Healing by Sault Minister Gets Study by New York Researcher," *Sault Daily Star* (May 7, 1958). Alex Holmes Bio file, United Church of Canada Archives.

13. "Julius Weinberger" *Encyclopedia of Occultism and Parapsychology* Leslie Shepard, ed. (Detroit: Gale Research, 1978), 978.

14. Sally Hammond, *We are All Healers* (New York: Harper & Row, 1973).

15. The *United Church Observer* gave a short and bemused account of a talk by Holmes to the Bay of Quinte Conference, during which a healing unexpectedly and "apparently" occurred. *United Church Observer* (July 1977), Alex Holmes Bio file, United Church of Canada Archives.

16. *I'm OK—You're OK* was a New York Times bestselling book first published in 1967 and written by a psychiatrist, Thomas A. Harris. It includes a section on Christianity that depends heavily on Paul Tillich to argue that authentic "religious experience" is rooted in an "awareness" that can only be accessed by an individual seeing the world for him or herself, without the help of tradition or teaching; ironically "transactional analysis" was a path to learn such awareness and access the "truth." Thomas A. Harris, *I'm OK—You're OK* (New York: Harper & Row, 1967). For a harsh review of Freud, see "News, Views, and Reviews," *Canadian Churchman* (June 3, 1954).

17. Rollo May, *Paulus: Reminiscences of a Friendship* (New York: Harper & Row, 1973), 108.

18. David Hein and Gardiner H. Shattuck Jr., *The Episcopalians* (Westport, CT: Praeger, 2004, 149. For Catholic charismatics, see Mary Jo Neitz, *Charisma and Community: A Study of Religious Commitment within the Charismatic Renewal* (New Brunswick, NJ: Transaction Books, 1987).

19. Hein and Shattuck trace the charismatic renewal to 1960 and make no reference to earlier examples such as Agnes Sanford. On myths of origin, see Joe Creech, "Visions of Glory: The Place of the Azusa Street Revival in Pentecostal History." *Church History* 63, no. 3 (1996), 406. See also Michael Wilkinson, "Canadian Pentecostalism: A Multicultural Perspective," paper delivered at the Canadian Society of Church History Annual Meeting, Vancouver, 2008; Michael Bergunder, "Constructing Indian Pentecostalism: On Issues of Methodology and Representation." In *Asian and Pentecostal: The Charismatic Face of Christianity in Asia.* Allen Anderson and Edmond Tang, eds. (Oxford: Regnum, 2005), 177–213, and Ann Taves, *Fits, Trances, and Visions: Experiencing Religion and Explaining Experience from Wesley to James* (Princeton, N.J.: Princeton University Press, 1999).

20. Morton Kelsey, *Healing and Christianity: A Classic Study.* 3rd rev. ed. (Minneapolis: Augsburg Fortress, 1995 [1973]), 309. See also, Morton Kelsey and Barbara Kelsey, *The Sacrament of Sexuality* (Warwick, NY: Amity House, 1986).

21. David Harrell, *All Things are Possible: The Healing and Charismatic Revivals in Modern America.* (Bloomington: Indiana University Press, 1979).

22. Gail Paton Grant, "Miracle Lore and Metamorphoses." in *Undisciplined Women: Tradition and Culture in Canada,* ed. Pauline Greenhill and Diane Tye (Montréal and Kingston: McGill-Queen's University Press, 1997), 202–212. See also, Marilyn Gail Grant, "Healing by Conviction: Charismatic Adjunctive Therapy." MA Thesis, York University, 1981.

23. Arthur N. Thompson, *Haelend: The Church's Ministry of Healing* (Winnipeg, MB: Charis Books, 1984).

24. Sanford's book also made it onto the *Observer's* "bestseller" list, *United Church Observer* (November 1973).

25. "Spiritual Healing," *Canadian Churchman* (May 3, 1956); "Training School in Spiritual Healing," *Canadian Churchman* (June 7, 1956); Other books favorably reviewed in the *Churchman* include Brian Hession, *The Gentle Step* (London: Peter Davies, 1958) written by an Anglican priest from the U.K.; "Spiritual Vitamin Pill," *Canadian Churchman* (March 1959); and a review of Episcopalian Bishop of Chicago Wallace Edmonds Conkling's, *Health and Salvation: A Guide for the Practice of Spiritual Healing* (New York: Morehouse Goreham, 1952), *Canadian Churchman* (November 20, 1952); Boole served as President of the School of Pastoral Care from 1999 to 2006.

26. Glenn Clark was himself an interesting mix of sacramentalism, "Eastern mysticism," and charismatic healing. Glenn Clark, *Be Thou Made Whole* (Saint Paul, MN: Macalester Park Publishing, 1953).

27. Agnes Sanford, *The Healing Light* (St. Paul, MN: Macalester Park Publishing, 1947), 30, 33.

28. Ibid., 35, 39.

29. Ibid., 36.

30. Ibid., 54.

31. Ibid., 95.

32. Ibid., 22.

33. Ibid., 87.

34. Sanford insisted, contrary to the advice of her friends, that confession was not the only sacramental path to healing. And contrary to the skepticism of a priest during her first confession, she later considered her postconfession emotions of a "high ecstasy of spirit" to be a reliable sign of God's healing vibrations. Sanford, *Healing Light*, 117, 121–122.

35. Ibid., 150, 158, 162.

36. For a critical review, see Oberton Stephens, MD, "The Healing Gifts," *Canadian Churchman* (January 1967); for her defenders see A. E. Streeter, "Regrettable Review," and E. Chapman, "Yes—Mrs. Sanford!" *Canadian Churchman* (February 1967). On Sanford's 1956 visit, see "Training School in Spiritual Healing," *Canadian Churchman* (June 1956). In 2006, the president of the school and the North American Director of the Order of St. Luke—both Canadian Anglican priests—announced that the Order of St. Luke was amalgamating the School of Pastoral Care under the name of the Order. Though her school is gone, Agnes Sanford remains as one of the few women—and certainly the first—to appear on the Order of St. Luke list of required reading for members, a list that also includes Du Vernet's admirer John Gaynor Banks and the charismatic Catholic and exorcism specialist Francis MacNutt.

37. Kelsey led a "diocesan day of prayer and renewal" at Christ Church Cathedral in Montreal in 1980, "Healers encouraged," *Canadian Churchman* (January 1980).

38. As early as 1962, the English cleric C. Hilary Butler, spoke at Christ Church Cathedral in Victoria, BC, to commend the work of sacramental healing as well as the "dedicated and commissioned lay-folk with natural healing gifts." He was careful, however, to warn against the twin dangers of heresy and

"personality-cults" that led to charlatanism. "The Divine Healing Ministry," *Canadian Churchman* (May 1962).

39. H. E. Taylor, "Heal the Sick," *Canadian Churchman* (January 1959 through September 1960).

40. "Psychiatry in a Mission Hospital," *Canadian Churchman* (February 16, 1950).

41. Daniel Cappon, "The Dying," *Psychiatric Quarterly* 33, no. 3 (1959): 466–489.

42. Daniel Cappon, "Physical, Mental, and Spiritual Healing," in *Handbook on the Healing Ministry of the Church* (Toronto: Office of the Bishop of Toronto, 1964), 5.

43. A review of Cappon's 1965 book, *Toward an Understanding of Homosexuality* (Englewood Cliffs: Prentice Hall, 1965) had this to say: "Cappon's book is a hodgepodge of psychiatry, sociology, pseudopsychoanalysis, therapeutic aggressiveness, and cloying piety." H. R. Blank, "Review of *Toward an Understanding of Homosexuality,*" *Psychoanalytic Quarterly* 35 (1966): 137–138.

44. The recommended reading list in the *Handbook on the Healing Ministry of the Church* included pastoral counseling and psychology of religion literature by Hiltner, Cabot and Dicks, Tillich, James, Leslie Weatherhead, and Percy Dearmer, and authors representing the Order of St. Luke. Very few women made the cut, and Agnes Sanford and Dorothy Kerin are absent.

45. Editorial, "Public Inquiry Needed," *Canadian Churchman* (November 1967); Kent Doe, "Churchman's 'Failure,'" *Canadian Churchman* (December 1967); John R. Thompson, "Morbid and Sadistic," *Canadian Churchman* (December 1967). See also, William N. Porter, "A Scapegoat?" *Canadian Churchman* (January 1968).

46. The Report, 24. The report was extensively summarized in the *Canadian Churchman* (July–August 1968).

47. The Report, 26, 28.

48. Ibid., 26.

49. Ibid., 13.

50. Ibid., 14. The Report cited the Prayer Book as requiring the priest to "pray for the sick and anoint them with oil that they may recover their *bodily* health" (emphasis original).

51. The Report, 39.

52. This is except for the advertisement for "Good Health" placed directly beside the article, which described the "science of sound health" to be found at an organic, whole foods, biblically based "nature cure health spa" in Carlsbad Springs, near Ottawa.

53. "Ein' Feste Burg" in *Book of Common Praise of the Anglican Church of Canada*, trans. Thomas Carlyle, (Toronto: Anglican Book Centre, 1938), 411; "Our God's A Fortress (Ein' Feste Burg)," in *The Hymn Book of the Anglican Church of Canada and the United Church of Canada*, trans. J. Macpherson (Toronto: n.p., 1971), no. 135. I am grateful to Prof. Jay Macpherson for sharing this story with me in a personal communication.

54. Steed, "Priest Tells of Cult Horror in Dad's Rectory."

55. Miriam Dobell, *Healing Happens: Experiences in the Church's Ministry of Healing* (Toronto: Anglican Book Centre, 1982), 59.

56. Ibid., 29.

57. Edward Aubert, *Belief and Health*. Conference on the Church's Ministry of Healing, Aurora, Ontario, September 1973, Diocese of Toronto. Burrswood now describes itself as a "holistic" place of healing that cares for "the whole person—body, mind, and spirit." http://www.burrswood.org.uk/about/intro.html. Accessed July 10, 2008. This phrase was also used in the interviews I conducted with doctors, psychologists, and nurses at Burrswood in April 2005.

58. Jocelyn Bell, *The Story of Five Oaks: Fifty Years in the Life of an Education Centre* (n.p., n.d.).

59. The Stuttgart Declaration of Guilt also drew upon metaphors of healing, using the word *Genesung* (convalescence, recovery) to describe what "tortured" humanity requires in the wake of the war. On the Stuttgart Declaration, see Matthew D. Hockenos, *A Church Divided: German Protestants Confront the Nazi Past* (Bloomington: Indiana University Press, 2004).

60. "The Urgency of the Gospel," and excerpts from "The New Life Movement," Booklet Number 1, Dept. of Evangelism, Board of National Missions; The Presbyterian Church, U.S.A., in "The Time of Healing," 22nd Annual Report, Board of Evangelism and Social Service, The United Church of Canada, Toronto, 1947. United Church Archives.

61. Editorial, *United Church Observer* (January 1, 1967).

62. Ernest F. Scott, *I Believe in the Holy Spirit* (Nashville: Abingdon Press, 1958), 39.

63. Ibid., 65, 70, 86.

64. Ernest F. Scott, "The Supernatural in Early Christianity," *The Journal of Religion* 10, no. 1 (1930), 94.

65. Scott, *I Believe in the Holy Spirit*, 88.

66. E. Brooks Holifield, *A History of Pastoral Care in America: From Salvation to Self-Realization* (Nashville: Abingdon Press, 1983), 197.

67. Seward Hiltner, "Three Contributions to Understanding Human Sexuality." *Pastoral Psychology* 24, no. 1 (1975), 35. Protestant writers shifted between body, mind, and *spirit* and body, mind, and *soul*, but spirit was the more common usage. One particularly clear example among many is found in John Pitts, *Faith Healing: Fact or Fiction* (Westwood, NJ: Fleming H. Revell, 1961), 114. This last quote is from a satirical article written by Hiltner, "The Durability of Docetism." *Christian Century* (April 10, 1974), 399.

68. The United Church still operates three acute care hospitals in northern British Columbia; see http://www.uchealth.ca/. Accessed January 30, 2009. Also see Bob Burrows, *Healing in the Wilderness: A History of the United Church Mission Hospitals* (British Columbia: Harbour Publishing, 2004). On medical missionaries see the article on United Church medical missionary to Angola, Sidney Gilchrist, "A Great, Good Man Goes Back," *United Church Observer* (February 1, 1968), and "My Africa: Why a Missionary Doctor, after Two Coronaries, Chooses to Go Back." *United Church Observer* (April 15, 1968); Also see, "The Moderator Looks at a Checkerboard of Our Missions in Canada, *United Church Observer* (January 15, 1967); Harvey L. Shepherd, "The New Doctors of the

Indian Frontier," *United Church Observer* (March 1, 1967); Patricia Clarke, "A Nurse's Diary from Troubled Angola," *United Church Observer* (June 15, 1967); "Our Healing Ministry . . . from Bonavista to Vancouver Island," *United Church Observer* (August 1, 1967). On abortion, see Ruth Ann Soden, "Is Abortion Always Wrong: Parliament May Soon Liberalize Abortion Laws. Here's Why the United Church Agrees," *United Church Observer* (October 15, 1968). Birth control was a topic that generated a lot of Protestant-Catholic conversations, such as Robert G. Hoyt, "Birth Control! The Catholic Church's Most Explosive Issue Reviewed by One of Its Most Outspoken Laymen," *United Church Observer* (November 1, 1967).

69. James N. Lapsley, "Seward Hiltner, 1909–1984," *Pastoral Psychology* 34, no. 1 (1985): 3–8.

70. For a discussion of competing notions of the self within psychiatric spirituality, including those of Cabot and Hiltner, see E. Brooks Holifield, "Ethical Assumptions within Clinical Pastoral Education." *Theology Today* 36, no. 1 (1979): 30–44.

71. Seward Hiltner, *Religion and Health* (New York: Macmillan, 1943), 64.

72. Ibid., 65–66.

73. Ibid., 96.

74. Ibid., 23.

75. This volume reprinted John Millet's "Body, Mind, and Spirit" and included chapters by psychiatrists and theologians including Carl Rogers, Paul Tillich, and Earl Loomis, the Director of the Program on Psychiatry and Religion at Union Theological Seminary.

76. Seward Hiltner, "Freud, Psychoanalysis, and Religion," in *Healing: Human and Divine*, ed. Simon Doniger (New York: Association Press, 1957), 91.

77. See, Andrew S. Finstuen, *Original Sin and Everyday Protestants: The Theology of Reinhold Niebuhr, Billy Graham, and Paul Tillich in an Age of Anxiety* (Chapel Hill: University of North Carolina Press, 2009).

78. E. Brooks Holifield, *A History of Pastoral Care in America: From Salvation to Self-Realization* (Nashville: Abingdon Press, 1983), 329. See also, "As a mediator between the two worlds [of psychology and theology], no one could surpass Paul Tillich." Holifield, *A History of Pastoral Care in America*, 288. For more on Tillich and his practice of psychology, see Terry D. Cooper, *Paul Tillich and Psychology: Historic and Contemporary Explorations in Theology, Psychotherapy, and Ethics* (Macon, GA: Mercer University Press, 2006).

79. "Word for the Broken-Hearted," *United Church Observer* (October 1973).

80. *United Church Observer* (November 1974).

81. Holifield, *A History of Pastoral Care*, 313. See also, C. Gertrude Cutler, "Tillich's Multi-dimensional View of Health: A Message of Holistic Healing," in *Theonomy and Autonomy*, ed. John J. Carey (Macon, GA: Mercer University Press, 1984), 171–189.

82. (Mrs.) D. Trotter, "Psychiatry Has Limits," *United Church Observer* (March 1, 1967).

83. For a largely Catholic version of this psychiatric spirituality that was simultaneously an experiment in communal living, see discussions of the Toronto-based Therafields community, which began in the 1960s, and which some former

participants have labeled a "cult." Grant Goodbrand, *Therafields: The Rise and Fall of Lea Hindley-Smith's Psychoanalytic Commune* (Toronto: ECW Press, 2010) and Philip Marchand, "Open Book by Philip Marchand: The Odd History of a 1960s Catholic Psychoanalytic Commune" *National Post,* October 1, 2010, http://arts.nationalpost.com/tag/therafields/ (Accessed February 15, 2011). I thank Peter Slater for bringing Therafields to my attention.

84. Ann Taves, "William James Revisited: Rereading *The Varieties of Religious Experience* in Transatlantic Perspective," *Zygon* 44, no. 2 (2009): 415–432.

85. "Notes and News," *Pastoral Psychology* 1, no. 1 (1950), 56.

86. Another "Clinical Training Course" for ministers was offered at McMaster University and featured lectures from the medical staff of the Mountain Sanatorium. *Canadian Churchman* (March 18, 1954). A comprehensive history of the intersection of Protestantism and psychiatry in Canada has yet to be written. For a brief account of the Maritimes situation, see Rodney Stokoe, "Clinical Pastoral Education," *Nova Scotia Medical Bulletin* (February 1974), 26–28. For a discussion of U.S. seminary programs in pastoral counseling, see Glenn T. Miller, *Piety and Profession: American Protestant Theological Education, 1870–1970* (Grand Rapids, MI: Eerdmans, 2007).

87. Stokoe, "Clinical Pastoral Education." Still largely run through Protestant seminaries, the IPT, now under the national umbrella organization, the Canadian Association for Pastoral Practice and Education, describes itself as less exclusively Christian and more "multi-faith," characterized by a "holistic approach to health care and personal development with a special focus on spiritual and religious care." http://www.cappe.org/index.html. CAPPE/ACPEP website. Accessed August 28, 2008.

88. Feilding's newsletter, printed out of his home, drew its inspiration from Reinhold Niebuhr's New York-based *Christianity and Crisis* and J. H. Oldham's Oxford-based *The Christian News Letter.* Trinity College Archives, Charles R. Feilding fonds (F2075), Accession No. 985-0021.

89. "Method: Whom Should we Address?" Preparatory document for the establishment of Canada and Christendom, 4. Trinity College Archives, Charles R. Feilding fonds (F2075), Accession No. 985-0021.

90. A full history of the TIPT has yet to be written, but this quote is taken from a 1964 pamphlet titled "Clinical Pastoral Training for Parish Ministers: A Program Open to the Clergy of all Churches Arranged by The Toronto Institute for Pastoral Training." Trinity College Archives, Charles R. Feilding fonds (F2075), unprocessed.

91. The goals of the Pastoral Institute, as listed in their constitution, included the following: "To provide as a special ministry of the Christian Church, education and group training for marriage and family life as well as personal counselling to help anyone who can make use of the services regardless of race, colour, religion or economic status" and "enlisting, through a selection and training program, the services of mature men and women for the work of counselling and education in marriage and family life." Dana Campbell, "Lifecycle Stages of the Pastoral Institute," unpublished paper, 2005. Another example is the psychiatric clinic that Toronto Western Hospital operated out of College Street United Church. *United Church Observer* (November 15 1968).

92. Samuel R. Laycock, *Pastoral Counselling for Mental Health* (Toronto: The Ryerson Press, 1958). Psychiatric spirituality was not solely Christian, as Heinze's analysis of the prominence of Jews among popular psychologists in the twentieth century demonstrates. Andrew R. Heinze, *Jews and the American Soul: Human Nature in the Twentieth Century* (Princeton, N.J.: Princeton University Press, 2004).

93. "Teach Mental Health," *United Church Observer* (January 15, 1968).

94. Brown's career is in contrast to that of John Chappel, the son of a United Church minister who was turned away for missionary work with the United Church and was openly critical of the Church's opposition to short-term medical missions. Chappel ended up studying community psychiatry and public health at Harvard University and working outside church contexts. John Chappel, as told to Patricia Clarke, "With Medico in Malaya," *United Church Observer* (March 15, 1965); John Chappel, "Psychiatry," in *The Cutting Edge: Reflections and Memories by Doctors on Medical Advances in Reno*, ed. Richard G. Pugh (Reno: University of Nevada Press, 2003), 143–154.

95. "Women in the Church," *Canadian Churchman* (March 1968). See also an earlier account of the Sisters' medical work that declared that "Our church may be well thankful . . . for the health of body and mind and soul of those who enter their excellent hospital." "The Noble Work of Healing," *Canadian Churchman* (May 1, 1952).

96. John A. P. Millet, "Body, Mind, and Spirit," *Pastoral Psychology* 1, no. 5 (June 1950), 15.

97. Susan E. Myers-Shirk, "'To Be Fully Human': U.S. Protestant Psychotherapeutic Culture and the Subversion of the Domestic Ideal, 1945–1965," *Journal of Women's History* 12, no. 1 (2000): 112–136.

98. R. Marie Griffith, "The Religious Encounters of Alfred C. Kinsey," *Journal of American History* (September 2008): 349–377.

99. David Mabell, "Strong Voices for Sex Education," *Albertan* (March 19, 1969), 1. United Church Archives; "Churches Sponsor Pow-wow," *Calgary Herald* (October 20, 1969). United Church Archives.

100. Laycock, *Pastoral Counselling for Mental Health*, 75.

101. William Nicholls, "Homosexuality: Changing the Laws Could Raise Morality," *Vancouver Sun* (July 6, 1965), 6.

102. Mervyn Dickinson, "The Church and the Homosexual," *United Church Observer* (November 15, 1965). A book now in the Emmanuel College Library collection was given to Dickinson by the Christian Education Committee of Fairlawn Church in Toronto, "in appreciation for a very helpful contribution to our study of spiritual healing." John Sutherland Bonnell, *Do You Want to Be Healed?* (New York: Harper & Row, 1968). See also J. Mervyn Dickinson, "The Rebirth of Pastoral Theology," *Canadian Journal of Theology* 9, no. 2 (April 1963): 126–132.

103. For an earlier, and less definitive, Protestant defense of homosociality (but not homosexuality), see George Chauncey, "Christian Brotherhood or Sexual Perversion: Homosexual Identities and the Construction of Sexual Boundaries in the World War I Era," in *Sexual Borderlands: Constructing an American*

Sexual Past, ed. Kathleen Kennedy and Sharon Rena Ullman (Columbus: Ohio State University Press, 2003), 187–217.

104. Seward Hiltner, "The Neglected Phenomenon of Female Homosexuality." *Christian Century* (May 29, 1974), 591–593.

105. In the U.S. context of public debate about homosexuality, Wendy Cadge has argued that "the mainline churches have opened up discussions about homosexuality to a broader range of the U.S. population and granted legitimacy to all sides of the debate." Wendy Cadge, "Vital Conflicts: The Mainline Denominations Debate Homosexuality," in *The Quiet Hand of God: Faith-Based Activism and the Public Role of Mainline Protestantism,* ed. Robert Wuthnow and John Evans. (Berkeley: University of California Press, 2002), 266.

106. E. Gilmour Smith, "Sickness and God." *United Church Observer* (February 15, 1969).

107. Tommy Douglas, who pioneered universal government-funded access to medical care when Premier of Saskatchewan and then pushed for its passing as leader of the Canadian Commonwealth Federation/New Democratic Party, was first a Baptist minister.

108. Will Oursler, *Religion: Out or Way Out* (Harrisburg, PA: Stackpole, 1968), 138.

109. Seward Hiltner, "Review of Health/Medicine and the Faith Tradition," *Theology Today* 40, no. 2 (1983), 200.

110. World Council of Churches, *Christian Perspectives on Theological Anthropology: A Faith and Order Study Document* (Geneva: WCC, 2005).

5. RITUAL PROXIMITY AND THE HEALING OF HISTORY

1. The apology was published in full in the *Anglican Journal* (September 1993) and can also be found at http://www.anglican.ca/Residential-Schools/re sources/apology.htm (accessed December 16, 2008).

2. Reiki is a Japanese-based healing modality that by some accounts has a Christian lineage; see P. D. Mitchell, *The Usui System of Natural Healing* (Coeur d'Alene, ID: The Reiki Alliance, 1985). Therapeutic touch is a hybrid Western/Eastern energy therapy invented by a U.S. nurse, Dolores Krieger, *The Therapeutic Touch: How to Use Your Hands to Help or to Heal* (Englewood Cliffs, NJ: Prentice-Hall, 1979). On health, healing, and the "new metaphysicals," see Courtney Bender, *The New Metaphysicals: Spirituality and the American Religious Imagination* (Chicago: University of Chicago Press, 2010).

3. The Web site is from the Lewis Memorial United Church in Turner Valley, Alberta. http://www.unitedchurchinthevalley.ca/messages.php (accessed December 18, 2008). The prayer is from Maren C. Tirabassi and Joan Gordon Grant, "Prayer with Christians Facing the Multiplicity of Spirituality," in *An Improbable Gift of Blessing* (Cleveland: United Church Press, 1998), 122.

4. Compiled by his wife, Gertrude, after Chambers's death in 1917, the text has become a classic of evangelical Christianity. Oswald Chambers, *My Utmost for His Highest* (Grand Rapids, MI: Discovery House Publishers, 1992).

5. See Walter Benjamin, "On the Concept of History," trans. Harry Zohn, in *Walter Benjamin: Selected Writings, vol. 4, 1938–40,* ed. Howard Eiland and Michael W. Jennings (Cambridge, MA: Harvard University Press, 2003).

6. "A Health Covenant for All the People of Canada," http://www.ccc-cce.ca/english/justice/health.htm (accessed December 18, 2008). The long-standing intersection of liberal Protestantism and the Canadian health care system is most famously embodied in Tommy Douglas, the leader of the Canadian Commonwealth Federation/New Democratic Party, a social gospel-influenced minister turned politician who played a key role in establishing state-funded health care system in Canada. Several scholars have accounted for the rise of state-funded health care in Canada, though rarely with a great deal of attention to church or other religious groups. The most detailed accounts include C. David Naylor, ed. *Canadian Health Care and the State* (Montreal and Kingston: McGill-Queens University Press, 1992); Malcolm Taylor, *Health Insurance and Canadian Public Policy: The Seven Decisions That Created the Canadian Health Insurance System and Their Outcomes.* 2nd ed. (Toronto: Institute of Public Administration of Canada, 1987); Carolyn Tuohy, *Accidental Logics: The Dynamics of Change in the Health Care Arena in the United States, Britain, and Canada* (New York: Oxford University Press, 1999); Raisa B. Deber, "Philosophical Underpinnings of Canada's Health Care Systems," in *National Health Care: Lessons for the United States and Canada,* ed. Jonathan Lemco (Ann Arbor: University of Michigan Press, 1994), 43–68.

7. John Evans, *Playing God? Human Genetic Engineering and the Rationalization of Public Bioethical Debate* (Chicago: University of Chicago Press, 2002). For theological perspectives, see Allen Verhey, ed., *Religion and Medical Ethics: Looking Back, Looking Forward* (Grand Rapids, MI: W. B. Eerdmans, 1996).

8. James B. Ashbrook, "Paul Tillich Converses with Psychotherapists," *Journal of Religion and Health* 11, no. 1 (1972): 40–72; "Canadian Ashram," *Canadian Churchman* (April 1, 1954). See also Harvey Cox, *Turning East: The Promise and Peril of the New Orientalism* (New York: Simon and Schuster, 1977).

9. Monica Furlong, *Genuine Fake: A Biography of Alan Watts* (London: Heinemann, 1986).

10. Sarah Strauss. "'Adapt, Adjust, Accommodate': The Production of Yoga in a Transnational World," *History and Anthropology,* 13, no. 3 (2002): 231–251; Wendy Cadge, *Heartwood: The First Generation of Theravada Buddhism in America* (Chicago: University of Chicago Press, 2004).

11. Arjun Appadurai, "The Past as a Scarce Resource," *Man* (N.S.), 16 (1981): 201–219; Arjun Appadurai, Paul Gilroy, and V. Bell, "Historical Memory, Global Movements and Violence," *Theory, Culture, and Society* 16, no. 2 (1999): 21–40.

12. Richard King, *Orientalism and Religion: Postcolonialism and the "Mystic East"* (London: Routledge, 1999), 4; Edward Said, *Orientalism: Western Conceptions of the Orient* (New York: Vintage, 1979); Peter van der Veer, *Imperial Encounters: Religion and Modernity in India and Britain* (Princeton, N.J.:Princeton University Press, 2001).

13. Dipesh Chakrabarty, "Minority Histories, Subaltern Pasts," *Postcolonial Studies* 1, no. 1 (1998): 16.

14. Ibid., 22.

15. Ibid.

16. Ibid., 28.

17. Ibid., 25.

18. Simon Coleman and Jon Elsner, "Tradition as Play: Pilgrimage to 'England's Nazareth,' " *History and Anthropology* 15, no. 3 (2004): 273–288.

19. For an account of Burrswood history and practices, see Michael Harper, "Burrswood: A Christian Hospital," *Christian Medical Fellowship,* http://www .cmf.org.uk/literature/content.asp?context=article&id=1584 (accessed January 20, 2009).

20. "Healing Centre," *The Eaglet* (Fall 2002), http://www.ssjd.ca/fall02.html (accessed July 25, 2008).

21. Interview with Ronald Van Auken, October 9, 2001.

22. J. M. Déchanet, *Christian Yoga,* trans. Roland Hindmarsh (New York: Harper, 1960); Strauss, "The Production of Yoga in a Transnational World."

23. J. M. Kubicki, *Liturgical Music as Ritual Symbol: A Case Study of Jacques Berthier's Taizé Music* (Leuven: Peeters, 1999).

24. Robert Wuthnow, *Creative Spirituality: The Way of the Artist* (Berkeley: University of California Press, 2001).

25. R. A. Cram, in J. F. White, *Christian Worship in North America: A Retrospective, 1955–1995* (Collegeville, MN: Liturgical Press, 1997), 278.

26. See Charles Stewart and Rosalind Shaw, eds. *Syncretism/Antisyncretism: The Politics of Religious Synthesis* (New York and London: Routledge, 1994), 18.

27. Sara Wuthnow, "Healing Touch Controversies," *Journal of Religion and Health* 36, no. 3,(1997) 221–229.

28. Qi or ch'i and prana are terms that mean life-giving energy or breath, within Chinese religion and Hinduism, respectively. On Hindu versions of universalizing religion, see King, *Orientalism and Religion*; and Arvind Sharma, *The Concept of Universal Religion in Modern Hindu Thought* (London: Macmillan, 1998).

29. I thank Jennifer Bailey, my research assistant, whose field notes informed this section on the meditation sessions.

30. Coleman and Elsner, "Tradition as Play," 283.

31. C. Faught, "John Charles Roper and the Oxford Movement in Toronto," *Journal of the Canadian Church History Society* 36 (1994): 113–133.

32. Roger Bastide, quoted in Susan Sered, "Taxonomies of Ritual Mixing: Ritual Healing in the Contemporary United States," *History of Religions* 47, no. 2 (2007): 221–238.

33. I first met John at his monastery in 2003 and interacted with Patrick and Nadia (pseudonyms) in various settings during 1999–2003. They all commented on an earlier version of this chapter.

34. John requested that I use his real name.

35. See also Nancy Roth, *A New Christian Yoga* (Cambridge, MA: Cowley, 1989).

36. Stephen Thomas, *Newman and Heresy: The Anglican Years* (Cambridge: Cambridge University Press, 1991), 2–3; N. Groves, "Society and Sacrament: The Anglican Left and Sacramental Socialism, Ritual as Ethics," *Buddhist-Christian Studies* 20 (2000): 71–84.

37. For another liberal Protestant perspective on Reiki that is less sacramentalist, see Bruce Epperly and Katherine Gould Epperly, *Reiki Healing Touch and the Way of Jesus* (Cleveland: Northstone, 2005). Epperly is something of a healing entrepreneur among liberal Protestants, as his website shows: http://www .bruceepperly.com (accessed December 18, 2008). For an interesting contrast to John's use of healing energy, see Birgit Meyer, "Beyond Syncretism: Translation and Diabolization in the Appropriation of Protestantism in Africa," in Stewart and Shaw, *Syncretism/Anti-syncretism*.

38. For a similar approach to energy from a Canadian SSJE member writing in 1975, see John Hemming's discussion of transcendental meditation and energy surges, *Canadian Churchman* (April 1975). See also the review of Anglican journalist Tom Harpur's approach to energy, in *Canadian Churchman* (June 1994).

39. John E. Booty, "The Anglican Tradition," in *Caring and Curing*, ed. Ronald Numbers and Darryl Amundsen (New York: Macmillan, 1986); Jennifer L. Hollis, "Healing into Wholeness in the Episcopal Church," in *Religion and Healing in America*, ed. Linda Barnes and Susan Sered (Oxford: Oxford University Press, 2005).

40. Edward Bouverie Pusey, "The Real Presence" in Owen Chadwick, *The Mind of the Oxford Movement* (Stanford: Stanford University Press, 1960), 197.

41. "Christianity and Modern Cults" *Canadian Churchman* (September 7, 1922); "Summary of Father Frere on Missions," *Canadian Churchman* (July 21, 1910).

42. John Webster Grant, "Blending Traditions: The United Church of Canada," *Canadian Journal of Theology* 9, no. 1 (1963): 50–59.

43. On Esalen, see Jeffrey Kripal, *Esalen: America and the Religion of No Religion* (Chicago: University of Chicago Press, 2007). Though dogged by controversy and financial uncertainty over its history, Five Oaks still functions as a center of ritual innovation. See Jocelyn Bell, *The Story of Five Oaks: Fifty Years in the Life of an Education Centre* (n.p., n.d.), 72–73; http://www.fiveoaks.on .ca/main.htm (accessed December 18, 2008).

44. Ruth Burgess and Kathy Galloway, eds. *Praying for the Dawn: A Resource Book for the Ministry of Healing* (Glasgow: Wild Goose Publications, 2000). Belle Oliver also noted the healing work of the Iona Community in her diaries.

45. Grant, "Blending Traditions," 59.

46. Peter Millar, quoted in W. Graham Monteith, "The Service of Prayers for Healing of the Iona Community: A Historical and Theological Perspective," in Burgess and Galloway, eds., *Praying for the Dawn*, 21.

47. Ian M. Fraser, "Purification of the Memory," in Burgess and Galloway, eds., *Praying for the Dawn*, 61–62.

48. Bruno Latour, *We Have Never Been Modern* (Cambridge, MA: Harvard University Press, 1993); Webb Keane, *Christian Moderns* (Berkeley: University of California Press, 2007).

49. Katharine Hockin, "My Pilgrimage in Mission," *International Bulletin of Missionary Research* 12 (January 1998): 23–28.

50. D. Zersen, "Parish Nursing: 20th-Century Fad?" *Journal of Christian Nursing* 11, no. 2 (1994): 19–21, 45; S. Matthaei and L. Stern, "A Healing Ministry: The Educational Functions of Parish Nursing." *Religious Education* 89, no. 2 (1994): 232; C. Scheffer, "Parish Nursing: Rediscovering the Healing Ministry," *Kansas Nurse* 69, no. 7 (1994): 3–4.

51. Jane Simington, Joanne Olson, and L. Douglass, "Promoting Well-Being within a Parish," *Canadian Nurse* 92, no. 1 (1996): 19; Joanne K. Olson, Margaret B. Clark, and Jane Simington, "The Canadian Experience," in *Parish Nursing: Promoting Whole Person Health Within Faith Communities*, ed. Phyllis Ann Solari-Twadell and Mary Ann McDermott (Thousand Oaks: Sage, 1999), 277–86; Mary Elizabeth O'Brien, *Spirituality in Nursing: Standing on Holy Ground* (Sudbury, MA: Jones and Bartlett, 2003), 9.

52. Deaconess Foundation, http://www.deaconess.org/Home.aspx?ContentID=15 (accessed June 26, 2007).

53. Parts of the section on parish nursing were written collaboratively with Jennifer Bailey, who also conducted one of the interviews with Debra, along with other interviews with parish nurses that informed my overall analysis.

54. Granger Westberg, *The Parish Nurse: Providing a Minister of Health for your Congregation* (Minneapolis: Augsburg Fortress, 1990), 17. Earlier uses of the phrase include an Anglican minister's call for parish nurses who would help doctors and increase church attendance, *Canadian Churchman* (November 24, 1910).

55. Leslie Van Dover and Jane Bacon Pfeiffer, "Spiritual Care in Christian Parish Nursing," *Journal of Advanced Nursing* 57, no. 2 (2006), 214.

56. For a United Church instructional text on how to blend these modalities, see Sharon Moon, *The Healing Oasis: Meditations for Mind, Body, and Spirit* (Etobicoke, ON: United Church Publishing House, 1998).

57. Lori Beaman, "Labyrinth as Heterotopia: The Pilgrim's Creation of Space," *Religion and the Social Order* 12 (2006): 83–104.

58. See, for example, http://www.unitedchurchinthevalley.ca/labyrinth.php (accessed December 19, 2008) and pamphlet from VST and http://www.labyrinthnetwork.ca/ (accessed December 19, 2008); http://www.labyrinth-enterprises.com/hospitals.html (accessed December 19, 2008); http://www.labyrinthnetwork.ca/torontostar.htm (accessed December 19, 2008). See Ingrid Bloos, "Using a Labyrinth in Spiritual Care," in *Spirituality and Health: Multidisciplinary Explorations*, ed. Augustine Meier, Thomas St. James O'Connor, and Peter Lorens VanKatwyk (Waterloo, ON: Wilfrid Laurier University Press, 2005), 149–166.

59. Charles Rosenberg, "Holism in Twentieth Century Medicine," in *Greater than the Parts: Holism in Biomedicine, 1920–1950*, ed. Christopher Lawrence and George Weisz (New York: Oxford University Press, 1998), 344.

60. Christian Medical Commission, *Healing and Wholeness: The Churches' Role in Health* (Geneva: World Council of Churches, 1990), 9.

61. There are many hostile conservative (and some mainstream) Christian accounts of the Canberra and Minneapolis gatherings on the Internet. For a range of other accounts of Chung's ritual performances, see Harvey Cox, *Fire

from Heaven: The Rise of Pentecostal Spirituality and the Reshaping of Religion in the 21st Century (Cambridge, MA: Da Capo Press, 2001), 213–242; Kirsteen Kim, *The Holy Spirit in the World: A Global Conversation* (Maryknoll, NY: Orbis Books, 2007).

62. Consultation on Faith, Healing, and Mission, http://www.oikoumene.org/en/resources/documents/wcc-commissions/mission-and-evangelism/08-12-02-consultation-on-faith-healing-and-mission-ghana.html (accessed December 3, 2008).

63. The authors of "The Healing Mission of the Church" advise that they are in agreement with earlier version of WCC statements on healing, including that of *Healing and Wholeness*, and that their paper should be read in conjunction with another WCC paper, "Mission as Ministry of Reconciliation," which urges Christians to repent for the "sin of violent colonization in the name of the Gospel." This recognition of colonialism is not part of "The Healing Mission of the Church." "The Healing Mission of the Church: Preparatory Paper No. 11," prepared for the WCC Commission on World Mission and Evangelism World Conference, Athens 2005, http://www.oikoumene.org/en/resources/documents/wcc-commissions/mission-and-evangelism/cwme-world-conference-athens-2005/preparatory-paper-n-11-the-healing-mission-of-the-church.html (accessed December 3, 2008); http://www.oikoumene.org/en/resources/documents/wcc-commissions/mission-and-evangelism/cwme-world-conference-athens-2005/preparatory-paper-n-10-mission-as-ministry-of-reconciliation.html (accessed December 3, 2008).

64. "The Healing Mission of the Church," 13

65. Ibid., 14. For a longer history of the interaction of traditional West African and Christian views of the spirit and exorcism, see Birgit Meyer, *Translating the Devil: Religion and Modernity among the Ewe in Ghana* (Edinburgh: Edinburgh University Press, 1999).

66. Aram I, "Healing: Empowering, Transforming, and Reconciling Act of God," http://www.oikoumene.org/en/resources/documents/wcc-commissions/mission-and-evangelism/cwme-world-conference-athens-2005/preparatory-paper-n-12-healing.html , accessed December 3, 2008.

67. On "affective communities" see Leela Gandhi, *Affective Communities: Anticolonial Thought, Fin de Siecle Radicalism, and the Politics of Friendship* (Durham: Duke University Press, 2006). For another perspective on Christian openness to religious difference see "Report on the Consultation 'What Difference does Religious Plurality Make?'" in *Shared Learning in a Plural World*, ed. Gerd Rueppell and Peter Schreiner (Piscataway, NJ: Transaction, 2003), 158–166.

68. Stan McKay and Janet Silman, *The First Nations: A Canadian Experience of the Gospel-Culture Encounter* (Geneva: World Council of Churches Publications, 1995).

69. For an earlier West Coast example see, Susan Neylan, *The Heavens Are Changing: Nineteenth-Century Protestant Missions and Tsimshian Christianity* (Montreal and Kingston: McGill-Queen's University Press, 2003). See also, James Treat, *Native and Christian: Indigenous Voices on Religious Identity in the United States and Canada* (New York: Routledge, 1996).

70. Ernie Willie, "Cree Priest Was Healer in Last Years of Ministry," *Canadian Churchman* (February 1977). A fuller version of Ahenakew's story is found in Alice Ahenakew, *Âh-âyîtaw isi ê-kî-kiskêyihtahkik maskihkiy [They Knew Both Sides of Medicine: Cree Tales of Curing and Cursing]*, ed., trans., and with a glossary by H. C. Wolfart and Freda Ahenakew (Winnipeg: University of Manitoba Press, 2000). Ahenakew's story is also prominent in Janet Hodgson and Jayant S. Kothare. *Vision Quest: Native Spirituality & the Church in Canada* (Toronto: Anglican Book Centre, 1990).

71. Salteaux's granddaughter, Beatrice, a United Church minister, brought First Nations rituals even more directly into her Christian services. See Tracy Trothen, "Canadian Women's Religious Issues," in *Encyclopedia of Women and Religion in North America*, ed. Rosemary Skinner Keller and Rosemary Radford Ruether (Bloomington: Indiana University Press, 2006), 1286–1287.

72. On the Jessie Saulteaux Resource Centre, see Melody McKellar, "The Talking Circle: A Model for Dialogue," in *Shared Learning in a Plural World*, ed. Gerd Rueppell and Peter Schreiner (Piscataway, NJ: Transaction, 2003), 93–97; and http://www.mts.net/~drjessie/ (accessed January 12, 2009).

73. Stan McKay, "First Peoples and the Churches: For Generations Yet to Come," The Cousland Lecture, Emmanuel College, Toronto, Ontario, March 7, 2007.

74. See http://www.youtube.com/watch?v=5Fns64BEtFA&feature=channel (accessed January 12, 2009).

75. Stan McKay, "An Aboriginal Christian Perspective on the Integrity of Creation," in Treat, *Native and Christian*, 51–55. See also, McKay and Silman, *The First Nations*; Louis Bird, *The Spirit Lives in the Mind: Omushkego Stories, Lives, and Dreams* (Montreal and Kingston: McGill-Queen's University Press, 2007); Eugene Richard Atleo (Umeek). *Tsawalk: A Nuu-chah-nulth Worldview* (Vancouver: University of British Columbia Press, 2004).

76. Robert Smith, "Apology to First Nations Peoples (1986)," http://www.united-church.ca/beliefs/policies/1986/a651 (accessed December 18, 2008).

77. http://www.united-church.ca/funding/healing (accessed December 18, 2008); http://generalsynod.anglican.ca/ministries/departments/mm/2005/winter/mm10.html (accessed December 18, 2008). Both Anglicans and United Churches are participating in the work of the Canadian Truth and Reconciliation Committee that began in 2008, joining South African, Guatemalan, and Rwandan precursors in a postcolonial embodiment of the desire to heal history through testimonial rather than violence. Marlene Brant Castellano, Linda Archibald, and Mike DeGagné, *From Truth to Reconciliation: Transforming the Legacy of Residential Schools* (Ottawa: Aboriginal Healing Foundation, 2008); Kevin Lewis O'Neill, "Writing Guatemala's Genocide: Truth and Reconciliation Commission Reports and Christianity," *Journal of Genocide Research* 7, no. 3 (2005): 331–349.

78. For discussions of syncretism, see Wade Clark Roof, "Religious Borderlands: Challenges for Future Study" *Journal for the Scientific Study of Religion* 37, no. 1 (1998): 1–14; Stewart and Shaw, *Syncretism/Anti-syncretism*; Andre Droogers, "Syncretism: The Problem of Definition, the Definition of the Problem," in: Jerald Gort, Hendrik Vroom, Rein Fernhout, and Anton Wessels, *Dia-*

logue and Syncretism: An Interdisciplinary Approach (Amsterdam: Editions Rodopi, 1989); David Frankfurter, "Syncretism and the Holy Man in Late Antique Egypt," *Journal of Early Christian Studies* 11, no. 3 (2003): 339–385.

79. Richard King, *Orientalism and Religion: Postcolonial Theory, India and the "Mystic East"* (London and New York: Routledge, 1999), 142. See also Thomas Tweed, "Who is a Buddhist? Night-Stand Buddhists and Other Creatures," in Charles Prebish and M. Baumann, *Westward Dharma: Buddhism beyond Asia* (Berkeley: University of California Press, 2002); Milton J. Coalter, John M. Mulder, and Louis B. Weeks, *Vital Signs: The Promise of Mainstream Protestantism* (Grand Rapids, MI: Eerdmans, 1996); D. McMahan, "Repackaging Zen for the West," in Prebish and Baumann, *Westward Dharma;* Sita Ram Goel, *Pseudosecularism, Christian Missions, and Hindu Resistance* (New Delhi: Voice of India, 1998); M. Dhavamony, *Hindu-Christian Dialogue: Theological Soundings and Perspectives* (Amsterdam: Rodopi, 2002); P. Guptara and A. Osmaston, *Yoga—A Christian Option?* (Cambridge: Grove Books, 1987).

80. For a range of perspectives, see Bron Taylor, "Earthen Spirituality or Cultural Genocide: Radical Environmentalism Appropriation of Native American Spirituality," *Religion* 17, no. 2 (1997): 183–215; Robert Young, *Colonial Desire: Hybridity in Theory, Culture and Race* (London: Routledge, 1995); Dhavamony, *Hindu-Christian Dialogue*, 168.

81. Stewart and Shaw, *Syncretism/Anti-Syncretism*, 7.

82. King, *Orientalism and Religion*, 84, 142.

83. Birgit Meyer, *Translating the Devil*; Webb Keane, "Sincerity, 'Modernity', and the Protestants" *Cultural Anthropology* 17, no. 1 (2002), 65–92. Webb Keane, *Christian Moderns: Freedom and Fetish in the Mission Encounter* (Berkeley: University of California Press, 2007), 5, 145. See also Matthew Engelke, *A Problem of Presence: Beyond Scripture in an African Church* (Berkeley: University of California Press, 2007).

84. Bill Phipps, "Apology to Former Students of United Church Indian Residential Schools, and to Their Families and Communities" 1998, http://www.united-church.ca/beliefs/policies/1998/a623, accessed February 1, 2011.

85. Bender, *The New Metaphysicals*.

86. See also Coleman and Elsner, "Tradition as Play."

87. Roof, "Religious Borderlands," 13.

CONCLUSION: CRITICAL CONDITION

1. Marilynne Robinson, "Onward, Christian Liberals," *The American Scholar* 75, no. 2 (2006): 51.

2. Robinson, "Onward, Christian Liberals," 48–49.

3. George Marsden, *Fundamentalism and American Culture*. 2nd ed. (New York: Oxford University Press, 2006), 202.

4. Donald A. Luidens, Dean R. Hoge, and Benton Johnson, "Lay Liberalism among Baby Boomers," *Theology Today* 51, no. 2 (1994): 249–55. For a self-consciously "mainstream Protestant" critique of lay liberalism as "a methodology [that] erodes both the basis of the gospel and the confidence to proclaim it," see Milton J. Coalter, John M. Mulder, and Louis B. Weeks, *Vital Signs: The*

Promise of Mainstream Protestantism (Grand Rapids, MI: Eerdmans, 1996), 129.

5. Other novelists known for their insightful (if often ribald) portrayals of liberal Christianity include the U.S. writer John Updike and the Canadian writer Robertson Davies. Scholarly defenders of liberalism include Leigh Schmidt and Gary Dorrien.

6. Monica Furlong, "With Love to the Church," in *The Restless Church: A Response to* The Comfortable Pew, ed. William Kilbourn (Toronto: McClelland and Stewart, 1966), 45. See also, Monica Furlong, *Genuine Fake: A Biography of Alan Watts* (London, Heinemann, 1986).

7. Furlong, "With Love to the Church," 46–47.

8. This history is well documented by James Treat in *Around the Sacred Fire: Native Religious Activism in the Red Power Era* (New York: Palgrave Macmillan/St. Martin's Press, 2003). Unlike historian Alan Hayes, who criticizes Hendry for his top-down nonconsultative mode, Treat describes Hendry's report as both "radical" and consultative of Native peoples. Alan L. Hayes, *Anglicans in Canada: Controversies and Identity in Historical Perspective* (Urbana and Chicago: University of Illinois Press, 2004).

9. Charles E. Hendry, *Beyond Traplines: Does the Church Really Care? Towards an Assessment of the Work of the Anglican Church of Canada with Canada's Native Peoples* (Toronto: The Ryerson Press, 1969), 83.

10. Courtney Jung, "Canada and the Legacy of the Indian Residential Schools: Transitional Justice for Indigenous People in a Non-Transitional Society" (April 8, 2009). Available at SSRN: http://ssrn.com/abstract=1374950 (accessed May 22, 2009).

11. On the "living apology" see http://www2.anglican.ca/rs/index.htm (accessed February 13, 2009). The full texts of the settlement can be found at http://www.residentialschoolsettlement.ca/settlement.html (accessed February 13, 2009).

12. Mark MacDonald, quoted in Marites N. Sison, "Churches Urged to Be 'on the Record' about Their Role in Residential Schools." *Anglican Journal* (January 10, 2008).

13. Arjun Appadurai, *Fear of Small Numbers: An Essay on the Geography of Anger* (Durham: Duke University Press, 2006), 136–137.

14. A. B. McKillop, *A Disciplined Intelligence: Critical Inquiry and Canadian Thought in the Victorian Era* (Montreal: McGill-Queen's University Press, 1979); Michel Foucault, "What is Critique?" in *The Politics of Truth*, ed. Sylvère Lotringer (Los Angeles: Semiotext(e), 2007), 50.

15. Michel Foucault quoted and translated by Ruth Marshall, *Political Spiritualities: The Pentecostal Revolution in Nigeria* (Chicago: University of Chicago Press, 2009), 46. See also Foucault, "What is Critique?"

16. Adam Gopnik uses the phrase "tragic consciousness" in *Angels and Ages: A Short Book about Darwin, Lincoln, and Modern Life* (New York: Random House, 2009). David Kim uses the phrase "melancholic freedom" to describe the "religious dimensions of projects of regenerating agency" in David Kyuman Kim, *Melancholic Freedom: Agency and the Spirit of Politics* (New York: Oxford University Press, 2007), 21.

17. For example, Elizabeth Povinelli offers a more pessimistic view of the process of reconciliation and atonement in the Australian context: "Mitigating the ongoing failures of the liberal common law through acts of public contrition and atonement simply provides a means of building a newer, deeper form of national self-regard and pride, a form freed from its tragic siblings, imperialism, totalitarianism, fascism." Elizabeth A. Povinelli, "Settler Modernity and the Quest for an Indigenous Tradition," in Dilip Parameshwar Gaonkar, *Alternative Modernities* (Durham: Duke University Press, 2001), 42.

18. See for example the work of the "10-40 Window" movement that directs its medical missions and healing prayer to those "lost" peoples living between 10° and 40° degrees north of the equator, between North Africa and China http://www.1040window.org/ (accessed February 13, 2009).

19. Other movements in which Canadian Anglicans and United Church members were central could provide further evidence, such coalitions pushing for divestment from South Africa in opposition to apartheid, the debate over the Mackenzie Valley pipeline in northern Canada, Nicaraguan and El Salvadorean solidarity movements, and, more recently, environmental justice movements.

20. See Alastair V. Campbell, *Health as Liberation: Medicine, Theology, and the Quest for Justice* (Cleveland: Pilgrim Press, 1995).

21. Miranda Hassett, *Anglican Communion in Crisis: How Episcopal Dissidents and Their African Allies Are Reshaping Anglicanism* (Princeton, N.J.: Princeton University Press, 2007); Mary-Jane Rubenstein, "Anglicans in the Postcolony: On Sex and the Limits of Communion," *Telos* 143 (Summer 2008): 133–160; Thomas Oden, *Turning Around the Mainline: How Renewal Movements Are Changing the Church* (Grand Rapids, MI: Baker Books, 2006). For a Canadian Anglican perspective on the debate over sexuality, see the letter by the Primate, Fred Hiltz, http://news.anglican.ca/news/stories/2026 (accessed February 13, 2009).

22. Catherine Gidney. *A Long Eclipse: The Liberal Protestant Establishment and the Canadian University, 1920–1970* (Montreal and Kingston: McGill-Queen's University Press, 2004), 148. For a more alarmed view, in which the demographic decline of Christianity in Canada is an indication that "our very civility is threatened," see Kurt Bowen, *Christians in a Secular World: The Canadian Experience* (Montreal and Kingston: McGill-Queen's University Press, 2004), 288.

23. For a discussion of anti-Semitism in twentieth-century Canadian Protestantism, see Alan Davies and Marilyn F. Nefsky, *How Silent were the Churches: Canadian Protestantism and the Jewish Plight during the Nazi Era* (Waterloo: Wilfrid Laurier Press, 1997).

24. Saba Mahmood, *The Politics of Piety: The Islamic Revival and the Feminist Subject* (Princeton, N.J.: Princeton University Press, 2005). See also, Saba Mahmood, "Secularism, Hermeneutics, and Empire: The Politics of Islamic Reformation," *Public Culture* 18, no. 2 (2006).

25. Aisha Khan, "Good to Think? Creolization, Optimism, and Agency," *Current Anthropology* 48, no. 5 (2007): 654.

26. Webb Keane, "Sincerity, 'Modernity,' and the Protestants," *Cultural Anthropology* 17, no. 1 (2002): 83.

27. Sheldon Pollock, Homi K. Bhabha, and Carol Appadurai Breckenridge, "Cosmopolitanisms," in *Cosmopolitanism*, ed. Carol Appadurai Breckenridge, Sheldon Pollock, Homi K. Bhabha (Durham: Duke University Press, 2002), 10.

28. Martin Marty, *Righteous Empire: The Protestant Experience in America* (New York: Dial Press, 1970).

Archives Consulted

Burke Library Archives, Union Theological Seminary, Columbia University Libraries

Diocesan Archives, Diocese of Toronto, Anglican Church of Canada

General Synod Archives, Anglican Church of Canada, Toronto

Mary Baker Eddy Library Archives, Boston

Special Collections, Doris Lewis Rare Book Room, University of Waterloo

Special Collections, Yale Divinity School Library

Trinity College Archives, University of Toronto

United Church of Canada Archives, Toronto

Vancouver School of Theology Archives

Selected Bibliography

Ahenakew, Alice. *Âh-âyîtaw isi ê-kî-kiskêyihtahkik maskihkiy = They knew both sides of medicine: Cree Tales of Curing and Cursing*, edited, translated, and with a glossary by H. C. Wolfart and Freda Ahenakew. Winnipeg: University of Manitoba Press, 2000.

Airhart, Phyllis D. "As Canadian as Possible Under the Circumstances: Reflections on the Study of Protestantism in North America." In *New Directions in American Religious History*, edited by Harry Stout and D. G. Hart, 116–40. New York: Oxford University Press, 1997.

———. *Serving the Present Age: Revivalism, Progressivism, and the Methodist Tradition in Canada*. Montreal and Kingston: McGill-Queens University Press, 1992.

———, and Roger C. Hutchinson. "Christianizing the Social Order: A Founding Vision of the United Church of Canada." Special Issue of *Toronto Journal of Theology* 12, no. 2 (1996).

Albanese, Catherine L. *A Republic of Mind and Spirit: A Cultural History of American Metaphysical Religion*. New Haven: Yale University Press, 2007.

———. *Nature Religion in America*. Chicago: University of Chicago Press, 1990.

Allen, Richard. *The View from the Murney Tower: Salem Bland, the late Victorian Controversies, and the Search for A New Christianity*. Toronto: University of Toronto Press, 2008.

Anderson, Benedict. *Imagined Communities: Reflections on the Origin and Spread of Nationalism*. London: Verso, 2006 [1983].

Anderson, Warwick. *Colonial Pathologies: American Tropical Medicine, Race, and Hygiene in the Philippines*. Durham: Duke University Press, 2006.

Appadurai, Arjun. *Fear of Small Numbers: An Essay on the Geography of Anger*. Durham: Duke University Press, 2006.

———. "The Past as a Scarce Resource." *Man (N.S.)* 16 (1981): 201–19.

————, Paul Gilroy, and V. Bell. "Historical Memory, Global Movements and Violence." *Theory, Culture, and Society* 16, no. 2 (1999): 21–40.

Appasamy, Dewan Bahadur A. S. *The Use of Yoga in Prayer.* Madras: The Christian Literature Society for India, 1926.

Appiah, Anthony. *Cosmopolitanism: Ethics in a World of Strangers.* New York: W.W. Norton, 2006.

Arendt, Hannah. *The Human Condition.* Chicago: University of Chicago Press, 1958.

Asad, Talal. *Formations of the Secular: Christianity, Islam, Modernity.* Stanford, CA: Stanford University Press, 2003.

————. *Genealogies of Religion: Discipline and Reasons of Power in Christianity and Islam.* Baltimore: Johns Hopkins University Press, 1993.

Austin, Alvyn. *Saving China: Canadian Missionaries in the Middle Kingdom, 1888–1959.* Toronto: University of Toronto Press, 1986.

————, and Jamie Scott. *Canadian Missionaries, Indigenous Peoples: Representing Religion at Home and Abroad.* Toronto: University of Toronto Press, 2005.

Balmer, Randall. *Grant Us Courage: Travels Along the Mainline of American Protestantism.* Oxford: Oxford University Press, 1996.

Bederman, Gail. "The Women Have Had Control of the Churchwork Long Enough: The Men and Religion Forward Movement of 1911–1912 and the Masculinization of Middle Class Protestantism." In *A Mighty Baptism: Race, Gender, and the Creation of American Protestantism*, edited by Susan Juster and Lisa MacFarlane, 107–40. Ithaca, NY: Cornell University Press, 1996.

Bellah, Robert. *Beyond Belief: Essays on Religion in a Post-Traditional World.* New York: Harper & Row, 1970.

Bender, Courtney. *The New Metaphysicals: Spirituality and the American Religious Imagination.* Chicago: University of Chicago Press, 2010.

————, and Pamela Klassen, eds. *After Pluralism: Reimagining Models of Religious Engagement.* New York: Columbia University Press, 2010.

Bendroth, Margaret Lamberts, and Virginia Lieson Brereton, eds. *Women and Twentieth-Century Protestantism.* Urbana and Chicago: University of Illinois Press, 2002.

Benn, Christoph, and Erlinda Senturias. "Health, Healing, and Wholeness in the Ecumenical Discussion." *International Review of Missions* 90, no. 356/357 (2001): 7–25.

Bergson, Henri. *Mind-Energy.* New York: Henry Holt, 1920.

Bhabha, Homi. *The Location of Culture.* London: Routledge, 1994.

Bland, Salem Goldworth. *The New Christianity or the Religion of the New Age.* Toronto: McClelland and Stewart, 1920.

Boddy, Janice. "Spirit Possession Revisited: Beyond Instrumentality." *Annual Review of Anthropology* 23 (1994): 407–434.

Bonnell, John Sutherland. *Do You Want to Be Healed?* New York: Harper & Row, 1968.

Bonner, Hypatia Bradlaugh. *Christianizing the Heathen: First-Hand Evidence Concerning Overseas Missions.* London: Watts and Co., 1922.

Bowen, Kurt. *Christians in a Secular World: The Canadian Experience.* Montreal and Kingston: McGill-Queen's University Press, 2004.

Brouwer, Ruth Compton. *Modern Women Modernizing Men: The Changing Missions of Three Professional Women in Asian and Africa, 1902–69.* Vancouver: UBC Press, 2002.

Brown, Wendy. *Regulating Aversion: Tolerance in the Age of Identity and Empire.* Princeton: Princeton University Press, 2006.

Browning, Don. "Immanence and Transcendence in Pastoral Care and Preaching." In *The Treasure of Earthen Vessels: Essays in Theological Anthropology,* edited by Brian H. Childs and David W. Waanders, 123–136. Louisville, KY: John Knox, 1994.

Bucke, Maurice. *Cosmic Consciousness: A Study in the Evolution of the Human Mind.* Philadelphia: Innes, 1901.

Bull, Malcolm. "Medicalization and Secularization" *The British Journal of Sociology,* 41, no. 2 (June 1990): 245–261.

Bultmann, Rudolf. *History and Eschatology: The Presence of Eternity. Gifford Lectures.* Edinburgh: University Press, 1957.

Burkinshaw, Robert K. *Pilgrims in Lotus Land: Conservative Protestantism in British Columbia, 1917–1981.* Montreal and Kingston: McGill-Queen's University Press, 1995.

Burrows, Bob. *Healing in the Wilderness: A History of the United Church Mission Hospitals.* Madeira Park, BC: Harbour Publishing, 2004.

Butler, Judith. "The Sensibility of Critique: Response to Asad and Mahmood." In *Is Critique Secular? Blasphemy, Injury, and Free Speech,* edited by Talal Asad, Judith Butler, Saba Mahmood, and Wendy Brown, 101–136. Berkeley: The Townsend Center for the Humanities, University of California, Berkeley, 2009.

Cabot, Richard C., and Russell L. Dicks. *The Art of Ministering to the Sick.* New York: Macmillan, 1959 [1936].

Cannell, Fenella. "The Christianity of Anthropology." *Journal of the Royal Anthropological Institute* 11, no. 2 (2005): 335–356.

Carrington, Philip. *The Anglican Church in Canada.* Toronto: Collins, 1963.

Carter, Sarah. *Capturing Women: The Manipulation of Cultural Imagery in Canada's Prairie West.* Montreal and Kingston: McGill-Queen's University Press, 1997.

Chakrabarty, Dipesh. *Habitations of Modernity: Essays in the Wake of Subaltern Studies.* Chicago: University of Chicago Press, 2002.

———. "Minority Histories, Subaltern Pasts." *Postcolonial Studies* 1, no. 1 (1998): 15–29.

Chauncey, George. "Christian Brotherhood or Sexual Perversion: Homosexual Identities and the Construction of Sexual Boundaries in the World War I Era." In *Sexual Borderlands: Constructing an American Sexual Past,* edited by Kathleen Kennedy and Sharon Rena Ullman, 187–217. Columbus, OH: Ohio State University Press, 2003.

Christie, Nancy. "Sacred Sex: The United Church and the Privatization of the Family in Postwar Canada." In *Households of Faith: Family, Gender and Community in Canada, 1760–1969,* edited by Nancy Christie, 348–376. Montreal and Kingston: McGill-Queen's University Press, 2002.

———, and Michael Gauvreau. *A Full-Orbed Christianity: The Protestant Churches and Social Welfare in Canada, 1900–1940.* Montreal and Kingston: McGill-Queen's University Press, 1996.

Church of England. *A Time to Heal: A Report for the House of Bishops on the Healing Ministry.* London: Church House Publishing, 2000.

Clarke, Brian. "English Speaking Canada from 1854." In *A Concise History of Christianity in Canada,* edited by Terrence Murphy and Roberto Perin, 261–360. Oxford: Oxford University Press, 1996.

Coalter, Milton J., John M. Mulder, and Louis B. Weeks. *Vital Signs: The Promise of Mainstream Protestantism.* Grand Rapids, MI: Eerdmans, 1996.

Coleman, Simon, and Jon Elsner. "Tradition as Play: Pilgrimage to 'England's Nazareth.'" *History and Anthropology* 15, no. 3 (2004): 273–288.

Comaroff, Jean. *Body of Power, Spirit of Resistance: The Culture and History of a South African People.* Chicago: University of Chicago Press, 1985.

Comaroff, John L., and Jean Comaroff. *Of Revelation and Revolution: The Dialectics of Modernity on a South African Frontier,* vol. 2. Chicago: University of Chicago Press, 1997.

Cook, Ramsey. *The Regenerators: Social Criticism in Late Victorian English Canada.* Toronto: University of Toronto Press, 1985.

Cox, Harvey. *Fire from Heaven: The Rise of Pentecostal Spirituality and the Reshaping of Religion in the 21st Century.* Cambridge, MA: Da Capo Press, 2001.

———. *The Secular City: Secularization and Urbanization in Theological Perspective.* New York: Macmillan, 1965.

Creech, Joe. "Visions of Glory: The Place of the Azusa Street Revival in Pentecostal History." *Church History* 63, no. 3 (1996): 405–424.

Csordas, Thomas J. *Body/Meaning/Healing.* New York: Palgrave Macmillan, 2002.

———. *The Sacred Self: A Cultural Phenomenology of Charismatic Healing.* Berkeley: University of California Press, 1994.

Cunningham, Raymond J. "From Holiness to Healing: The Faith Cure in America, 1872–1892." *Church History* 43, no. 4 (1974): 499–513.

———. "James Moore Hickson and Spiritual Healing in the American Episcopal Church." *Historical Magazine of the Protestant Episcopal Church* 39, no. 1 (1970): 2–16.

———. "The Emmanuel Movement: A Variety of American Religious Experience." *American Quarterly* 14, no. 1 (1962): 48–63.

———. "The Impact of Christian Science on the American Churches, 1880–1910." *The American Historical Review* 72, no. 3 (1967): 885–905.

Curtis, Heather. *Faith in the Great Physician.* Baltimore: Johns Hopkins University Press, 2007.

Dean, Joanna. *Religious Experience and the New Woman: The Life of Lily Dougall.* Bloomington: Indiana University Press, 2006.

Dearmer, Nancy. *The Life of Percy Dearmer.* London: Book Club, 1941.

Dearmer, Percy, ed. *Christianity and the Crisis.* London: Victor Gollancz, 1933.

———, ed., *The Fellowship of the Picture: An Automatic Script Taken Down by Nancy Dearmer.* New York: E. P. Dutton, 1920.

————. *Body and Soul: An Enquiry into the Effects of Religion upon Health, with a description of Christian Works of Healing from the New Testament to the Present Day*. London: Sir Isaac Pitman & Sons, Ltd., 1910.

————. *Everyman's History of the Prayer Book*. London: Mowbray, 1912.

de Certeau, Michel. "The Scriptural Economy." In *The Certeau Reader*, edited by Graham Ward, 158–176. Oxford and Malden, MA: Blackwell Publishers, 2000.

de Vries, Hent, ed. *Religion: Beyond a Concept: The Future of the Religious Past*. New York: Fordham University Press, 2008.

Dobell, Miriam. *Healing Happens: Experiences in the Church's Ministry of Healing*. Toronto: Anglican Book Centre, 1982.

Dorrien, Gary. "American Liberal Theology: Crisis, Irony, Decline, Renewal, Ambiguity." *Cross Currents* 55 (2006): 456–481.

————. *The Making of American Liberal Theology: Crisis, Irony, and Postmodernity, 1950–2005*. Louisville, KY: Westminster John Knox, 2006.

Dougall, Lily. *The Christian Doctrine of Health: A Handbook on the Relation of Bodily to Spiritual and Moral Health*. London: Macmillan, 1916.

Douglas, Mary. "Anthropology in the Old Testament." In *Anchor Bible Dictionary*, edited by David Noel Freedman. Toronto: Doubleday, 1992.

Droogers, Andre. "Syncretism: The Problem of Definition, the Definition of the Problem." in *Dialogue and Syncretism: An Interdisciplinary Approach*, edited by Jerald Gort, Hendrik Vroom, Rein Fernhout, and Anton Wessels, 7–25. Amsterdam: Editions Rodopi, 1989.

Dumont, Louis. *Essays on Individualism: Modern Ideology in Anthropological Perspective*. Chicago: University of Chicago Press, 1986.

Du Vernet, Frederick. *Out of a Scribe's Treasure*. Toronto: Ryerson Press, 1927.

————. *Spiritual Radio*. Mountain Lakes, NJ: The Society of the Nazarene, 1925.

DuVernet, Sylvia, ed. *Portrait of a Personality: Archbishop Frederick Herbert DuVernet*. Toronto: Sylvia DuVernet, 1987.

Dyck, Ian. "Founding of the Anthropology Division at the National Museum of Canada: An Intertwining of Science, Religion, and Politics." In *Revelations: Bi-Millennial Papers from the Canadian Museum of Civilization*, edited by Robert B. Klymasz and John Willis, 3–34. Hull, QC: Canadian Museum of Civilization, 2001.

Eddy, Sherwood. *Doubt or Practical Suggestions for Those Having Intellectual Difficulties Regarding the Christian Faith*. New York: Association Press, 1920.

————. *Eighty Adventurous Years: An Autobiography*. New York: Harper, 1955.

————. *Facing the Crisis: A Study in Present Day Social and Religious Problems*. New York: Association Press, 1922.

————. *The New Era in Asia*. New York: Missionary Education Movement of the United States and Canada, 1913.

————. *You Will Survive After Death*. Surrey: Omega Press, 1954.

Edwards, Gail. "'The Picturesqueness of His Accent and Speech': Methodist Missionary Narratives and William Henry Pierce's Autobiography." In

Canadian Missionaries, Indigenous Peoples: Representing Religion at Home and Abroad, edited by Alvyn Austin and Jamie S. Scott, 67–86. Toronto: University of Toronto Press, 2005.

Elbourne, Elizabeth. *Blood Ground: Colonialism, Missions, and the Contest for Christianity in the Cape Colony and Britain, 1799–1853.* Montreal and Kingston: McGill-Queen's University Press, 2002.

Engelke, Matthew. *A Problem of Presence: Beyond Scripture in an African Church.* Berkeley: University of California Press, 2007.

———, ed. *The Objects of Evidence.* Oxford and Malden, MA: Wiley-Blackwell, 2008.

Fairbairn, R. Edis. *Faith Healing.* Toronto: Ryerson Press, 1923.

Falby, Alison. "The Modern Confessional: Anglo-American Religious Groups and the Emergence of Lay Psychotherapy." *Journal of History of the Behavioral Sciences* 39, no. 3 (2003): 251–267.

Farmer, Paul. *Pathologies of Power.* Berkeley: University of California Press, 2004.

Fairweather, Eugene R. "Christianity and the Supernatural: I. The Meaning of the Supernatural" *Canadian Journal of Theology* 9, no. 1 (1963), 12–19.

Fairweather, Eugene R. "Christianity and the Supernatural II. Historical Notes on Christian Supernaturalism" *Canadian Journal of Theology* 9, no. 1 (1963), 95–102.

Fast, Kerry. "But What a Strange Commixture Am I": Borders of Self and Religion in the Making of Women's Lives. PhD Dissertation, University of Toronto, 2008.

Faure, Bernard. *Double Exposure: Cutting Across Buddhist and Western Discourses,* translated by Janet Lloyd. Stanford: Stanford University Press, 2004.

Flatt, Kevin. "The Survival and Decline of the Evangelical Identity of the United Church of Canada, 1930–1971." PhD Dissertation, McMaster University, 2008.

Foucault, Michel. *The Birth of the Clinic: An Archaeology of Medical Perception.* New York: Vintage Books, 1975.

Foucault, Michel. "The Crisis of Medicine or Antimedicine?" *Foucault Studies* 1 (2004): 5–19.

———. *History of Sexuality.* New York: Vintage Books, 1980.

———. *Introduction to Kant's Anthropology.* Los Angeles: Semiotext(e), 2008.

———, and Ludwig Binswanger. *Dream and Existence,* translated by Jacob Needleman. Atlantic Highlands, NJ: Humanities Press International, 1986.

Fox, Richard Wightman. "The Culture of Liberal Protestant Progressivism, 1875–1925." *Journal of Interdisciplinary History* 23, no. 3 (1993): 639–660.

———. "The Niebuhr Brothers and the Liberal Protestant Heritage." In *Religion and Twentieth-Century American Intellectual Life,* edited by Michael J. Lacey, 94–115. Cambridge: Cambridge University Press, 1989.

———. *Reinhold Niebuhr: A Biography.* 2nd ed. Ithaca, NY: Cornell University Press, 1996.

Frankfurter, David. "Syncretism and the Holy Man in Late Antique Egypt." *Journal of Early Christian Studies* 11, no. 3 (2003): 339–385.

Freeman, E. G. D. "The Church and Social Reconstruction." In *Four Addresses of the Church of the Air Series*. Toronto: United Church of Canada, 1941.

Gagan, Rosemary R. *A Sensitive Independence: Canadian Methodist Women Missionaries in Canada and the Orient, 1881–1925*. Montreal and Kingston: McGill-Queen's University Press, 1992.

Gandhi, Leela. *Affective Communities: Anticolonial Thought, Fin de Siecle Radicalism, and the Politics of Friendship*. Durham: Duke University Press, 2006.

Gaonkar, Dilip P. *Alternative Modernities*. Durham: Duke University Press, 2001.

Gardner, Charles. *In Defence of the Faith*. Oxford: Basil Blackwell, 1927.

Garriott, William, and Kevin Lewis O'Neill. "Who is a Christian? Toward a Dialogic Approach in the Anthropology of Christianity," *Anthropological Theory* 8 (2008): 381–398.

Gauvreau, Michael. *The Evangelical Century: College and Creed in English Canada from the Great Revival to the Great Depression*. Montreal: McGill-Queen's University Press, 1991.

George, Carol V. R. *God's Salesman: Norman Vincent Peale and the Power of Positive Thinking*. Oxford: Oxford University Press, 1993.

Gidney, Catherine. *A Long Eclipse: The Liberal Protestant Establishment and the Canadian University*. Montreal and Kingston: McGill-Queen's University Press, 2004.

Gifford, Sanford. *The Emmanuel Movement (Boston, 1904–1929). The Origins of Group Treatment and the Assault on Lay Psychotherapy*. Cambridge, MA: Harvard University Press, 1996.

Gill, Gillian. *Mary Baker Eddy*. Reading, MA: Perseus Books, 1998.

Gitelman, Lisa. *Scripts, Grooves, and Writing Machines: Representing Technology in the Edison Era*. Stanford: Stanford University Press, 1999.

Gordon, Deborah. "Tenacious Assumptions in Western Medicine." In *Biomedicine Examined*, edited by M. Lock and D. Gordon, 19–56. Dordrecht: Kluwer Academic, 1988.

Gottschalk, Stephen. *Rolling Away the Stone. Mary Baker Eddy's Challenge to Materialism*. Bloomington: Indiana University Press, 2006.

———. *The Emergence of Christian Science in American Religious Life*. Berkeley: University of California Press, 1973.

Grant, Gail Paton. "Miracle Lore and Metamorphoses." In *Undisciplined Women: Tradition and Culture in Canada*, edited by Pauline Greenhill and Diane Tye, 203–212. Montreal: McGill-Queen's University Press, 1997.

Grant, John Webster. "Blending Traditions: The United Church of Canada" *Canadian Journal of Theology*, 9(1, 1963), pp. 50–59.

Grant, John Webster. *Moon of Wintertime: Missionaries and the Indians of Canada in Encounter since 1534*. Toronto: University of Toronto Press, 1984.

Gray, Donald. *Percy Dearmer: A Parson's Pilgrimage*. Norwich, Norfolk: Canterbury Press, 2000.

Griffith, R. Marie. *Born Again Bodies: Flesh and Spirit in American Christianity*. Berkeley: University of California Press, 2004.

———. "A 'Network of Praying Women': Women's Aglow Fellowship and Mainline American Protestantism." In *Pentecostal Currents in American Protestantism*, edited by Edith L. Blumhofer, Russell P. Spittler, and Grant A. Wacker, 131–151. Urbana and Chicago: University of Illinois Press, 1999.

———. "The Religious Encounters of Alfred C. Kinsey." *Journal of American History* 95, no. 2 (2008): 349–377.

Hacking, Ian. "Our Neo-Cartesian Body in Parts." *Critical Inquiry* 34 (2007): 78–105.

———. *Rewriting the Soul: Multiple Personality and the Sciences of Memory*. Princeton: Princeton University Press, 1995.

Hale, Nathan G. Jr. *Freud and the Americans: The Beginnings of Psychoanalysis in the United States, 1876–1917*. New York: Oxford University Press, 1971.

Hammond, Sally. *We are All Healers*. New York: Harper & Row, 1973.

Hangen, Tona. *Redeeming the Dial: Radio, Religion, and Popular Culture in America*. Chapel Hill: University of North Carolina Press, 2002.

Hann, Chris. "The Anthropology of Christianity per se" *Archives Européennes de Sociologie* 48, no. 3 (2007), 391–418.

Harper, Margaret Mills. "Nemo: George Yeats and her Automatic Script." *New Literary History* 33 (2002): 291–314.

Harrell, David. *All Things are Possible: The Healing and Charismatic Revivals in Modern America*. Bloomington: Indiana University Press, 1975.

Harrington, Anne. *Reenchanted Science: Holism in German Culture from Wilhelm II to Hitler*. Princeton: Princeton University Press, 1996.

Harrington, Anne. *The Cure Within: A History of Mind-Body Medicine*. New York: W. W. Norton, 2008.

Harris, Thomas A. *I'm OK—You're OK: A Practical Guide to Transactional Analysis*. New York: Harper & Row, 1969.

Harrison, Peter. *The Bible, Protestantism, and the Rise of Natural Science*. Cambridge: Cambridge University Press, 1998.

Hassett, Miranda. *Anglican Communion in Crisis: How Episcopal Dissidents and Their African Allies Are Reshaping Anglicanism*. Princeton, N.J.: Princeton University Press, 2007.

Hatch, Nathan O. "The Puzzle of American Methodism." *Church History* 63, no. 2 (1994): 175–189.

Hau, Michael. "The Holistic Gaze in German Medicine, 1890–1930." *The Bulletin of the History of Medicine* 74 (2000): 495–524.

Hauerwas, Stanley. "Practicing Patience: How Christians Should be Sick." In *Beyond Mere Health: Theology and Health Care in a Secular Society*, edited by Hilary Regan, Rod Horsfield, and Gabrielle McMullen, 80–102. Melbourne: Australia Theological Forum, 1996.

———. "Salvation and Health: Why Medicine Needs the Church." In *The Hauerwas Reader*, edited by John Berkman and Michael Cartwright, 539–555. Durham: Duke University Press, 2001.

Hayes, Alan L. *Anglicans in Canada: Controversies and Identity in Historical Perspective*. Urbana and Chicago: University of Illinois Press, 2004.

Hayward, Rhodri. "Demonology, Neurology, and Medicine in Edwardian Britain." *Bulletin of the History of Medicine* 78, no. 1 (2004): 37–58.

Hein, David, and Gardiner H. Shattuck Jr. *The Episcopalians*. Westport, CT: Praeger, 2004.

Heinze, Andrew. *Jews and the American Soul: Human Nature in the Twentieth Century*. Princeton: Princeton University Press, 2004.

Hilmes, Michele. "Rethinking Radio." In *Radio Reader: Essays in the Cultural History of Radio*, edited by Michele Hilmes and Jason Lovigli, 1–20. New York: Routledge, 2002.

Hiltner, Seward. *"Freud, Psychoanalysis, and Religion."* In *Healing: Human and Divine*, edited by Simon Doniger, 71–100, New York: Association Press, 1957.

———. *Religion and Health*. New York: Macmillan, 1943.

Hocking, William Ernest. *Human Nature and Its Remaking*. New, rev. ed. New Haven: Yale University Press, 1923 [1918].

———, and the Commission of Appraisal. *Re-Thinking Missions: A Lay-Man's Inquiry after One Hundred Years*. New York: Harper, 1932.

Holifield, Brooks. *A History of Pastoral Care in America: From Salvation to Self-Realization*. Nashville, TN: Abingdon Press, 1983.

———. *Health and Medicine in the Methodist Tradition: Journey Toward Wholeness*. New York: Crossroad, 1986.

Hollinger, David A. "'Damned for God's Glory': William James and the Scientific Vindication of Protestant Culture." In *William James and a Science of Religion: Reexperiencing the Varieties of Religious Experience*, edited by Wayne Proudfoot, 9–30. New York: Columbia University Press, 2004.

Hollis, Jennifer L. "Healing into Wholeness in the Episcopal Church." In *Religion and Healing in America*, edited by Linda Barnes and Susan Sered, 89–102. Oxford: Oxford University Press, 2005.

Huber, Mary Taylor, and Nancy C. Lutkehaus. *Gendered Missions: Women and Men in Missionary Discourse and Practice*. Ann Arbor: University of Michigan Press, 1999.

Huisman, Frank, and John Harley, eds. *Locating Medical History: The Stories and Their Meanings*. Baltimore: Johns Hopkins University Press, 2004.

Hutchison, William. *Errand to the World: American Protestant Thought and Foreign Missions*. Chicago: University of Chicago Press, 1987.

———. "Liberal Protestantism and the End of Innocence." *American Quarterly* 15, no. 2, part 1 (1963): 126–139.

———. *The Modernist Impulse in American Protestantism*. Durham: Duke University Press, 1992.

Iacovetta, Franca. *Sisters or Strangers? Immigrant, Ethnic, and Racialized Women in Canadian History*. Toronto: University of Toronto Press, 2004.

Illich, Ivan. *Medical Nemesis*. Edinburgh: Edinburgh University Press, 1974.

Jakobsen, Janet R., and Ann Pellegrini, eds. *Secularisms*. Durham: Duke University Press, 2008.

James, William. "The Energies of Men" *Science, N.S.* 25, no. 635 (1907): 321–32.

———. *Pragmatism: A New Name for some Old Ways of Thinking*. New York: Longman Green and Co., 1907.

———. *Pragmatism and Other Writings*, edited by Giles B. Gunn. New York: Penguin Classics, 2000.

———. *The Varieties of Religious Experience: A Study in Human Nature*. Cambridge, MA: Harvard University Press, 1985.

Jardine, Lisa. *Ingenious Pursuits: Building the Scientific Revolution*. London: Little, Brown, 1999.

Jasen, Patricia. "Mind, Medicine, and the Christian Science Controversy in Canada, 1888–1910." *Journal of Canadian Studies* 32, no. 4 (1998): 5–22.

Johnson, Mark. *The Meaning of the Body: Aesthetics of Human Understanding*. Chicago: University of Chicago Press, 2007.

Jung, Courtney. "The Burden of Culture and the Limits of Liberal Responsibility." *Constellations* 8, no. 2 (2001): 219–35.

———. *The Moral Force of Indigenous Politics: Critical Liberalism and the Zapatistas*. New York: Cambridge University Press, 2008.

Kant, Immanuel. *Anthropology from a Pragmatic Point of View*, translated and edited by Robert Louden. Cambridge: Cambridge University Press, 2006.

Katerberg, William H. *Modernity and the Dilemma of North American Anglican Identities, 1880–1950*. Montreal, Kingston: McGill-Queen's University Press, 2001.

Katerberg, William H. "Redefining Evangelicalism in the Canadian Anglican Church: Wycliffe College and the Evangelical Party, 1867–1995." In *Aspects of the Canadian Evangelical Experience*, edited by George Rawlyk, 171–188, McGill-Queen's University Press, 1997.

Keane, Webb. *Christian Moderns: Freedom and Fetish in the Mission Encounter*. Berkeley: University of California Press, 2007.

———. "The Evidence of the Senses and the Materiality of Religion." *Journal of the Royal Anthropological Institute*, 14, no. 1 (2008): 110–127.

———. "Sincerity, 'Modernity,' and the Protestants." *Cultural Anthropology* 17, no. 1 (2002): 65–92.

Keller, Rosemary Skinner, Louise L. Queen, and Hilah F. Thomas, eds. *Women in New Worlds: Historical Perspectives on the Wesleyan Tradition*. Nashville, TN: Abingdon Press, 1982.

Kelm, Mary-Ellen. *Colonizing Bodies: Aboriginal Health and Healing in British Columbia, 1900–1950*. Vancouver: UBC Press, 1998.

Kerin, Dorothy. *The Living Touch*. Tunbridge Wells, UK: KSC Printers, 2002 [1914].

Khan, Aisha. "Good to Think? Creolization, Optimism, and Agency." *Current Anthropology* 48, no. 5 (2007): 653–673.

King, Richard. *Orientalism and Religion: Postcolonial Theory, India and the "Mystic East."* London and New York: Routledge, 1999.

King, William McGuire. "An Enthusiasm for Humanity: The Social Emphasis in Religion and Its Accommodation in Protestant Theology." In *Religion and Twentieth-Century American Intellectual Life*, edited by Michael J. Lacey, 49–77. Cambridge: Cambridge University Press, 1989.

Klassen, Pamela E. *Blessed Events: Religion and Home Birth in America.* Princeton: Princeton University Press, 2001.

———. "Radio Mind: Christian Experimentalists on the Frontiers of Healing." *Journal of the American Academy of Religion* 75, no. 3 (2007): 651–683.

———. "Textual Healing: Mainstream Protestants and the Therapeutic Text, 1900–1925." *Church History* 75, no. 4 (December 2006): 809–848.

Kleinman, Arthur. *Writing at the Margin: Discourse between Anthropology and Medicine.* Berkeley: University of California Press, 1995.

Kollar, Rene. *Searching for Raymond: Anglicanism, Spiritualism, and Bereavement between the Two World Wars.* Lanham, MD: Lexington Books, 2000.

Kosek, Joseph K. *Acts of Conscience: Christian Nonviolence and Modern American Democracy.* New York: Columbia University Press, 2009.

Kripal, Jeffrey. *Esalen: America and the Religion of No Religion.* Chicago: University of Chicago Press, 2007.

Lake, Kirsopp. *The Religion of Yesterday and To-morrow.* Boston: Houghton Mifflin, 1926.

Lambuth, Walter R. *Medical Missions: The Twofold Task.* New York: Student Volunteer Movement for Foreign Missions, 1920.

Lapsley, James N. *Salvation and Health: The Interlocking Processes of Life.* Philadelphia:.Westminster Press, 1972.

Larson, Edward J. *Summer for the Gods: The Scopes Trial and America's Continuing Debate over Science and Religion.* New York: Basic Books, 1997.

Larson, James S. "The World Health Organization's Definition of Health: Social vs. Spiritual Health." *Social Indicators Research* 38 (1996): 181–192.

Latour, Bruno. *We Have Never Been Modern.* Cambridge, MA: Harvard University Press, 1993.

Lawrence, Christopher, and George Weisz, eds. *Greater Than the Parts: Holism in Biomedicine, 1920–1950.* New York: Oxford University Press, 1998.

Laycock, Samuel R. *Pastoral Counselling for Mental Health.* Toronto: The Ryerson Press, 1958.

Lazarus, Barry A. "The Practice of Medicine and Prejudice in a New England Town: The Founding of Mount Sinai Hospital, Hartford, Connecticut." *Journal of American Ethnic History* 10, no. 3 (1991): 21–41.

Lears, T. J. Jackson. *No Place of Grace: Antimodernism and the Transformation of American Culture, 1880–1920.* New York: Pantheon Books, 1981.

Lenoir, Timothy. "Inscription Practices and Materialities of Communication." In *Inscribing Science: Scientific Texts and the Materiality of Communication*, edited by Timothy Lenoir, 1–19. Stanford: Stanford University Press, 1998.

Leys, Ruth. "Traumatic Cures: Shell Shock, Janet, and the Question of Memory." *Critical Inquiry* 20, no. 4 (1994): 623–662.

Litsios, Socrates. "The Christian Medical Commission and the Development of the World Health Organization's Primary Health Care Approach." *American Journal of Public Health* 94, no. 11 (2004): 1884–1893.

Livingstone, Grover. *Through Sickness to Life.* Toronto: The Ryerson Press, 1954.

Lock, Margaret. "Cultivating the Body: Anthropologies and Epistemologies of Bodily Practice and Knowledge." *Annual Review of Anthropology* 22 (1993): 133–155.

———, and Deborah. R. Gordon. *Biomedicine Examined*. Dordrecht and Boston: Kluwer Academic Publishers, 1988.

Loeb, Lori. "Beating the Flu: Orthodox and Commercial Responses to Influenza in Britain, 1889–1919." *Social History of Medicine* 18, no. 2 (August 2005): 203–224.

Louw, D. J. *A Mature Faith: Spiritual Direction and Anthropology in a Theology of Pastoral Care and Counseling*. Louvain: Peeters Publishers, 1999.

Luckhurst, Roger. *The Invention of Telepathy*. Oxford: Oxford University Press, 2002.

Lyon, David, and Marguerite Van Die, eds. *Rethinking Church, State, and Modernity: Canada between Europe and America*. Toronto: University of Toronto Press, 2000.

MacFarlane, Mary Anne. "Faithful and Courageous Handmaidens: Deaconesses in the United Church of Canada, 1925–1945." In *Changing Roles of Women within the Christian Church in Canada*, edited by Elizabeth Gillian Muir and Marilyn Fardig Whiteley, 238–260. Toronto: University of Toronto Press, 1995.

Maffly-Kipp, Laurie F., Leigh E. Schmidt, and Mark Valeri, eds. *Practicing Protestants: Histories of Christian Life in America, 1630–1965*. Baltimore: Johns Hopkins University Press, 2006.

Mahmood, Saba. *The Politics of Piety: The Islamic Revival and the Feminist Subject*. Princeton: Princeton University Press, 2005.

Mao Tse-tung. *Serve the People: In Memory of Norman Bethune; The Foolish Old Man who Removed the Mountains*. Peking: Foreign Languages Press, 1967.

Marcus, George E., ed. *Rereading Cultural Anthropology*. Durham: Duke University Press, 1992.

Marshall, David B. "Canadian Historians, Secularization, and the Problem of the Nineteenth Century." *Historical Studies* 60 (1993–1994): 57–81.

Marshall, Ruth. *Political Spiritualities: The Pentecostal Revolution in Nigeria*. Chicago: University of Chicago Press, 2009.

Martin, Dale. *The Corinthian Body*. New Haven: Yale University Press, 1995.

Marty, Martin E. *The Religious Press in America*. New York: Holt, Rinehart, and Winston, 1963.

———. "Tradition and the Traditions in Health/Medicine and Religion." In *Health/Medicine and the Faith Traditions: An Inquiry into Religion and Medicine*, edited by Martin E. Marty and Kenneth L. Vaux, 3–26. Philadelphia: Fortress, 1982.

Masuzawa, Tomoko. *The Invention of World Religions*. Chicago: University of Chicago Press, 2005.

———. "Troubles with Materiality: The Ghost of Fetishism in the Nineteenth Century." *Comparative Studies in Society and History* 42, no. 2 (2000): 242–267.

May, Rollo. *Paulus: Reminiscences of a Friendship*. New York: Harper & Row, 1973.

McComb, Samuel. "Psychotherapy." In *The New Schaff-Herzog Encyclopedia of Religious Knowledge*, vol. 9. New York: Funk and Wagnalls, 1911.

McGuire, Meredith B., and Debra Kantor. *Ritual Healing in Suburban America*. New Brunswick, NJ: Rutgers University Press, 1988.

McMullin, Stan. *Anatomy of a Séance*. Montreal and Kingston: McGill-Queen's University Press, 2004.

Meador, Keith G. "'My Own Salvation': The Christian Century and Psychology's Secularizing of American Protestantism." In *The Secular Revolution*, edited by Christian Smith, 269–309. Berkeley: University of California Press, 2003.

———, and Shaun C. Henson. "Growing Old in Therapeutic Culture." In *Growing Old in Christ*, edited by Stanley Hauerwas, Carole Bailey Stoneking, and Keith G. Meador, 90–111. Grand Rapids, MI: Eerdmans, 2003.

Meyer, Birgit. *Religious Sensations: Why Media, Aesthetics, and Power Matter in the Study of Contemporary Religion*. Amsterdam: Faculteit der Sociale Wetenschappen, Vrije Universiteit, 2006.

———. *Translating the Devil: Religion and Modernity among the Ewe in Ghana*. Edinburgh: Edinburgh University Press, 1999.

Miedema, Gary R. *For Canada's Sake: Public Religion, Centennial Celebrations, and the Re-making of Canada in the 1960s*. Montreal: McGill-Queen's University Press, 2005.

Milbank, John. "Liberality versus Liberalism." In *Religion and Political Thought*, edited by Michael Hoelzl and Graham Ward, 225–236. New York: Continuum, 2006.

———. *Theology and Social Theory: Beyond Secular Reason*. 2nd ed. Malden and Oxford: Blackwell, 2006.

Miller, Donald E. *Reinventing American Protestantism: Christianity in the New Millennium*. Berkeley: University of California Press, 1997.

Miller, J. R. *Shingwauk's Vision: A History of Native Residential Schools*. Toronto: University of Toronto Press, 1996.

Millet, John A. P. "Body, Mind, and Spirit." *Pastoral Psychology* 1, no. 5 (June 1950): 9–16.

Moore, R. Laurence. *In Search of White Crows: Spiritualism, Parapsychology, and American Culture*. New York: Oxford University Press, 1977.

———. *Religious Outsiders and the Making of Americans*. New York: Oxford University Press, 1986.

Moorshead, R. Fletcher. *The Way of the Doctor: A Study in Medical Missions*. London: The Carey Press, 1926.

Most, Andrea. "The Birth of Theatrical Liberalism." In *After Pluralism: Reimagining Religious Engagement*, edited by Courtney Bender and Pamela Klassen, 127–155. New York: Columbia University Press, 2010.

Mullin, Robert Bruce. *Miracles and the Modern Religious Imagination*. New Haven: Yale University Press, 1996.

———, and Russell E. Richey. *Reimagining Denominationalism: Interpretive Essays*. New York: Oxford University Press, 1994.

Murphey, Murray G. "On the Scientific Study of Religion." In *Religion and Twentieth-Century American Intellectual Life*, edited by Michael J. Lacey, 136–171. Cambridge: Cambridge University Press, 1989.

Myers-Shirk, Susan E. "'To Be Fully Human': U.S. Protestant Psychotherapeutic Culture and the Subversion of the Domestic Ideal, 1945–1965." *Journal of Women's History* 12, no. 1 (2000): 112–136.

Naylor, C. David, ed., *Canadian Health Care and the State*. Montreal and Kingston: McGill-Queens University Press, 1992.

———. *Private Practice, Public Payment: Canadian Medicine and the Politics of Health Insurance, 1911–1966*. Montreal and Kingston: McGill-Queen's University Press, 1986.

Neitz, Mary Jo. *Charisma and Community: A Study of Religious Commitment within the Charismatic Renewal*. New Brunswick, NJ: Transaction Books, 1987.

Nelson, Siobhan. "From Salvation to Civics: Service to the Sick in Nursing Discourse." *Social Science & Medicine* 53, no. 9 (2001): 1217–125.

———. *Say Little, Do Much: Nurses, Nuns, and Hospitals in the Nineteenth Century*. Philadelphia: University of Pennsylvania Press, 2001.

Newbigin, Lesslie. *The Healing Church: The Tuebingen Consultation*. Geneva: World Council of Churches, 1965.

Neylan, Susan. *The Heavens Are Changing: Nineteenth-Century Protestant Missions and Tsimshian Christianity*. Montreal and Kingston: McGill-Queen's Press, 2003.

Niebuhr, Reinhold. *Leaves from the Notebook of a Tamed Cynic*. Louisville, KY: Westminster John Knox Press, 1990 [1929].

Numbers, Ronald, and Darrel W. Amundsen, eds. *Caring and Curing: Health and Medicine in the Western Religious Traditions*. Baltimore, Johns Hopkins University Press, 1998 [1986].

Nutt, Rick. "G. Sherwood Eddy and the Attitudes of Protestants in the United States toward Global Missions." *Church History* 66, no. 3 (1997): 502–521.

———. *The Whole Gospel for the Whole World: Sherwood Eddy and the American Protestant Mission*. Macon, GA: Mercer University Press, 1997.

O'Brien, Mary Elizabeth. *Spirituality in Nursing: Standing on Holy Ground*. Sudbury, MA: Jones and Bartlett, 2003.

Oliver, Belle Choné. *Anandi's Question: For Parents of Little Children*. Madras, Allahabad, Rangoon, and Colombo: Christian Literature Society for India, 1930.

———. *Tales from the Inns of Healing of Christian Medical Service in India, Burma, and Ceylon*. Canadian edition. Toronto: The Committee on Missionary Education, The United Church of Canada, 1944 [1942].

O'Neill, Kevin. *City of God: Christian Citizenship in Guatemala*. Berkeley: University of California Press, 2009.

O'Neill, Kevin L. "Writing Guatemala's Genocide: Truth and Reconciliation Commission Reports and Christianity." *Journal of Genocide Research* 7, no. 3 (2005): 331–349.

Opp, James. *The Lord for the Body: Religion, Medicine, and Protestant Faith Healing in Canada, 1880–1930*. Montreal: McGill-Queen's University Press, 2005.

Orsi, Robert "Snakes Alive: Religious Studies between Heaven and Earth" *Between Heaven and Earth*. Princeton: Princeton University Press, 2006, 177–204.

Orsi, Robert. *Thank You St. Jude: Women's Devotion to the Patron Saint of Hopeless Causes*. New Haven: Yale University Press, 1996.

Osborne, Peter. "Modernity Is a Qualitative, Not a Chronological, Category." *New Left Review*, I, no. 92 (March–April 1992): 65–84.

Ostrander, Rick. *The Life of Prayer in a World of Science: Protestants, Prayer, and American Culture, 1870–1930*. Oxford: Oxford University Press, 2000.

O'Toole, Roger. "Canadian Religion: Heritage and Project." In *Rethinking Church, State, and Modernity*, edited by David Lyon and Marguerite Van Die, 34–51. Toronto: University of Toronto Press, 2000.

Owen, Alex. *The Place of Enchantment: British Occultism and the Culture of the Modern*. Chicago: University of Chicago Press, 2004.

Pearce-Higgins, J. D., and G. Stanley Whitby, eds., *Life, Death and Psychical Research: Studies on Behalf of the Churches' Fellowship for Psychical and Spiritual Studies*. London: Rider, 1973.

Pescosolido, Bernice A., and Jack K. Martin. "Cultural Authority and the Role of American Medicine: The Role of Networks, Class, and Community." *Journal of Health Politics, Policy and Law* 29, nos. 4–5 (2004): 735–756.

Peterson, Derek. "The Rhetoric of the Word: Bible Translation and Mau Mau in Colonial Central Kenya." In *Missions, Nationalism, and the End of Empire*, edited by Brian Stanley, 165–179. Grand Rapids, MI: Eerdmans, 2003.

Phillips, Paul T. *A Kingdom on Earth: Anglo-American Social Christianity, 1880–1940*. University Park: Pennsylvania State University Press, 1996.

Poloma, Margaret. "A Comparison of Christian Science and Mainline Christian Healing Ideologies and Practices." *Review of Religious Research* 32, no. 4 (June 1991): 337–350.

———. *Main Street Mystics: The Toronto Blessing and Reviving Pentecostalism*. Walnut Creek, CA: Alta Mira, 2003.

Porterfield, Amanda. *Healing in the History of Christianity*. Oxford: Oxford University Press, 2005.

Powell, Lyman P. *Mary Baker Eddy: A Life-Size Portrait*. New York: Macmillan, 1930.

Pratt, James Bissett. *Matter and Spirit: A Study of Mind and Body in their Relation to the Spiritual Life*. New York: Macmillan, 1922.

Putney, Clifford. *Muscular Christianity: Manhood and Sports in Protestant America, 1880–1920*. Cambridge, MA: Harvard University Press, 2001.

Puxley H. L. "The Church and the Paranormal." In *The Psychic Force*, edited by Allan Angoff, 219–228. New York: G. P. Putnam, 1970.

Riches, David. "The Holistic Person; Or, the Ideology of Egalitarianism." *Journal of the Royal Anthropological Institute*, N.S. 6 (2000): 669–85.

Rieff, Philip. *The Triumph of the Therapeutic: Uses of Faith after Freud*. New York: Harper & Row, [1966] 1987.

Robb, J. Wesley. "Hendrik Kraemer versus William Ernest Hocking." *Journal of Bible and Religion* 29, no. 2 (1961): 93–101.

Robbins, Joel. "Anthropology and Theology: An Awkward Relationship?" *Anthropological Quarterly* 79, no. 2 (Spring 2006): 285–294.

———. *Becoming Sinners: Christianity and Moral Torment in a Papua New Guinea Society.* Berkeley: University of California Press, 2004.

———. "Continuity Thinking and the Problem of Christian Culture: Belief, Time, and the Anthropology of Christianity." *Current Anthropology* 48, no. 1 (2007): 5–38.

Roberts, Jon H. "Psychoanalysis and American Christianity, 1900–1945." In *When Science and Christianity Meet*, edited by David C. Lindberg and Ronald Numbers, 225–244. Chicago: University of Chicago Press, 2003.

Rogaski, Ruth. *Hygienic Modernity: Meanings of Health and Disease in Treaty-Port China.* Berkeley: University of California Press, 2004.

Roof, Wade C. "Religious Borderlands: Challenges for Future Study." *Journal for the Scientific Study of Religion* 37, no. 1 (1998): 1–14.

———. *Spiritual Marketplace: Baby Boomers and the Remaking of American Religion.* Princeton: Princeton University Press, 1999.

Root, John D. "Science, Religion, and Psychical Research: The Monistic Thought of Sir Oliver Lodge." *Harvard Theological Review* 71 (1978): 245–263.

Rosenberg, Charles. "Framing Disease: Illness, Society, and History." In *Framing Disease: Studies in Cultural History*, edited by Charles E. Rosenberg and Janet Golden, xiii–xxvi. New Brunswick, NJ: Rutgers University Press, 1992.

———. "Holism in Twentieth Century Medicine." In *Greater than the Parts: Holism in Biomedicine, 1920–1950*, edited by Christopher Lawrence and George Weisz, 335–56. New York: Oxford University Press, 1998.

———. *Our Present Complaint: American Medicine, Then and Now.* Baltimore: Johns Hopkins University Press, 2007.

Sanford, Agnes. *The Healing Light.* St. Paul, MN: Macalester Park Publishing, 1947.

Sapir, Edward. "The Meaning of Religion." In *Selected Writings in Language, Culture, and Personality*, edited by David G. Mandelbaum, 346–356. Berkeley: University of California Press, 1949.

Satter, Beryl. *Each Mind a Kingdom: American Women, Sexual Purity, and the New Thought Movement.* Berkeley and Los Angeles: University of California Press, 1999.

Saul, John Ralston. *A Fair Country: Telling Truths about Canada.* Toronto: Penguin, 2008.

Schmidt, Leigh. *Hearing Things: Religion, Illusion, and the American Enlightenment.* Cambridge, MA: Harvard University Press, 2000.

Schmidt, Leigh. *Restless Souls: The Making of American Spirituality.* San Francisco: HarperSanFrancisco, 2005.

Schoepflin, Rennie B. *Christian Science on Trial: Religious Healing in America.* Baltimore: Johns Hopkins University Press, 2003.

Scott, Ernest F. *I Believe in the Holy Spirit.* New York and Nashville, TN: Abingdon Press, 1958.

Scott, Munroe. *McClure: A Biography.* Toronto: Penguin Books Canada, 1979.

Selden, Charles. *Are Missions a Failure?* New York: Fleming H. Revell, 1927.

Semple, Neil. *The Lord's Dominion: The History of Canadian Methodism.* Montreal: McGill-Queen's University Press, 1996.

Sered, Susan. "Taxonomies of Ritual Mixing: Ritual Healing in the Contemporary United States." *History of Religions* 47, no. 2 (2007): 221–238.

———, and Linda Barnes, eds. *Religion and Healing in America.* Oxford: Oxford University Press, 2005.

Shiels, W., ed. *The Church and Healing: Papers Read at the Twentieth Summer Meeting and the Twenty-first Winter Meeting of the Ecclesiastical History Society.* Oxford: Basil Blackwell for the Ecclesiastical History Society, 1982.

Shuman, Joel J., and Keith G. Meador. *Heal Thyself: Spirituality, Medicine, and the Distortion of Christianity.* Oxford: Oxford University Press, 2003.

Skrine, John Huntley. *The Survival of Jesus: A Priest's Study in Divine Telepathy.* New York: Hodder & Stoughton, 1917.

Smith, Jonathan Z. *Relating Religion: Essays in the Study of Religion.* Chicago: University of Chicago Press, 2004.

Smuts, Jan C. *Holism and Evolution.* London: Macmillan, 1926.

Sontag, Susan. *Illness as Metaphor and AIDS and Its Metaphors.* New York: Farrar, Strauss and Giroux, 1989.

Stanley, Brian. "The Legacy of George Sherwood Eddy," *International Bulletin of Missionary Research*, 24, no. 3 (2000): 128–131.

Stark, Rodney. "The Rise and Fall of Christian Science." *Journal of Contemporary Religion* 13, no. 2 (1998): 189–214.

———, William Sims Bainbridge, and Lori Kent. "Cult Membership in the Roaring Twenties: Assessing Local Receptivity." *Sociological Analysis* 42, no. 2 (1981): 137–162.

Starr, Paul. *The Social Transformation of American Medicine.* New York: Basic Books, 1982.

Stebner, Eleanor J. "More Than Maternal Feminists and Good Samaritans: Women and the Social Gospel in Canada." In *Gender and the Social Gospel*, edited by Wendy J. Deichmann Edwards and Carolyn De Swarte Gifford, 53–70. Champaign: University of Illinois Press, 2003.

Sterne, Jonathan. *The Audible Past: Cultural Origins of Sound Reproduction.* Durham: Duke University Press, 2003.

Stewart, Charles, and Rosalind Shaw, eds. *Syncretism/Antisyncretism: The Politics of Religious Synthesis.* New York and London: Routledge, 1994.

Stocking, George W. Jr. *Victorian Anthropology.* New York: Free Press, 1987.

Stout, Harry, and D. G. Hart, eds. *New Directions in American Religious History.* New York: Oxford University Press, 1997.

Stout, Jeffrey. *Democracy and Tradition.* Princeton: Princeton University Press, 2005.

Strauss, Sarah. "'Adapt, Adjust, Accommodate': The Production of Yoga in a Transnational World." *History and Anthropology* 13, no. 3 (2002): 231–251.

Szabo, Jason. "Seeing is Believing? The Form and Substance of French Medical Debates over Lourdes." *Bulletin of the History of Medicine* 76 (2002): 199–230.

Tambiah, Stanley. *Magic, Science, Religion and the Scope of Rationality.* Cambridge: Cambridge University Press, 1990.

Taves, Ann. *Fits, Trances, and Visions: Experiencing Religion and Explaining Experience from Wesley to James*. Princeton, N.J.: Princeton University Press, 1999.

———. "William James Revisited: Rereading *The Varieties of Religious Experience* in Transatlantic Perspective." *Zygon* 44, no. 2 (2009): 415–432.

Taylor, Bron. "Earthen Spirituality or Cultural Genocide." *Religion* 27, no. 2 (1997): 183–215.

Taylor, Charles. *A Secular Age*. Cambridge, MA: Harvard University Press, 2007.

Thompson, Arthur N. *Haelend: The Church's Ministry of Healing*. Burlington, ON: Welch Publishing, 1985.

Thuesen, Peter. *In Discordance with the Scriptures: American Protestant Battles over Translating the Bible*. New York: Oxford University Press, 1999.

Tillich, Paul. *The Eternal Now*. New York: Scribner, 1963.

———. *The Interpretation of History*. New York: Scribner, 1936.

———. *Systematic Theology*. Chicago: University of Chicago Press, 1973.

Tomes, Nancy. "Merchants of Health: Medicine and Consumer Culture in the United States." *The Journal of American History* 88, no. 2 (2001): 519–547.

Treat, James. *Around the Sacred Fire: Native Religious Activism in the Red Power Era*. New York: Palgrave Macmillan/St. Martin's Press, 2003.

———. *Native and Christian: Indigenous Voices on Religious Identity in the United States and Canada*. New York: Routledge, 1996.

Turner, Bryan. *The Body and Society: Explorations in Social Theory*. London and Thousand Oaks, CA: Sage Publications, 1996.

Tweed, Thomas, ed. *Retelling U.S. Religious History*. Berkeley: University of California Press, 1997.

———. "Who is a Buddhist? Night-Stand Buddhists and Other Creatures." In *Westward Dharma: Buddhism beyond Asia*, edited by Charles Prebish and M. Baumann, 17–33. Berkeley: University of California Press, 2002.

Valverde, Mariana. *The Age of Light, Soap and Water, 1885–1925*. Toronto: McClelland and Stewart, 1991.

van der Veer, Peter. *Conversion to Modernities: The Globalization of Christianity*. New York: Routledge, 1996.

———. *Imperial Encounters: Religion and Modernity in India and Britain*. Princeton, N.J.: Princeton University Press, 2001.

Van Die, Marguerite. *An Evangelical Mind: Nathaniel Burwash and the Methodist Tradition in Canada, 1839–1918*. Montreal and Kingston: McGill-Queen's University Press, 1989.

———, ed. *Religion and Public Life in Canada: Historical and Comparative Perspectives*. Toronto: University of Toronto Press, 2001.

Vaudry, Richard W. "Evangelical Anglicans and the Atlantic World: Politics, Ideology, and the British North American Connection." In *Aspects of the Canadian Evangelical Experience*, edited by G. A. Rawlyk, 154–70. Kingston and Montreal: McGill-Queen's University Press, 1997.

Vaughn, Megan. *Curing Their Ills: Colonial Power and African Illness*. Stanford: Stanford University Press, 1991.

Vipond, Mary. *Listening In: The First Decade of Canadian Broadcasting, 1922–1932.* Montreal and Kingston: McGill-Queen's University Press, 1992.

Viswanathan, Gauri. *Outside the Fold: Conversion, Modernity, and Belief.* Princeton: Princeton University Press, 1998.

Wacker, Grant. *Heaven Below: Early Pentecostals and American Culture.* Cambridge, MA: Harvard University Press, 2001.

———. "The Holy Spirit and the Spirit of the Age in American Protestantism, 1880–1910." *Journal of American History* 72, no. 1 (1985): 45–62.

———. "A Plural World: The Protestant Awakening to World Religions." In *Between the Times: The Travail of the Protestant Establishment in America, 1900–1960,* edited by William R. Hutchison, 253–277. Cambridge: Cambridge University Press, 1989.

———. "The Waning of the Missionary Impulse." In *The Foreign Missionary Enterprise at Home,* edited by Daniel H. Bays and Grant Wacker, 199–205. Tuscaloosa: University of Alabama Press, 2003.

Ward, James E. *The Commonwealth of the Soul: A Study of the Reason behind Spiritual Healing.* Toronto: Wm. Tyrrell, 1921.

———. *The Window of Life.* Toronto: Macmillan, 1925.

Warner, John Harley. "Grand Narrative and Its Discontents: Medical History and the Social Transformation of American Medicine." *Journal of Health Politics, Policy, and Law* 29, nos. 4–5 (2004): 757–780.

Warner, Michael. "Is Liberalism a Religion?" In *Religion: Beyond a Concept: The Future of the Religious Past,* edited by Hent de Vries, 610–617. New York: Fordham University Press, 2008.

Weatherhead, Leslie D. *Life Begins at Death.* Nashville, TN: Abingdon, 1969.

———. *The Mastery of Sex through Psychology and Religion.* Toronto: McClelland and Stewart, 1936.

Weber, Max. *The Protestant Ethic and the Spirit of Capitalism.* New York: W. W. Norton & Co., 2009 [1930].

———. "Science as a Vocation." In *From Max Weber: Essays in Sociology,* edited by H. H. Gerth and C. Wright Mills, 129–56. London: Routledge, 1991 [1948].

Westfall, William. *Two Worlds: The Protestant Culture of Nineteenth Century Ontario.* Montreal and Kingston: McGill-Queen's University Press, 1989.

White, Christopher. "Minds Intensely Unsettled: Phrenology, Experience, and the American Pursuit of Spiritual Assurance, 1830–1880." *Religion and American Culture* 16, no. 2 (2006): 227–261.

———. *Unsettled Minds: Psychology and the American Search for Spiritual Assurance, 1830–1940.* Berkeley: University of California Press, 2009.

Whiteley, Marilyn Fardig. *Canadian Methodist Women, 1766–1925: Marys, Marthas, Mothers in Israel.* Waterloo, ON: Wilfrid Laurier University Press, 2005.

Wigger, John. *Taking Heaven by Storm: Methodism and the Rise of Popular Christianity in America.* Oxford: Oxford University Press, 1998.

Winslow, J. C. *Christian Yoga.* Printed by request for the Society for the Propagation of the Gospel. Croydon: Roffey and Clark, 1923.

———. "Mahatma Gandhi and Aggressive Pacifism." In *Mahatma Gandhi: Essays and Reflections on His Life and Work,* edited by S. Radhakrishnan, 314–316. London: George Allan and Unwin, 1939.

Worcester, Elwood, and Samuel McComb. *Body, Mind, and Spirit.* New York: Charles Scribners, 1932.

———, and Isador Coriat. *Religion and Medicine: The Moral Control of Nervous Disorders.* New York: Moffat, Yard, 1908.

Wuthnow, Robert. *The Restructuring of American Religion: Society and Faith since World War II.* Princeton: Princeton University Press, 1988.

Wuthnow, Robert, and John H. Evans, eds. *The Quiet Hand of God: Faith-based Activism and the Public Role of Mainline Protestantism.* Berkeley: University of California Press, 2002.

Young, Robert. *Colonial Desire: Hybridity in Theory, Culture and Race.* London: Routledge, 1995.

Zammito, John. *Kant, Herder, and the Birth of Anthropology.* Chicago: University of Chicago Press, 2002.

Index

Adele (St. Luke's laywoman), 170–171, 176, 182, 184
affective communities, 18, 202, 259n59, 277n67
Africa, xii, xiv, xix, 24, 53, 67, 75, 105, 201, 202; North Africa, 281n18; South Africa, 44, 71, 88, 194, 278n77, 281n19; West Africa, 277n65
agency: anthropology and, 41, 216, 280n16; divine agency, 16, 34, 175–176
Ahenakew, Andrew, 203–204, 213, 278n70
Ahlstrom, Sydney, 102
Airhart, Phyllis, 241n26, 250n147
Albanese, Catherine, 11, 102
Allen, Richard, 225n23
ancestors, 182, 191, 206–208
Anderson, Benedict, 27
Anderson, Webb, 105–106
Anglican Church of Canada, contrasted with United Church of Canada, 25, 26, 111, 123, 139, 154, 189. See also Anglo-Catholicism; church newspapers; Evangelical Anglicans
Anglicanism: definition of, 20–22; Anglican Journal, 27, 272n1. See also church newspapers
Anglo-Catholicism, 13, 20–21, 24, 56, 178, 182, 187, 229n51. See also High Church
anointing, 20, 24, 26, 77, 90, 114, 169, 171, 178–179, 183, 185, 203, 205, 251n159, 267n50; prayer for Anointing of the Sick, 151, 168. See also unction

anthropology: and ancestral history, 206–208; of Christianity, xiii, 18, 32–36, 206, 221n23, n25; of healing, 4, 14, 200–202; and holism, 41, 44–45; and human nature, 37–38; and liberalism, 216–217; liberal Protestants and, 5, 8, 51, 162, 168, 222n26, 231n8, 233n23; medical, xx–xxi, 48, 55, 227n36; Paul Tillich and theological, 49–50, 52, 64; of religion, xiii, xix–xxi, 34–36, 105, 216–217; as a secular discipline, 34–35, 175–176; of the spiritual body, xiii–xiv, xxiii, 20, 30–57, 142–143, 157, 171, 209, 218; theological, xix–xxii, 33–38, 193
anti-Catholicism, 19, 21, 76
anti-Judaism, 76, 94, 175, 216, 281n23
anxiety, xv, 13, 15, 93, 121, 159, 162, 234n39
apartheid, xi, 25, 281n19
apology (for residential schools), 7, 169, 172, 204–205, 207, 209, 213, 272n1, 280n11
apostolic succession, 20, 25, 77, 111
Appadurai, Arjun, 42, 174, 243
Appasamy, Dewan Bahadur A.S., 115–116, 118, 135
appropriation, xxii, 77, 135, 170, 169, 186, 190, 205, 206, 207
Arendt, Hannah, 38
Asad, Talal, 34, 222n27, 232n17
Aubert, Edward, 153–154, 268n57

authenticity, xviii, 61, 77, 117, 120, 166, 174–175, 187, 206–207, 217, 265n16
autocritique, 104–107, 112, 209–218
automatic writing, 46, 91, 92, 119–120, 136, 260n83, 261n99. *See also* spiritualism

baptism, 58, 98, 215
Barth, Karl, 37–38, 142, 233n23, n27
Bateson, Gregory, 188
belief, xviii, 118, 127, 140, 142, 154. *See also* disbelief, 8, 17, 139
Bender, Courtney, 207, 272n2
Benjamin, Walter, 102
Benn, Christoph, 54, 233n32
Bergson, Henri, 20, 104, 256n15
Berton, Pierre, 211–212
Bethune, Norman, 30–31, 44, 59, 231n2
Bhabha, Homi, 7, 61, 69, 248n111
Bible, the, 20; anthropology and, 233n23; as artifact, 71; Belle Oliver and, 113; and healing, 59, 65, 66–68, 71, 72–73; Holy Ann and, 86; and literacy, 58–59; Percy Dearmer and, 84; and ritual reading, 24, 32, 65, 68; as standard for healing, 60, 83, 84, 201, 238n100; as talisman, 61; translation of, 20, 61, 70, 239n10
Biblical citations: *Acts*, 19, 248n117; *1 Corinthians*, 12, 144; *1 Corinthians*, 15, 30, 192; *Deuteronomy*, 10, 190; *Deuteronomy*, 18, 92; *Exodus*, 1, 192; *James*, 5, 100; *Jeremiah*, 14, 154; *John*, 14, 244n55; *Luke*, 14, 149; *Matthew*, xi, 10; *Nehemiah*, 2, 224n14; *Romans*, 6, 58; *1 Thessalonians*, 5, 46, 201, 235n55; *2 Timothy*, 4, 244n55
Biomedicine: definition, xvi–xvii; authority of, 5–6, 7, 10, 14–19, 52–56, 62–65, 72, 82–83, 168, 227n35; Burrswood Christian Hospital and, 177–178; critique of, 199–201; liberal protestant relationship to, xi–xvii, xxiii, 7, 9–10, 12, 13, 42–43, 60–61, 67, 74, 78, 91, 98, 136, 144, 170, 172–174, 188, 209, 224n19; parish nursing and, 192–198
biopower, xvi, 64
Bland, Salem, 31
Boas, Franz, xx, 37, 109
body, xiii–xiv, 33–34, 42–45, 72, 74, 209, 233n22; Agnes Sanford and, 146–147; Belle Oliver and, 1–3, 60, 66, 104; Debra and, 198; as fetish, 104–105; and health, 77–83; and yoga, 115–188. *See also* embodiment

body, mind, spirit. *See* holistic trinity
bodyprayer, 196
British Columbia, xii, xv, xx, 3, 108, 111, 116, 147, 268n68; University of, 164
British Empire, 24, 107, 117
Brouwer, Ruth Compton, 223n5
Brown, Karen McCarthy, 6
Bucke, Maurice, 125, 253n185
Buddhism, healing and, 9, 14; Christianity and, 9, 10, 14, 71, 182, 183, 185–187; meditation and, 10, 173, 183, 185–186; and proselytizing to western audience, 173, 174, 205; syncretism and, 173, 186
Bull, Malcolm, 64–65
Bultmann, Rudolf, 100–101, 125
Burrswood Christian Hospital, 29, 123, 153, 176, 177–178, 189, 268n57, 274n19

Cabot, Richard, 47, 157, 267n44, 269n70
Caledonia, Diocese of, xii, 3, 5, 108–109, 129
Canadian Association for Pastoral Practice and Education, 270n87
Canadian Churchman, 6, 9, 26, 45, 66–99, 101, 108, 130, 131, 145, 147–148, 150, 151, 152, 161, 203. *See also* church newspapers
Canadian Commonwealth Federation (CCF), 11, 272n107, n6
Canadian Council of Churches, 13, 20, 151, 172. *See also* ecumenism
Canadian Medical Association, 90, 251n155
Canadian Mental Health Association, 161
Canadian Nurses Association, 56–57, 194
Cannell, Fenella, 34
Canterbury, Archbishop of, 21, 147, 148, 153
capitalism, xv; liberal protestant critique of, 12, 13, 51, 62, 81, 96, 102, 111, 119, 143, 217, 260n79; and public health care, 10, 266, 201
Cappon, Daniel, 40, 148–149, 164, 234n35, 267n43
Cartwright, Mabel, 9–10, 18, 105, 224n14, n15
Chakrabarty, Dipesh, xv, 135, 175–176, 181
charismatic authority, 14, 24, 88, 123
charismatic Catholics, 265n18, 266n36
charismatic gifts (especially gifts of healing), 40, 60, 85, 122, 123, 144, 178 187, 203, 266n36, n38
charismatic healing, 15, 21–24, 40, 43–44 55–57, 60, 72, 122, 138, 142–158, 170, 178, 182, 193, 266n26; charismatic renewal, xxii, 42, 143–148, 154, 165

China: missions to, xii, xiv, 24, 25, 54, 67, 69, 71, 75, 135, 243n41, n47, 281n18; Anna Henry and, 58; Belle Oliver and, 106; James Hickson and, 88; Norman Bethune and, 30; Robert McClure and, 112; Sherwood Eddy and, 104; William Smith and, 70–71

Chown, Alice, 95–96, 253n185

Chown, S.D. 71, 73–74

Christian citizenship, xi, 62 66, 240n14

Christian Guardian, 6, 26–27, 66–99, 124. *See also* church newspapers

Christian imagination, xii, 4, 28, 129

Christian Medical Commission, 54–56, 199–201. *See also* World Council of Churches

Christian Science, 7, 15, 20, 28, 42, 72–82, 83, 87, 92, 97–99, 110, 131, 190, 244n55, n56, 246n83; liberal Protestant critique of, 56, 60–62, 66, 73, 74–77; 83, 87

Church Missionary Gleaner, the, 108–109. *See also* church newspapers

church newspapers, 26–28, 66, 87, 92 ; *Anglican Journal*, 27, 272n1; *Canadian Churchman*, 6, 9, 26, 45, 66, 74–75, 76, 78, 89, 90–91, 93, 95, 101, 108, 130, 131, 145, 147–148, 150, 151, 152, 161, 203; *Christian Guardian*, 6, 26–27, 66, 68, 71, 72–73, 75, 83, 85, 86, 87, 89, 90–91, 92–93, 94, 95–96, 98, 124; *Church Missionary Gleaner, the*, 108–109; *New Outlook, the*, 27, 126; *United Church Observer*, 27, 128, 159, 165, 194, 203, 237n95, 265n15

church union, 25, 103, 124

churches, All Peoples' United Church (Sault Ste. Marie, Ontario), 139; Calgary Centre United Church (Calgary, Alberta), 161, 163; Christ Church Cathedral (Montreal), 266n37; Christ Church Cathedral (Victoria, British Columbia), 266n38; Church of Christ the Healer (England), 177–178; Church of the Divine Revelation (St. Catherine's, Ontario), 124, 261n106; Divine Science Church (Seattle, Washington), 113; Emmanuel Episcopal Church (Boston, Massachusetts), 78, 82, 236n64; Lewis Memorial United Church (Turner Valley, Alberta), 197, 272n3. *See also* Toronto churches

civilization, Christian mission and, xvii, 66–67, 71, 109, 133, 204

civil rights movement, 13

colonialism, anthropology of religion and, xix–xxi, 34–35; anti-, xv, 105–106; and healing, 172, 212–218; and holism, 44, 54–55, 129; and India, 259n59; and medicalization, xvi, 6, 199; and medical missions, 88, 102; and syncretism, 135, 199–206

Commission on World Mission and Evangelism, 52, 200, 277n63. *See also* World Council of Churches

commissions on healing, 88, 90–91, 148–153

communication technologies, xiv, 26–28, 97, 101–104, 109, 135–136, 174

communication, xx, 27–28, 32; with the dead, 84, 92, 118, 124, 126; with the divine xiv, 42, 112, 135; and healing, xiv, 174; with spirits, 46, 92, 101, 104, 118, 124, 126, 128. *See also* spiritualism; telecommunication

Confederation Street (United), Toronto, ·29, 174, 190–192

confession, 47, 78, 214; confession and healing, 80, 210, 266n34; confession and psychoanalysis, 130, 156

Congregationalism, xiv, 11, 12, 18, 25, 188

conservative Protestantism, xix, 4, 17, 57, 105, 113, 186, 210; critique of liberal Protestantism, 32, 163, 167, 199, 201, 211, 215, 231n8, 226n34, 276n61

consumer culture, xvi, 135, 206. *See also* materialism

conversion: colonialism and, 215, 217; medical missions and, xii, 25, 61, 69, 106, 114; psychoanalysis and, 130

Coriat, Isador 46, 78, 227n37

cosmic, consciousness, 46, 49, 95, 125, 188, 253n185; dimension of health, 83, 102, 158, 168; guilt, 155, 167

cosmology, biomedical, 64, 83; text-based cosmology, xxii, 60–62, 86, 91, 97. *See also* texts

cosmopolitanism, xiv, xvii, xxi, 18, 29, 32, 106, 202, 209–211, 229n48, n49; optimism and, 214–217; and virtue ethics, 34–35

Creighton, W. B., 27, 89–90, 230n65

critique: anthropological, xxi, 34–35; of charismatic healing, 75, 87, 92, 104–105; liberal Protestant sensibility of, xx–xxiii; socialist, 8, 12, 50, 102; of therapeutic culture, xvi–xviii, 64–65. *See also* autocritique

Csordas, Thomas, 227n36

Curtis, Heather, 121

Dante 9, 58

Darby, George, 70, 243n44

deaconesses, 15, 16, 21, 65, 68, 93–97, 192–193, 252n173

Dearmer, Nancy, 91, 119, 120–121, 261n99

Dearmer, Percy, 119–21; on body, mind and spirit, 78, 119; criticism of, 120; and critique of Christian Science, 78; and Gandhi, 126; and holism 45; and prayer, 104; and sacramentalism, 119, 121, 130, 251n159; and socialism, 21, 121, 260n79; and Society for Psychical Research, 91, 119, 120; and spiritualism, 119–120, 128, 261n99; and textuality, 83–84, 91, 118

Debra (parish nurse), 196–198, 276n53

deCerteau, Michel, 83, 248n111. See also scriptural economy

decline, narrative of Protestant, 17–19, 211–218, 281n22. See also secularization

demonic spirits, 40, 137, 145, 170, 171, 173, 178, 201; Paul Tillich and, 49–52, 146, 156, 159, 237n81

denominations, 11–12, 14, 18, 25, 113, 226n24

Dickinson, Mervyn, 162, 164, 165, 271n102

Dicks, Russell , 47, 157, 267n44

disease, xiv, 40; colonialism and spread of, xvi; mastery over, 53, 77, 117, 121, 166; mental, 40, 244n55; moral cause of, 79; sexually transmitted, 66, 93. See also pathology

disenchantment, 4, 61, 103; biomedicine and, 199

divine healing, 23, 43, 60, 72, 82–3, 84–87, 90, 104, 108, 110, 122, 144, 146–148, 150. See also charismatic healing; faith healing

Dobell, Miriam, 152–153, 178

Doctors without Borders, xv

Dorrien, Gary, 8, 224n12, 225n22, 280n5

doubt, liberal Protestants and, 13, 31, 81, 127–128, 210, 262n116

Dougall, Lily, 45, 118–119, 121–123, 261n93

dreams, 47, 144, 148

dualism, 34, 38, 42–43, 44, 45, 48, 53, . 122, 233n28, 234n42

Dumont, Louis, 44, 219n3

Du Vernet, Frederick, xii, xiv, xx, 3–4, 5, 8, 17, 28, 29, 30, 39, 56, 107, 116, 117, 118, 122, 124, 125, 126, 129–130, 132, 133, 135, 137, 142, 146, 187, 203,

223n5, 254n3, 257n31, n35, 258n43, 266n36; and First Nations, xii, xx, 3, 108–109 257n31, n35; and spiritual radio, 33, 101–102, 103, 106, 108–112, 114, 144, 147, 156, 170

ectoplasm, 126, 128

ecumenism, xix, 3, 8, 13, 20, 24, 113, 117, 129, 161, 173, 189, 201–202, 212, 215, 254n3; ecumenical associations, 13, 15, 20, 54, 106, 123, 172, 173, 179, 189, 200; the United Church of Canada and, 11, 18, 215

Eddy, Mary Baker, 28, 60, 72–76, 98, 123, 244n55. See also Christian Science

Eddy, Sherwood, 56, 104, 125–129, 135, 236n76, 262n111; and ecumenism, 125, 126

electricity, xxii, 4, 5, 23, 101–103, 124, 146, 156

Emmanuel Movement, the, 15, 45, 46, 47, 72, 78–82, 85, 88, 104, 131, 156, 227n37

embodiment, liberal Protestantism and, 14, 17, 31–32, 103, 112, 119, 173, 187, 235n43

emotionalism, 23, 61, 88, 139, 142

energy, 81, 91, 101–111, 121, 136, 174, 198, 205, 207; Agnes Sanford and, 146; Alex Holmes and, 174; Elwood Worcester and, 80–81; Frederick Du Vernet and, 4, 101–102, 109–111; odic energy, 49

energy sacramentalism, 179–188, 272n2, 274n28, 275n37, 275n38

Engelke, Matthew, xiii, 33, 221n23, 231n6

England: Burrswood Christian Hospital and, 176–177; charismatic healing and, 145, 161–162; Church of, 20–21, 88, 212; experimentalism in, xxii, 217–218; Jack Winslow and, 117; James Ward and, 134; John Wesley and, 192; Lily Dougall and, 119, 121; Oxford Movement and, 182, 185

Enlightenment, the, 11, 64, 176, 200, 202

ethnography, xxi, 6, 217

etiology, 40, 46, 142, 145, 168

etymology, 74, 157–158

Eucharist, 20, 77, 115, 121, 148, 152, 184, 186–187

Evangelical Anglicans, 20–23, 24, 26, 40, 94, 104, 177, 178, 182, 189, 215

evangelical Christianity, 28, 113, 159, 200, 211, 272n4

Evangelical Lutheran, 193
Evangelical United Brethren, 25
Evangelism, xiii, xv, 24, 60, 113, 154, 179
exorcism, xii, 14, 15, 33, 138, 144, 145,
    149–151, 156, 168, 178, 200–202,
    266n36, 277n65
experience: anthropology and religious, 33,
    35, 37, 41; authenticity of, 265n16; and
    experimentalism, 103, 110, 118, 127; of
    God, 43, 126, 145, 155, 174, 189,
    235n55; of healing, 47, 48, 57, 72, 86,
    102, 122,146; liberal Protestants and,
    156, 205, 209, 254n3; reason and, 8, 13;
    text as test of, 86, 102
experimentalism, 7–29, 102–112, 172–188,
    217–218, 254–55n3, 256n20, 263n124,
    263n126

Fairbairn, Robert, 103, 124–125
Fairweather, Eugene R., xii–xiii, 219n1
faith cure, 33, 79, 113, 224n19
faith healing, xxii, 4, 8, 14–15, 24, 32, 43,
    52, 56, 72, 77, 84–85; Protestant
    critique of, 90, 124, 139, 150–151, 182;
    United Church and, 142, 154, 174. See
    also charismatic healing, divine healing
Falby, Alison, 17
Farmer, Paul, xx
feminism, 157, 163, 198, 215, 216, 235n43
feminist theology, 199, 200
feminization, 72–75, 81, 93–97, 132, 200,
    251n168
First Nations, liberal Protestants and,
    203–218; Anthony Wallace and, 36–37;
    Du Vernet and, xii, 3–4, 107–109, 133;
    Edward Sapir and, xx; healing practices
    and, xiv, 10, 13, 14, 142, 176, 199–202;
    278n71; and Hendry Report, 212–213,
    280n8; medical missions and, xv, 62, 69,
    95, 257n35. See also Native Anglicans;
    residential schools
Five Oaks Education and Retreat Centre
    (United Church), 189, 275n43
Foucault, Michel, xvi, 64, 214, 240n17
freedom, xviii, 37, 58, 59–60, 100, 105,
    133, 155, 206, 214, 216–218, 280n16
Freud, Sigmund, xx, 45–46, 50, 81, 118,
    130, 158, 265n16; psychoanalysis and,
    48, 129, 130, 220n16; psychoanalytic
    theory and, 47, 130, 154
Furlong, Monica, 212

Gandhi, Leela, 18, 259n59. See also
    affective communities

Gandhi, Mohandas K., 116, 117, 119, 126,
    135, 259n65
gender, xix, 74, 163, 235n43. See also
    feminization
gendered difference, 44, 67–68, 80, 120,
    136
genealogy, xxiii, 34, 42, 144, 192, 222n26,
    232n17
General Synod (Anglican Church, Canada),
    213
Gidney, Catherine, 216
Globe, Katherine, 137–139, 148, 151–152
glossolalia, 143, 144, 145
God, communion with, 48, 77, 85, 99, 104,
    110, 117; in dwelling of, xiii; healing
    power of, xii, xii, xiv, 3–4, 10, 24, 33,
    43, 53, 73, 78, 82–85, 88, 100–105,
    110–111, 121–123, 138–139, 145–147,
    153, 166, 168–169, 183, 201, 266n34;
    love of, 101–113, 146, 164; presence
    of, 1, 35, 49, 57, 74, 93, 235n55; spirit
    of, xiv, 24, 33, 35, 80, 118, 121, 125;
    theological anthropology and, xiii, 5, 8,
    34–45, 38, 57, 138, 204; and the Trinity,
    40, 43; will of, 67, 98, 117, 120, 190;
    word of, 61, 68
Gordon, Deborah, 64
grace, xiii, 20 42–43, 88, 98, 100, 105, 144,
    159
Grant, John Webster, 189, 257n35
Griffith, Marie, 34, 163, 228n45, 238n105
Guild of Health, the, 21, 22, 26, 78, 121,
    145
guilt, 153–155, 167–168, 213, 268n59;
    cosmic guilt, 167

Harrington, Anne, 39, 233n28, 234n35;
Harris, Thomas, 43, 156, 265n16
Harvard University, 3, 49, 185, 271n94
Hatch, Nathan, 17
Hauerwas, Stanley, xviii
healing: definition of, xi–xv; changing
    concepts of, 32–33, 40–42, 52–56; as
    metaphor, xi, 39, 189, 267n50; as a
    political program, xi–xii, 26, 134, 189,
    209–218. See also charismatic healing;
    faith healing
Healing Fund, 25, 172, 204, 213
healing revivals, 15, 28, 89, 98, 142,
    155
health, 54–56, 217–218; emotional, 14,
    161, 167, 183; gospel of, 60; Seward
    Hiltner and, 157–158, 167; texts and,
    97–99

health care, xv, 52, 54–55, 172, 173, 192,
     199, 235n49, 270n87. *See also* public
     health care
hegemony, xix, xxiii, 107, 218. *See also*
     imperialism
Heinze, Andrew, 46, 271n92
Hellaby, Hilda, 95, 253n181
Hendry, Charles (and the Hendry Report),
     212–213, 280n8
Henry, Anna, 58–59, 68–69, 70, 94
heresy, xix, xxii–xxiii, 6, 13, 56, 74–76, 84,
     124, 125, 170, 187, 199, 206, 236n74,
     266n38
Hickson, James (Moore), 21, 24, 86–89,
     117, 140, 142, 145, 250n138
High Church, 20, 22, 77, 123, 145, 177,
     219n1. *See also* Anglo-Catholicism
Hiltner, Seward, 156–158, 160, 162, 163,
     165, 167, 267n44, 268n67, 269n70
Hinduism, liberal protestant openness to,
     10, 14, 181–186; Mary Baker Eddy and,
     76–77; and universal religion, 274n28.
     See also yoga
historicity, 15, 100–101, 175–176,
     217–218
Hocking, Ernest, 3, 101, 104, 105
Holiness movement, 23–24
holism, xiv–xv, 40–42, 53–55, 148–150,
     151, 166, 168, 233n32, 234n35,
     235n49, 268n57, 270n87; Edward
     Aubert and, 153–154, 268n57; Jan
     Smuts and, 44; Paul Tillich and, 159;
     Pentecostal healing and, 43, 235n55;
     Seward Hiltner and, 158
holistic trinity (body, mind, and spirit),
     38–49, 52, 142–143, 168; as motto,
     39–40, 55, 160
Holmes, Alex, 139, 140–143, 154, 174,
     265n15
"Holy Ann," 86
Holy Communion. *See* Eucharist
Holy Spirit, 31, 46, 86, 142, 155, 158, 159,
     170, 171, 186, 209; as part of Trinity,
     40, 115
homophobia, 172
homosexuality, xxii, 6, 13, 37, 46, 144,
     164–166, 212, 215, 271n103, 272n105
hospital chaplaincy, 17, 38, 40, 47, 65,
     151, 160
hospitals, liberal Protestants and, xv, 5, 9,
     16–17, 21, 25, 52, 54, 65, 68, 93–94,
     156, 178, 268n68, 271n95; religious
     professionals in, 5, 25, 38, 65, 79,
     87–88, 96, 160

human nature, xiii, 8; anthropology and, xx,
     8, 33, 35–36, 38; Karl Barth and, 38;
     liberal Protestants and, 37, 43, 103;
     Pentecostals and, 45
humanism, xiii, 159, 211
humanitarian aid, xv, 106
Hutchison, William, 8, 225n22, 256n22
hybridity, 7, 42, 106, 186, 188, 206, 272n2
hygiene, 1, 62, 98, 212, 223n1; deaconess
     orders and, 93–94

Illich, Ivan, xvi
I'm OK—You're OK, 43, 142. *See also*
     Thomas Harris
imagined communities, 6, 27, 60
immigrants (to Canada), 12, 19, 24;
     deaconness orders and, 62, 94–96;
     Norman Bethune and, 31, 59
imperialism, Christian, xii, xvi, 3, 9,
     105–107, 129, 133–134, 143, 171,
     173, 206; spiritual, 207. *See also*
     pathologies of modernity
India: Belle Oliver and, xii, 1, 3, 25, 39, 107,
     114–115, 223n5; Brother John and,
     185–186; colonialism and, 259n59;
     experimentalism in xxii, 105, 115–116,
     135, 148, 173–174; Father Patrick and,
     182; Florence Nichols and, 148; Jack
     Winslow and, 116–117; James Hickson
     and, 88; missions to, xii, xiv, 24, 25, 61,
     67, 75, 243n41; mysticism of, 76; Percy
     Dearmer and, 118–119, 260n79; Robert
     McClure and, 112; Sherwood Eddy
     and, 126
individualism, anthropology and, 219n3;
     biomedicine and, 64, 83; liberalism and,
     xvii–xviii; liberal Protestantism and,
     38, 106 210–211; as pathology of
     modernity, 90, 143, 154, 199, 167;
     therapeutic culture and, xvii, 265n16
injustice, liberal protestant critique of,
     10–11, 18, 102, 106, 136, 167, 172,
     178, 190, 199, 202, 216, 260n79
Iona Community, 189, 275n44

James, William, xvii, 3, 37, 39, 42, 46, 58, 72,
     81, 104, 115, 118, 160, 233n22, 236n64,
     244n54, 246n79, 261n99, 267n44
Japan, 24, 30, 88, and Reiki 183, 272n2
Jesus, divinity of, 25–26; and energy, 166; as
     example, 30–31, 79, 128, 147, 155, 158;
     as healer, xi, xii, xv, 8, 14–15, 77, 79, 85,
     86, 104, 113, 227n37; as historical
     figure, 79, 186, 187; incarnation of, 74;

indigenization of, 115; resurrection of, 84, 125, 128; in ritual proximity, 187; stories about, 50; teachings of, xii, xvi, 73, 110, 122, 149–150, 157–159; transubstantiation and, 20; and tripartite anthropology, 22, 45, 46, 147

Jesus prayer, 183

Jesus Seminar, 170

John (SSJE Brother), 184–188, 194, 198, 274n33, n34

Johnson, Mark, 42–43, 44, 235n43

Judaism, and healing, xvii, 46, 65, 78, 161, 216, 271n92

Jung, Carl, 45, 130, 132, 144

Jung, Courtney, xxiii, 10

justice: health and, 201, 202, 203, 273n6; love and, 166, 188; peace and, 37, 54, 209. See also injustice; social justice

Kant, Immanuel, xx, 35, 46, 233n14

Keane, Webb, 32, 41, 206, 217, 220n8, 221n25, 228n44, 231n6. See also semiotic ideology

Kerin, Dorothy, 21, 29, 45, 84, 122–123, 153, 176–178, 180, 185, 267n44

Khan, Aisha, 216–217

Kinsey, Alfred, 163

labyrinth, 15, 26, 169, 189, 195, 196–197, 199, 276n58

lament, of Christian inheritance of healing, 14–19, 215–216

Latour, Bruno, 190

liberal humanism, 211

liberal subjects, xviii, xix–xx, 222n31

liberalism, definition, xviii–xix, xxii; as practice, xviii, xxiii, xix, 19, 215, 217; Protestant, xix, 8–13, 18–19, 22, 38, 156, 199–200, 210–211, 216–218, 224n12, 225n23, 279n4, 280n5; supernatural, xiii–xiv, xviii, xx, xxiii, 3, 29, 62, 82, 112–115, 125, 129, 134, 170, 215; as tradition, xviii, 210, 216, 218

liberation theology, xix, xx, 180

literacy, 59, 61, 66, 68–71, 239n10, 244n50

Livingstone, Grover, 31–32, 33, 47–48, 157, 185

Lodge, Oliver, Sir, 91–92, 114

Long, Charles, 11

love, xiv–xv, xxii, 42, 60, 62, 101, 105–112, 116, 121, 136, 144, 164, 188, 212–215, 244n55; vibrations of, 146–148

Low Church. See Evangelical Anglicans

Luidens, Donald, 211

Luther, Martin, 137, 152, 159

Lutheranism, 161, 192, 193, 206

MacNutt, Francis, 15, 266n36

Mahmood, Saba, 216–217

Maines, Frederick, 124–125, 126

mainstream Protestantism, 12–13, 17, 22, 97, 143–144, 226n27, 228n44, 228n45, 238n105, 276n61, 279n4

Mao Tse-Tung, 30, 231n1

Marjorie (United Church minister), 174, 190–192, 195, 207

Marsden, George, 210–211, 215

Marshall, Ruth, 214

Martin, Dale, 34, 53, 234n36

Marx, Karl, xx, 50, 159

masculinity, Christian healing and, 23, 73, 80–81, 89, 132

materialism, xiii, xvii, 50, 76, 78, 87, 91, 135, 154, 155, 166, 199, 201

materiality, 32, 33, 42, 48, 62, 74, 77–78, 122, 217. See also semiotic form

materialization of belief, 140, 142

May, Rollo, 51, 143

McClure, Robert, 106, 112, 237n93

McComb, Samuel, 45, 78, 80, 81

McGilvray, James, 53–54

McKay, Stan, 203–204

McPherson, Aimee Semple, 89, 112, 123, 125

Mead, Margaret, xx, 37, 38, 162

medical education, xii, 5, 16, 25

medical materialism. See monism

medical missions, xii, xv, xix, 5, 7, 9, 15, 25, 52–55, 65, 67–71, 75, 91, 105–106, 112–114, 117, 134, 148, 156, 170, 195, 199, 204, 215, 237n93, 268n68, 170–71n94, 281n18; deaconess orders and, 93–97; medicalization, liberal Protestants as agents of, xi, xxii, 5, 14–18, 62–65, 218, 240n20; Michel Foucault and, xvi, 62, 64

medicalized enchantment, 15–16, 56

mediums. See spirit mediums

metaphysical, 11, 35–6, 39, 45, 50, 102, 146, 167

Methodism, definition of, 22–26

Meyer, Birgit, 33, 206, 277n65. See also sensational forms

Milbank, John, xxi

Milliken, Robert, 58, 98

mind, 42–44, 48–49, 66, 72–73, 77, 102, 104, 130–133, 235n43, 244n54, n55; mind cure, 72; mind-reading, 132–133. See also body, mind, spirit; subconscious

miracles, xiv; charismatic healers and, xiii, 122, 235n55; Jesus and, 8, 79, 84–86, 101–102, 192, 209
modernity, definition of, xv–xvi; liberal protestants and, 12–13, 35, 45, 101–102, 135, 156, 176, 189, 254n3; pathologies of, xi–xxii, 11, 90, 102, 143, 171, 192, 210–214, 220n8; secular modernity, 4, 6
monasticism, Anglican, 21, 29, 162, 184–186; ecumenical, 179, 189
monism, 42, 45, 135, 246n79
Moore, Laurence, 12
moral clinic, the, 80–81
morality, liberal protestants and questions of, xxii, 7, 14, 62, 64–65, 71, 73–74, 97, 98, 128, 143, 154, 160, 164, 209–210, 215; as force for healing, 62, 79–80
Morison, Odille, xx, 109, 257n33
Mullin, Robert Bruce, 251n159
Murphey, Murray, 36
Muskoka, Ontario, Canada, 29, 31, 185
Mysticism, 73–76, 115–116, 123, 126, 135, 142, 160, 175, 188, 212, 266n26

Nadia (St. Luke's yoga teacher), 179–181, 182, 183, 185, 194, 274n33
National Council of Churches, 28, 179, 183, 189, 191
Native Anglicans, 204, 212–213
New Age, 17, 39, 170, 177, 202
Newbigin, Lesslie, 52–53, 237n86
New Democratic Party. See Canadian Commonwealth Federation (CCF)
New Outlook, 27, 126. See also church newspapers
New Thought, 46, 82, 113, 130, 142
New York City, 164, 191. See also Union Theological Seminary
Nichols, Florence, 148
Niebuhr, Reinhold, 17, 49, 126, 129, 263n125, 270n88

occultism, 42, 48, 92, 115, 121, 136, 160, 260n75
Oliver, Belle, xii, 1–3, 4, 25; and body, mind, spirit, 1, 39; and conversion, xii, 1; and ecumenism, 113–114, 117; and Jesus, 113; and literacy, 59; and medical education, 1, 114, 117; and medical missions, xii, 25, 68, 105, 106, 107, 112–114, 117; and modern healing, xii, 3, 104, 113–114, 275n44; and prayer, 114, 116; and sex education, 1, 39, 60,

163, 223n1; and supernatural liberalism, 112–115, 223n5
O'Neill, Kevin, 34, 240n14, 278n77
opium addiction, 58, 68, 243n43
Opp, James, 43, 72, 224n19, 238n105, 248n110, n118, 251n168
optimism, xxi, 8, 13, 40, 48, 91, 129, 135, 155, 171; cosmopolitan, 214–217
Order of St. Luke, 22, 144–145, 193, 266n36, 267n44
orientalism, 107, 175, 188, 205–206
Orsi, Robert, 6, 224n19
Osler, William, 98, 261n99
Oxford Movement, the, 21, 79, 182, 185–187

parish nursing, xix, xxvii, 6, 15, 26, 38, 56, 170, 192–198, 199, 238n100, 276n53, n54
pastoral counseling, 33, 40, 52, 57, 142, 154, 156–159, 160–164, 174, 178, 267n44, 270n86, 271n92
Pastoral Institute, the (Calgary), 161, 163, 270n91
pathologies of modernity, xi–xxii, 11, 90, 102, 143, 171, 192, 210–214, 220n8
Patrick (Anglican priest), 10, 29, 171, 174, 179, 181–184, 185, 191, 194, 198, 274n33
Paul (the Apostle), 128, 159; and the body, 77, 146; and spiritual gifts, 85, 144; tripartite anthropology of, 43, 45, 46, 235n55; words of, 59, 73, 244n55, 248n117
Peers, Michael, 169, 172, 204
Pentecostalism, 143–144, 265n19; Adele and, 171, 176, 184; Nigerian, 214; and spiritual healing, 43–62, 72–89, 230n65, 234n37, 235n55, 241n26
phrenology, 156
Pincock, Jenny, 124, 125
Pollock, Sheldon, 217
postbiomedical bodies, 16
postcolonial studies. See affective community; historicity; hybridity; orientalism
Powell, Lyman, 78, 98
practice, liberal Protestantism as, xviii, 7, 11–12, 173–174, 216–218, 225n22; ritual, 172–198
prayer, 104, 124, 195–196; Alex Holmes and, 140, 143; Anna Henry and, 59–60, 68, 69; for the Anointing of the Sick, 151, 168; Belle Oliver and, 104,

114–115; "bodyprayer" 196; efficacy of, 56, 85, 91, 189; and healing, 3, 4, 5, 16, 23, 26, 99, 100, 102, 117, 121, 125, 148, 151, 154, 178, 238n100, 281n18; Jesus prayer, 183; as magic, 104, 116; meditation and, 10, 30, 179, 183; prayer meetings, 6, 10, 29, 113; as sensational form, 33; St. Mathias prayer group, 137–138, 143, 152; as technique of devotion, 32, 48; as telepathy, 104, 136, 110. *See also* Taizé

Presbyterianism, xiv, 6, 11, 12, 18, 19, 25, 113, 161, 188, 191, 193, 207, 230n65

Price, Charles, 87–90, 250n147, 148

primary health care movement, 54–55. *See also* Christian Medical Commission

print culture, and healing, 27, 60. *See also* texts

progress, liberal Protestants and, 8, 78, 103, 207, 216; as pathology of modernity, xiii, xvi

Protestant principle, the, 50, 214

Psyche, 17, 34, 43, 44, 40, 46, 51, 112, 130, 157, 167

psychiatry, 36–37, 47, 49, 148–164, 177, 265n16, 267n43, 270n86, n91, 271n94

psychiatric spirituality, 158, 163, 269n70, n83, 271n92

psychic research, xii, 61, 82, 91–92, 102, 112, 116, 118, 120, 129, 154, 260n75, 263n125

psychoanalysis, xxii, 7, 8, 13, 38, 48, 56, 82, 102, 121, 148–149, 156, 209, 220n16, 267n43

psychoanalytic theory, 47, 129–130; Christian theology and, 40, 156–159

psychology: liberal Protestant embrace of, xvii–xviii, 3, 17, 39–52, 82, 102, 129–136, 142, 156–168, 193; biomedical authority of, xxii, 5, 62, 65; Edward Aubert and, 153–154, 268n57; Elwood Worcester and, 45, 46, 79–82; Frederick Du Vernet and, 3–4, 109–112; Grover Livingstone and, 47–48; Jack Winslow and, 116–117; James Ward and, 130–133, 136; Marjorie and, 174, 191; para-, 8, 141; and pastoral counseling, 154–166, 267n44, 271n92; as pathology, xvii; Paul Tillich and, 49–50, 155, 156, 158–160, 269n78; Percy Dearmer and, 119–121; Seward Hiltner and, 158; and sexuality, 163–166, 172

psychotherapy, 15, 17, 42, 65, 82, 86, 89, 190, 215

psychotherapeutic culture, 163, 237n79

public health care, xi, xii, 4–5, 10, 16, 26, 31, 65, 96, 166, 188, 195, 230n64, 254n189, 273n6

purity, 17, 66, 93, 113–114, 206, 214–215, 242n30

racism xi, xiii, 13, 18, 44, 101, 172, 189, 212

radical Orthodoxy, xxi

radio, 27, 61, 91, 124, 97, 100, 134, 255n13. *See also* spiritual radio

radio mind. *See* spiritual radio

rationality: critique of charismatic healing as irrational, 83, 85; liberal protestants and, xii–xiv, 8, 13, 21, 57, 61, 64, 73, 175, 200

Rauschenbusch, Walter, xix, 227n37

reconciliation, xi, 7, 202, 277n63, 281n17. *See also* Truth and Reconciliation Commission

Red Cross, the, xv, 105, 106

Reiki, xv, xxii, xxvii, 7, 10, 29, 169, 174, 183–185, 196, 201, 202, 205–206, 209, 272n2, 275n37

relaxation, 80–81, 115, 146, 177, 180, 184

religion: anthropology of, xiii, xix–xxi, 34–36, 105, 216–217; as concept formed through medicalization, 62, 64–65; study of comparative, 50, 105; world, 134–136, 215

religious diversity/difference, xiv, 8, 10–14, 67, 73–76, 88, 105–107, 112, 126, 173, 185–186, 199–202, 277n67; purification and, 189–190

residential schools, 3, 18, 22, 25, 109, 133, 167, 172, 204–205, 207, 213

responsibility: liberal Protestant sense of, 8–13, 14, 105–106, 208, 210, 214; for residential schools, 25, 167, 171–172, 175

Riddell, Hanna, 9, 224n18

Rieff, Philip, xvii, 220n16, 221n17

Robbins, Joel, xx, xxi, xxvi, 34

Robinson, Marilynne, 210, 214, 215

Rogers, Carl, 38, 50, 237n79, 269n75

Rogers, Marjorie, 138, 151–152

Roman Catholicism, xiv, 5, 6, 12, 19–21, 47, 48, 65, 75–77, 78, 84, 87, 93, 94, 143, 144, 163, 173, 180, 182, 189, 192, 193, 201, 202, 224n19, 229n51, 247n108. *See also* Anglo-Catholicism; charismatic Catholics

Routley, T.C., 251n155
Roof, Wade Clark, 207, 278n78
Rose, Nikolas, 10

sacraments, healing and, 40, 77, 79, 88,
    130–131, 178, 266n26, 266n38. See
    also anointing; baptism; confession;
    Eucharist; unction
sacramentalism: Agnes Sanford and,
    146–148, 266n34; Anglicans and,
    32, 77, 79, 144, 176, 187; Emmanuel
    Movement and, 85; energy sacramental-
    ism, 184–189; Order of St. Luke and,
    144, 145, 179; Oxford Movement
    and, 79, 182, 186; Percy Dearmer and,
    119, 121; technological sacramentalism,
    118
sad Christians, 43–44, 57, 238n105
Sanford, Agnes, 40, 141, 145–147, 149,
    150, 151, 170, 265n19, 266n24, n34,
    n36, 267n44
Sapir, Edward, xx, 222n26
Saul, John Ralston, 257n35
Saulteaux, Jessie, 203, 278n72
Schleiermacher, Friedrich, xix, 238n103
Schmidt, Leigh, 11, 118, 280n5
science, as verification of Christian healing,
    xi, xix, 4, 8, 16–17, 37, 44, 53, 56, 66,
    78, 81, 84, 87, 90, 101, 107–110, 120,
    124, 127, 129, 131, 134, 136, 141–142,
    146, 157, 181, 186, 200, 209
scientific method, 16, 53, 60–61, 82–97,
    102, 104, 210
scientific spirit, xv, 58, 60–62, 67, 74, 83,
    93, 95, 98, 103
scriptural economy, 82–92
secular faith, 36–37
secularization, xvii–xviii, 16, 17, 19, 36,
    57, 211–213, 215–216, 218, 281n22;
    biomedicine and, 52–54, 64–66, 114,
    252n174
semiotic ideology, 32–33, 41, 231n6
sensational forms, 33, 59, 97, 98, 102, 135,
    174, 183, 199,
Senturias, Erlinda 54, 233n32
Seventh Day Adventists, 64–65
sex education, 1, 39, 60, 66–67, 128, 161,
    163, 165, 223n1, 242n30
sexism, 13, 172; hetero-, 18
sexual abuse, 22, 138
sexuality, 29, 49, 60, 119, 132, 143, 152,
    157, 163–166, 167, 172, 173, 189,
    281n21
Smith, Adam, 31, 71

Smith, G. Moore (Canon), 137–139, 140,
    142, 147, 148–152, 157, 264n10
Smith, Jonathan Z., 11
Smith, William E., 17, 70–71, 112
Smuts, Jan, 44
social gospel, 3, 4, 12, 13, 24, 25, 27, 51,
    85, 93, 94, 154, 227n37, 252n179,
    273n6
socialism, xv, 8, 11, 12, 13, 16, 21, 50, 51,
    95, 98, 111, 112, 119, 121, 126, 178
social justice, xi, xv, 8, 22, 124, 167, 189,
    191, 202, 281n19
Society for Psychical Research, 91, 118,
    119, 120, 124; Journal of the, 124
Society of St. George, 134
Society of St. John the Evangelist (SSJE),
    184–185, 275n38
spirit, definitions of, 44, 48, 51, 118
spirit mediums, 42, 46, 111–112, 119, 124,
    126–128
spirit possession, 46–47, 49, 51, 231n66
spiritual equilibrium, xxii, 31, 38, 40–42,
    49, 52–53, 102, 142–143, 152, 153,
    156, 159, 166–168, 173–174, 198,
    234n36. See also spiritual intervention
spiritual intervention, xxii, 38, 40–43, 49,
    52–56, 84, 101–102, 152, 153,
    166–168, 170–171, 173–174, 196, 200,
    202, 234n36; St. Matthias and,
    138–148. See also spiritual equilibrium
spiritualism, 4, 46, 49, 52, 84, 86, 91–92,
    103, 115–129, 141–144, 178, 207
spirituality: authentic, 117, 129, 175; First
    Nations, 13, 204; and healthcare,
    48–56, 151, 192, 192–202, 238n100;
    liberal Protestant, 174; universal, 106,
    109, 112, 134–136, 171
spiritual radio, xii, xiv, xx, xxii, 4, 17, 26,
    28, 33, 39, 57, 101–112, 114, 118,
    135–136, 141, 144, 156, 178, 203, 209,
    263n124
Stanley, Brian, 129
St. James' Cathedral (Anglican), Toronto, 87
St. John the Divine, Sisterhood of, 93, 96,
    162, 178
St. John's Medical Mission, 93–94
St. John's Rehabilitation Hospital, 94, 96,
    162
St. Luke's (Anglican), Toronto, 29, 170–171,
    174, 178–184, 185, 196
St. Matthias (Anglican), Toronto, 137–139,
    142, 143, 148, 150–154
St. Stephen-in-the-Fields (Anglican),
    Toronto, 130, 131, 133, 134

St. Paul's Cathedral (Anglican), Toronto, 87
Stout, Jeffrey, xviii
subconscious, xvii, 4, 129; Elwood
    Worcester and, 45–47, 79, 81; Frederick
    Du Vernet and, 110–111, 146; James
    Ward and, 130–132, 134; Paul Tillich
    and, 50
subjectivation, 214
Sue (parish nurse), 194–196
suggestion, power of, 51, 72–73, 79–80, 86,
    89–90, 104, 109–110, 121, 130–132
Sullivan, Winnifred Fallers, 56
supernaturalism, xii–xiv, xx, 42, 91,
    217–218; Belle Oliver and, 3–5,
    112–115; Frederick Du Vernet and,
    101–102, 223n5; historicity and,
    175–176; Iona community and,
    189–190; Jack Winslow and, 117; James
    Moore Smith and, 149, 264n10; loss of,
    36–37; psychic, 118–129; Sherwood
    Eddy and, 125–129; technological,
    101–111, 134, 142
supernatural liberalism, xiii–xiv, xx, xxiii,
    62, 82, 111–112, 170, 215
superstition, xiv, 6, 51, 69, 91, 154,
    243n41
syncretism, 18, 73, 75, 116, 173–74,
    176–188, 199–208, 278n78. See also
    religious diversity/difference

Taizé, 28, 179, 183, 189, 191, 274n23
Taves, Ann, 160, 251n168, 260n75
Taylor, Mark Lewis, xx
techniques of the self, 214
techniques of devotion, 31–33, 52
technologies of the self, 10, 209
telecommunication, xiv, 4, 103, 108, 110,
    132, 141
telepathy, 8, 92, 102, 104, 108–10, 121,
    128–130, 132–133, 135–136
texts: Anglicans and, 23–24; -based
    cosmology, xii, 60–62, 86, 91, 97; as
    healing tools, 60, 66–72, 239n7; and
    imagined communities, 60; liberal
    protestants and, 58–99; Methodists and,
    241n26; as proof, 77–78, 82–97;
    and the scientific method, 60–62; as
    sensational form, 59–60, 97; as
    talismans, 61–62, 239n9. See also Bible;
    church newspapers; literacy; tracts
therapeutic culture, xvi–xvii, 13–4, 18, 40,
    163,
therapeutic touch, 169, 174, 181, 195–196,
    199, 274n27

theological colleges: Anglican Theological
    Seminary, 89; Emmanuel College, 162,
    194, 271n102; General Theological
    Seminary, xiii; Jessie Salteaux Resource
    Centre, 203; Princeton Theological
    Seminary, 142, 157, 162; Queen's
    Theological Seminary, 155; Trinity
    College, 26; Union Theological
    Seminary, 38, 49, 51, 126, 143, 155,
    157, 201, 212; Wycliffe College, 108,
    137
Tillich, Paul: on anxiety, 49, 53, 159;
    Christianity and psychology and,
    155, 156, 158–159, 160, 265n16,
    267n44, 269n78; on the demonic,
    50–52, 146, 156, 159, 237n81; and
    glossolalia, 143; and healing, 49, 53,
    149; Mark Johnston on, 42–43; and
    pastoral counseling, 40, 159; and
    Protestant liberalism, xix, xx, 219n1;
    and the Protestant principle, 214; Rollo
    May on, 143; Seward Hiltner on,
    157–158; and superstition, 51;
    theological anthropology of, 49, 51,
    52, 269n75; and the ultimate, 49, 51,
    159; and Zen Buddhism, 173
Tisdall, Douglas, 137, 138–139, 151
Toronto churches: Church of the Holy
    Trinity (Anglican) 197; Confederation
    Street (United), 29, 174, 190–92;
    Fairlawn United Church, 271n102;
    Parkdale United Church, 139, 140,
    142; St. James' Cathedral (Anglican),
    87; St. John's Garrison Church
    (Anglican), 93–94; St. Luke's (Anglican)
    29, 170–171, 174, 178–184, 185, 196;
    St. Matthias (Anglican), 137–139, 142,
    143, 148, 150–154; St. Paul's Cathedral
    (Anglican), 87; St. Stephen-in-the-Fields
    (Anglican), 130, 131, 133, 134
Toronto Institute for Pastoral Training,
    150, 160–161, 270n90, n91
Toronto, 26, 29, 78, 98, 172; Alex Holmes
    and, 139, 140, 142; James Hickson
    and, 87; and Katherine Globe affair,
    137–141, 148–150, 152–153, 160,
    164; Sherwood Eddy and, 126. See also
    Toronto churches
Toronto Star, 137, 139, 140, 141, 152, 194
Toronto, University of, 25, 40, 87, 138, 148,
    150, 160, 212, 220n8
tracts, missionary distribution of, 59, 60,
    61, 69–71, 112, 121
transcendental meditation, 169, 275n38

Trelawney, Edward, 89–90
triumphalism, xii, 3, 7, 9, 10, 25, 112,
    172–73, 181, 190
Trumpour, H.R., 89
Truth and Reconciliation Commission
    (Canada), 205, 213, 278n77. See also
    reconciliation
Tübingen, Germany, 52, 53, 54
Turner, Bryan, 64

unction, 21, 47, 77, 78, 85, 119, 148
United Church, contrasted with Anglican
    Church of Canada, 25, 26, 111, 123,
    139, 154, 189; hospitals, xv. See also
    church newspapers; church union
United States: and influences on Canadian
    Protestant healing practices, xiv, 47, 78,
    87, 89, 126, 144–145, 154, 160, 162,
    185, 193–194, 212; liberal Protestant-
    ism in, 11–12, 17, 21–22, 81, 126,
    167, 210
unity, xiii–xv, 4, 8, 144, 155; of the spirit
    (Tillich), 49–52. See also ecumenism
universal humanity, xiv, xv, 8, 18, 35, 50,
    112, 235n43. See also human nature
universal spirituality, 106, 109, 112,
    134–136, 171
universalism, xxiii, 5, 117, 126, 182–188,
    198, 238n100, 274n28; and healing,
    205, 209; and prayer, 104
University of Toronto. See Toronto,
    University of

Wacker, Grant, 106, 241n26
Wallace, Anthony F. C., 36–37
Ward, James, 28, 130–134, 136, 156, 157
Warner, Michael, xix
Watts, Alan, 173, 188, 212
Weatherhead, Leslie, 48–49, 160, 161,
    236n75, n76, 267n44
Weber, Max, 4, 223n7

Weinberger, Julius, 141–142
welfare state, xv, 16, 53. See also public
    health care
Wesley, John, 19, 22–23, 26, 76, 102, 159,
    192
Westberg, Granger, 193, 198
White, Christopher, 156, 220n16, 223n6,
    234n39, 236n62, 251n157, 254n3
Wholeness. See holism
Wilson, Lois, 199, 261n103
Winslow, Jack, 106, 116–118, 135, 257n29
Worcester, Elwood, 32, 49; on body, mind
    and spirit, 81, 236n59; on Christian
    Science, 246n83; Emmanuel Movement
    and, 78–82, 104, 156, healing and, 80,
    81; on homosexuality, 164; on Jesus,
    46, 79–80, 227n37; and the moral clinic,
    78, 80; and psychology, 79–80, 82,
    121; and sacramentalism, 79, 121;
    and spirits, 46, 51; and suggestion, 80,
    121; and virility, 81; on William James,
    80, 236n64; and women, 80, 88
World Council of Churches (WCC), 13,
    20, 53–54, 56, 173, 199–202, 238n102,
    277n63. See also Christian Medical
    Commission; Commission on World
    Mission and Evangelism; ecumenism
world wars, 7, 101
World War I, 86, 91, 119, 133–134,
    271n103; post-, 42, 112, 118
World War II, 40, 185; post-, 42, 52,
    144–145, 148, 154, 157

yoga, xv, xix, xxii, xxvii, 6, 7, 8, 10, 28,
    28, 39, 102, 169, 170, 171, 173, 176,
    178–184, 188, 190, 194, 195–196, 199,
    201, 202, 205, 209, 215; Christian yoga,
    6, 10, 15, 42, 106–112, 115–116, 118,
    170
Young Men's Christian Association
    (YMCA), 104, 115, 124, 125, 126, 158

TEXT
10/13 Sabon

DISPLAY
Sabon

COMPOSITOR
Westchester Book Group

PRINTER AND BINDER
IBT Global